Lesbian Intimacies and Family Life

Lesbian Intimacies and Family Life

Desire, domesticity and kinship in Britain and Australia, 1945–2000

Rebecca Jennings

BLOOMSBURY ACADEMIC
LONDON • NEW YORK • OXFORD • NEW DELHI • SYDNEY

BLOOMSBURY ACADEMIC

Bloomsbury Publishing Plc, 50 Bedford Square, London, WC1B 3DP, UK
Bloomsbury Publishing Inc, 1385 Broadway, New York, NY 10018, USA
Bloomsbury Publishing Ireland, 29 Earlsfort Terrace, Dublin 2, D02 AY28, Ireland

BLOOMSBURY, BLOOMSBURY ACADEMIC and the Diana logo are
trademarks of Bloomsbury Publishing Plc

First published in Great Britain 2024
This paperback edition published in 2025

Copyright © Rebecca Jennings, 2024

Rebecca Jennings has asserted her right under the Copyright, Designs and
Patents Act, 1988, to be identified as Author of this work.

For legal purposes the Acknowledgements on p. viii constitute an
extension of this copyright page.

Cover image © Denise Jennings

All rights reserved. No part of this publication may be: i) reproduced or
transmitted in any form, electronic or mechanical, including photocopying,
recording or by means of any information storage or retrieval system without
prior permission in writing from the publishers; or ii) used or reproduced
in any way for the training, development or operation of artificial intelligence
(AI) technologies, including generative AI technologies. The rights holders
expressly reserve this publication from the text and data mining exception
as per Article 4(3) of the Digital Single Market Directive (EU) 2019/790.

Bloomsbury Publishing Plc does not have any control over, or responsibility for, any third-
party websites referred to or in this book. All internet addresses given in this book were
correct at the time of going to press. The author and publisher regret any inconvenience
caused if addresses have changed or sites have ceased to exist, but can accept no
responsibility for any such changes.

A catalogue record for this book is available from the British Library.

A catalog record for this book is available from the Library of Congress.

ISBN:	HB:	978-1-3503-5887-4
	PB:	978-1-3503-5890-4
	ePDF:	978-1-3503-5888-1
	eBook:	978-1-3503-5889-8

Typeset by Integra Software Services Pvt. Ltd.

For product safety related questions contact productsafety@bloomsbury.com.

To find out more about our authors and books visit www.bloomsbury.com
and sign up for our newsletters.

For Vicky, Ben and Ada, the inspiration for this book

Contents

Acknowledgements		viii
Introduction		1
Part One		
1	Desire and sex	17
2	Domesticity	45
3	Marriage and commitment	77
Part Two		
4	Lesbians and the nuclear family	101
5	Creating a family	127
6	Parenting	165
7	Family, kinship and support	201
Conclusion		227
Notes		231
Select bibliography		268
Index		276

Acknowledgements

This book could not have been written without the collaboration of the many women who generously gave their time and shared their experiences of lesbian intimacy and family life. I am profoundly grateful and hope that I have done justice to these inspiring stories.

I have benefitted from the advice, support and intellectual generosity of many scholars during the course of this project. I am particularly grateful to Julia Miller, for her research assistance and to Robert Reynolds, Shirleene Robinson, Tanya Evans, Hsu-Ming Teo, Leigh Boucher, Michelle Arrow and my other former colleagues at Macquarie University, Sydney. This project was conceived and initiated in Australia and I acknowledge the support of an Australian Research Council Future Fellowship in funding the research, as well as the enthusiasm and support of many Australian friends and colleagues, including Barbara Baird, Yorick Smaal, Carla Pascoe Leahy, Graham Willett, Lisa Featherstone, Carroll Pursell, Sandra Mackay, Leonie Noyce and the Pride History Group, Sydney.

The book was completed at University College London and I would like to thank Chloe Ireton, Joe Cozens, Lo Marshall and other colleagues there, particularly Florence Sutcliffe-Braithwaite, whose unfailing interest and insightful comments on drafts have been invaluable and my doctoral students, Samuel Vermote, Ellen Durban and Beth Charlton, for many interesting conversations about lesbian motherhood and history. This book has been strengthened by the feedback and support of fellow historians of sexuality, Liz Millward and, in the UK, Alison Oram, Amy Tooth Murphy, Craig Griffiths, Mo Moulton, Jana Funke, Justin Bengry and E-J Scott.

Finally, I owe a huge debt of gratitude to my partner, Vicky, for her research assistance, comments on many drafts and endless patience, support and enthusiasm for the project, as well as for sharing the joys and challenges of lesbian motherhood with me.

Introduction

In the decades following the Second World War, a proliferation of experts, media and self-help literature – as well as family, friends and wider social networks – advised, supported and exhorted women to approach their intimate lives in particular ways, telling women how to find and keep the ideal man; how to maintain a successful marriage; when and how to have sex; at what stage and with whom to have children; and in what circumstances and ways to raise those children. Our understanding of the decades between the 1940s and 1990s is shaped by powerful narratives about the profound shifts in heterosexual intimate and family life which occurred during this period.

Those who found themselves attracted to their own sex, however, lived much of their lives without such scripts. Prior to the mid-1960s, only a handful of books and no magazines existed to tell such women how to find any woman, never mind the 'ideal'; they knew no role models for building a 'successful' lesbian relationship; and becoming a lesbian parent seemed an impossibility. The individual stories of intimacy explored in this book demonstrate that forging intimate lives without cultural scripts can be a liberating experience, filled with radical potential, but it can also be extraordinarily difficult and lonely. *Lesbian Intimacies* charts the diverse ways in which British and Australian women have created, sustained and lost sexual and loving relationships with other women through the second half of the twentieth century. It shows how women have managed the challenges of forging intimate relationships in secret, without reference to any cultural or personal role models of lesbian love and desire and in the absence of social and legal frameworks recognizing or sustaining their relational and family forms. Finally, by tracing these histories, it aims to provide cultural scripts for those who come after.

I first began to work on this book in the late Australian summer of 2010. I was on maternity leave, caring for my two-month-old son and, after a long and circuitous journey to have him, I was trying to make sense of what it meant to be a lesbian mother. I was no stranger to uncharted territory. When my partner and I had first got together twelve years before, we had few reference points for how to create a positive and lasting same-sex relationship: we just made it up as we went along, hoping that respect and communication would get us through the highs and lows. Parenthood seemed a whole new challenge, however, both for me as an individual and for us as a couple, and I found myself wanting to know how other women had approached this challenge before us. We were fortunate that, just before our son was conceived, NSW had amended legislation to recognize both lesbian parents on the birth certificate of a child born by clinical artificial insemination, so we had the unprecedented security of knowing that we were both legally recognized as his parents from the moment of his birth. However, the social context of lesbian parenting remained unpredictable and sometimes hostile. A generally positive antenatal experience was marked by instances of overt and unconscious discrimination, while the announcement of my pregnancy had impacted on our wider family relationships in positive and negative ways. Perhaps the overwhelming experience of early motherhood for me was the endlessly repeated need to come out as a lesbian: to health professionals; to the mother and baby group to which I was assigned when my son was born; to the uniformly church-run playgroups where I took my children as toddlers and to an apparently never-ending stream of total strangers who suddenly became invested to varying degrees in our lives because we had children. All of these assumed that I had a husband and that our children had a father and all needed to be disabused of that presumption, many reacting with incomprehension, discomfort or ignorance. It was difficult to know how to manage these multiple tensions in our lives while coping with the emotional upheaval of new parenthood and, although we had many supportive friends to whom we owe a great deal, we knew no other lesbian mothers with whom we could share our experiences of parenting and its impact on ourselves and on our relationship. This research was an attempt to reach out to the many women I knew had come before us: to hear their stories and understand how lesbian love and desire and family formation have fitted into and challenged the recent history of intimacy in Australia and Britain.

By the time I had secured funding and begun research on the project, my son was nearly eighteen months old and my partner had given birth to our daughter, so I embarked on the interviews and archival research for this book with a toddler and a new-born baby at home. I cannot overstate the many practical, physical and emotional challenges this situation posed. Both our children were what babycare guru, Miriam Stoppard, disingenuously described as 'wakeful' babies and I was chronically sleep-deprived for years. Having both been born in the UK, my partner and I had no family of origin within a 10,000 mile radius and in any case our children refused to be left with anyone except ourselves. Research trips were conducted together as a family, with my partner stuck in self-catering accommodation with the children while I crammed in two, or sometimes three, interviews a day. Practical obstacles were not the only challenges which needed to be negotiated. Researching this book was also an emotional rollercoaster. As other historians have noted before, both archival research and oral history interviewing can be an emotionally intense and confronting experience and this project proved to be both in many ways.[1] During the interview process, I experienced acts of kindness I will never forget: gifts of cooked meals to help us through the challenges of a newborn baby; affirmation that what we were attempting to achieve was valuable and potentially even revolutionary; as well as encouragement that we would survive this exhausting and turbulent period of our lives as others had before us. However, the research was also at times profoundly troubling and forced me to confront many difficult questions about my own identity and experience as a lesbian and a parent. Inevitably assumptions were made about my sexuality and politics; opinions were offered about the rights and wrongs of lesbians raising children, and especially boys; and I heard many heart-breaking stories of trauma and loss which fuelled my own fears and vulnerabilities around being a lesbian and a mother in a still often hostile world. This book, therefore, is both an attempt to trace and make sense of a history of lesbian relationships and parenting, and a product of my own intimate and emotional journey as a lesbian, a historian and a mother.

Methodology

Addressing these twin academic and personal concerns, *Lesbian Intimacies* seeks to do two things. It maps out the diverse ways in which women who desired and loved other women understood and expressed intimacy and family in the second half of the twentieth century, foregrounding individual stories and analysing the interplay between social and cultural frameworks and subjective experience. Reading these stories against the larger narratives of intimacy in modern Australia and Britain, it also seeks to demonstrate how lesbian practices of intimacy have reflected and subverted relational ideals in this period; how they have acted as catalysts for changing models of relationships and family; and how writing same-sex desire into our historical accounts of modern intimacy profoundly changes many of our accepted truths.

Personal testimonies are at the heart of this book. It draws on seventy-six oral history interviews conducted by myself with self-identified British and Australian lesbians. Recruited by adverts in the local and gay press; by contacting a range of lesbian organizations; and through word of mouth, participants were drawn from across Australia and Britain and ranged in age from their twenties to their eighties. Their social and economic and educational backgrounds were diverse, as were their fields of employment. Although many live or lived in larger cities such as Sydney, Melbourne and London, others lived in regional towns or rural areas and their stories reflect the diversity of located lesbian histories.

Oral history has long occupied a central place in methodologies of modern lesbian history and there is a growing scholarship on the practice and theories of interviewing in queer history.[2] Building on the work of feminist oral historians, queer historians have emphasized the principle of shared authority in lesbian oral history practice and the importance of establishing common ground between interviewers and participants in order to foster a safe and collaborative context for the interview.[3] Amy Tooth Murphy has written persuasively on the impact and value of insider status in queer oral history interviewing and the interviews I conducted for this book confirmed the value of building trust through a process of sharing personal experience and affirming common cultural reference points.[4] Both during the recruitment process and immediately prior to the interview itself, participants often wanted to understand in detail my motivations for the research and sought confirmation of my sexual identity, parenting experience, politics and other issues. Establishing that I was a lesbian and a mother was seen by many of the women I spoke to as a crucial indicator that I could be trusted to treat their precious and deeply personal memories with respect and understanding and I hope that I have achieved that. However, it is never possible to achieve complete shared identification between interviewer and participant and we should not overstate the potential of lesbian commonality. My other identities as a white, middle-class, academic historian in my mid-thirties, with a British accent undoubtedly impacted on how participants responded to me and articulated their own stories in dialogue with me. There were moments in interviews when I could see this intersubjective tension in operation. At times I witnessed a participant being jarred from their sense of comfort in our shared sexuality by the sudden realization that I could not immediately recognize the experience they were recounting because I was too young, or because I had been born and raised in Britain. At others, participants' comments revealed assumptions about my sexual experience or political viewpoints which pointed to the possibilities of misrecognition in lesbian interviewing. This sense of outsider status was particularly apparent in relation to race. Dan Royles has written thoughtfully on the ways in which dynamics of racial difference between interviewer and participant can shape the narrative (and silences) produced in particular ways.[5] In this project, my own racial identity as white impacted most significantly at the recruitment stage: despite considerable efforts to reach a racially diverse sample of narrators, most were white, of Anglo or European background and a small minority were Asian, suggesting that I had failed to identify the best channels to reach lesbians of colour or to foster the necessary trust to encourage participation. Conscious of the distortions which would arise from an absence of these and other less well-represented voices in the research, I have used archived oral history collections such as the Hall Carpenter Collection, From a Whisper to a Roar and Haringey Vanguard, in addition to published collections of personal testimonies, to provide a broader range of perspectives and to reach back to the early post-war decades, which few participants were old enough to recall.

The unique and rich body of oral history sources utilized in this book provides an insight into the emotional and subjective histories of lesbian intimacy in this period, both demonstrating the huge variety in women's experiences and enabling shifting patterns of relationship and family formation to be traced across the late twentieth century. In combination with these personal testimonies, a wide range of archival sources are used to explore the ways in which changing political and cultural concepts of sexuality impacted on individual and collective attitudes and practices of intimacy. Representations of lesbian intimacy are analysed in medical literature, the media and literary texts; lesbian and gay media and feminist journals and texts; as well as organizational records and private papers. These sources illuminate the wider cultural context of shifting medical, legal and social attitudes to female same-sex desire in which women were forging intimate relationships, as well as illustrating the ways in which lesbian networks and organizations fostered new concepts and practices of lesbian intimacy.

Lesbian Intimacies focuses on the period between the end of the Second World War and the late 1990s, a period which has been characterized by historians as one of profound change in patterns of intimacy. While sociological and legal studies have mapped out debates around same-sex marriage, intimacy and parenthood since 2000 and traced the significant changes which have occurred in this sphere in the twenty-first century, the historical background to those recent shifts has been largely neglected and this book addresses that gap. The book takes a transnational approach, exploring the distinct and entangled histories of Britain and Australia in this period. The historic cultural links between Australia and Britain were maintained at this time by the high numbers of British migrants to Australia and the common practice of young Australians travelling to, and sometimes settling in, Britain. The two countries shared common social and cultural values and traditions which shaped the experience of lesbians in similar ways, making a transnational approach valuable and enriching. Against this broader cultural backdrop, strong lesbian and feminist transnational networks, which developed from the 1960s onwards, make a transnational study of the two contexts particularly productive, highlighting the role of those connections in fostering change in each country.[6] Many of the women interviewed for this project had lived in both countries and key developments, such as the adoption of reproductive technologies as a route into lesbian motherhood, emerged as a result of knowledge sharing between British and Australian lesbians. While studying the entangled British and Australian experience therefore furthers our understanding of each national context, the cultural and environmental specificity of each country also produced some differences in concepts of family and intimacy and the book draws attention to the impact on this history of varying legal and material frameworks as well as cultural differences.

Defining lesbian intimacies

The question of how to define lesbianism in the past has exercised lesbian historians for decades, with different perspectives being influenced by shifting political and feminist approaches as well as by changing theoretical and methodological frameworks in the wider field of history. The particular challenges faced by historians of sexuality are also shaped by the context of the specific historical period under consideration, so questions of definition look very different to a twentieth-century historian than to a medievalist. Laura Doan has suggested that, although sexuality is often understood as central to modern conceptualizations of the self, evidence of sexual selfhood or subjectivity is patchy in the early twentieth century. She argues that 'examination of archival materials relating to women, work, and the First World War indicates that ordinary people did not generally name or self-name' and case studies of individual women demonstrate that 'as late as the 1930s some women understood themselves and were perceived by others in relation to gender and class yet manifested little interest in, or seemed to have limited access to, the technologies or subjectivities of sexuality'.[7] By the years after the Second World War, a proliferation of discourses of selfhood, sexuality and love had established the cultural linkage of sexuality and selfhood much more firmly in popular attitudes and many women understood their desires for other women in these terms. However, exceptions remained, and oral histories and personal papers evidence the persistence of same-sex desire and sexual acts being practised unconnected to a notion of lesbian identity well into the post-war period. Despite shifting notions of sexuality more broadly, the cultural silences around female same-sex desire meant that some women still did not have an understanding of female homosexuality or lesbianism as a category of the self, while others took time to develop an awareness of lesbian subjectivity as a possibility. In this context, a theoretical approach foregrounding practice, rather than identity, allows scope to include women in a broader lesbian history who entered into intimate emotional and sexual relationships with other women without developing a sense of lesbian selfhood. Judith Bennett's concept of 'lesbian-like' is helpful in this context. In her work on the medieval period, she suggests:

> I would therefore like to play with the implications of naming as lesbian-like a range of practices that impinge on our own modern – and very variable – ideas about lesbianism. If women had genital sex with other women, regardless of their marital or religious status, let us consider that their behavior was lesbian-like. If women's primary emotions were directed toward other women, regardless of their own sexual practices, perhaps their affection was lesbian-like. If women lived in single-sex communities, their life circumstances might be usefully conceptualized as lesbian-like. If women resisted marriage or, indeed, just did not marry, whatever the reason, their singleness can be seen as lesbian-like. If women dressed as men, whether in response to saintly voices, in order to study, in pursuit of certain careers, or just to travel with male lovers, their cross-dressing was arguably lesbian-like. And if women worked as prostitutes or otherwise flouted norms of sexual propriety, we might see their deviance as lesbian-like.[8]

Such an approach might also be used productively in the mid-twentieth century to interpret the behaviours of women who did not develop or articulate a sexual subjectivity.

The difficulties of taking an identity-based approach to lesbian history do not diminish with the dissemination of discourses of lesbian selfhood from the 1960s, however. As the vibrancy of work in the history of sexuality has shown, 'lesbian' is not and never has been a monolithic category. There have always been many ways to be a lesbian or to do lesbianism and this book documents the richness of that diversity in the second half of the twentieth century. Seeking a single, coherent definition of the identity category 'lesbian' in that context is therefore as counterproductive as it is impossible. Doan urges historians of the interwar period to pay attention to the ways in which historical subjects may have resisted the drive to 'know' the sexual self and Heather Murray demonstrates the persistence of this refusal into the post-war period. In her analysis of correspondence sent by North American women to a lesbian collective and counsellor in the 1970s, Murray argues that letter writing enabled women to escape the constraints of an affirmative lesbian feminist identity model and to express more complex and ambivalent emotional responses to their same-sex desires.[9] For those women who accepted a lesbian subjectivity in some form, the precise nature of that category was contested throughout the late twentieth century. As Chapter 1 explores, the significance of sexual desire and practice in defining lesbianism was an area of ongoing debate from the 1960s onwards, with questions raised over whether a woman constituted a lesbian if she was having a sexual relationship with a man or if she was not in a sexual relationship with a woman. The intersections of gender and sexuality also produced a range of conceptualizations of lesbian identity. Many feminist approaches to lesbianism centred around the notion of lesbians as 'women' but a narrow or essentialist definition of the category 'woman' can exclude or marginalize many historical subjects who might have understood themselves, or whom historians might wish to consider within the category 'lesbian'. Levi CR Hord suggests that a reworking of the concept of lesbian specificity, taking into account the contemporary example of the non-binary lesbian, can move us beyond essentialist notions of the lesbian grounded in gender difference. Reading Monique Wittig's assertion that lesbians are not women because they refuse the naturalized relation of women to men and her insistence that lesbians and gay men move beyond notions of gender difference, alongside Judith Butler's insight that the 'I' proclaiming an identity always exceeds the boundaries of that identity category, Hord argues that a new model of lesbian specificity must move beyond an understanding of identity based on exclusions and instead focus on the excess which overspills identity boundaries. In doing so, Hord claims, we might find a model of 'liberated desire' as 'specific desire – desire for certain bodily formations, certain constructed or intentional gendered aesthetics, for certain affective relations, or certain politically guided orientations' which need not be connected to an essentialist notion of womanhood.[10] Such an approach enables recognition of the complex interplay of gender and sexuality in the second half of the twentieth century and the broad range of lesbian gender identities articulated in this period, from the butch lesbian and 'female husband' at one end of the spectrum to the femme and, potentially, the 'married lesbian' at the other.

Drawing on these insights, and therefore recognising both the categories 'lesbian' and 'woman' as contingent, I have taken a methodological approach which seemed to offer potential to capture the widest range of 'lesbian' experience. In addition to women who self-identified as lesbian through their participation in lesbian oral history projects, I have considered women who implicitly opted into this category by participating in lesbian communities such as magazines, activist and support groups as well as those whose practices of intimacy seemed to suggest a desire for or commitment to a loving relationship with another woman. Many of these women understood their sexuality in different ways at different stages in their lives or lacked the language or cultural framework to articulate a sense of sexual selfhood at all. Others, either historically or more recently, may not have understood themselves within normative categories of womanhood. In including their stories, I do not seek to 'claim' them as lesbians in any definitive way, or to minimise alternative potential readings of their subjectivity, but simply to consider some aspects of their behaviour as expressing lesbian possibilities and thereby to acknowledge a more expansive and fluid and less boundaried conceptualisation of lesbian history.

Intimacy

Practices of intimacy have been widely debated by scholars in recent decades, but the question of how we might conceptualise lesbian intimacies historically has received much less attention. In his review of historical scholarship on intimacy in modern Britain, George Morris defines intimacy as encompassing, amongst other forms, 'love, friendship, family, touch, sexuality, and privacy' and suggests that these types of intimacy are inter-related.[11] Many of these themes, he notes, have been the subject of sustained historical enquiry by scholars in the fields of the history of sexuality, history of privacy and history of emotions, as well as those concerned with histories of selfhood. However, few historians have worked explicitly with notions of 'intimacy' or considered the interconnections between different forms of intimacy and how this might contribute to our historical understanding of its conceptualisation and practice. As a category of historical analysis, he argues, 'Intimacy runs the risk of being so capacious as to cease to be useful, but this flexibility is also part of its analytic usefulness; it allows us to consider the boundaries and slippages between feelings, bodies and practices.'[12]

Insights from the history of emotions have begun to inform the ways in which historians have understood shifts in models of intimacy in the modern period. While some scholars have presented love and other emotions as primal forces, many historians of emotion have considered the meanings of affect to be culturally constructed and therefore historically contingent. Barbara Rosenwein asserts: 'feelings can never be known out of context. They depend on the values and situations that elicit them, on the narratives that people use to make sense of themselves and their world, and on the accepted or idiosyncratic modes of expression that are employed to communicate them.'[13] William Reddy similarly argues that emotions cannot be separated from the cultural context in which they are expressed, but takes a different approach, suggesting that 'emotives' (forms of emotional expression) either call into being or call into question the feeling they evoke. For Reddy, therefore: '"Love" is not a separable feature of human experience independent of social life. Emotions do not exist prior to social organisation or cultural form, but arise from an interaction between social organisation and cultural form on the one hand, and our capacity to feel, on the other.'[14] Recent work on the modern history of love and heterosexuality has reflected these approaches, suggesting that the twentieth century witnessed profound shifts in relational ideals. In his study of modern love, Marcus Collins argues that 'mutuality' was a central feature of heterosexual love in modern Britain, reaching a height in the 1960s, before declining in the wake of a feminist pursuit of autonomy.[15] Hera Cook, however, claims that feminist advances towards gender equality, coupled with more readily available and effective means of contraception, enhanced the possibility of mutuality from the 1970s onwards.[16] Alana Harris and Timothy Willem Jones suggest that the period between the publication of Marie Stopes' *Married Love* in 1918 and Alex Comfort's *The Joy of Sex* in 1972 constituted the heyday of modern love and romance.[17] In Australia, Hsu-Ming Teo argues that romance became increasingly aligned with American practices of consumer culture in the mid-century.[18] In its emphasis on the interconnections between social structures, cultural forms and individual emotion, much of this literature has assumed a heterosexual framework and the ways in which homosexual forms of intimacy have been felt or articulated in the twentieth century have received little attention from historians.

Since the publication of Anthony Giddens' influential work, *The Transformation of Intimacy* in 1992, however, the rapidly shifting legislative and social landscape around same-sex relationships has prompted extensive research and lively debate amongst sociologists. Building on his earlier work on the late modern emergence of the reflexive self, Giddens proposed that a shift was occurring away from an older model of intimacy based on romantic love as the foundation for a permanent marital union towards new forms of intimacy characterised by what he termed the 'pure relationship'. He defined a pure relationship as: 'a social relation [which] is entered into for its own sake, for what can be derived by each person from a sustained association with another; and which is continued only in so far as it is thought by both parties to deliver enough satisfactions for each individual to stay within it.'[19] For Giddens, this shift coincided with a parallel emergence of a new model of 'active, contingent' love, which he termed 'confluent love'.[20] Giddens considered lesbians and gay men to be at the vanguard of this shift, as their exclusion from the institution of marriage and the arguable absence of gender inequalities and differences in same-sex relationships fostered models of intimacy based on equality and negotiation between partners. The notion of lesbian relationships as 'pure relationships', defined by equality and an absence of difference, has been similarly urged by Gillian Dunne, while Weeks, Heaphy and Donovan have characterised same-sex relationships as transforming practices of intimacy.[21] Lynn Jamieson, however, has critiqued Giddens' model for its failure to fully account both for the impact of structures of gender inequality on heterosexual relationships and the evidence of wider intimate networks and strategic use of silence in same-sex relationships.[22] Yvette Taylor has also problematised the notion of the pure lesbian relationship, pointing to the ways in which class differences and inequalities impact on individual relationships and noting that relational choices are also shaped by legislative contexts which privilege certain forms of intimacy. She argues: 'The dominant academic position tends to emphasise individual agency, creativity, autonomy and choice as re-shaping intimate biographies. However, other factors such as poverty, unemployment, not having enough and just "getting by" all have an impact on "picking and choosing".'[23] In her work on patterns of intimacy within lesbian families, Jacqui Gabb has also critiqued notions of the pure relationship. Taking issue with the stratification of emotions and intimate relations into socially given categories (most notably, for Gabb, the distinction between adult, sexual relationships and instinctive mother-child relationships), Gabb points to the variety of forms of lesbian intimacy:

> Within lesbian relationships, frequently and problematically identified as often lacking in sex, the boundaries between friendships and lovers are often blurred. It is not uncommon for lesbians to befriend and "fall in love" with someone to whom they are attracted before embarking on a sexual relationship. Or in line with traditional heterosexual courtship, a relationship may start with dating and/or sex from which love may grow. Where the hetero- and homosexual paths substantively

diverge, is that lesbians are far more likely to retain loving relationships with past sexual partners than any other category. Their intimate network often ranges across the sexual spectrum from platonic friendship, to ex-lovers, to current sexual partnerships.[24]

The blurring of boundaries between friendship, desire, sex and commitment in adult lesbian relationships and between parent-child and adult-adult love in lesbian family models is, as Gabb notes, a significant and unique aspect of lesbian forms of intimacy. This points to the importance of gender in shaping the specificities of lesbian forms of intimacy, both in comparison to heterosexual and gay male practices. In its reliance upon a presumed absence of gender difference in same-sex relationships, the notion of a pure relationship posits a simplistic account of equality within lesbian relationships which fails to take account of the ways in which gender differences between 'women' mediate power differentials within lesbian relationships. It also fails to take account of the ways in which wider social categories of gender produced structural inequalities that shaped the possibilities for lesbian forms of intimacy in similar ways to the class, economic and racial inequalities noted by Taylor. As *Lesbian Intimacies* explores, the reduced earning potential, lower social status and legal constraints faced by those occupying the social category of 'woman' in late twentieth-century Britain and Australia shaped lesbian relational forms in specific ways.

The attention to what is different about same-sex forms of intimacy, which has characterised much of the sociological work on lesbian relationships, has much to offer historical studies. George Morris reminds us that: 'Historical subjects were always imbricated in complex networks of intimacy', suggesting, 'It matters that the parents a child reacts against in their own romantic life, for example, were once young lovers themselves.'[25] The interconnections he points to in the extant historiography, however, like his own example, largely assume a heteronormative frame which is less useful in making sense of lesbian forms of intimacy in the past. As Heather Murray notes, in her work on gay kinship in post-war America, notions of familial intimacy relied on an intergenerational exchange of personal experiences of heterosexual love, marriage and parenting. In the absence of this shared experience – or in the face of deliberate concealment of homosexual desire by lesbian and gay daughters and sons – the processes by which familial intimacy might be attained were ruptured.[26] Throughout the post-war period and later in the century, British and Australian lesbian patterns of intimacy were created in a context of silence, hostility and denial which profoundly disrupted conventional models of family, friendship and desire. In addition to the histories of love, romance and parental affection which historians have contributed to our understanding of modern histories of intimacy, therefore, we need to pay attention to the impact of a different cultural and emotional landscape on lesbian forms of intimacy in the twentieth century. Doing so requires us to consider the interconnections between emotions such as love, desire and longing, which have been the focus of much scholarly attention to date, and other emotions such as shame, jealousy, fear, loneliness and loss.

Shame, as a constituent element of queer affect, has been widely analysed by queer theorists. Eve Kosofsky Sedgwick suggests that gay shame derives from the experience of nonrecognition of oneself and one's sexual difference, which is common to queer people, as well as other socially marginalized groups, and impacts on the nature of interpersonal communication and ongoing relations with family, friends, colleagues and others.[27] For Sedgwick, both queer identity and queer resistance are rooted in the experience of shame and 'The forms taken by shame are not distinct "toxic" parts of a group or individual identity that can be excised; they are instead integral to and residual in the processes by which identity itself is formed.'[28] The relationship between gay shame and the politics of both gay pride and, later, queer activism has been widely theorised with many critics similarly noting that it is not possible simply to locate shame in the past and move beyond it to an affirmative politics.[29] Heather Love urges instead:

> Although there are crucial differences between life before gay liberation and life after, feelings of shame, secrecy, and self-hatred are still with us. Rather than disavowing such feelings as the sign of some personal failing, we need to understand them as indications of material and structural continuities between these two eras …
>
> Modern homosexual identity is formed out of and in relation to the experience of social damage. Paying attention to what was difficult in the past may tell us how far we have come, but that is not all it will tell us; it also makes visible the damage that we live with in the present.[30]

Accepting that what Love terms 'backward feelings', such as shame, loss and regret, are integral to queer identity and queer affect in both the past and present enables us to consider the specificities of lesbian intimacy. In his work on emotional histories of homosexualities, Benno Gammerl argues that historians need to reflect on how the emotional and sexual interact in the past and to ask how the nature of emotions has shifted over time. Gammerl points to how fear, as an integral aspect of homosexual experience, underwent qualitative change in the post-war period, from a fear of detection in the 1950s and 1960s, to a fear of attack in the 1970s and a fear of shyness and failure in the 1980s and 1990s.[31] As Joanna Bourke notes in another context, there are many different forms of fear and this is apparent in the histories of lesbian intimacy traced in this book: while fear of loneliness shaped many lesbian interactions in the 1950s and 1960s, a fear of loss defined both the structure and emotional experience of lesbian parenting throughout the late twentieth century.[32]

It should be stressed, as Heather Love argues, that the intertwining of these affects with lesbian love and desire does not indicate an inherent failing in queer intimacy, but points to the historical and ongoing ways in which social and cultural attitudes and possibilities have shaped the conceptualisation and experience of queer emotion and sexuality. As Love maintains:

> Same-sex desire is marked by a long history of association with failure, impossibility, and loss. I do not mean by this that homosexual love is in its essence

failed or impossible, any more than regular love is. The association between love's failures and homosexuality is, however, a historical reality, one that has profound effects for contemporary queer subjects.[33]

Tracing the connections between social structures and cultural representations of lesbianism in the past and individual women's subjective experiences allows us to explore the ways in which lesbian affect has been historically constituted and is central to the approach taken in this book. This is perhaps most apparent in relation to the less well-theorised emotion of jealousy, which was central to post-war medical and cultural conceptualisations of female homosexuality and became embedded in complex ways in lesbian narratives and politics of sexual intimacy from the 1950s to the 1980s. Considering the complex interactions between social and cultural attitudes to gender and sexuality, emerging lesbian political and cultural forms and individual notions of sexual selfhood and family, *Lesbian Intimacies* demonstrates the significance of the late twentieth century in redefining marriage, parenting and the family and traces the emergence of relationship models which continue to shape contemporary society.

Book structure

Lesbian Intimacies explores patterns of continuity and change in lesbian relationship models between 1945 and 2000. In the immediate post-war decades, while some women sought discreet, long-term partnerships, others adopted gendered butch/femme roles. Although these relationship models have persisted up to the present day, alternative conceptualisations of intimacy were also adopted by some women from the 1970s onwards. After decades of relative silence regarding female same-sex desire, new visible forms of lesbian identity and culture entered public debate for the first time in this decade. These vibrant new political and social communities were productive of new patterns of lesbian intimacy and sometimes heated debates about expressions of lesbian desire and commitment which continued into the 1980s and 1990s. The first part of the book traces these shifts, exploring questions such as the longevity of women's relationships and the importance attached to monogamy as an ideal in relationships; the emotional, financial and behavioural roles adopted by women within same-sex relationships and the degree of equality aimed for and achieved between partners; the significance and expression of sex and romance; and whether marriage offered a model for relationships between women. Sexual practice and desire between women in the past have received little scholarly attention and Chapter 1 addresses this gap, assessing the impact of cultural tropes about lesbian sex on individual women, tracing a range of ways in which women across the period expressed desire and considering how individual women's sexual practice and appetite has shifted through their life course. Chapter 2 considers the ways in which relationship structures shaped and reflected the domestic environment of the home. Social and economic constraints on women's access to housing have influenced options for the development of lesbian relationships, while notions of gender have shaped the roles and distributions of power within relationships. Paying close attention to the material dimension of lesbian homes through an examination of the type of housing and spatial layout helps to illuminate the ways in which women have conceived of their relationship structures, and the chapter shows how the traditional private home of discreet post-war lesbian couples was challenged by collective living and non-monogamous sexual practice in the shared houses and squats of the 1970s. Chapter 3 explores the extent to which lesbians, individually and collectively, valued and strove for commitment and longevity in relationships. While legally recognized same-sex partnerships and marriage did not become available in Britain or Australia until the twenty-first century, there is a long pre-history of private ceremonies and demands for relationship recognition throughout the period in both countries, which this chapter traces.

Although the possibility that lesbians could be mothers was rarely acknowledged in Britain or Australia in this period, Part Two uncovers a rich history of lesbian parenting and family life since 1945, considering the extent to which lesbians have been mothers in this period and the context in which they became parents and raised their children; individual women's attitudes to motherhood as a social and personal role; and the family structures and parenting roles adopted by same-sex attracted women. The nuclear family has been one of the most persistent symbols of post-war British and Australian society, dominating popular narratives and academic studies of the period. Focusing on the ubiquitous but largely invisible figure of the married lesbian, Chapter 4 explores the experience of women who married despite, or prior to acknowledging their same-sex desires and the extent to which post-war marriage allowed space for the expression of those desires. For those women who conceived children within marriage, the marital home often represented a site of conflicting emotion in which dreams of autonomy and desire battled with maternal love, fear and loss and this chapter traces histories of lesbian mothers' custody battles. Chapter 5 maps the various routes lesbians took into parenting in late twentieth-century Britain and Australia. It traces a shift from heterosexual marriage as the primary means of becoming a mother towards the use of assisted reproduction to create lesbian families. Debates about the possibility of lesbian motherhood, both within lesbian communities and more widely, fostered the construction of a discourse of lesbian-parented children as uniquely 'wanted', 'planned' and 'chosen' and this chapter explores the development of this largely white, middle-class narrative and reflects on the ways in which it has erased the stories of women whose families were not planned. The daily practice of lesbian parenting posed significant challenges to normative concepts of the ideal heterosexual nuclear family in both Britain and Australia in this period. Chapter 6 traces a variety of approaches lesbians have taken towards parenting and family structure in the context of wider social hostility, exploring changing notions of the role of the 'mother' and 'co-mother' and the practice of collective parenting as a lesbian family form. It considers the impact of feminist concepts of gender norms and the nuclear family; medical and social attitudes towards child development; as well as the effect of wider social and economic structures on women's choices. Underpinning the exploration of lesbian relationships and parenting is a broader examination of notions of the family and

Chapter 7 reflects on how British and Australian lesbians have understood 'family'; from whom they have sought and found emotional and material support in daily life and in times of crisis; and the extent to which lesbians have redefined the concepts of family and kinship in this period.

Both my own and wider social concepts and practices of lesbian intimacy have changed profoundly in the more than a decade since I began work on this book. My children are fast approaching adolescence; we, as a family, have relocated to the UK and I am working in a very different context in British academia. Significant shifts have occurred in the legal framework surrounding lesbian intimacy: same-sex marriage rights have been won (bitter struggles notwithstanding, in Australia particularly) and other advances have been achieved in the legal recognition of lesbian relationships and parents. In many ways, there is greater social awareness and acceptance of lesbian forms of intimacy and family, but we also find ourselves in a moment of increased hostility to gender and sexual dissonance. In the UK, levels of hate crime against LGBTQ+ people have increased markedly in recent years and in both countries social and cultural anxieties are being played out in academia, the media and politics through the medium of a divisive and virulent attack on gender diversity. In tracing a history of lesbian intimacies in Britain and Australia in the late twentieth century, this book seeks both to provide some context to these current debates and to assert the rich diversity and cultural and social significance of lesbian practices of desire, domesticity and kinship.

Part One

1

Desire and sex

As a young woman in Brisbane in the early 1960s, Chloe 'realised that [she] was a lesbian' when some queens she had met put her in contact with 'an older dyke whose job it was to introduce all the new girls'. She recalled: 'She was probably in her forties and I was 20. As soon as she took me to bed, I knew that this was it. This is what I was'.[1] Julie also described her first sexual encounter with a woman as the defining moment in her understanding of her lesbianism. In early 1960s London, after struggling to make sense of her sexuality for some years, Julie had decided to approach a sex counsellor. She recalled:

> So I went to see him and … he started with his talk of sex counselling and then he simply got into practical details, like he showed me genitals, pictures first, then the real thing, then he got me into bed with a woman. I'm sure he enjoyed every minute of it! And I can't say I didn't enjoy it. But I mean, it was really, it was a really, it was a good way to learn … [and] it just gave me … the certain knowledge that I was gay.[2]

Other women recalled a persistent cultural belief that a woman could not be a lesbian if she had not experienced sex with another woman. Jenny argued that, in 1970s Australia, 'women's sexuality was seen as contingent on someone else in general'. When she joined the Gay Women's Group in Melbourne in 1973, she remembered 'one of the women at one of the first meetings was going, "So if I break up with X do I stop being a lesbian and then only become a lesbian again when I'm on with X?" … The idea of being a lesbian by yourself wasn't really, really there'.[3] Ellen confronted similar attitudes when she took the decision that she was a lesbian and chose to share this with friends at a South London women's group in the mid-80s. Her friends refused to accept her declared sexuality, maintaining that she could not be a lesbian if she had not had sex with a woman. When Ellen informed them that she had had a sexual relationship with another woman six or seven years previously, another friend objected that she could not be a lesbian if she was not currently in a relationship with a woman.[4]

While these women emphasized the importance of sex in defining lesbianism, others downplayed it, advocating love and commitment and sometimes celibacy as closer to their concept of a lesbian identity. Mirroring this range of views and experiences articulated in personal accounts, the significance of genital sexuality in defining lesbian relationships in the past has been hotly debated by historians since the 1980s. In their work on intimate female friendships in the eighteenth and nineteenth centuries, lesbian feminist historians Lillian Faderman and Carroll Smith-Rosenburg argued that respectable middle and upper-class women's 'romantic friendships' were typically non-sexual, despite the passionate language some women used with each other in letters and poetry.[5] Martha Vicinus has proposed that from the late eighteenth-century onwards, a distinction began to be made between respectable, non-sexual friendships between women and increasingly marginalized Sapphic relationships.[6] Sharon Marcus, however, has suggested that, in the nineteenth century, some middle- and upper-class women used the sexual language of 'marriage' to describe their committed relationships with other women and were typically accepted by their wider social circles on these terms.[7] These debates were partly a response to the empirical problem of stating with any certainty whether specific relationships in the past contained a sexual element, which has prompted Martha Vicinus to ask: 'does it really matter so much … what someone born a hundred or two hundred years ago did in bed?'[8] Jack Halberstam, however, answers this question in the affirmative, arguing that the sexual practices of women in the past are indeed important, not least given the modern tendency to conceal or de-sexualize the lesbian.[9]

These debates have largely focused on the nature of intimate relations between women living prior to the twentieth century, reflecting a presumption that the impact of sexological theories on understandings of sexuality and lesbian identity from the turn of the century onward would have rendered it impossible for women in the twentieth century to remain unaware of the possibility of desire and sex between women. However, research on both the influence of sexology and on popular understandings of sexual identity in the first half of the twentieth century throws doubt on this assumption.[10] In Britain, sexology remained a marginal field until the mid-twentieth century and sexological texts, although available to some wealthy and intellectual women, were largely inaccessible to middle and working-class women, whose conceptualizations of sexuality continued to be shaped by wider cultural assumptions of female desire as, at most, reactive. In Australia, highly restrictive censorship laws prohibited the importing of texts which referred to homosexuality and restricted access to sexological texts to medical professionals.[11] As a result, many of the questions raised in the romantic friendship debate remain pertinent into the post-war period. Taboos around the discussion of female sexuality continued to operate throughout the second half of the twentieth century and constrained some women's ability to articulate the sexual aspects of their relations with other women and their actual sexual practice. These inhibitions remain powerful in the narratives many women have constructed about their relationships in oral history interviews and other personal narratives. Despite direct questioning about the significance and nature of genital sexuality in their same-sex relationships, some women registered narrative discomfort in exploring these issues, answering such questions briefly and vaguely, redirecting the discussion elsewhere or simply refusing to respond. Reflecting on a similar methodological challenge she faced in her research into the queer history of San Francisco, Nan Alamilla Boyd has argued that what narrators consider to be sayable is shaped both by perceptions of queer oral history as a political project involving 'the self-conscious production of a particular kind of representation – a representation fit for public consumption' and by assumptions about the positionality of the interviewer.[12] For those narrators who, unlike Boyd's, had not been active participants in a distinct urban queer subculture, the lack of a discursive framework in which to locate sexual practice might add further constraints on speech.

Moreover, even in the second half of the twentieth century, historians cannot presume an automatic connection between same-sex desire and the claiming of a lesbian identity. As Sally Newman notes, discussions of the place of genital sexuality in intimate female relationships in the past have relied upon the 'assumption ... that sexual activity, lesbian identity, and guilty self-consciousness are organically connected in sequence'.[13] However, post-war personal narratives of female same-sex intimacy demonstrate that no inevitable connection existed between sexual activity, lesbian identity and guilt. While some women in both Britain and Australia, like Chloe and Julie cited above, presented their first same-sex sexual encounter as a defining moment in their awareness and adoption of a lesbian identity, others maintained sexual relationships with other women for decades without claiming a lesbian identity. Similarly, while some narratives include explicit and implicit accounts of crippling guilt which inhibited women's ability to articulate or act upon their same-sex desires, other women presented their sexual encounters with women as 'natural' and even inconsequential. This diversity of experience and practice has been obscured by scholarly attempts to define a single coherent lesbian subject in the past. In calling for greater scholarly attention to the variety of categories and identities under which we might understand desire between women in any given historical period, Jack Halberstam has argued:

> Once we establish that the kinds of sexual desires and acts that the term 'lesbian' claims to represent are multiple and various, the category itself comes under serious pressure. The desires and sexual instincts of a cross-dressing female husband are in no way similar to the desires and sexual instincts of the women she attempts to seduce, and the desires and sexual acts shared by romantic friends may be far different from the sexual relations between masculine women and their married lovers.[14]

Halberstam's point is undeniable and one aim of this chapter is to point to the diversity of same-sex sexual practice which existed in post-war Britain and Australia. Cultural scripts and sexual identities helped to define how some women understood and acted upon their sexual desires and it is necessary to map out a more expansive range of cultural frameworks or categories for understanding sexual instinct and practice in the past. However, as historians of affect have highlighted in recent years, sexual practice was also a somatic experience and it is important to pay attention to the embodied dimension of desire.[15] Personal narratives and other accounts indicate that historical subjects not only shifted between different available cultural categories at different moments, in different spaces and at different stages of their life course, adapting their sexual practices accordingly, but also that such categories were adopted or performed in different ways by each subject. Physiological factors such as age, health and individual libido impacted on desire, while subjective factors such as personal experience and previous interactions shaped individual responses to cultural categories. Mapping out a range of discourses and experiences of same-sex sexual desire, therefore, this chapter will make three central claims: firstly, that sex matters in intimate relations between women; secondly, that the dominant interpretative frameworks through which historians and others have sought to understand female same-sex desire have tended to obscure rather than elucidate that history; and thirdly, that individual women adapted, subverted and interpreted available cultural scripts of same-sex sexuality in multiple ways – or bypassed them completely – leaving us with a picture of sexual experience in this period characterized primarily by fluidity and variety.

Discourses of female sexuality in the post-war period

In the immediate post-war decades, constraints on open discussion of sexuality had a significant impact on many women's attitudes towards and understanding of sex. Obscenity laws prevented the publication of explicitly sexual material and sex was therefore rarely mentioned in literature, the press or other cultural forms. Sex education in schools remained limited and frequently parents were reluctant to raise the subject with their children. In Australia, despite a proliferation of sex-education texts produced by churches, medical professionals and the state in the post-war decades, sex education was considered a private concern and, as Lisa Featherstone has suggested, 'many young men and women found that coming of age in the late 1940s and 1950s meant sexual matters were not discussed at home or at school' leading to a lack of basic biological information.[16] In Britain, oral history studies suggest that sex and childbirth were 'such "taboo" subjects that they were not discussed within most families' and that this reticence continued into the 1960s.[17] Homosexuality was not included in sex-education curricula in either Britain or Australia and, in Britain, the enactment of Section 28 of the Local Government Act 1988, which prohibited the 'promotion' of homosexuality as a 'pretended family relationship', further inhibited even informal references to homosexuality in many schools and municipal contexts.[18] The absence of discussion around female sexuality more broadly, and lesbian sexuality in particular, impacted on individual women's experience of their sexuality, sometimes delaying the expression of physical desire and undermining women's confidence in their sexual practice. Nina, who was born in Jersey in 1933, recalled that 'I didn't have a genital relationship with a woman until I was twenty-seven and I actually had a sexual relationship with a man just before that in the same year.' Describing herself as a 'late developer', Nina explained this as the result of a lack of knowledge about the possibilities of lesbian sex:

> So in a sense, I felt emotionally I'd been in relationships with women, but I read Radclyffe Hall's *The Well of Loneliness* when I was in my early twenties and one of the things that I hold against that book is that she says women can't make love to each other and, I think, somewhere I believed that. I didn't have the courage to explore for myself.[19]

Nina's belief in the impossibility of lesbian sex had an impact on her early relationships with other women, and she recalled that when she 'met somebody when I was training as a teacher ... we were in a sexual but not genital relationship'.[20] Bella, who fell in love with a girl at school in 1951, was more open to sexual exploration but similarly felt that she lacked sexual knowledge. She recalled: 'We knew nothing about sex, had no idea about the clitoris, masturbation, penetration. We just kissed and I loved her breasts.'[21] Margaret, who grew up in Devon in the 1940s and 1950s, made a similar distinction between forms of physical intimacy such as kissing and cuddling, with which she was familiar, and genital sexuality, of which she remained ignorant for longer. Recalling her first sexual encounter with another woman in her late teens, she remembered:

> The people at school were just sort of lots of long kisses and you know big cuddles and walking around and being very close to each other and things like that so it wasn't until I was about 17 and a half and I was very nervous. I mean these other two friends of mine had had sexual relations ... [and] they confided in me ... I mean I'd had no sex education whatsoever really, all I'd got is what I'd learned from other people at school and that was a mixed bunch.

Margaret's account suggested that, in the absence of formal sex education, she was ultimately able to acquire some information about the possibilities of genital sex from her peers at school and, in particular, two close friends who were also attracted to other girls, but she considered these sources inadequate.[22] Diana, who was an only child and had no access to either formal or informal sex education, described her early sexual relationships in late 1940s Bristol as experimental affairs. Responding to a question about whether she knew anything about lesbian sexual practice, Diana recalled:

> Oh, good heavens no! Oh no! It was all a complete mystery to me ... although I was desperately in love with Jean and although in fact we went to bed together I hadn't the faintest idea what I was supposed to be doing with her and ... it was all very vague and groping.[23]

Religious taboos on extramarital sex and homosexuality also shaped women's knowledge and attitudes towards sex in the post-war decades. Margaret, who was raised in a Roman Catholic family in Sydney in the 1930s and 1940s, recalled: 'I was in fact virginal until I was twenty-one. As a proper devout Catholic should be'. Despite being taught that extramarital sex and pregnancy were immoral, Margaret's sex education was so vague that, when her employer sexually assaulted her in a motel, she did not realize she had experienced sexual intercourse until she later discovered she was pregnant.[24] Sylvia, who began attending a High Anglican church while training to be a teacher in the 1940s, also described how her religious beliefs shaped her attitudes towards sexual feelings:

> It was ... in my next teaching job, that I fell in love with a member of staff and she fell in love with me. She was more experienced than I was, and she knew

how to arouse me. Then I saw the danger signal and I was absolutely terrified. She wanted to get me into bed and I refused. I was terrified of the idea. I thought she might do something to harm me, either physically or psychologically. I was so ignorant, you see. It was quite agonising really, because I felt so guilty about the whole thing.[25]

In addition to constraining women's understanding of the possibilities and mechanics of lesbian sexual practice, the absence of a public discourse about sex in this period also inhibited many women's discussion of sex with their lovers. Some women internalized taboos around lesbian sex, feeling that it was a shameful act which should not be acknowledged, even in private. Nina recalled that, in her 20s, she was:

Fairly closeted, really. That's one of the things I find painful to look back on – I realise now that I was quite afraid then. It would have been an awful shock to me if the first woman I loved actually made love to me. I was quite prejudiced in a way – I thought it wasn't normal. It took me some years to accept same-sex love.[26]

Ellen, a Turkish Cypriot Londoner who had married at sixteen and had two children before her marriage broke down, described similar feelings of shame in her first brief relationship with another woman in 1972.[27]

The place of the erotic in lesbian relationships

The extent to which women's intimate relationships included genital sexuality varied widely throughout the period, depending on individual women's libido and the dynamic within each relationship, as well as women's stage in the life course or in a long-term relationship and physiological factors such as illness, pregnancy, disability or tiredness.

Some women described how sexual fantasy had played a catalytic role in prompting them to seek out intimate relationships with other women. When Susan began to acknowledge to herself that her married life in 1980s Sydney was not a success, her realization that she wanted a relationship with a woman was reinforced by suppressed memories of earlier same-sex fantasies. She reflected:

[A]t around about 11 o'clock at night [SBS] would put on the B rated Italian movies. These are wonderful movies because they have these voluptuous Italian women in sheer negligees and topless and I'd be sitting there going 'Oh my God, mmm!' and I clearly remember thinking: 'Susan, you shouldn't be looking at their breasts. Not their nipples – no! You shouldn't be looking at that. You shouldn't be doing that'. And I'd tell [myself] 'No, no, no, I'm not, I'm fine, I'm normal, I'm normal, I'm normal.'[28]

While Susan's fantasies were based on television romances, other women imagined sexual encounters with women they knew in daily life. Rachel first became aware of her desire for a same-sex relationship when she 'fell head over heels in love' with her supervisor at university in 1970s Tasmania. Although 'nothing much' happened between the two women, Rachel recalled having 'all sorts of fantasies' about a possible relationship. She explained:

> Well for a while she had this beaut flat with a big fireplace and a sheepskin rug and I fantasised about making out on the rug in front of the fire and things like that. I didn't actually imagine I'd live with her or anything like that, but I did imagine having sex with her.[29]

For some women, the first acknowledgement of a lesbian identity was accompanied by a period of sexual experimentation, in which they had multiple short-term sexual partners. Nakissa, who came out on the London lesbian scene in the mid-1990s, after a short-lived marriage to a man, reflected that she had felt free to experiment sexually with other women, unconstrained by cultural scripts about appropriate sexual behaviour:

> One of the things I discovered is I could have a sexuality. I could have a sexuality and express that sexuality without fear of having a reputation. It was really interesting because as a straight woman or as a woman living a straight life you have to guard your sexuality ... I didn't have to worry about that anymore, I could just be me and go, 'Right, I just wanna learn about myself sexually, I wanna learn about other people sexually, I want to explore' and I just did. I did and it was a really great time for me.[30]

Maxine described a similar experience of experimentation when she was a student in the 1980s. She rang Gay Line in Perth in search of other lesbians and remembered being 'very, very interested in sexual exploration'. While Maxine felt that sex has 'always been a really strong driving force in my life and a really strong part of any relationship that I'm in', her early twenties were particularly characterized by multiple affairs and 'sexual hunger'.[31]

Some women, like Maxine, found that a strong desire to express their passion for women sexually continued throughout their lives. Margaret, born in the Midlands in 1930, similarly described a lifetime of relatively long-term committed relationships with a few women, punctuated by numerous brief sexual affairs with other women. She reflected:

> I had lots of different girlfriends. Lots and lots of girlfriends ... All the way through. I've been a bit – I've not been absolutely 100 per cent. I've been a bit naughty. You know, little bits on the side as you do. Well you don't but I did. Not too bad ... People I've worked with or something. Got to like. Nothing serious.[32]

For Margaret, her understanding of herself as 'a bit naughty' was central to her sexual identity. As her aside, 'Well you don't but I did', implies, this was an aspect of her experience which she considered to be potentially unique to her, rather than characteristic of a shared lesbian identity. Certainly, other women represented sexual desire as less important than emotional intimacy in their relations with women. Chloe claimed that: 'I've never been a person who's had a great libido or anything. I've never been one who's been driven by the libido. It's more emotion, been emotional attachments really – unless I'm in a bit of denial about lust!'[33] Although the individual sexual drive of the women involved was important in defining the significance of sex within a relationship, the dynamic between the women was also a determinant factor. Megg, whose first lesbian relationship had been almost entirely platonic, described her next relationship as 'all about physical contact'. She recalled that 'from the very beginning, we could walk – she'd be at one end of the pub, I'd be at another – and you could feel, we could fuck each other across the room with our eyes. It was an incredibly sexual relationship.'[34]

The frequency and significance of sex within a relationship could also shift over time for a variety of reasons. Many women described the beginning of a relationship as an intensely erotic period, when women were likely to be sexually intimate often. Recounting the history of their relationship to a lesbian magazine, Sam and Wendy described meeting at a Trades Union Congress women's summer school in London in 1991. Wendy recalled that, after an evening of pool and Budweiser:

> Then, around about midnight she looked at her watch, grabbed my hand and said 'It's time for bed.' At the lift I said, 'Where are we going?' She said, 'Up to my room.' So we got in the lift and we kissed. In Sam's room she said, 'Pull the curtains and get yer kit off.' We spent the rest of the week having mad, passionate sex. Everyone else on the course thought we'd been together for years and years and years. I went home black and blue ... At the end of the week, Sam went back to the Elephant and Castle, I went back to Eastbourne ... We arranged to meet next day cos it was Pride ... and had sex, standing in the middle of the crowd in front of the main stage.[35]

Some women maintained frequent or regular sexual intimacy throughout their relationships, while others found that the physical aspect of their relationship dwindled over time. Marit reflected that, after twenty eight years with her partner, Sally, the sexual aspect of their relationship had decreased. 'Ideally', she said, 'I think we'd probably still like to express ourselves sexually, weekly. But we've probably – we might not do it for a month sometimes.' Comparing this with the early years of their relationship, Marit commented: 'I've heard it likened to, that in the first year if you put a smartie in a jar for each time you made love, you'd fill it, and then, thereafter, you took one out, you'd never empty the jar.'[36] Jean felt that, in her experience, the frequency of sex had declined with age. She commented:

> I used to like sex two or three times a week ... But these days it's once a week and it's perfectly fine for both of us and we're not in lust – we're way beyond the 'Oh, I can't keep my hands off you' kind of thing, but we're still sexually attracted to each other and I think that's an important aspect. So I'm very glad.[37]

Throughout the course of a relationship, certain events, such as illness or the birth of a child, could act as an obstacle to sex. Louise, whose partner became pregnant about ten years into their relationship, recalled:

> [D]uring pregnancy, then, of course, the sexual side of it was intermittent, and then wasn't comfortable. She was tired and I was tired, and I'm just trying to think whether she had much morning sickness. I don't think too much. She had varicose vein issues and those sorts of things. Then, of course, once [the baby] was born, it was full-on ... So sex was not something we thought of.[38]

Louise's experience that pregnancy and the physical and emotional pressures of caring for small children limited opportunities and desire for sex was echoed by many other lesbian mothers, while other women discussed the impact of illness and disability on sexual relationships. In an article describing her frustrations with the ways in which the lesbian community related to disabled lesbians, Kirsten Hearn told British radical feminist journal, *Trouble and Strife*:

> Different women with different disabilities have different needs and abilities before, during and after sex. Some of us can only lie in certain positions or may have to use different parts of our bodies. Some of us have more strength and energy than others ... Many lesbians with disabilities, taking in the oppressive ideologies that we do not deserve, wanting and needing to be loved, will find ourselves under-confident, over-anxious to please and willing to submit to almost anything the other woman wishes us to do or have done to us.[39]

In addition to the specific issues of strength and ability she described, Kirsten also noted that disabled lesbians, in common with other disabled people, were widely assumed to have no sexuality or sexual desire, and that their ability to form sexual relationships was restricted by the difficulties of identifying partners and overcoming able-bodied lesbians' assumptions and prejudices.

Cultural constructions of lesbian sex

Despite individual variations in sexual instinct, many women drew on current cultural models of same-sex sexuality in making sense of their sexuality. In the immediate post-war decades, available discourses of lesbian sex were muted and frequently originated in mainstream depictions of homosexuality such as those by medical and social commentators and journalists but, by the 1970s, lesbian communities and subcultures were constructing an increasing variety of sexual models. While the literature on lesbianism in the 1950s and 1960s was limited in comparison to the attention devoted to male homosexuality by a range of 'experts' and the press, those commentaries that were published tended to emphasize the sexual aspect of lesbian identity and practice, typically representing lesbians as either dangerously promiscuous or possessing a weak sexual impulse. Albertine Winner, drawing on her experience in the British women's services to describe homosexuality in women in 1947, made a distinction between the typically under-sexed lesbian and the dangerous promiscuous type. She observed:

> The great majority of homosexual relations among women, including many of the true 'love affairs,' are not associated with anything that could be described as sexual intercourse. There may be a good deal of love-making, caressing, love-play, but mutual masturbation, any real attempt at producing orgasm, is not at all common.[40]

However, she warned that a small minority of lesbians posed a much greater threat to society through their uncontrolled sexuality:

> There is, however, a second and much more dangerous type, the promiscuous Lesbian who, passing quickly and lightly from affair to affair, usually with physical relations, may cause great harm and unhappiness … Some are psychopathic heterosexuals themselves (or rather, bisexuals) who, bored and dissatisfied with promiscuous and purely sensual relations with men, take to going with women to find novelty and satisfaction. It is with them that we find the grosser perversions and elaborate physical practices, not the general run of Lesbians.[41]

In his 1959 study of male and female homosexuality, *Odd Man Out*, British psychiatrist, Eustace Chesser, dedicated one of only two chapters on lesbianism solely to a discussion of 'lesbian love' and similarly drew on both of these tropes. Chesser also characterized the 'true invert' as aggressively sexual. In one of four lesbian case histories, Chesser described an innate lesbian who was characterized by her masculine attitude and appearance. She had enjoyed a successful career in the WRAF before her intense sexual urges prompted her dismissal. Chesser recounted:

> The incident which lead to her discharge was an indecent assault on another girl with whom she shared a room. It occurred while her roommate was undressing. She suddenly embraced her and became so excited she was quite unable to restrain herself.
>
> This was not the first time she had behaved in a similar manner. There had been trouble at school and she was expelled.[42]

Medical and broader popular associations of lesbianism and promiscuity impacted on some women's attitudes towards their own same-sex desires in the 1950s and 1960s. When Australian, Margaret, had her first affair with another woman on board a ship to Europe in the 1950s, she found the experience enjoyable but possessed no knowledge of the concept of lesbianism. Instead, she recalled assuming that the woman who had seduced her was 'deviant; over-sexed', reflecting the broader cultural impact of such notions of lesbianism.[43] Sydney lesbian, Sandra, described in her memoir her fears that her sexual partners would consider her excessively interested in sex. As a result, she felt inhibited in expressing her sexual desires, even in private, and felt that this impacted negatively on her relationships. Recalling visits from two lovers in the mid-1950s, Sandra explained:

> I knew the hour each was due to arrive at my door, I knew the purpose of the knock on the door, but my greeting would be so rigidly formal. An invitation to a cup of tea, then an invitation to join me in bed. I was always ready for a rejection of the offer. No touching beforehand, no caressing, not even a kiss until we were undressed and hidden in the bed itself. There, out of sight of the world, I could relax and say the things I should have said earlier as between friends. I was fearful to show just how anxious I was to touch and kiss, lest others deem me a sex maniac of sorts. I was fearful to show any emotion at all. But as emotion was constantly raging through me, my attempts at repression were most painful. And incomplete. So I remained a tense, stiff, hurting individual who could bring no pleasure to others.[44]

In Britain, the medical characterization of lesbians as hypersexual was reflected in broader cultural representations of lesbian sex practice which helped shape popular attitudes towards lesbian sexuality in the post-war period. British journalist, Bryan Magee, who produced a television documentary on lesbians in 1965 and a book on male and female homosexuality in 1966, again emphasized the sexual aspect of lesbian relationships. In his book, *One in Twenty*, the section on lesbians began with a chapter entitled 'What Lesbians Do' which enumerated the different sexual positions (mutual masturbation, cunnilingus and tribadism) that he considered to be commonly practised by lesbians and he claimed that lesbians experienced more orgasms than heterosexual women.[45] That his views reflected not only medical but broader public assumptions about lesbianism is apparent in attitudes lesbians encountered in this period. When British lesbian magazine, *Arena Three*, was launched in 1964, one of the founding members, 'DMC', commented with surprise on how many men had requested sample subscriptions to the magazine in the hope of finding erotic titillation. This response implied, she argued, that the public image of the lesbian was less of a woman whose sole sexual interest was in women, than of a woman 'skilled in bizarre sexual practices'.[46] Her comments may have been a reference to the association of lesbianism with the use of sex toys which emerged in cultural references to lesbianism at this time. Bryan Magee was one of a handful of British journalists who began to explore the subject of lesbianism in the 1960s, frequently reiterating this and similar themes.[47] In 1963, Dilys Rowe claimed in the *Twentieth Century*:

> On the seamier side there are the dingy clubs where, so a member of one of them told me, pick-ups are made, gossip is circulated about other people's affairs, the latest news from the homosexual clubs in Holland is put about, as well as information about the latest 'aides' to homosexual practice from the continent. (She spoke about them wistfully, as some women would talk about the new Paris line, without much hope of being able to buy it over here this season.)[48]

Although media representations of lesbianism were much more limited in Australia in the 1960s, notions of lesbians as over-sexed and addicted to the use of sex toys were circulating in some medical circles in this period. When an Adelaide lesbian activist consulted a gynaecologist at the request of her mother in the early 1970s, she was confronted with a similar assumption. She recalled: 'He was surprised to learn that few lesbians use dildoes.'[49]

Throughout the 1960s, individual women and magazines such as *Arena Three* sought to counter such representations of lesbianism as erotic with a more respectable, desexualized image. Commenting on the subscription requests from would-be male readers of *Arena Three*, DMC observed: 'The most unfortunate aspect of this unholy mesalliance between lesbianism and pornography is that it diverts attention from the really important problems, which are social, to the comparatively minor ones of sexuality.'[50] She reiterated this point in an article for *Family Doctor* in 1965, observing 'Women do not appear, superficially at any rate, to have the same urgent physical desires which lead men into trouble and into promiscuity.'[51] Like many other homophile magazines of the period, *Arena Three* itself avoided publication of any explicitly sexual content, focusing instead largely on the social aspects of lesbianism.[52] In so doing, the magazine echoed another familiar post-war medical trope – the insignificance of physical intimacy in lesbianism.

In his 1959 comments on female homosexuality, Eustace Chesser argued that 'the sexual instinct in a woman is not nearly so concentrated on genital contacts' and her 'sexuality is far more diffuse, hence the greater importance she attributes to kisses and caresses. Moreover, she is less easy to arouse through a purely physical approach. She does not merely desire the relief that intercourse can give, she wants to feel that she is loved.'[53] As a result, many women, he suggested, found an outlet for their lesbian urges through expressions of close friendship, such as sharing a bed and kissing, without ever acknowledging their homosexuality. Despite the recurrent figure of the predatory, over-sexed lesbian, many medical commentators in the 1950s and early 1960s similarly tended to emphasize the low sexual drive of the majority of lesbians. D.J. West, in his widely read Pelican volume on homosexuality, reissued several times between 1955 and 1968, observed:

> Physical contacts between lesbians most often arise out of strong friendships or protracted sentimental attachments, and for a long time they may be limited to kissing and caressing without any attempt at mutual masturbation or sexual orgasm.[54]

Anthony Storr, in his 1964 work, *Sexual Deviation*, claimed that, in contrast to homosexual men, women, 'whether they be homosexual or heterosexual, are not so violently driven by their sexual impulses that they cannot generally postpone their need for satisfaction.' Therefore, he maintained, 'feminine homosexuality is often confined to the psychological level, with perhaps no physical manifestations at all beyond the tender embraces which our society generally accepts as being a natural accompaniment of friendship between women.'[55]

Post-war lesbian sexual practice

Such representations of lesbian sexuality as insignificant impacted on the attitudes of individual women towards their own desires. Reflecting on her early engagement with the 'public myths' of lesbianism, in a paper given at the First National Homosexual Conference in Melbourne in 1975, Barbara Creed recalled the impact of Storr's words on her nineteen-year-old self:

> This disturbed me because while I didn't experience this so-called *violent* sexual urge (which has amused many of my male homosexual friends who are still waiting to be seized by it!) I certainly experienced sexual feelings which were quite intense and which were inextricably bound up with other feelings of love and warmth. Furthermore my relationship was clearly sexual and didn't just involve 'tender embraces'. Did this mean in fact that what I thought was a fairly normal sexual drive was really a violent sexual urge? I had no way of knowing. No-one to ask. No-one to talk to. Was I *even* more abnormal than Mr Storr thought other lesbians were?[56]

This tendency to dismiss the physical side of lesbian intimacy reflected broader attitudes to female sexuality dating from the nineteenth and early twentieth century, which emphasized the procreative function of sex and characterized female sexuality as passive or reactive.[57] By the post-war period, sexual advice experts in both Britain and Australia were promoting the vaginal orgasm as the ideal and only true expression of marital sexuality, which combined the possibility of mutual, simultaneous orgasm with the potential for conception.[58] Within this context, many post-war medical and cultural commentators found it difficult to conceptualize the possibility that sex between women could accord its participants sexual satisfaction. Thus, one Australian woman, describing a visit she had made to a gynaecologist in the early 1970s at the instigation of her concerned parents, told activist magazine, *Boiled Sweets*:

> Throughout the interview he refused to accept that a woman can be spontaneously sexually aroused by another woman, although he conceded that digital manipulation of the clitoris might induce a clitoral orgasm. However, he insisted that only nature's triumph of design, the penis, could induce a true vaginal orgasm … He was amazed and, I suspect, sceptical when I said that lesbians could have not just one, but several orgasms in a love-making session. He implied that, as I had never been properly fucked, I was probably mistaking extreme pleasure for orgasm.[59]

While medical and mainstream cultural assumptions about lesbian sexuality shaped some women's conceptualizations of their own desire and sexual practice in this period, an alternative discourse emerged from lesbian communities. For women who found lovers and formed relationships in the context of butch/femme subcultures in the 1950s and 1960s, a cultural framework structured their sexual encounters with other women. Subsequent lesbian feminist critiques of butch/femme represented such women as victims of an oppressive era, who had unthinkingly adopted the unequal and exploitative interactions of heteropatriarchal relationships. Butch/femme lesbians were accused of maintaining a power dynamic in which feminine lesbians were sexually objectified by their masculine partners and lacked agency in the expression of their sexual desires and pleasures.[60] However, butch/femme culture and relationships were much more complex and deeply layered than this depiction suggests. Historic assumptions about women's sexual passivity rendered the assertion of lesbian desire extremely problematic and butch/femme culture provided a language in which to articulate the erotic aspect of same-sex relationships. In her 1982 critique of lesbian feminist approaches to butch/femme, Wendy Clark argued: 'Sexual visibility in the sense of assertion of one's sexuality and sexual needs was something that was allowed only to men. If a woman wished visibly to assert her sexual needs the only model was the male one.'[61] US fem lesbian, Joan Nestle, made a similar point in 1984, arguing: 'a butch lesbian wearing men's clothes in the 1950s was not a man wearing men's clothes; she was a woman who created an original style to signal to other women what she was capable of doing – taking erotic responsibility.'[62] For Nestle, femme style was equally important as a form of erotic communication, signalling a femme's passion and sexual power to butch women and, when in the company of her butch lover, explicitly declaring their sexuality to the world.

Sexual practice in butch/femme communities similarly represented a significant departure from heterosexual models which continued to prioritize male sexual needs in this period. As Wendy Clark noted, the feminist assumption that binary notions of active/passive roles in heterosexual sex could be mapped onto butch/femme sexuality resulted in some serious misconceptions of butch/femme sexual practice by later critics:

> By means of a crude assumption the passive/active of heterosexual sex is passed on to lesbian sex. Whereas in heterosexual sex, because of the present influence of social relations between women and men and the history of those relations, active = taking = men; while passive = receiving = women, in lesbian sexual practice the reality of active/passive can be experienced differently. In lesbian sex the active is the one giving the pleasure to the other as well as possibly obtaining pleasure from the act as well. Even the passive is in a way active. Having pleasure can be an active thing, even though its heterosexual meaning is not that.[63]

This notion of the butch partner as giving sexual pleasure resulted in a unique form of sexual practice which many British and Australian women who engaged in butch/femme sexual encounters in this period recalled. Marion explained:

> It was not all right for a butch to be touched sexually and it is only recently that I've been able to be touched and I sometimes feel awkward about that. Do not assume that this has meant that my sex life has ever been anything but amazing and wonderful! I have always had a strong sex drive and I've shared that with some great women. And learning to be touched hasn't made sex 'better,' only different.[64]

Karen, a Sydney butch lesbian, gave historian Yorick Smaal a more detailed account of the types of sexual practice which were considered acceptable for butch lesbians in this context, explaining:

> I would be on top I would perhaps put my breast in her mouth and as I stimulated her I would rub myself off on her leg or I learned how to have an orgasm by the pleasure of the woman I was pleasuring. Without stimulation ... And of course knowing that I was giving pleasure was giving pleasure to me.[65]

In some communities, the expectation that butch partners would take an active role in sex was strictly policed through gossip and even a degree of bullying or ostracism of women who failed to conform. Londoner, Pat James, recalled that in the community centred on the Gateways club in the late 1940s and early 1950s:

> I remember there was one very butch-looking woman there who had a terrible reputation because she used to get into bed with women and not do anything, and we all used to think it was terribly funny, which we shouldn't really. But your reputation got around – what you were like, what you weren't like, and you were petrified of losing your reputation if it was a good one.[66]

Sydneysider, Karen, used more extreme terms to describe the repercussions of failure to take an active role in her community in the 1960s. She explained:

> If you were in the butch role, then you were never on the bottom, never. It was just known that you were the butch. And if anyone ever heard or got wind (this is in the group), if you had sex in the reclined position there was hell to pay. You were called Willy the cockroach, terrible, terrible degrading things happened to you.[67]

However, the rules were not always completely inflexible. After several years of taking the active role in sex, Pat James experienced a sexual encounter in her late twenties which altered her attitude to butch sexuality. She recalled:

> I felt happy in my butch role and not at all constrained by it. But when I was about twenty-six or twenty-seven, I remember I met a feminine, attractive woman and when we went to bed I didn't really feel attracted to her at that moment. Then I was shocked to find that she was making love to me. And I didn't mind, I rather liked it and it turned out very well with two active people making love. But I was petrified and told her not to tell anyone, which shows the atmosphere of the time ... But, in fact, I discovered that it was much better for both to be active, you know.[68]

Pat James did not experience any repercussions as a result of this encounter and, if both partners exercised discretion, there was scope for more flexibility in sexual practices. Marion Paull stressed that in her Melbourne community in the early 1960s, there was a strong emphasis on keeping the details of sexual encounters private, which inevitably opened up possibilities for sexual exploration between individual women.[69]

While butch/femme culture provided a relatively clear framework within which some women could imagine and enact their sexual desires in this period, other women who were not part of these communities described a variety of attitudes and approaches to sex. Few women at this time had been exposed to any cultural representations of lesbian sexuality and this discursive absence could pose obstacles to women articulating sexual desire or, alternatively, open up potential spaces for unfettered and experimental sexual expressions. Julie, who experienced crushes on girls in England in the late 1950s and early 1960s, recalled her lack of awareness of the sexual potential of her feelings. She explained:

> Something in my background meant that I just never thought about sex with them. I mean I can say now I fancied them but at the time I don't know what I would have called it, I think I would have called it a crush but it didn't have anything to do with sex somehow, because I never thought about sex! And then I fell in love with my boss at work, in one of the libraries I worked in. I kind of knew that was love, but again I didn't really think about sex. I suppose I'd stand close to her and I'd think, 'I wonder what she'd do if I put my hand on her arm?', but you know I didn't think about her being undressed or us kissing each other or anything like that. I don't know why, perhaps it was the Catholic school or the fact my parents never talked about it, I just don't know.[70]

Barbara Bell, on the other hand, described her active and varied sex life in London in the 1940s and 1950s. Recounting her affair with a woman, Jessie, whom she had met at a club in Mayfair, Barbara reflected: 'She was a wonderful lover. She taught me a few things – she knew everything about sex. I didn't know much. That was part of the excitement in those days. You learnt a new trick. And the next person you were with, you passed on the new trick.' In Barbara's recollection, individual sexual encounters represented both an opportunity to develop a personal sexual repertoire and a way of constructing a collective lesbian sexual culture through shared practice. This sexual culture was remarkably varied and Barbara recalled that, in addition to showing her oral sex, sado-masochism and using a homemade dildo, Jessie also 'showed me how delightful a bath could be together. Never thought of that before. She showed me how sexy long hair can be when you're making love.'[71] For Barbara, sexual roles were a performance, which varied between different relationships and according to the shifting desires of individuals. She commented:

> That's what is so nice about lesbian relationships … You might be two feminine-looking women, you might be two butch-looking women, but when you get stripped of your clothes, of the façade that you're walking about in, it doesn't matter. Maybe your femininity will come out in your love-making. Maybe the other side. You can follow your mood. Maybe you're in the midst of some affair and you're the dominant one. Then you see somebody else and think, I'd like her to do things to me – I'd like her to be the boss. Okay. Be all feminine. Put on your false eyelashes. Make up your face. Play the part.[72]

Barbara's account of her sexual experience emphasized the pleasurable and playful aspects of erotic relationships with other women.

Feminist approaches to lesbian sex

In the late 1960s and early 1970s, a new generation of women began to approach the theory and practice of sex between women in the context of feminism. In Australia, where radical feminist ideas were very influential in the women's movement, sex and intimacy were widely debated and theorized in the early 1970s. The Melbourne Radicalesbians, formed in 1973, produced a number of conference papers and other writings exploring sex and intimacy between women, which questioned the connections between genital sexuality and normative models of intimacy such as marriage, commitment and monogamy and promoted the importance of individual women's sexual agency. Barbara articulated these ideas in her paper delivered at the 1973 Radicalesbian conference when she claimed:

> The radicalesbian challenges the idea basic to a patriarchal society that women exist for men and that their sexuality can only be defined in terms of response to a male's sexuality ... She rejects completely the assumption that sexuality is the gift of the male and violates willingly the male-female social contract (nuclear family, consumerism, etc.). She understands completely her own sexuality and sensuality: her clitoris her body. She is able to enjoy sexual relating with other women and should be able to discuss problems of sexuality with her lover – usually a silent topic between men and women. She also understands how to relate to herself – 'masturbation is better than oppressive mating'.[73]

Challenging earlier assumptions of female sexual passivity, radical feminist approaches to sexuality emphasized women's knowledge of and control over their own bodies and desires and located women as active agents in the exploration of their sexual desires.

This theoretical perspective fostered a culture which encouraged women to express and act upon their desires for each other and Australian and British lesbian feminist communities in the early 1970s promoted the practice of non-monogamy and sexual exploration. Laurene, who lived a radical lesbian feminist lifestyle in Australia in this period, recalled:

> Monogamy was an imitation of heterosexuality and we had to break down any imitations. So ... we were very promiscuous, a lot of us ... The whole thing about safe sex and stuff wasn't an issue for women – or pregnancy or contraception. So I think we had wild sex. That was one of the greatest things, I think, that was about being a lesbian back then when everyone was lesbians and the Radicalesbians – sex was absolutely magnificent because it was uninhibited.[74]

Influenced by psychoanalytic and counter-cultural notions of the self, feminist theory and practice of this period emphasized the importance of individual women reflecting on their own attitudes and assumptions, with the aim of challenging internalized patriarchal notions of sexuality. For some, consciousness-raising groups provided a context in which women would share and examine their sexual attitudes, while others read and debated literature or engaged in discussion and experimentation with friends and lovers. Dorothy recalled that, in her left-wing political circle in Belfast,

> [W]e were all reading really stimulating kinds of things to do with the ego and personal relationships. We were reading things like Alan Watts, or Laing – I can't remember what else but things that made you think about what your personal identity was and what your sexual identity was. And it seemed a really obvious thing that you could become sexually involved with either sex.

A few years later, Dorothy and her then lover, Nora, became involved in organizing a Women and Socialism conference on sexuality in London. Nora spoke about the challenges of multiple relationships, which both women were experimenting with, and the conference led to the formation of a discussion group on multiple relationships, which Dorothy joined. She recalled:

> I think what we were trying to do was find a way you could have more than one relationship and not go round the twist! [laughs] Yeah, I mean, at that period it was all very intense and part of the time, you were just like trying to examine what was going on in all of the different relationships and accusing each other of not behaving in the way that we thought you had to behave for the thing to work.[75]

Dorothy described an ongoing practice over several years of individual and collective examination of her own attitudes towards and experience of sexuality, which both opened up new possibilities for her and was a source of conflict in her life. Liz similarly described extensive self-reflection on multiple relationships as an arduous and sometimes disempowering experience. When her feminist involvement prompted her to broach her same-sex desires with her husband, their discussion ultimately resulted in an attempt to have a three-way relationship with another woman. Liz explained:

> I think we were very – naively, but very seriously – trying to explore issues around sexuality and issues around possessiveness and jealousy and friendship and how those things come together and don't. And we spent hours, I mean probably, if you added them all up, it would add up to weeks, kind of talking through the minutiae of all of this … But I increasingly felt I was going crazy in this relationship, because what we talked about wasn't what I felt was actually happening.[76]

Despite the widely noted emotional cost of this culture of non-monogamy, assumptions that women who were already in a sexual relationship with one woman should feel free to have casual or more long-term sexual relationships with other women as well shaped the behaviour of many women in feminist and counter-cultural communities. Gilli Salvat, who was involved in lesbian feminist circles in London in the late 1970s, recalled that when she met her lover, Louie:

> I was going out with four other women at the time. All at different stages of breaking up or getting it together or whatever! One was throwing bottles at my head and Carol Lee was sleeping with half the dykes in Brighton and I was upset about that. And there was this other woman who was 8 and a half months pregnant! Who was a Buddhist and all things like that. And I met Louie at a disco and we finally got off with each other and it was really good, sexually.[77]

In this context, some women described feeling under a degree of pressure, both from themselves and the women around them, to accept and enable their partners' sexual encounters with other women. Sylvia described a sexual relationship she was in with a younger woman in Adelaide who 'was always flirting with other women and it was very painful. But this was the year of no monogamy and you should have open relationships'. Her lover became 'obsessed' with another woman and, during a feminist conference, went out to dinner with this woman and stayed out all night. The following morning, she returned to the place she and Sylvia were staying, upset because the night had not been a success, sexually, and Sylvia was expected to counsel her through her experience. Sylvia explained: 'Anyway, she got into bed and we then talked about it. I had to comfort her because it had been a disappointment. That's the level of politics we were at. Painful – oh, god, the pain.'[78]

Theoretical discussions of sex and intimacy framed jealousy as 'meaningless' and a hangover from patriarchal notions of sexual possessiveness.[79] Many women, like Sylvia, therefore strove to overcome feelings of jealousy and hurt arising from their partners' practice of non-monogamy; often with limited success. Some women, however, felt particularly vulnerable to the emotional repercussions of non-monogamous sexual practice as a result of their individual emotional make-up or their past experiences. Shirani, who was involved in a lesbian feminist circle in Brighton in the early 1970s, recalled: 'I tried to adopt those ideas about non-monogamy and actually they caused me an incredible amount of pain and grief. I've had a lot of loss in my life already, loss of friends, I've had no stability really, and it didn't provide that.'[80] Non-monogamy was also potentially problematic if one partner in a longer-term relationship was more interested in practicing non-monogamy than the other. By the 1980s, there was growing recognition in lesbian feminist circles that, while some women were able to embrace the practice of non-monogamy enthusiastically, others found it emotionally challenging. This ideological shift was articulated in a range of literature exploring lesbian feminist ethics and emphasizing the importance of lesbian feminists treating their lovers with respect.[81]

Feminist critiques of heteropatriarchal sexual models also helped to frame the ways in which women in lesbian feminist circles practised sex with each other. In the 1950s and 1960s, influential feminist texts such as Simone de Beauvoir's *The Second Sex* and Monique Wittig's novel *Les Guerilleres* had articulated a powerful critique of earlier sexological work which had defined penetrative sex as the quintessential sexual act and prioritized the vaginal orgasm.[82] Instead, feminist sexual politics celebrated the clitoris as the locus of sexual pleasure for women and penetrative sex came to be understood as an invasion of a woman's body and a crucial means of her subordination.[83] Lesbian sex, in contrast, was framed as potentially much more equal; a move away from active and passive roles towards a non-hierarchical model of sex. Reflecting on her personal journey from heterosexual feminist to lesbian feminist, Sue Roxon told the *Sydney Women's Liberation Newsletter*:

> I guess the basic attraction for me in being sexually involved with women was that I felt that it would entail total involvement. Unlike with men, with women I felt that I wouldn't be able to just lie back and take it. There wouldn't be a hierarchy automatically established by our sexes. There is no lesbian equivalent of the missionary position![84]

The 'total involvement' Sue envisaged would arise from the unique friendship and intimacy women were capable of experiencing with each other. Nett Hart articulated this view in her essay on a radical feminist lesbian separatist perspective on sexuality, arguing:

> If the one with whom you are sexual is someone you love, someone you know and who knows you, someone of whom you are not afraid, then it will be impossible to Objectify. We can welcome the whole package of who we are and who our partner is … [T]he sex created by intimacy is a movement to engage the beloved physically, psychically, and emotionally in ways that spring from our knowing connection. It is this wild, unarticulated sexuality that opens us to the possibility of our deeply life-loving connections in co-passion.

At the heart of this connection was mutual trust and respect which was made possible both by the friendship the individual women felt for each other and, more broadly, the social equality which was assumed to exist between two women.[85] Australian lesbian feminist, Jan Smith similarly argued: 'The essential point of Lesbianism, and that which is usually overlooked, is that it involves not just sex, but love between women: love between equals – a potentially far healthier proposition than the typical heterosexual equivalent.'[86] The assumption that love between women was inevitably equal, however, ignored concerns about power imbalances raised by many working-class and disabled lesbians and lesbians of colour. Hope Massiah told the authors of *Lesbians Talk: Making Black Waves*: 'Relationships with White women are fraught with difficulties. I've been in relationships with White women, and although they were good, the issue of racism was always there.' Femi Otitoju similarly felt that inequalities could be a problem, arguing 'In general relationships with White women are fine. In reality I see a tremendous amount of abuse – abuse of power and lack of respect from White women.'[87]

For those lesbian feminists influenced by ideas of women's innately nurturing and creative qualities, women were inevitably superior lovers. Jan claimed: 'Women are more tender, more sensitive and considerate of the feelings of others, and while this may be due to our conditioning it makes for a better lover.'[88] These inherent qualities also rendered women's loving instinctive, so that, as Marilyn McLean put it in a letter to *Lesbian Newsletter*: 'Lesbian love needs no "practice" in its sexual aspects, coming naturally and spontaneously. It cares for oneself and the other woman one is in a loving relationship with.'[89] Some women found this sexual culture to be exciting and full of possibilities. Recalling her sexual relationships in the context of lesbian separatist communities in Australia, Britain and Europe in the late 1970s, Laurene commented: 'That was before the notion you had to have toys or anything like that. It was just passion and intensity, I guess, is my experience. I can't say that's everyone's, eh? But I'll tell you it was mine. I had some fabulous sex!'[90] Others, however, found the approach restrictive and felt that the prioritizing of specific forms of sexual practice inhibited their freedom of expression. Sylvia, who was involved in lesbian feminist communities in Adelaide in the 1970s, complained:

> [R]elationships were supposed to be very respectful, very vanilla, if you like to put those phrases on it … no violence, no aggression, it was even hard to talk about – I did this and got a little bit of flack – vibrators were a bit iffy, let alone dildos. Right? So lesbians, whether they did it or not, there was certainly no one would've admitted strapping on a dildo – my God, so awful.[91]

Women who began to have sexual relationships with other women for the first time in this cultural context often described particular difficulties or concerns in conforming to expected sexual practice. Annie and Susan referred to this issue in an interview on Gaywaves Radio in Sydney in 1980, in which they were reflecting on the nature of lesbian relationships. Susan claimed:

> When women realise they are lesbians, it doesn't mean that they instantly achieve total sexual liberation and find themselves able to direct some sort of womanly sexuality to other women. Many women struggle with the question of passivity – that's a joke among lesbians actually, that many women are so passive that they don't get around to having lesbian relationships, because both partners are so passive they can't get around to talking about it to each other.

Annie agreed, adding: 'There is a double-bind in that too, as there's the thing about being passive, and there's also the fear of being seen in that male wooing/chasing/hunting role.'[92]

By the late 1970s, the growing emphasis on political lesbianism was responsible for the development of a number of different feminist perspectives on lesbian sex. In their hugely influential essay, 'Woman-Identified Woman', the New York Radicalesbians had attempted to replace conventional post-war definitions of lesbianism in terms of sexuality with a more constructed identity model, representing a lesbian primarily as a woman who was trying to create an identity outside of the conventionally feminine (something all radical feminists aimed to do).[93] The Radicalesbians therefore positioned lesbians as like heterosexual feminists, but ahead of them on the feminist journey: pioneers of the feminist revolution.[94] This positioning of lesbians at the vanguard of feminism created both a sexual hierarchy which valued lesbians as more committed to the women's movement than heterosexual women and a belief that sexuality was a choice which women could make to align their intimate lives with their feminist politics. These ideas influenced British and Australian feminists throughout the 1970s and a number of women took the decision to become lesbians for political reasons at this time. Sand, a New Zealander who lived in lesbian feminist communities in Australia and Britain in the 1970s, made this choice. She recalled:

> Once I came across lesbians it was just like 'Oh, this is just far too much fun! Combine business with pleasure' and off we went ... I certainly am not of the opinion that I was born a lesbian ... It was very much a political choice and that was where I chose to put my time and energy and along the way just came across all these other women that had also decided to.[95]

While Sand framed her decision in terms of a coming together of political commitment and sexual pleasure, by the end of the decade a less sexualized form of political lesbianism was being strongly advocated in some feminist circles, a model which helped shape historiographical questioning of the importance of genital sexuality in the lesbian relationships of the past. In Britain, the debate about the relationship between feminism and lesbianism was brought into the open by the Leeds Revolutionary Feminist Group, whose essay, 'Political Lesbianism', was published in *WIRES*, the national newsletter of the British women's movement, in 1979. The essay sought to spark an explicit debate on a topic which the authors felt had been suppressed in the movement for a number of years: the question of whether 'all feminists should be lesbians'.[96] Supporting this position, the Leeds Revolutionary Feminist Group argued that: 'it is specifically through sexuality that the fundamental oppression, that of men over women, is maintained' and that therefore 'Every woman who lives with or fucks a man helps to maintain the oppression of her sisters and hinders our struggle.' Acknowledging that many women would find it difficult to 'give up men', the authors argued: 'We do think that all feminists can and should be political lesbians. Our definition of a political lesbian is a woman-identified woman who does not fuck men. It does not mean compulsory sexual activity with women.'[97] For these revolutionary feminists, political lesbianism was therefore defined by a decision not to engage in sex with men, rather than a positive choice to engage in sex with women. Not only was eroticism between women downplayed, but celibacy was embraced as an equally valid option for political lesbians.[98]

'Sex positive' culture

By the early 1980s, frustrations with the perceived de-eroticization of political lesbianism and some women's dissatisfaction with lesbian feminist forms of sexual practice prompted an increasingly contentious debate around the meanings of lesbian sexuality and the types of sexual fantasy and sexual practice enacted by lesbians. The 1981 publication of *Sex Heresies*, a US feminist periodical, which explored a range of lesbian sexual forms from sadomasochism (SM), masturbation and erotica to butch/femme relationships and celibacy, sparked controversy in the United States and influenced debate in Britain and Australia as well. Kimberley O'Sullivan has noted the eruption of a further debate in Australia the same year, when the Leeds Revolutionary Feminist Group's pamphlet, *Love Your Enemy?*, was distributed in Australia.[99]

In Britain, Susan Ardill and Sue O'Sullivan claimed in 1986: 'the struggle around sexuality has been muted and spasmodic, though accompanied by often violently intense reactions.'[100] These reactions took the form of conflict between a number of lesbian feminists (revolutionary feminists amongst the most vocal) and lesbians advocating sadomasochism or supporting a liberal stance towards sexuality.[101] In the winter of 1983–4, the *London Women's Liberation* Newsletter refused to publish a notice about a meeting called by SM Dykes to discuss sadomasochism and in 1985 a lengthy dispute was carried on over whether lesbian SM groups should be allowed to meet in the newly opened London Lesbian and Gay Centre.[102] Throughout these debates, revolutionary feminists and other lesbian feminists – some of them members of the group Lesbians Against Sado Masochism – represented SM sex as violent, racist, fascist, oppressive and fundamentally 'male'.[103] Groups such as SM Dykes and the Sexual Fringe, on the other hand, represented 'deviant' forms of sexuality as the only exciting erotic possibilities, dismissing 'vanilla' sex as boring. In Australia, a similar divide emerged between lesbian feminists and 'sex radical' dykes, but manifested less in the outright exclusion of SM dykes from lesbian space than in continued vocal and angry debates at lesbian events.[104] Reflecting, in 1991, that the 'lesbian nation' was now split into tribes, many of whom were fundamentally divided from each other, Kimberley O'Sullivan recalled:

> At the first heat of the [sex positive] 1991 Ms Wicked competition, no sooner had contestant number one left the stage than the place erupted. While the MC valiantly tried to regain control, a non-stop torrent of abuse flew between members of the audience. Some women loudly objected to the nature of the fantasy shown, while others objected to the attempted censorship of the woman's performance.[105]

The intensity of feeling in both Australia and Britain meant that it dominated lesbian debate and spaces for a period in the 1980s and early 1990s and individual women often felt obliged to take a clear stance on the issue.

While SM tended to attract the most vitriolic criticism, Sue O'Sullivan and Susan Ardill argued that: 'To some extent, SMers have captured the market of sexual description' and SM became a catch-all term to refer to a much broader range of lesbian sexualities which began to be articulated in the 1980s. The increased publication of literature and films about lesbian sex in this decade point to a growing desire on the part of lesbians for information about and depictions of lesbian sex, but this was a gradual shift and it was not until the second half of the decade that a lesbian sex radical culture fully emerged in Australia and Britain.[106] In Britain, the late 1980s saw the founding of Britain's first lesbian sex magazine, *Quim*, and the publication of a British collection of lesbian erotica, *Serious Pleasure*. Edited by the Sheba Collective, *Serious Pleasure* included a mixture of American and British erotic short stories and poetry prefaced by an introduction which explained the collective's feminist approach to erotica. Sue O'Sullivan, a member of the collective, recalled:

> We wanted a book which was inclusive of black lesbians, lesbians of different ages, we wanted a mix of pretty hard sexy raunchy stuff and nice vanilla stuff, we wanted a whole, you know, we wanted it to be a book that somebody would find something that they found quite exciting.[107]

The book was a commercial success and played an important role in opening up a new space for the representation of lesbian sexuality.[108] In contrast to the inclusive approach adopted in *Serious Pleasure*, *Quim* was envisaged as a direct and confronting challenge to lesbian feminist sexual theory and practice. The magazine discussed SM, butch/femme and prostitution and included erotic photographs, short stories and a number of controversial sexual fantasies, referring to under-age sex and lesbian rape.

In tandem with the gradual increase in production of lesbian erotica, a lesbian sex radical scene was beginning to emerge in Britain and Australia in the mid-1980s. In London, radical lesbians living in squats in Brixton and Hackney founded lesbian fetish club, Chain Reaction, in 1987. Siobhan Fahey recalled that the club, which had a 'sex cabaret' show each week, attracted controversy from women who disagreed with the sexual politics but this contributed to the club's success and it was 'always packed out'.[109] Jamie recalled Chain Reaction as her first introduction to the leather scene in the 1980s. She reflected:

> I was scared to death. I remember going in and just getting a drink, and I was sweating buckets. I think I was wearing black jeans and a leather jacket. But I was so nervous that somebody was going to leap out and make me do things that I really wanted to do, but I was scared. And nobody did anything, it was a little disappointing. No, they had cabarets and they had … it was just a safe, fun, raunchy place to be.[110]

At the same time, Brixton Women's Centre hosted a night called 'Systematic' which promoter, Yvonne Taylor, said attracted 'a whole range of different types of women: black, white, young, old, butch and femme'.[111] Chain Reaction closed in 1990 but was soon replaced by The Clit Club, which attracted SM lesbians and hosted live sex performances.[112]

In 1984 a small group of Sydney women had formed Sexually Outrageous Women for 'all women interested in exploring/experimenting in diverse sexual activities (including SM)' and organized public events including readings of sexual fantasies, demonstrations of sex toys and an SM demonstration. The group folded within a year but, in 1988, Australian lesbian sex magazine, *Wicked Women*, was founded in Sydney and became a focal point for lesbian sex radicals. The following year, the magazine began to organize parties, known as Be Wicked parties. Kimberley O'Sullivan recalled:

> The first, Be Wicked 1, was held in an old warehouse with lesbian porn gracing the walls, spaghetti wrestling, a public sex space and even an a cappella singer. When the police raided in the early hours of the morning and the 300 or so dykes and a sprinkling of gay men were herded out, the infamy of Wicked Women events was assured ...
>
> A typical Wicked Women party had its own resident DJ, SM and bondage performances, enlarged and projected sex slides and non-stop video porn all evening. There was always lots of erotic artwork and performances from the confronting to the totally obscure.[113]

Wicked Women went on to found the Ms Wicked competition in 1990, in which contestants, performing at heats across Australia, were judged on their ability to demonstrate 'wickedness' in their sexual fantasies.[114]

Sex performances became increasingly widespread at lesbian nights in the early 1990s. In an attempt to open up debate about this development and inform their readers about the meanings and aims of these performances, Melbourne lesbian newspaper, *Labrys*, interviewed a number of performers, who described their acts and reflected on their personal motivations. Rene, whose performances at the Tote were described as having 'generated a great deal of interest and discussion about lesbian sexuality', explained:

> I wore chaps which exposed my bum and my breasts were also exposed. I eroticised with myself, feeling my body and looking into a full length mirror – enjoying the look and feel of my body. I fantasised about wearing / having a penis (I wore a dildo) and masturbated my penis [dildo], I also licked my riding boots in front of the mirror.[115]

Rene went on to discuss another, particularly controversial performance in which she and her lover Mace enacted a fantasy where Mace was a gay male prostitute and Rene was a gay male undercover police officer posing as a potential client. The women wore men's clothing and moustaches and the act involved the use of a knife and handcuffs. Her account hints at the connections between gay male and lesbian sexual culture and practice in this period. While lesbian feminist critiques of lesbian sex radical culture as sexist or patriarchal inhibited open discussion of the ways in which gay male sexual culture might influence lesbian sexual practice, some shared venues offered opportunities for exchange, such as the Sex Subculture parties in Sydney where C. Moore Hardy documents that 'lesbians performed alongside queers and homosexuals'.[116]

Despite the development of lesbian sexual culture in magazines and venues in the 1980s and 1990s, however, many lesbians continued to feel that it was not possible to discuss lesbian sexuality and their own sexual experiences openly. In their book, *Lesbians Talk: Making Black Waves*, Valerie Mason-John and Ann Khambatta argued that the focus on SM had prevented discussion of other sexual matters:

> The arguments about SM in the lesbian community have masked the need for safe, open debates about lesbian sex and sexuality. Too many discussions have been polarised along the line of where individuals stood regarding SM, with no space to talk about the realities of lesbian sex in a way that includes the fact that it is not always a glorious experience. Neither has there been room to discuss the fact that lesbians can and do abuse each other in ways that have nothing to do with consent.[117]

Mason-John and Khambatta highlighted the polarizing effect of the 'sex wars', suggesting that these debates made it impossible to discuss forms of sex other than SM. However, SM itself also seemed to remain largely taboo in discussion of personal sexual experience in the 1980s and 1990s. The Hall Carpenter lesbian and gay oral history collection, which was created in this period, is indicative of the inhibiting effect the politicization of SM seems to have had on discussion of sexual practice. Lesbian-identifying participants did not discuss personal engagement in SM practices and this remains a feature of more recent oral history collections, in which narrators might describe involvement in an SM club scene, but not personal sexual practice. Narrators' perception that lesbian feminist or academic researchers would disapprove of such practices, or that they were not appropriate for the public record, might have prevented oral history participants from discussing this experience.[118] In Britain, this reluctance to detail personal engagement in SM sex may also have been influenced by the wider political and legal climate in the late 1980s and 1990s. In a context of heightened homophobia fed by fears about HIV/AIDS and the right-wing political emphasis on 'family values', the Operation Spanner case demonstrated the potential legal consequences of participation in SM sexual practice, when police used a videotape and recorded admissions from participants to convict sixteen gay men of assault for engaging in consensual SM.[119]

Feminist and lesbian conferences in Australia and Britain did provide some space for discussion of sex in the 1980s, including opening up conversations about previously taboo sexual trauma, such as child abuse and lesbian rape.[120] However, personal testimonies and other accounts also suggest that, despite the proliferation of discourses around lesbian sexuality after the 1970s, individual women continued to experience difficulties in articulating their personal sexual desires and practices and discussing sexual problems. The development in the 1970s of magazines aimed at young women, such as *Cleo* in Australia and *Cosmopolitan* in Britain, opened up greater discussion of female sexuality more broadly and some women utilized the 'problem pages' and 'agony aunt' columns to voice their personal experiences of same-sex desire, but these forums rarely encouraged or attracted questions of a specifically sexual nature. Specialized sex magazines provided a more targeted space for raising sexual problems and, in the 1970s, some Australian lesbians wrote to *Forum* magazine seeking advice on sexual matters. The magazine offered non-judgmental advice on a wide array of sexual problems and offered a space in which readers of all sexual preferences could recount, and seek information and guidance on, their particular sexual practices.[121] However, only a handful of correspondents raised lesbian sexual problems in the magazine and the absence of discussion of personal sexual experience in specifically lesbian magazines such as *Arena Three* and *Sappho* suggests a general reluctance to raise personal sexual issues in a public forum.

Conclusion

The rich and varied history of lesbian desire and sexual practice in this period demonstrates that sex did and should matter to our understanding of lesbian intimacy. Whether, how frequently and in what ways women were expressing their desire for other women varied enormously according to personal preference, physiological factors and cultural and historical attitudes. Cultural discourses around lesbian sexuality emerged from medical and sexological literature and increasingly from lesbian communities themselves in this period and both the presence and absence of such scripts shaped some women's experience of sex. Nevertheless in various ways, lesbian sex and desire remained and remains a taboo topic which challenges historical attempts to interpret it.

2

Domesticity

The meanings of 'home' were complex for women who were attracted to other women in the post-war period. A substantial scholarship has stressed the pervasive culture of domesticity which dominated post-war British and Australian societies, noting the centrality of the housewife to British political and cultural discourse and the power of the Australian suburban dream in the years after the war.[1] By the 1960s, the emerging Women's Movement was reacting against this idealization of the home, articulating a powerful critique of women's domestic roles as restrictive, isolating and monotonous.[2] However, as the work of a number of feminist historians has shown, this literature primarily reflected the experience of middle-class, educated, white British women for whom the decline of domestic service meant an increase in household labour and a perceived loss of status. For some working-class women, as Judy Giles and Carolyn Steedman have argued, the mid-twentieth century witnessed the final fulfilment of their dreams of acquiring a home of their own and the liberty to dedicate their time and energies to caring for that home.[3] As working-class women were gradually integrated into the discourse of respectable domestic femininity, the meanings of home were further complicated by race. Wendy Webster has demonstrated that, while the 'good home was a central image of national progress', Black women 'experienced serious difficulties in securing any sort of domestic comfort or familial life, regardless of class'.[4] If Black women were largely constructed as external to the home in this period, so too was the homosexual. As Matt Cook has claimed in his discussion of queer domesticity in 1950s London: 'The upsurge of discussions about the homosexual, the prostitute and the immigrant conjured these figures especially as the threatening "others" to the "normal" home and "normal" family'.[5] It is plausible to add lesbians to this list, pointing to the many post-war novels which located lesbians outside of the family, rootlessly haunting the urban streets, or the numerous sociological studies which depicted unmarried women as trapped in miserable, isolated bedsitters, lacking the comforts and company of 'home'.[6] But the relationship between lesbians and the home cannot be reduced to a simple picture of exclusion.[7] On the one hand, the gendering of the home as a particularly feminine space meant that on some level, all women were constructed in relation to and influenced by the material and discursive concept of the home in this period. On the other, the resistance of female same-sex desire to categorization and the absence of explicit cultural discussion of female homosexuality meant that many women experienced and acted on desires for other women without claiming the identity of 'lesbian' or without identifying themselves to others as such.[8] These women occupied domestic space and forged relationships as daughters, sisters, wives and friends, drawing on a wide range of familial and social frameworks to make sense of their domestic arrangements. Paying attention to the complexities of these relational dynamics allows us to explore the ways in which women's same-sex intimacies impacted on and were shaped by the material environment of the home in this period.

This chapter will begin by exploring some of the ways in which the concept or dream of the home worked its way into the romantic imaginings of women who desired other women in the decades after the war. If a home of one's own was central to many women's dreams of marital happiness in this period, then to what extent and how did the home figure in the fantasies and realities of women's same-sex intimacies? As this discourse shifted in response to feminist and counter-cultural critiques of the nuclear family in the 1960s and 1970s, how did this impact on same-sex relationships and lesbian homes? Geographers Alison Blunt and Robyn Dowling have noted: 'One of the defining features of home is that it is both material and imaginative, a site and a set of meanings/emotions.'[9] Utilizing this concept of the home, this chapter will suggest that the domestic and the intimate were interrelated in two key ways in lesbian lives. Firstly, the material spaces in which women enacted their intimate relationships often reflected women's conceptualisation of those relationships.[10] Women who modelled their relationship on binary gender roles might live as 'husband and wife' in a shared flat or house, while women who pursued a relationship discreetly whilst presenting an alternate double life to family and friends often gave this material expression by maintaining two flats or two bedrooms to give the impression of platonic friendship. Secondly, the possibilities open to women in expressing desire and love for other women were shaped and constrained by their domestic environments. Younger women still living in the family home might be unable to bring lovers into their domestic space while, for married women, the marital home could be a site of same-sex passion or intimacy only at certain times when the family was elsewhere. Tracing the domestic context of lesbian relationships through the mid and late twentieth century, I will suggest that the material environment was intricately related with the structure of women's relationships and that broader cultural attitudes towards gender, the family and the home shaped both.

An imagined home

The post-war idealization of domesticity impacted on the ways in which women imagined their relationships with other women in this period, and the home figured repeatedly in lesbian fantasies of the 1950s and 1960s in both Britain and Australia. Recalling her dreams of potential relationships with other women when she was a young woman in the late 1960s, Anglo-Australian, Jennie, noted: 'They were sort of nice dreams, comfortable, companion like dreams, spending the rest of our lives together in perfect harmony. They were sort of loving, domestic relationships.'[11] Miss J.S. from Birmingham, a fifteen-year-old girl who wrote to British lesbian magazine,

Arena Three, in 1969 in response to an invitation to younger readers to share their experiences, also placed domesticity at the heart of her lesbian fantasies. She explained: 'I hope to get a job in electrical engineering, get some money, meet someone I could live with and "settle down", so to speak.'[12] A decade later, a self-described 'late-night feminist' poet wrote in to Australian feminist journal, *Rouge*, reflecting on her earlier ideas of the perfect lesbian relationship, before she encountered feminism: 'A few years ago/ All I could see/ For the future/ As far as my so-called/ Personal life was concerned/ Was being in a settled/ Couple relationship/ Like any old married couple,/ The only difference being/ That my partner/ Would be a womin … I suppose it would be/ Quite nice/ The little house in the country/ The few close friends/ The warmth of each other/ In the autumn years.'[13] In Britain, such personal fantasies were reinforced by a shared discourse of lesbian domesticity articulated in lesbian magazines such as *Arena Three*. In 1966, Miss D.F. from Kensington argued in *Arena Three*, 'The ideal lesbian life is, then, one of sharing home and bed with a partner who reciprocates affection and sexual desire in approximately equal degree.'[14] The following year, a pretty cottage in the country with a rose-filled garden was also central to the idyllic life shared by couple Vida and Margaret in the short story, *Compact*, published in the magazine.[15]

On meeting a lover, many women quickly made these fantasies a reality. When Sandra met her lover, Barbara, at a Salvation Army hostel in Sydney in the early 1950s, she immediately set about finding a flat for the women to share in Bondi, convinced that living together would cement their relationship.[16] Similarly, when Cynnie and Julie met in London in 1963, they decided early in their relationship to live together. In a media interview promoting British lesbian organization, Minorities Research Group, they told the *Sunday Times*: 'Five days after we met we decided we were in love – we were travelling through Ipswich on a train at the time.' The article continued: 'They agreed to wait six weeks before living together, to make sure it wasn't a mistake. They have been together now for nearly two years.'[17] For these women, a domestic context to their intimacy was essential to give a sense of validity and permanence to the relationship.

The interconnectedness of the material home with the emotional aspect of intimacy in women's minds also emerged in many women's responses to obstacles in their relationships. In a mid-1960s short story describing one woman, Jay's discovery that her partner has had an affair with another woman, the dilemma of how to react is resolved by reference to the couple's shared domestic environment. After an emotional scene between the two women, they go to sleep, but Jay awakes in the night and, looking at a figurine of Sappho she possesses, takes the decision to forgive her partner and continue the relationship: 'On the way through the living room she picked up the statue, smiled down at it and set it carefully back in its accustomed place on the table beside the window. After all, it was a very lovely statue. She had looked for it a long time, paid a dear price for it, and saw no reason to part with it for one flaw.'[18] The investment of time and energy in creating a home together was understood by many women as an expression of their commitment to each other. This is underscored by an article which appeared in the *Kilburn Times* a year later. The paper reported the case of a forty-year-old traffic warden who had been charged with arson after she had set fire to some of the furniture in a home she shared with another woman. She reportedly told a fireman: 'I did it deliberately. You see, we are both lesbians, and she was carrying on with another woman … I just wanted to destroy the home we had built together.'[19]

The material environment

The creation of a shared home can be understood as more than a simple indication of commitment in a relationship, however. The material form which that home took often reflected the ways in which women conceived the structure of their relationship and the roles each woman played within it, as well as the relationship model they hoped to communicate to others. Many women who embarked on relationships with other women in the post-war decades chose to live together in a variety of contexts and types of accommodation. Assumptions about spinsters' desires for companionship and limited cultural awareness of the possibilities of same-sex desire enabled many women to live together as 'friends' in the post-war decades without arousing the suspicions of landlords or neighbours. Mabel Hills and her friend, who met when they were in neighbouring beds in hospital, set up home together in an English village just after the Second World War, in a house bought for them by the friend's father. The two women obtained jobs in the local community and attended church and Mabel recalled that 'nobody ever said … people never thought [anything of our relationship]'.[20] This outward discretion mirrored the unspoken nature of the two women's intimacy. Reflecting on their partnership years later, Mabel commented that although she didn't consider their relationship to be 'anything out of the ordinary' and she and her friend 'took it as a matter of course' that they were sexually intimate, the two women 'never discussed it as anything. We never discussed it, shall we say, neither one way or t'other'. Similarly, Rene Sawyer, who moved in with her lover in 1957, remembered that, although her mother was 'a bit hurt by this, you know, her only chick going out of the nest', her parents visited often and assumed the two women were flatmates:

> They'd come round and visit and Terri would put on a little meal for them and everything else and it was all very nice, you know, sort of like the in-laws coming to have a meal and that. Although mum and dad most probably didn't feel that way. They just thought it was quite natural for two girls to live in a bedsit together because a lot of girls did that in that day, well they do it now – it's cheaper rent-wise and that, so everything was alright, there was no problems.[21]

By the late 1960s, however, such attitudes were beginning to be troubled in Britain as increased public discussion of female homosexuality raised awareness of the issue. Lesbian communities themselves played a role in this shift with sometimes contentious results. In 1965, Miss AMAJ and Miss TH wrote to *Arena Three* to complain:

> We think that too much publicity about your club's activities in the popular press is making it very difficult for two women to live together unnoticed, without being viewed with suspicion. My friend and I have lived together now for four years,

during which time we have worked with normal people, who thought nothing unnatural about 2 women living together. Since those articles have been appearing in the Sunday Press and on TV we have noticed an increasing (but morbid) interest in our relationship with each other.[22]

In an attempt to deflect any potential suspicions from family and friends, some women took the precaution of maintaining two bedrooms or two homes as a cover. When Margaret met her lover, Jann, in 1950s Sydney, Margaret was living alone in a bedsitter in Eurong Street, near Hyde Park, and Jann was living with her parents. As the relationship developed, the two women decided to live together but planned to conceal the fact from their families. Margaret explained:

So then she got an apartment in Elizabeth Bay, ostensibly she got it, but we got it, but I still lived ostensibly in my apartment … I didn't want it to be seen that I and Jann were living together so I lived in Eurong Street for all appearances. Of course, I was there [in Elizabeth Bay] all the time but I'd come back to Eurong Street and when I was talking to anyone I'd talk about home, meaning Eurong Street and 'the flat', and 'me', and 'it' and not 'us'.[23]

This domestic arrangement reflected the women's wider strategy of leading double lives, telling their families stories of boyfriends and even going on occasional 'dates' with men as cover for their relationship. However, Margaret linked this practice of deception with a parallel insecurity in the women's relationship, which ultimately broke up when Jann decided to marry one of the men she had dated as cover. Margaret reflected: 'But there was never any quarrel really, or great anger on my part, it just seemed to me that that was how the whole thing would have to end up. We couldn't live together or be who we were because of all the restrictions and anxiety and lies.'[24] For Margaret, the women's inability to live together openly and present themselves as a couple to their family and friends weakened the relationship from the outset and made it inevitable that the affair would not last. British women also described leading double lives at this time and Cynnie gave a similar account of her relationship with a woman she had met at college in the late 1950s:

When we left college, we both moved to London and we set up officially two separate households, so that I could shield my family from the knowledge that we were actually still together, but we did in fact have a flat together as well, which in those days became rather expensive to try and run 2 bedsitting establishments, but we managed that somehow. And for the next 2 or 3 years, we both worked in London, lived together and continued the relationship.

As with Margaret and Jann, however, the inability to live together openly placed a strain on the relationship. Cynnie recalled:

But it clearly became an unsatisfactory relationship from her point of view and I think she hankered after the respectability of a marriage to a man and a proper family. Her father was a serving officer in the forces and a fairly conventional background of course and I think she began to get involved with one or two men. Nothing very serious but obviously that upset me, and there were continual traumas of this nature, that clearly we were not going to be happily living together for the rest of my life as I had at one time envisaged we might.[25]

While for Cynnie, Margaret and others, the discretion which structured their presentation of their relationship was mirrored in their domestic circumstances, other women drew on more explicit models in constructing their relationships. In Britain in the decades after the war and in Australia, from the 1960s onwards, urban lesbian subcultures located around bars, coffee shops and nightclubs fostered butch/femme relationship roles which drew on the presentation of opposing gendered identities to express same-sex sexual desire and organize social interactions.[26] For women who participated in these communities, butch/femme culture offered a model on which to draw in structuring their relationships, with shared expectations about the appearance and behavioural practices adopted by each partner. Many women confined their performance of butch identities to specific locations such as lesbian bars or their own homes and presented a more conventional feminine appearance at work and elsewhere. For these women, butch/femme roles were therefore practised discreetly in the privacy of their own homes but did not impact on the women's ability to present a conventional appearance to landlords and neighbours. However, for some butch women this was not an option and alternative strategies were required to secure housing. In Australia, in particular, some women in these circumstances chose to pass as a heterosexual married couple. Marion Paull described doing this when she was in a butch/femme relationship in Melbourne in the early 1960s. She recalled:

> It was during this relationship that I lived as a man. Well, we lived as a married couple actually. It seems to be much easier to be accepted as a man when you're with a girl ... The flat we lived in was in fact the upstairs part of a terrace house. The landlady thought it was a bit odd that I did the ironing, but nice odd. She used to introduce us to her friends.

Marion initially worked as a man too, but when she obtained a job as a woman, managing the different roles in her life became difficult. She explained:

> The other problem was changing clothes. Obviously, I couldn't leave our little love nest in a dress, nor could I be seen in the neighbourhood like that, as many people knew us by sight, at least. So I used to pack my skirt and shoes in a little bag and take the train to the other side of Melbourne. If the carriage was empty, I'd change on the train as quickly as possible and then get off. On a busy day, I'd have to stay on for quite a way, and when I got off the train, I'd change in the ladies lavatory.[27]

By the 1960s and 1970s, however, women were increasingly choosing to live openly as a lesbian couple. In larger cities, this might pass unremarked by neighbours and landlords, but the practice typically attracted more attention in smaller and remote towns and rural communities. In an interview with historian, Dino Hodge, Aboriginal gay man, Gurra, recounted his memories of a woman in Darwin who lived openly with her female partner in the 1960s. He recalled:

> She was one of the first Aboriginal people in Darwin to go down south and get qualifications. She'd come back and was working as a teacher at the school opposite my school ... and she was obviously living with this girl, woman, who I thought was a man. I thought it was a very attractive blonde man and then you could see it was an attractive woman. She had a sports car, a green MG, and they looked absolutely fabulous together. This black haired, attractive Aboriginal woman, slim, with this blonde haired woman.
>
> They lived openly in Darwin, and amazingly, no problem. Even the old Darwin families, they may have talked about them behind their back, but not openly.[28]

Gurra suggests that it was this woman's strength and her standing in the local community which enabled her to live openly as a lesbian in a cultural context which was typically hostile to both same-sex and inter-racial relationships. Similar themes were echoed in Megg's account of her openly butch/femme relationship with a local woman while on a teaching posting in country WA in the 1980s. Again, her reputation as a respected teacher enabled her to confront the disapproval which was initially voiced.[29]

These experiences were unusual, however, and many others encountered considerable hostility from neighbours or landlords who were aware of their lesbian relationship. Chris recalled being evicted from a rented property in Melbourne in the late 1970s when the landlord discovered that she and her friends were lesbians: 'I got thrown out of a house – actually I was living in a lesbian household. We were obviously only lesbian. Some local yobbos painted "lesbian" on the front of the house as a way of persecuting us. So the landlord threw us out.'[30] Kukumo Rocks recalled that when she moved from her marital home to a lesbian household in Edinburgh in the 1980s or early 1990s: 'We get people down at the house shouting at us when we come out of the house and that's part of the rejection that lesbians feel in society.'[31] The visibility of shared lesbian households could render them particularly vulnerable to hostility from neighbours or landlords. However, women living alone or with lovers or children also experienced discrimination. Margaret described the years of ongoing harassment she and her wife experienced from neighbours on their street in Balmain, Sydney in the 1970s and 1980s:

> But we were vilified in this street ... [I]t must have come to them that we were lesbians ... Well! Now that distressed them ... [and the] neighbour in house number 1, he was one of the good old Balmain Catholics ... But he was in fear from us and hated us and became so obstructive ... he would park his car right in front of his house, so that we couldn't get past his to get to our house ... Well, oh it was terrible. Years and years this went on ... And all the other folks knew ... and there was that sense of isolation, of aloneness, of insular, of being disliked, not being part of anything and being actively, physically, hated

and the desire of somebody to physically hurt you and damage you because of the sexuality that you choose ... and it was a bad time and I think that impacted on us.[32]

For Margaret, the working-class, Catholic character of the local community was an important factor in shaping the attitudes of her neighbours. Al, who experienced hostility from neighbours in Leeds in the same period, suggested that harassment from neighbours was linked to social deprivation. She had been the target of abuse while living in a lesbian collective household in the Chapeltown area in the late 1970s and then moved to Beeston in the early 1980s with her daughter. She recalled:

It was okay to start with but then as the recession hit ... and generally it became an open warfare situation. And it only needs a couple of households harassing and other people to shut their doors – horrendous. And there was one particularly bad house, people who were basically, they had nothing going for them in life and so they'd pick on someone else who was vulnerable and that was us. And my car was vandalised, we had eggs thrown at the window. The last three months there, there was shit on the door when I came home from work. It was really, really bad ... One night, there was a man, the house faced on to the park, and a man sat on the bench in the park and every time I turned off my bedside light, he shouted 'Lesbian! Lesbian!' in a drunken voice but for some reason he didn't when I turned the bedside light on, so I had it on all night.[33]

Many women described the negative impact of this type of ongoing harassment on their mental well-being and relationships. Jayne Egerton, Chair of the British lesbian and gay charity, Stonewall's Housing Association, claimed in 1990 that:

I once advised a Glaswegian lesbian in her seventies who had been driven from one squalid and impermanent home after another as a result of harassment from neighbours. Her family would have nothing to do with her and her only friend had been her lover who had recently died. She had never experienced the pleasures of a genuine 'home' in her entire life and had taken tranquillizers for 'depression' for twenty years.[34]

Al explained that the hostility she described from neighbours had forced her lover to move out of the house, while Margaret felt that the toll ongoing harassment had taken on her wife's mental health had been a factor in the breakdown of their twenty-year relationship.

Finding a home

The ability of women to establish a domestic context to their relationship in the post-war decades was also constrained by a number of practical obstacles. The dominance of the male breadwinner model continued to shape assumptions about women's financial independence until the 1970s, making it difficult for single women to purchase housing. In Britain, women were unable to obtain a mortgage without a male guarantor in this period and, in Australia, similar attitudes forced women buying alone or in same-sex couples to obtain loans at poor rates of interest.[35] Women who rented housing on the private rental market were often vulnerable to discrimination by landlords and felt under pressure to conceal the nature of their relationship. Reflecting on the experience of lesbians in post-war Australia in a 1975 conference paper, Barbara Creed observed: 'no-one would wish to always have to be discreet if she lived in a rented house or flat in case she was reported and asked (politely – of course) to leave.'[36] Housing shortages were also a problem in Britain where the destruction of many houses in wartime bombing and the post-war increase in the birth rate exacerbated long-term shortages. Despite housing being a central issue in the 1945 general election, ambitious projects for public housing were held back by a shortage of building materials and housing remained an issue for decades after the war.[37] Unmarried women were particularly affected by this adverse housing situation. Families were regarded as a priority in the design and construction of post-war homes and the domestic needs of single women were repeatedly sidelined. In 1955, the National Council of Women's conference recognized this situation as a pressing problem, when it passed a resolution calling on the Minister of Housing and Local Government to make more provision for single women in housing projects. Reluctance to consider the housing needs of single women was exacerbated by characterizations of the single woman in opposition to domesticity. Speaking at the conference, Mrs C.G. Stanley of the Moral Welfare Committee echoed these views when she observed that 'a great block of flats occupied entirely by women would be a most unnatural thing'. She invited her listeners to 'Suppose that one of them wanted to ask a man to tea, or for the evening. She would see all those women looking out of their windows.'[38] Her comments reflected the views of a range of social commentators of the period who represented the domestic sphere as a bleak, restrictive and unnatural environment for unmarried women.[39] The difficulties of locating housing as a lesbian or single woman continued into the 1970s and 1980s in London, in particular. Jayne Egerton argued in 1990 that these problems were largely economic and 'Women's access to decent accommodation is frequently determined by their relationship with a male wage earner. Single, divorced and widowed women invariably have greater financial and housing problems than married or cohabiting women.'[40] The Conservative national government's privatization of public housing exacerbated these problems in the 1980s and Sarah Green claimed that, in her research into lesbian feminist communities in London in the late 1980s: 'Impermanence was also a part of women's personal lives. Housing was a chronic problem and almost all the women I met spoke of their difficulties in finding housing in London, and many lived in temporary accommodation. Only a fraction of the women I met owned their own homes.'[41]

In Australia, post-war urban expansion, which led to the creation of new suburbs on the outer edges of Australian cities, was similarly problematic for single women or lesbian couples. John Murphy and Belinda Probert's interviews with men and women who lived in these new suburbs in the 1950s and 1960s demonstrate the dominance of these areas by young married couples, who forged community organizations and facilities according to highly gendered and heteronormative assumptions about the needs of the community. Residents who did not fit this model, such as single mothers, faced acute isolation and social exclusion. One single mother, whose husband had abandoned her and their two young children, bought a cottage with her mother in the Melbourne suburb of Armadale in the 1950s and recalled: 'For the neighbours not to know that I didn't have a husband, I'd be sneaking out the back gate and up the back lane [to work], and I was a mystery to everyone in the street. To be on your own with a child and pregnant, you were almost like a leper.'[42]

Difficulties obtaining suitable housing were exacerbated for some women by other factors such as racial discrimination. As Kennetta Hammond Perry notes, men and women of colour found that the racist attitudes of private landlords and the residency requirements of public housing combined to severely restrict access to housing, particularly for recent migrants to Britain. In London, housing advertisements frequently explicitly declared: 'No Irish, Blacks or Dogs' or 'White Tenants Only', while other landlords turned applicants of colour away on the doorstep. Dorothy Cooper, who moved from Belfast to London in the early 1970s, described the difficulties she experienced as an Irish woman finding accommodation:

> I remember certainly arriving in London and the difficulty, certainly, of finding somewhere to live. I came with Nora, the woman I was involved with, and we went to stay with some friends from Belfast who'd come over earlier. And we were only there a couple of nights and the landlord evicted us at midnight, making remarks about how the Irish were just like the Indians – you let a flat to one and the next minute there's 30 of them. And he threw us out on the street at midnight … And after that I went to stay with a cousin I knew. But it took months and months and months to find a bedsit to live in.[43]

For those women who were able to find accommodation, conditions were often appalling, with exorbitant rents, and both rooms and bathrooms shared between large numbers of people.[44] Unmarried women were particularly vulnerable to the impact of this housing situation and Bryan, Dadzie and Scafe noted that in the late 1970s and 1980s: 'Because of the discriminatory policies of local authorities, growing numbers of Black women were being housed in high rise blocks on 'problem' estates – particularly if they were single parents.'[45]

These issues were compounded for lesbians of colour who experienced the combined effects of racial discrimination and hostility towards lesbians. In an article for *Arena Three*, Pet Brien offered an allegorical account of the hurdles she had faced in setting up home with her white lover in 1960s London:

> Nurse White and Nurse Black paired off from the start. After their graduation they decided to share a flat. Nurse White rented, later moved nurse Black in. As would be expected, they were asked to leave as soon as the landlady had found out about nurse Black.

There came another flat, that time from a Jewish landlord who did not care if the tenant was an octopus. Now, neighbours complained and out went the two friends.

It was nurse White who decided to 'come down' as society would call it and move in nurse Black's community. Alas, the trouble did not stop. There, it was nurse White who was not welcome. Except for the landlord who slapped his tongue with the 'Once they go with black woman they want black man' theory in mind and the other tenants made life miserable for the two young women. As Mr Landlord did not get his way, he asked the young ladies to leave. So out they went, from flat to flat, to single roomed nurses hostel, back to flats.

Ground down by this experience, the two women 'tried to "break it up" for the other's sake' but felt unable to do so and ultimately decided to leave Britain 'for some remote part of the world. Each of them totally disowned by their friends and relations'.[46]

Women's freedom to set up home with another woman could also be constrained by familial obligations or other relationship commitments. Social expectations that unmarried daughters would take on the care of ailing parents or simply provide company for a widowed mother after the death of their father meant that a number of women described being pressured into living in the family home and prevented from establishing a domestic context to their same-sex relationships. When Margaret met her friend, Iris, in Coventry in the late 1940s, Iris came to stay with Margaret at Margaret's mother's house. Margaret described this as a wonderful environment in contrast to the small 'box room' which Iris had been living in at home:

> Of course when I met her I loved her and I gave her lots of love and she came to stay at my house and I'd got a proper big bedroom and nice things. Well they were nice. There was a lot of love there anyway. We spent a lot of time together and she'd come and stay. I remember I told her I loved her. She said she loved me so that was absolutely wonderful.

Although Margaret did not refer to any constraints on their relationship caused by living in Margaret's family home, Margaret's subsequent description of when the relationship became sexual suggests that the family home was not an environment in which they felt able to express much physical affection. Margaret explained:

> My grandma leant me her cottage because she was away somewhere. She'd got a cottage out in Brinklow – that's a little village just outside Coventry. I said to [Iris] ... come and stay with me there. So we went and that's when we ... it must have been the first time we got together because I was putting my arms around her and tucking her in at night and all that. A little kiss on the cheek and it got more and more. Yes, it did.
>
> It was wonderful [at the cottage]. We didn't have any time. We didn't have any clocks. We stopped the clocks. We just lived as we felt like. If we were hungry we'd eat. We'd get up when we were ready. We'd go to bed when we were ready.[47]

Margaret's vivid recollection of the week or two she and Iris spent in her grandma's cottage reinforces the sense of this experience as a brief period in which the young women felt they had both the space and the time to freely express their intimacy. In her work on heterosexuality and the home, geographer Carey-Ann Morrison notes:

> The dominant scripting of home has been in terms of monogamous heterosexual coupling, institutionalised in marriage, social discourse and public policy. This means that home, both materially and imaginatively, is deemed to be the natural and normal place for bodies to touch and feel. Likewise, touch between loving, monogamous heterosexual couples is the 'typical' framework for intimacy at home. In this way, touch works to reproduce hegemonic and naturalised notions about the relationship between heterosexuality and domestic space.[48]

In a cultural context which linked the home with heterosexuality, lesbian desire could be difficult to express as Margaret and Iris found. Isabel Miller's classic 1969 lesbian novel, *Patience and Sarah*, which was widely read and reviewed in British and Australian lesbian feminist circles, pointed to this same difficulty in the last scene, when the women finally attained a long-desired home of their own, but felt too overwhelmed by this unaccustomed space to express physical intimacy in their new bed.[49]

Wider social hostility towards female same-sex desire could pose obstacles to lesbian intimacy, even when a material space was available. During the 1970s and 1980s, previously married lesbian mothers who sought custody or access to their children through the courts were frequently required by judges to abstain from the expression of affection towards their lovers while their children were in the house. Young women also often described their relationships foundering in the context of the constraints imposed by parental surveillance. Gilli Salvat recalled the obstacles imposed on her passionate relationship with a schoolfriend, Anne, when she was in her teens, by the lack of private space in which to express themselves. The girls initially met at Anne's family home, where Anne's bedroom afforded sufficient privacy for them to be able to engage in 'kissing and snogging' and be 'very, very intense with each other'. However, when Anne's mum read her diary and realized the romantic nature of their relationship, Gilli was banned from the house. After a painful separation, the girls were able to find some time to themselves in Gilli's family home by playing truant from school when Gilli's parents were at work. However, Gilli recalled that again, the pair were interrupted:

> We went back to my parents' flat because I knew that they would be at work and it was like one of the few times that we'd got into bed together. And I was really getting into it, like exploring her body and stuff and it was just so exciting you were almost fainting you know. And there was all this knocking at the door and luckily I'd bolted the door … And it was my poor mum, and she'd come home from work ill, and she couldn't get in the flat … And so I got Anne and you know she sort of had her bra undone and everything and I just threw her blouse at her and everything and I just got her out of there, half dressed, with her clothes under her

arm, pushed her up the fire escape, which led to the roof. And she had to stay on the roof! My mum came back with the caretaker and I just made up this story that I felt really ill and all that and she was okay about that because she believed me. But what I had to do then was make up another story that I felt alright, so that I could let her off the roof – so I had to make up all this bullshit, get me school clothes on, go down the stairs, walk along the road so she saw me disappear, then double back, creep up the stairs, passed the door where my mum was in the flat, up the fire escape and let her out. And she's just like, she's completely freaked out and crying and everything and I had to shut her up and get her out of there.

Gilli recalled that, although she never read anything negative about lesbianism, it was incidents like this which 'affected me thinking about that relationship because everything was screaming at me that it was wrong'.[50] June described similar challenges finding space to express physical affection with her girlfriend, Shirley, in 1970s Glasgow. She recalled:

I was still at home and she was still at home and so it was difficult. We had nowhere to go and there used to be a great big billboard up from Dundas Street bus station that we'd nip behind. We'd go for a drink and later on if we wanted to have a bit of a kiss and a cuddle we'd go there. I'm standing there in all this rubbish, this crap and I'm thinking – to hell with this.[51]

Such difficulties continued into the 1980s and 1990s in Britain and Australia. In 1993, Northern Territory magazine, *Lesbian Territory*, printed a letter from a university student describing her situation: 'Only a select few know I am a lesbian. My family is not even vaguely aware of my lesbianism. Thus, when sister lesbians call me at home, we speak to each other in special codes.'[52] 'Asphy Xia', a seventeen-year-old Victorian lesbian, also wrote to a lesbian paper in the early 1990s describing her difficulties living at home with homophobic family members. She told *Labrys* readers: 'My family does not know I am gay, due to excessive homophobia on their part. This makes life at home feel a little stifling.'[53]

Collective housing

By the early 1970s, emerging counter-cultural ideas about the family were beginning to open up new possibilities for the structuring of both intimate relationships and domestic space. White feminist and lesbian and gay activists in the 1970s critiqued the nuclear family as oppressive of women, enforcing the roles of wife and mother and dividing women from each other into small patriarchal units. Instead, lesbian feminists sought to foster equal and supportive relationships between women, in which sexual intimacy was simply another expression of friendship and sisterhood. Monogamy and other relationship forms which mirrored that of marriage were regarded as oppressive of women and liable to lead to emotional dependency, and lesbian feminists therefore sought to replace the 'couple' with non-monogamous relationships.[54] In British and

Australian lesbian feminist networks, the practice of non-monogamy was closely connected with communal forms of living, centring on shared houses and, in the UK, squats. Urban houseshares and other forms of collective living were relatively common in the late 1960s and 1970s in Australia, while in the UK, the large numbers of abandoned and partially derelict houses in inner cities were increasingly taken over as squats by proponents of alternative lifestyles. Communal living had been embraced by members of the counter-culture and New Left from the 1960s onwards, as part of an ideological commitment to the sharing of labour and resources, whilst inner-city houseshares were increasingly common amongst student populations. The anti-capitalist rejection of material culture which was a central aspect of this movement radically challenged earlier post-war understandings of the home as an environment in which residents invested considerable energy and resources. In contrast to the culture of consumerism which encouraged home-makers to acquire material possessions in an attempt to create domestic comfort and as an expression of individuality, these new communal living spaces were characterized largely by functionality and a focus on the structuring of interpersonal relationships within them.[55] In feminist and lesbian feminist circles, women-only shared houses and squats developed alongside a broader commitment to separatism and feminist activism and, for many women, their engagement with feminist politics and culture was mediated through their domestic lives as residents in lesbian feminist collective houses. In cities across Australia and the UK, women established houseshares along feminist principles, aiming to share responsibility for household chores; pool financial resources; take decisions collectively; and build a woman-centred community.[56] From the mid-1970s onwards, similar principles were applied to the formation of rural women-only communities, the largest of which were established in NSW in Australia and in Wales in the UK.[57]

Residence in lesbian feminist communal housing in this period fostered a particular model of lesbian identity and shared houses and squats were a key site for the enactment of feminist ideals and practices of intimacy. Women who had previously participated in other models of lesbian domesticity understood these shared houses as representative both of a radically new living environment and a commitment to a very different form of intimacy. In an article entitled 'Conflicts ... on becoming a lesbian feminist', published in *Rouge* magazine, the author explained that she had been introduced to lesbian feminism when she moved into 'a household where 2 radical feminists lived', following the break-up of her long-term lesbian relationship. In her previous relationship, they had, she recalled, '[kept] quiet about our lesbianism' and:

> Lived a life identical to any heterosexual couple, the only difference being that my partner was a womin, not a man. We styled ourselves on 'normal' heterosexual relationships, fitted into society, received society's benefits, had good jobs, kept ourselves to ourselves, and a house in the suburbs ... We saved our money from the good jobs, for material things, and planned for our future together by feathering our consumer goods nests.

Her former circle of lesbian friends had regarded feminism with considerable suspicion, and she recalled that she and her ex-girlfriend had joked about the risks of indoctrination incurred by those staying in a lesbian feminist house.[58] The influence of this environment was confirmed by the article: after a year living in the radical feminist houseshare, this woman's understanding of her sexuality and relationships with individual women and society had altered significantly and she had become actively involved in feminist politics. Another Australian, Chris, explicitly linked the different perspective offered by feminist shared houses with the material environment of the house, when she described her move from a house shared with her lover Anne in suburban Epping to a feminist shared house in inner city Redfern. She recalled:

> I remember walking in this, it was a pretty decrepit house in Redfern, and there were … 2 couples and a couple of other people, they had a spare room out back, and I walked out and it was, had been spray-painted, you know 'Publish Women or Perish' and 'Lesbianism. Why Settle for Less?' and stuff like that. So that was our bedroom … And you know, there was sea grass all over the floor and you know, it was just an entirely different kind of set up – we had shagpile at our house in Epping … It was … just a different world for me.

For Chris this new world with sea grass on the floor and motorbikes in the hall was interconnected with a new approach to intimacy and she described the impact which living in the house had on her attitude towards relationships:

> when we were all in that house together, everybody started having relationships … and in the meantime I was also having another, a relationship with a woman that I had met in New Zealand as well … Because you know in those days … it went on quite a bit … Yeah and Anne and I had gone off to a CR group that was held in Stanmore in the 70s … and we went there and met a few women, but one woman in particular that I fell madly in love with and so started a relationship with, whilst I was still involved with Anne. And then left to go and have that relationship.[59]

While the practices of intimacy in collective housing were often reflected in the décor of the house, they might also be embedded in the material structure of the building. In his work on the gay male squats in Brixton in the 1970s, Matt Cook has explored the ways in which the terraced housing was opened up to create communal living spaces, reflecting the commitment to collective living.[60] Christine Wall, in her work on feminist squats in Hackney in the same period, has noted that 'much early feminist writing analysed the oppressive architecture of nuclear-family households in both suburban and metropolitan settings'. 'The antithesis of suburban life', she argues, 'was found in the everyday, lived experience of women's squatted communities, which enabled collective living, shared childcare and the means to live outside dominant power relations'.[61] Residents of Australian shared houses also suggested that the internal organization of the houses they lived in facilitated the swapping of partners, as typically each woman was allocated her own room or bed. Alex, who lived in a commune on Crystal St in Sydney in the early 1970s, recalled: 'there'd be a lot of kind of musical beds around the house'.[62] Reflecting on her own experience of non-monogamy in Melbourne, Chris explained: 'I remember, for example, I was in a relationship with one woman. Then I would have another sexual encounter … and we would all go home, and she'd go up with her partner. I'd go into my room with the other one. You could sort of swap around, and it was sort of accepted.'[63]

While many women recalled their own commitment to the ideal of non-monogamy, in practice it could lead to considerable emotional tensions, both for individuals and within the house, where jealousy and emotional upset over the break-up of relationships were felt but could not always be expressed. Dorothy Cooper, who lived in a large women's squat at 35 Hillthrop Road, Islington, in the 1970s, recalled:

> The main thing I remember about that house was that, I think it had quite an aura really. We were sort of famous, people used to visit us quite a lot … People envied us I think, that we seemed to be a very kind of er, I don't know, a fun group. And we were to some extent and then the other side of that was a terrible kind of intensity that went on and some people started sexual relationships with each other in the house and various multiple ones, and those kinds of complications. And it became, I think, a very stifling place to be and I was really glad when I left it in the end.[64]

These sorts of tensions were sometimes exacerbated by a sense of collective pressure to conform to a non-monogamous ideal in one's own relationships. Sandra, who lived in a number of lesbian feminist houses in Sydney in the 1970s, recalled: 'there was a kind of fair bit of pressure, self, self-imposed, to try and break down those sort of ideas and so on. And it was not easy. Yeah and I probably had a lot of relationships or sexual encounters in those years, as did a lot of the women that were in that sort of scene.'[65] While Sandra recalled the pressure to reject monogamy as self-imposed, lesbian feminist collective houses undoubtedly also acted as spaces which enforced a degree of conformity to shared ideals. In their analysis of lesbian identities in domestic environments, Lynda Johnston and Gill Valentine argued that the shared lesbian home 'is a site where a lesbian identity must be performed, but it is also a site where this identity comes under surveillance from other lesbians. "Political correctness", which has come to haunt the lesbian feminist landscape, or other "orthodoxies", can be invoked by some women to regulate the performance aspects of others' lesbian identities within the domestic environment.'[66] Helen, who lived in a lesbian feminist house in Melbourne in this period, remembered pressure from other members of the household to conform to ideals of non-monogamy, and described her own attempts to conduct a covert monogamous relationship with another woman, Chris, while living in the house. She explained: 'we actually didn't declare, because you weren't meant to be in "couples" we actually decided the easiest way not to be in a couple was not to tell … anyone in the house that we were on together. So we actually, whilst we were quite public out of the house, we were completely closeted within lesbian circles.' Lesbian feminist critiques of heteropatriarchal models of intimacy extended to a rejection of butch/femme roles in lesbian relationships and the danger of being seen to enact these roles was a matter of particular concern to Helen. She recalled that despite having not declared their relationship to their housemates: 'Chris and I used to get up in the morning and decide whether we were putting dresses or trousers on that day' to ensure that they did not inadvertently adopt opposing styles which might give the appearance of a butch/femme relationship.[67]

When women from urban lesbian feminist communities founded rural women-only communities in NSW and Wales in the 1970s, they brought with them similar collective principles and ideas of intimate sisterhood.[68] In the Radicalesbian Manifesto, drafted in 1973 by Melbourne lesbian feminists who went on to establish the NSW women's lands, it was stated:

> We want to overcome the division between women – to touch, relate, to give strength and validity to each other. We want women to be able to relate to women on all levels. We want to relate as individuals, not as elements in a correct ideology. Fucking with another woman just removes one more barrier in our minds, enables us to learn to love our woman-selves in another woman.[69]

Physical affection, emotional intimacy and sexual intimacy were understood as existing on a spectrum of woman-identification which was the basis of a women-only community. Sand, who lived in both communities at different times, recalled:

> A lot of energy went into relationships and exploring monogamy and non-monogamy and how that would all work and friendships within all of that. And there were some amazing passionate friendships and – with elements of a sexual dynamic – but also just sort of a potency because some of the women would have sexual relationships but there was also just that energy between everybody … and it made life kind of vital. And everybody was always aware of what was sort of going on with everybody else to some extent. And so we were really putting a lot of time and energy into trying to come up with ways of relating and being with each other that were fair and fun and quite wild and adventurous as well. There was also that sense of caring for the whole and so there was a group dynamic that was really strong.[70]

Influenced by these ideas, a variety of models of intimacy were practised on the women's lands, ranging from long-standing couples to serial monogamy, 'bed-hopping' or clusters of non-monogamous lovers. Chris recalled:

> Sometimes there were these groupings, where there would be one particular popular woman, and she would have a number of partners. They would all – because they idealised this one woman so much, they would tolerate the other partners, and they saw themselves as a kind of a family. I can think of one instance where that's happened, and they saw themselves as a family with – it was almost – in one instance, it seemed to me almost like a cult leader.[71]

Other women moved fairly rapidly from one sexual partner to another, participating in a succession of fairly brief, overlapping affairs.

These fluid relational forms were facilitated by the structureless material environment of the communities. In Wales, women slept together in barns and Sand recalled: 'We'd always make a row of beds, some women would get that together, some women would do the fire and the food and we'd all just be in a row.'[72] When the first NSW rural community, Amazon Acres, was established in 1974, the 1,000 acre plot included two old loggers' huts or shacks and these were used as shelter by some women while others slept in tents or other temporary structures. In the late 1970s, the women began building a large hexagonal structure, known as the 'hex', which was used as a communal space for meetings, cooking and other shared activities, but it was not until the mid-1980s that individual women began to build yurts and other dwelling places to sleep in.[73] The building of individual shelters occupied by single women or couples reflected a gradual shift in practices of intimacy on the lands from non-monogamy to more settled couple relationships.

In the late 1980s and 1990s, many women began to move away from collective styles of living. However, the ideological framework which had drawn lesbian feminists to communal lifestyles and forms of intimacy continued to influence individual women's domestic choices in a number of ways. The feminist emphasis on retaining autonomy in relationships had prompted an expectation in Australian lesbian feminist circles that women would always maintain independent domestic space separate from their lovers. In her paper 'Rules and Relationships' presented at the Radicalesbian conference at Sorrento, Victoria in 1973, Jenny included in her list of agreed rules (put together after consultation with women in Adelaide): 'Feminist lesbians who are fucking together don't … live together/sleep together every night.'[74] A number of women noted this as a widely held expectation in lesbian feminist communities which continued throughout the 1980s and 1990s. Reflecting on her lesbian relationships from the late 1980s onwards, Jean noted that she had not lived with a lover for fourteen years, instead taking it in turns to spend a few nights each at each other's houses. When Jean began a new relationship in the early 1990s, the two women again initially lived apart for ideological reasons. Jean recalled: 'We'd been living apart, because it was sort of one of the rules in the lesbian community, that I kind of liked, that you didn't live with your lover. It meant you could be totally independent really.' Although Jean presented this understanding as a 'rule' in the 1970s, by the 1990s she suggested that the situation had softened:

> There weren't any rules in the 90s as there were in the 70s and 80s. 70s and 80s, rules were written up in the newsletters. Also, I'd never gone by the rules anyway, but it suited me to be living on my own. That was the major reason I lived on my own. It gave me the necessary space to do my writing without having to worry about somebody else in the house.

A few years into their relationship, however, Jean and her lover began to consider the possibility of living together, while retaining a strong sense of the importance of autonomy. Jean explained:

> So when she and I were contemplating living together, her household had just broken up and she was looking for another place to stay and she was going to buy

a little place for herself, and she moved in here just temporarily. I said, you know, perhaps we should just look at – we could perhaps live together, just for a while, and if it doesn't work out, she can just move on again. We liked living together, and being older I think, the trailing backwards and forwards – and she did actually buy herself a little place and that's her bolt-hole – if she needs to go there, she can go there, sort of thing.[75]

Sylvia recalled experiencing considerable difficulties over personal space during her relationship with a German feminist, Edda, whom she had met at a festival in South Australia in the late 1980s. After a period of maintaining a long-distance relationship, Sylvia agreed to go and live with Edda in Germany, but found that her own ethics of autonomous space differed from those of her partner. Sylvia explained to Edda the 'politics of having your own room':

You've got your own – you do it yourself. It's yours … if you come into something from someone else, they've got their place and you need your space. So the politics of having your own room would be you create it to your space and she would have her space, so you'd be respectful. And as you get older – there are a lot of issues with older women and relationships to do with snoring and various other things and many women do actually have their own room.

Although Edda had responded to Sylvia's request by setting aside a room for Sylvia with 'a couch that you could sleep on and … a desk and everything', it was clear that the two women approached the issue from different perspectives. Sylvia recalled that she 'felt like I was a visitor all the time. I didn't feel like I could do what I wanted to' because Edda did not approach their relationship from the same political viewpoint:

But living in the same house – I hadn't lived with a partner, except for Jim, for many years. So that was a challenge. And she was no good at sharing. Everything was hers and I fitted in. There was no sense, no – she hadn't got any of the politics that I had grown up with in the women's movement. She didn't – she was feminist, but she didn't have those relationship politics. She didn't understand them and she'd had trouble with all her relationships, in exactly the same way.

Well, for instance, she didn't want me to use the washing machine. She just wanted me to put the washing in the basket, because she liked to do it in her way. Right? She didn't want me to wash dishes, but I could dry them. Right? It was just restrictive.[76]

Although women who had been involved in Australian lesbian feminist circles in the 1970s and 1980s typically recognized this ideological commitment to autonomy and independent space, these concepts were less familiar to women who had not been actively engaged in feminist politics. Megg, a Sydney lesbian feminist, experienced difficulties around domestic space when she entered a relationship with a woman she described as 'an old fashioned bar dyke'. The women met in a bar in Perth in the 1980s, when Megg was a student, and they began a passionate four-year relationship, ultimately moving into a flat together in a small goldmining town in country WA.

Despite the strong sexual attraction between the women, some tensions arose in the relationship because, as Megg explained: 'we didn't have anything in common'. Domestic space became one key dimension of conflict and Megg recalled: 'She was a very conventional dyke, so she was horrified at having two bedrooms. So the fact that I asked for two bedrooms then becomes a sign of rejection.'[77]

Even for women who shared a similar ideological approach to relationships and domesticity, setting up house together could involve difficult negotiations. When Sally and her partner, Marit, first moved in together after being in a relationship for six years, they lived in a house which Marit had bought. The domestic context of their relationship had been complicated at the outset by Sally's need to leave her marriage and subsequently to maintain a home for her three children at a time, in the 1980s, when many lesbian mothers lived in fear of losing custody of their children. Ultimately, Sally and Marit decided to leave Melbourne, where they had met, and move to country Victoria. Marit moved first, buying a house and finding work in the hope that Sally would be able to join her. Sally recalled that, despite Marit's attempts to make her feel that the house was shared, she found it difficult to move into a home which she did not regard as her own. She recalled that moving in together:

> Was quite difficult. We had been together quite a while at that stage. We were quite a stable couple. However, I had never lived in another woman's house … I have a lot of issues because of being in my grandparents' house [when I was younger]. My grandfather was not welcoming … So I've always had issues being in other people's houses. So although Marit was incredibly generous and when she had bought the house she had put my name on the title. I didn't put a cent towards it. So she did everything she could to make me feel comfortable about it. But I still struggled with that issue. So yes that was very difficult. Trying to imagine where I had to cooperate and discuss decisions about my physical environment. Whereas I had just been running the place for so many, many years.[78]

Not all women wanted or had access to independent space, however, as this often required financial resources or a choice of housing stock which was not universally available. Jai Forde described how, when she was forced by homophobic abuse to move out of the estate in Willesden, NW London where she had been living, she was allocated housing by the lesbian and gay charity, Stonewall. Hoping for her own space, she initially moved into a house in Lordship Park, where she shared a bathroom and kitchen on the top floor with another woman, but when the man downstairs accidentally set fire to the building, she was relocated to another Stonewall house where she shared living space with a larger group of people.[79]

Domesticity and power

Many scholars have pointed to the importance of the home as a site of 'identity management', whose privacy enables its residents to bring together 'diverse identity-fragments, materially embedding a holistic sense of self within domestic space'.[80]

bell hooks and others have posited the home as a space of sanctuary from racial discrimination and a site where nurturing relationships can validate marginalized identities and Andrew Gorman-Murray has extended these insights to all lesbian and gay homes.[81] However, as Johnston and Valentine note, lesbians do not always experience the home as a safe or validating space and discrimination and power inequalities can inhibit the home's ability to provide sanctuary.[82] Feminist theorizing of the home and family typically located domestic power inequalities in social structures of class or gender. Feminist activism in Britain and Australia in the 1970s and 1980s was therefore instrumental in promoting awareness of and developing responses to women's lack of social and economic power in the home and vulnerability to domestic abuse. However, the emphasis on gender hierarchies as a factor in domestic violence meant that abuse in lesbian relationships did not begin to be widely acknowledged in British and Australian lesbian communities until the early 1990s. Megg described the difficulties she herself and her wider network of lesbian feminist friends in Alice Springs experienced in recognizing her lover's behaviour towards her as abusive:

> I'd be abused in front of people, verbally. So it wasn't physical abuse but it was, 'you're stupid' – all of those kinds of things. People didn't see it ... and then after we broke up, a couple of women immediately came to see me and said look, what was going on? Because previous lovers had walked out going 'My God' and they hadn't quite believed it ... It seems to be that it's a, so not meant to be part of lesbian culture that ... it's invisible, even when it's happening in front of your face ... At some point, I had, another lesbian in town saw it one night and she actually invited me for lunch. Then she just said two words, domestic violence. I went, 'Don't be ridiculous!' I mean I was part of that too. It doesn't exist in the lesbian community, that's what men do to women.[83]

In a review of a US edited collection, *Naming the Violence: Speaking out about Lesbian Battering*, for Melbourne's *Labrys Newspaper*, Jan Rawlins-Tully suggested that the lesbian community's reluctance to acknowledge domestic abuse in lesbian relationships stemmed from a perceived threat to the ideal of lesbian relationships and a tendency to unite as a community against external threats. She concluded:

> The lesbian who experiences violence in an intimate relationship is caught on the one hand between the homophobia of society which says that such relationships are bound to be destructive because of their deviant nature and on the other hand the lesbian community which encourages a conspiracy of silence on such matters in an attempt to avoid any such criticism.[84]

Many women described feeling unable to escape abusive relationships either because their lesbian friends would not believe them or because they were isolated from lesbians or other support networks and felt unable to ask for help.[85]

Lesbian and feminist analyses of lesbian domestic violence from the 1990s onwards theorized abuse in relation to power. Writing in *Labrys*, Gaye McCulloch argued: 'Violence is used for the express purpose of gaining power over, and therefore oppressing another – in this case our lovers.'[86] Vera Ray's 1991 article in the *Journal of Australian Lesbian Feminist Studies*, which was widely cited in Australian debates on the issue, contended that, unlike in domestic violence perpetrated by men against women, lesbian perpetrators saw themselves to be in an inferior or insecure position in the relationship and used domestic abuse in an attempt to equalize the power balance.[87] This analysis was supported by a number of women who had been subjected to domestic abuse, but did not reflect the experience of all. Jennie described the abusive relationship she experienced as one in which her abusive partner was widely regarded as a successful and powerful individual. She recalled: 'Sandy is a very powerful person within the Health Department', whereas 'I felt like the little wifey at home.' This unequal distribution of power outside of the home was reflected in the distribution of domestic tasks within the home. Jennie explained: 'Sandy is, was a brilliant cook, a gourmet cook, but I was the one that did the dishes, cleaned the toilet, that sort of thing. Sandy got the praise for great cooking and stuff and indeed her dinners were gorgeous, but certainly not equality.' This perception of inequality in domestic labour escalated, a few years into the relationship, into ongoing physical and psychological abuse. Jennie recalled:

> It was sort of punches and waking me in the middle of the night and hitting me around the head. Punching me on my body where bruises were left and other people couldn't see and it was just frustration. And there were a few other habits that I didn't particularly like, like being sick on the floor and leaving it, and sort of other things – putting, excuse the expression, putting shit all over the toilet and not cleaning it up …
>
> At one point she took my purse with my credit cards and everything, all my bank cards, everything. She took them away and said I'm not giving you these back. So I couldn't get any money, I couldn't get any food, I couldn't get anything, any fuel. I had to borrow from friends to get fuel to get to work … and I had to open a different account so my wages were paid into a different account.[88]

Jennie interpreted the physical violence and psychological abuse she experienced at the hands of her partner as a continuation of the power imbalance in their relationship and described a breach between her partner's external success and her anxieties around being seen to be in a lesbian relationship.

The distribution of labour within the home

Feminist historians have analysed the domestic sphere and housework in relation to gendered hierarchies of power and as a feature of capitalist societies.[89] While the allocation of domestic labour in same-sex relationships has not been the focus of research by historians, a number of sociological studies have explored the issue, questioning the importance of gender as a conceptual framework for individuals' and couples' approaches to housework. Although noting that 'contained within [an] ideal discourse of domesticity is an assumption that the home is a space in which men and women take on separate, gendered roles', Carla Barratt claims that an absence of gender scripts in lesbian relationships has resulted in a more flexible and negotiated approach to the apportioning of domestic roles in same-sex relationships.[90] Susan Kentlyn similarly assumed that gender would not be a factor in the allocation of domestic labour in same-sex households, but found that most of the respondents in her research on same-sex couples in Queensland understood domestic labour as aligned with femininity, low in status and susceptible to power relations of domination and subordination. For lesbian couples in particular, she argued, this produced a complex dynamic:

> The modulation of gender performance in lesbian couples appears much more complex [than in gay male couples], driven by many competing factors and conflicted desires. The women seemed to be torn by the need to acknowledge the value of 'women's work' whilst also seeing it as symbolic of women's oppression and position of subordination within gendered relations of power.[91]

Examined from a historical perspective, it is clear that many British and Australian women in same-sex relationships in the post-war period understood the allocation of domestic labour as an expression of power or powerlessness in their relationships and drew on or sought to contest gendered assumptions about the appropriate performance of domestic roles.

Feminist critiques of butch/femme relationships since the 1970s have frequently focused on the distribution of domestic labour between butch/femme couples, arguing that relationships structured in this way reproduced the unequal apportioning of housework apparent in archetypal post-war marriages. Certainly some women in butch/femme relationships in the post-war period described their allocation of domestic labour in this way. Rene Sawyer, who lived in a butch/femme relationship with her lover, Theresa, in Ealing in the 1950s, described their domestic roles as closely modelled on gendered roles. She recalled:

> Well one thing's for certain, you never had a butch really that ever did any cooking. I myself never knew really how to boil an egg until I was about 27/28 … My role as a butch was: I sat at the dinner table and my dinner was put down in front of me, as my father before me and my grandfather before that. And that was the role that we took on. Whereas the femme always took the role on as being the housewife and the mother.[92]

Rene's account suggests that her ability to model her domestic role on one she had witnessed her father and grandfather performing gave her a sense of security and confidence in what was expected of her. Sixteen-year-old Sandra, who moved into a flat in Sydney, with her lover, Barbara, in the 1950s, described a similar assumption that parental roles could provide a pattern for domestic structures. She recalled:

> We found a flat for rent at Bondi Beach, took it and moved in, despite the high cost. And my relationship with Barbara ran straight into difficulties. I was living out the role of husband with Barbara as wife, without having previously had a good

role model of a husband-wife team to copy. My experience with my own parents should have warned me about this, but it didn't ... I thus got into every role-playing game in any book. I expected Barbara to prepare the breakfast porridge and was surprisingly impatient when she burnt it. When I took over the preparation myself, I wondered how she would react. She, however, was not caught up in the game.[93]

As young women, with no connection to a broader lesbian community, Sandra and Barbara's domestic roles were shaped, initially, by familial and wider social roles and, ultimately, when this distribution of labour proved unsuccessful, by taking a more flexible skills-based approach. Sandra's account is also indicative, however, of the ways in which domestic labour distribution reflected power hierarchies within relationships. Looking back on this relationship in her memoir, written decades later, Sandra noted:

Barbara never confided in me. I still do not know what her inner thoughts were about me ... She never commented on anything I did or said. She went her way, thinking her own thoughts into which I had no insight. She would thank me for the chocolates I bought each pay day, and would murmur 'No' when I wanted to make love just once too often. Apart from that, I had little concept of her as an individual. She was a projection of my own desires, my 'wife' or my 'love'. Her identity lay in what she could offer me – being kind and unselfish, tolerant and persevering, affectionate – a homogenous glob of 'goodness' which bore the name of Barbara ... When I made love with her, I thought this made us lovers while she was but being carried along by a stronger will than her own.[94]

Re-evaluating her relationship with Barbara subsequently, Sandra located the allocation of roles in their relationship in the context of a broader power inequality, which enabled her to dictate the distribution of domestic labour and the terms on which the relationship was structured. For women whose relationships were located in the broader social context of a lesbian butch/femme bar scene or social network in this period, however, gendered expectations of domestic roles were often reinforced by the shared culture they participated in. Respect and status within wider social networks could derive from a demonstrated performance of expected domestic as well as public roles and some women described being conscious that a failure to fulfil these roles could impact not just on their immediate relationship but on their wider reputation in the community.[95] Others, however, indicated that they and their partners adopted a more flexible approach to gendered roles in private.[96]

Women who were not involved in a butch/femme community typically described their domestic roles in more varied and flexible terms. Some women strongly articulated a commitment to demonstrating equality in their distribution of domestic labour. Sharley recalled that, when she began a relationship with another woman in 1950s London, she and her lover, Georgina, discussed domestic roles:

Georgina would say to me, 'What shall we do?' And I'd say, 'What do you want to do?' You know, in the beginning. And I said, we must both take responsibility. I don't want to pressurize you into doing things and I don't want to be pressurized by you. I think we should be equal. Now she loved cooking, and I certainly didn't object to her cooking and she was more domesticated than I, but it didn't mean to say that she was into a domestic scene rather than I. She was certainly tidier! But … it was by mutual consent and it wasn't into a role-playing thing.

Sharley linked this emphasis on mutual consent with the political perspective she and Georgina shared, noting: 'But you see, again, Georgina was political. Maybe not quite as far committed as I was, but her politics also taught her that as a woman she has got to be a responsible person.' This was in contrast, she felt, with many of their contemporaries who 'are not at all political, or if they are political they're very, very wishy-washy sort of politics' and therefore approached the question of domestic labour in a different way. She commented: 'Most of my lesbian friends of my age-group, there is a certain degree of role-playing. And it seems to work. They seem to be happy the way they are, so, you know, people like this. Maybe it gives them comfort, maybe they know where they stand.'[97]

By the mid-1960s, a belief in the importance of taking a non-gendered approach to domestic labour was gaining influence in lesbian circles. Critiquing a letter in *Arena Three* which argued that lesbian relationships were characterized by partners who were psychologically masculine and feminine, Anne Hughes claimed:

It is an observable fact that in many female menages, one partner drives the car, the other does the cooking, but this division of labour is, I would suggest, sorted out on a practical rather than a quasi-psychological level. Contrary to what your correspondent believes, I think that much of the damage done to our image is done by those playing at being 'man' and 'woman' and not two women relying on each other for satisfaction on all possible levels.[98]

A married woman who had left her husband to set up home with another married woman echoed these sentiments in the magazine a few years later. Describing her relationship with her lover, she wrote: 'We believe in security, stability, love, sharing the load equally, and are both capable of working while our children are at school.'[99] The absence of such equality in a relationship was increasingly interpreted as a failing in this period. Diana Chapman, reflecting on her relationship with *Arena Three* editor, Esme Langley, in the mid-1960s, voiced her dissatisfaction with this partnership with reference to her perception of its inequality. She recalled: 'it was pretty one-sided. I was working, paying a lot of the bills, cleaning up the flat, doing the cooking. Esme was poncing around, doing *Arena Three*.'[100]

Such attitudes reflected the growing impact of feminist critiques of housework as one of the key areas in which women were exploited in a sexist society. British and Australian feminists contributed to an extensive international debate on the various ways in which social expectations about housework as women's work impacted on women's autonomy and the possible solutions to this issue.[101] The transnational campaign for 'Wages for Housework' represented the most recent manifestation of a longer-standing argument that women should be paid for their domestic labour, while others advocated a solution in which men were made to take responsibility for their own domestic needs and perform an equal share of housework.[102] The underlying assumption in many of these approaches was that housework was undesirable and demeaning work which women were forced to, rather than chose to perform. In a lesbian feminist context, debates demonstrated the tensions between a reluctance to exploit other women by relying upon their domestic labour and a personal rejection of the denigrated role of 'housewife'. In an article on feminist theory and practice for *Scarlet Woman* magazine, Australian lesbian feminists Kerryn Higgs and Barbara Bloch used collective houses as an example of the ways in which many women abused some of the fundamental principles of feminism. They argued that: 'the feminist desire for freedom from the oppressions of this society leads us into an unquestioning elevation of the idea of doing exactly what we want to do all the time'. In the context of collective living, they suggested, this could result in quite inconsiderate behaviour. They noted: 'At the most basic level, necessity is never removed. We need to eat, wash, clean up our wastes and support ourselves. There is no freedom from these obligations unless we leave them for someone else to do.'[103] A contributor to *Rouge* magazine, writing on the experience of living with other women, reinforced this point, although in a less critical way. She claimed:

> Another thing I like about living with a group of wimin is (when it happens) the sharing of responsibility for things like housework, cooking, wimin visitors, cars, boring it-bits – paying of bills etc. Actually what this sharing of responsibility means often is that things don't get done – but for me the good feelings that come when it does happen make group living a preferable lifestyle.[104]

Dorothy, who lived in a women's squat in Islington in the 1970s, compared her experience of shared labour there favourably with a previous bad experience at a mixed squat on the same road. Whereas at the mixed squat, she recalled: 'There was a lot of conflict around the communal things like who cleaned the toilets and who bought the toilet roll and all that. It was continual conflict', at the women's collective: 'There was a rota for housework and a rota for making dinner and it was no mean feat to make dinner for 10 people, plus guests.'[105]

In the context of a couple, the pressure to try to conform to feminist ideals of shared domestic labour could sometimes become oppressive. Clare recalled that, when she and her partner moved back to Sydney from London with their three children in the 1980s, she felt obliged by her feminist politics to divide the domestic labour equally, despite also working as the main breadwinner:

> We shared the jobs around the house. When we came here, Linda didn't have residency … so she couldn't work. So I worked and then I bought a chemist shop, so I worked incredibly hard and long hours. So that meant she was home with the children. This is from about '88 till '95 or something.
>
> A lot of the time, she worked part time. But I was the main breadwinner. We still shared all the domestic stuff, cleaning and stuff – again, based on politics and personality. I definitely would feel I had to do my share when I came home. I was exhausted, let me tell you. I was exhausted for years … It was this sort of neurotic non-division of labour. So hard, all of that, not able to be dealt with.[106]

Although Clare recalled her and her partner's shared feminist politics as a block to discussion about the distribution of domestic labour in their relationship, other couples practised negotiation as an explicitly feminist approach. When Sally and her partner moved in together to a country property in Victoria, Sally described their allocation of domestic labour as an evolving process based on constant negotiation:

> Yeah, we talked a lot about it, and especially beforehand … We shared the household tasks. She's always been really great at building construction and anything mechanical. So I guess – and heaps of energy which I haven't had. So AD did a hell of a lot of work … We came – we hit upon a solution with those sorts of tasks, with building and construction and external maintenance that one or another would lead the job. The other one would help. Because when we were both trying to lead the job it was just a nightmare.
>
> We've had lots of spirited discussions. We often disagree on nearly everything. We go back and forth, back and forth, back and forth for days if not weeks. So it's very tiring at times but we get there in the end.
>
> It was – and it evolved over time – so many years and we did talk a lot about that stuff. So our roles changed. We were aware that it was really hard to create roles for a lesbian relationship, and that's what we thought we had to do.

Sally described the process of intense discussion that she and her partner adopted as a conscious effort to create roles for themselves in the context of an absence of prescribed domestic roles for lesbian couples. Her account points to an underlying assumption that domestic labour should be distributed equally, but also a strong feminist commitment to making decisions through a process of collective discussion. Despite Sally's suggestion that the couple were attempting to 'create roles for a lesbian relationship', she recognized that these roles changed during the relationship. Reflecting on the work each woman did around the house, Sally commented: 'With the housework I think I probably did a bit more [at the beginning]. I don't know – certainly we did close on even. At that stage I think I used to do more of the cooking. But that's changed now and AD does most of the cooking now.'[107] While Sally drew on a self-consciously feminist perspective in her approach to the question of domestic roles, other women lacked an explicitly ideological framework, utilizing instead the skills which each woman possessed. Lou, who began renting a house together with her partner in Canberra in the mid-1990s, recalled:

> I always cooked. No, we shared everything but cooking and she did the ironing because I'm not good at that. But, no, it just – everything seemed to just intertwine. We just – it just worked from the beginning … I'm very handy with tools and that and I taught her how to use a drill and things like that because growing up I did all the handy work – Mum did and then taught me so I'm not afraid of a drill or saw and that. Then I showed her … and, yeah, so it was just natural. We'd fix the fence or do something around the house that needs fixing and we just taught each other.[108]

Women's approaches to the issue of finance in their relationships were similarly guided by considerations of autonomy and power. In the early post-war decades, women who envisaged their relationships as long-term, committed partnerships typically merged their financial resources. Andrée and Grace met in the late 1940s in Essex, when Andrée went to work for Grace in her dog kennels. Andrée had recently run away from home to avoid an unwanted marriage and, when her mother located her and recognized that Andrée would not be marrying her fiancé, she gave Andrée the money saved towards the wedding to invest in Grace's kennel business. The two women ultimately sold this business and bought a small farm together, subsequently moving a few times and jointly purchasing a succession of houses. By the 1960s, Grace's health was too poor to allow her to work and Andrée worked two jobs until she retired to support them both.[109] Although jointly purchasing properties or businesses was an option available only to middle-class women and those with family support, women with fewer financial resources sometimes expressed commitment by renting flats or bedsits together and sharing wages. In the absence of other legally recognized forms of commitment, such as same-sex marriage, jointly owned assets took on a particular significance as an expression of women's intentions towards their lovers. In 1969, C.E. and V.G. from Kent raised the issue of the division of finances in a letter to *Arena Three*. Having read a series in the *Guardian* newspaper, titled 'Money and the Middle Class', which featured a (male) homosexual couple who kept their finances separate, C.E. and V.G. wondered if they themselves were unusual in their shared approach. They explained:

> We ourselves regard our money as 'ours', and don't divide it into hers and hers. It's a little confusing at times, as our salaries are paid into separate bank accounts, but this is merely for appearances' sake. We promptly transfer our money to a joint Giro account, and ignore the raised eyebrows behind the local Post Office counter.[110]

Although this couple were concerned to protect their employment by avoiding any suspicion of lesbianism, it was nevertheless sufficiently important to them to merge their finances that they were willing to risk comments in their local Post Office. In a subsequent issue of *Arena Three*, another reader responded confirming that she and her partner adopted a similar approach:

> I feel that a 50-50 basis is the only way to derive complete security, especially where a home is involved. My Friend and I have been together now for seven years. From the outset we combined our earnings. We haven't got a posh home, by some standards, but started from scratch and everything is 'ours'. There's never been one moment in those seven years when we've had to worry as to who will be paying the telephone bill, the rental on the TV set, or buying the next stick of furniture, etc.[111]

This reader's comments suggest that the desire to merge finances may have reflected wider social assumptions about women's financial dependence in a period when a high proportion of adult women were heterosexually married and at least partially reliant, economically, on the support of a husband.

Such assumptions were increasingly problematized in the 1970s, however, in the context of a feminist valorization of independence and a growing recognition that economic dependence restricted women's autonomy in a variety of ways. Women who left heterosexual marriages to establish relationships with other women were often particularly sensitive to the potential risks of merging finances with a partner and were therefore more likely to insist on maintaining separate bank accounts and avoiding joint property purchases. Jan, who left a long-standing marriage in the 1970s when she realized her attraction to other women, explained that since her marriage and a subsequent 'disastrous' early attempt to co-own a house with another woman:

> I've only ever had separate finances ... It's partly an age group thing. It's partly that I was so much older when I got involved in living with other women. Partly having been through divorce once. It's too complicated all that stuff.[112]

However, this emphasis on autonomy was, to an extent, in tension with the feminist commitment to collectivity. The influence of left-wing, anti-capitalist ideologies on feminist theorizing and practice in the 1970s and early 1980s meant that feminist shared houses, squats and rural separatist communities were typically organized around an assumption of shared financial resources. In an interview with feminist journal, *Refractory Girl*, in 1974, the residents of a radical lesbian feminist shared house on Crystal Street in Sydney explained:

> Food money is pooled; people with money always help out.
> No one has ever had to leave because they haven't had enough money. This is just about rock bottom; if they can't live here they can't live anywhere! (laughter).
> If someone's got a good reason why they haven't got money, we pay rent for them.[113]

Similarly, the rural women's lands in Northern NSW were established on the basis of shared access for all women. Land for the first community, Amazon Acres, was purchased collectively with a small number of larger donors and other contributions raised through fundraising events, but the community operated on the principle that any woman had the right to visit or live on the land regardless of her ability to make any financial contribution. Despite the shared commitment to a principle of collective finances, the reality could sometimes fall short of women's ideals, leading to exploitation or conflict within communities. Lava, who was a resident at the Welsh women's land, Cefn Foellat, in the late 1970s, recalled:

> It actually belonged to an Englishwoman who at some point said 'Oh yeah, we can open this place and everybody is welcome to come' and then the first lot of women came and that was the people, the women we met in the South of France. But then they actually all left ... and then us new wave came ... But to be very honest, we

weren't very respectful of her ownership, we sort of just took over. This was really just a bunch of German women and we just took over the place and the woman who actually owned it, she left for London.[114]

The tension between the vigorous denial of property rights which informed Lava's friends' approach to collective living and the softer concept of sharing envisaged by the English owner resulted in considerable conflict, which Lava believed had left the owner unable either to reclaim her land or to qualify for state benefits as an individual without any means of financial support.

Differences in personal experience and socio-economic background also rendered attempts at financial sharing problematic. Janet Wahlquist told *Scarlet Woman* magazine in 1976 that an attempt she made to live collectively with a group of women from her consciousness-raising group was ultimately undermined by financial tensions. She explained:

> We talked about our collective before we went into it, it wasn't just a matter of needing a place to live. We decided that we would share our incomes, that we would have weekly meetings where any problems would be discussed, and where we would try to build up a strong rapport within the collective. The decision to share money was a demonstration of the goodwill we felt towards each other and our interest in making the collective work.
>
> The money sharing turned out to be a major source of conflict … Some of us couldn't cope with sharing money because of the way we had been taught to regard money as children and adolescents. Our diversity of experience etc went beyond differences in our attitudes to sharing money. This diversity of experience proved to be a great problem, not because diversity itself is a problem, but because we didn't accept that there was such a diversity and try to work out a way of coming to terms with this.[115]

The difficulties Janet identified were sufficiently serious to break apart the collective she described, but many other women complained of less significant frustrations in attempts to pool resources in the home.[116]

Conclusion

Whether or not to share clothes, food, money and indeed domestic space with lovers was a question which occupied the minds of many British and Australian lesbians in the second half of the twentieth century. Their decisions reflected personal preference and aspiration and the accessibility of resources, as well as being shaped by shifting political and cultural constructions of 'home'. The post-war culture of domesticity impacted significantly on the ways in which women imagined and structured their same-sex relationships in the decades after the war. The home figured repeatedly in women's fantasies of lesbian partnerships and many women regarded a shared home as a sign of commitment. The material environment of women's homes often reflected the structuring of their forms of intimacy, although, for some women, lack of access to a shared domestic space placed considerable pressure on their relationships. In the 1970s, feminist critiques of monogamy and the nuclear family coincided with broader counter-cultural attacks on the concept of the home as a site of consumption to produce radically different forms of domesticity and intimacy. While, for some women, a feminist commitment to autonomy continued to define attitudes towards the domestic context of relationships into the 1980s and 1990s, for others a shared home provided an essential backdrop to intimacy.

3

Marriage and commitment

In 1999, Australian journalist and gay rights activist Julie McCrossin gave a talk to the Sydney Institute in which she claimed that same-sex marriage was 'a topic very few people in the gay or lesbian, transgender or transsexual communities are willing to openly discuss' and in fact, she had 'never heard anybody else [advocate it] publicly'. She continued: 'I think it's fair to say many people, including human rights advocates that I greatly respect, would say that "real" marriage is an unachievable goal for same-sex couples.'[1] This view has been asserted repeatedly since, both by activists and academic commentators, who have represented calls for marriage equality as only the most recent stage in successive post-war campaigns around lesbian and gay rights. In her consideration of the same-sex marriage debate in Australia, feminist academic Barbara Baird has dated the origins of Australian campaigns for marriage equality to the mid-1990s, when, she argues, Liberal Prime Minister John Howard's conservative family values ideology reshaped the aspirations of lesbian and gay activists.[2] This view of lesbian and gay marriage campaigns as a move away from the more radical politics of the 1970s towards a quest for respectability and acceptance has been widely voiced by gay and queer theorists in recent decades, building on Lisa Duggan's 2002 claim that lesbian and gay marriage constitutes a 'new homonormativity'. Arguing that neoliberal policies in the United States and Britain have forged 'a politics that offers a dramatically shrunken public sphere and a narrow zone of "responsible" domestic privacy', Duggan describes marriage equality as 'public recognition of a domesticated, depoliticized privacy' and claims that the quest for lesbian and gay marriage 'does not contest dominant heteronormative assumptions and institutions but upholds and sustains them'.[3] For Duggan and other queer critics of the marriage rights movement, the concentration on this issue risks removing the radically transformative potential of queer sexuality from lesbian and gay activism and further outlawing those queer subjects whose sexual practices cannot be encompassed within the framework of the new homonormativity.[4]

While these debates have situated campaigns for marriage equality within a post-Millennium political framework (culminating in legislation enabling same-sex marriage in the UK in 2013 and in Australia in 2017), historians have demonstrated that same-sex marriage and calls for state recognition of same-sex relationships have a much longer history. In her work on women's gender-crossing in twentieth-century British culture, Alison Oram has documented a historical tradition of marriage between women dating back to the turn of the nineteenth century, while Ruth Ford has uncovered evidence of same-sex marriages in Australia in the interwar period.[5] Analysing butch fem marriage practices in post-war Toronto, El Chenier has asked how we are to read these historical weddings in the light of recent critiques of same-sex marriage. Chenier's earlier work attempted to locate such weddings in a lesbian and gay scholarship which understood butch fem culture as a form of 'public gay community life' that constituted 'acts of resistance against sexual oppression'. However, more recently, Chenier has argued that 'a reconsideration of butch fem postwar weddings in light of contemporary critiques of the gay marriage movement illuminates two particular issues: the limits of "resistance" as a category of analysis, and the way that familial practices, traditionally located in the "private sphere", are undervalued and overlooked'.[6] The emphasis of feminist and queer activism and scholarship on visible, public and oppositional activities has, they suggest, obscured stories of the domestic and familial. Similarly, this chapter will suggest, the focus on metropolitan communities centred on bar subcultures and political activism and the neglect, until recently, of rural and suburban histories of sexuality have distorted our understanding of sexual cultures and identities in the past. In contrast to the Canadian butch fem weddings, which Chenier reads as a form of pleasure practice located in urban bar communities, the comparable post-war British and Australian ceremonies were typically private affairs practised by socially isolated or geographically remote women without reference to a broader community. This chapter will suggest that the practice of same-sex marriage in Britain and Australia, and the emergence of a discourse which advocated state or Church recognition of same-sex marriage, was located largely outside of the urban and activist lesbian and gay communities for much of the post-war period and thus developed in tension with an alternative feminist and left-wing discourse critiquing marriage and the nuclear family, articulated from the late 1960s onwards.

Marriage as a model in lesbian relationships

In the immediate post-war decades, a broader cultural emphasis on marriage and motherhood as ideal goals for women meant that marriage offered a readily available model for women in same-sex relationships. Jeffrey Weeks has noted that, in the 1950s, 'Marriage rates were high, divorce rates were low, and marriage remained the gateway to respectable adulthood.'[7] In this context, as Chapter 4 explores, many women entered into heterosexual marriages in the hope that it would 'cure' them of same-sex desires, or without clearly recognizing that they were attracted to other women. For those women in same-sex relationships, the pervasive discourse of marriage provided a possible framework through which to structure their own patterns of intimacy. Personal accounts of women's same-sex relationships in the 1950s and 1960s, in particular, make explicit reference to the ways in which some women modelled their relationships on the heterosexual marriages of their parents or friends or drew on discourses of marriage which were circulating in culture more broadly. In the 1940s and 1950s, these models were potentially conflicting, as expectations of the marital relationship shifted after the war. Historians have noted the interwar emergence of the 'companionate marriage', in which the marriage relationship began to be reinterpreted as a partnership in which the man and the woman should have complementary, not dependent roles. In the post-war period, this ideal gradually replaced an older model in which women had been expected to take a more dependent and subservient role. Nevertheless, the fundamental aspects of the marriage relationship as a monogamous and life-long commitment remained uncontested.

In referring to their same-sex relationships in this period, some British and Australian women utilized both the language and conceptual frameworks of marriage. Sandra Willson, who formed two committed relationships with other young women in 1950s Sydney, recorded her relationships in a diary which she described as 'a history of my marriages'. In adopting the terminology of marriage, Sandra reflected a practice which was relatively common in same-sex relationships of this period. Recalling her relationship with another woman during the 1940s and 1950s, Myrtle Soloman explained: 'I lived with a woman called Marie for fifteen years. I met her during the war in the factory, so that was quite a long marriage.'[8] This practice may have been prompted in part by a lack of suitable terminology to refer to the women one loved and shared one's life with. In 1969, Miss D.P. from Hants wrote to British lesbian magazine *Arena Three*, complaining about the inadequacy of available terms. She wrote:

> I have a pet aversion: the word 'affair'. There appear to be two schools of thought on the definition of this word:- (a) a temporary liaison, or (b) a permanent relationship. Insofar as (b) is concerned, it has been said that one can hardly introduce one's partner as 'This is my friend', knowing that it goes much deeper than this. And society being what it is at the moment, one can hardly say 'my wife' or 'my husband' – hence the use of 'This is my affair'. An 'affair' is surely something of a temporary nature only, so why use it to describe a permanent partnership.[9]

Robyn Kennedy made a similar point in her paper at the First National Homosexual Conference in Melbourne in 1975, arguing: 'The social denial of the validity of the homosexual relationship is reflected in the absence of vocabulary to describe the partners of such a relationship.'[10]

However, marriage was not simply a convenient term: its centrality as a social institution meant that it carried with it specific meanings, which women drew on in a variety of ways in applying it to their relationships. Describing her marriage to fellow teenager, Barbara, whom she had met at the Salvation Army hostel where they both lived in 1950s Sydney, Sandra Willson explained:

> I was living out the role of husband with Barbara as wife, without having previously had a good role model of a husband-wife team to copy. My experience with my own parents should have warned me about this, but it didn't. They had played games of living together as a unit, of keeping the family together, which just didn't gel with the reality of me.[11]

Sandra did not regard her own parents' marriage as a positive model as it had ultimately ended in divorce, but nevertheless, in drawing on it as a pattern for her own relationship, she indicated her sense of what a marital relationship should be. The model she utilized was based on a domestic partnership embodying two distinct, gendered roles. A similar image of a same-sex marriage was presented in a short story published in *Arena Three*, in 1967. The story centred on a couple, Vida and Margaret, whose idyllic life in a peaceful cottage was shattered when Margaret was injured – perhaps fatally – in a car crash. Their relationship was portrayed in terms which in many ways reflected the ideal of a heterosexual marriage of the period. The reader was told:

> Vida worked in her advertising agency, coming home thankfully each night to the semi-rural peace of their Green Belt home and flower-filled garden. Margaret, an excellent manager, ran the house, hung out the washing on the line, did the shopping, met other young housewives for coffee, cooked delicious meals and filled the little house with folksong.[12]

Not all women, however, regarded marriage as necessarily involving distinct roles. For some, use of the term 'marriage' indicated an expectation of longevity and commitment in the relationship. Eileen, who moved in lesbian circles in Sydney and Melbourne from the 1950s onwards, used the word to describe her longest relationship, with Vivienne, which lasted from 1961 until Vivienne's death in 1976. Reflecting on her failure to have any further relationships after Vivienne's death, Eileen observed: 'When you're married to star quality everything else is second best. [My friend] Val used to try and marry me off to various people but nothing stuck. I just didn't bother.'[13] In 1977, J. and C. from Merseyside wrote to *Sappho* magazine declaring: 'We are writing to tell you about our happiness together. Thanks to you we are no longer lonely and unhappy. We started corresponding six months ago and have not looked back. We are now engaged and about to settle down together, which means that you will be one subscriber short.'[14] Describing her first relationship with another woman in 1970s' Cessnock, NSW, Fleur also used the term to indicate commitment. She recalled:

> She was about sixteen years older than me. She took me for a ride. Really, I mean I was so young, and she sort of knew everything, and we bought a car and everything like that, and she ended up with it 'cause I was so naïve about things. I thought it was the relationship I was going to be in for all the rest of my life, as far as I knew I was going to be married to her.[15]

The sense of permanence and life-long commitment inherent in mainstream understandings of marriage was central to its appeal to many women in same-sex relationships in this period. This was particularly the case in the immediate post-war decades, when cultural and medical representations of lesbian relationships typically constructed them as unstable, short-lived and prone to jealousy, in contrast to heterosexual marriages which continued to be regarded as enduring and stable. In 1959, British psychiatrist Eustace Chesser claimed: 'There is a distinctive homosexual temperament in which jealousy, possessiveness and sadomasochism predominate. The overt Lesbian suffers from a basic insecurity and a constant fear that the loved one may be seduced into heterosexuality.'[16] These views were continuing to be voiced in the press into the 1970s. In January 1978, Mary Gibbs wrote in to the *Manchester Daily Express* to complain about Jean Rook's argument that lesbian relationships are 'often more neurotic, passionate, jealous and highly-sexed than a standard marriage', while the *News of the World* reported on a new book by sex counsellor, Tim LaHaye, in which he claimed that 'fidelity among homosexuals is almost unknown' and that once 'an affair has run its course, the youthful homosexual is dumped'.[17] The desire of women to overcome these stereotypes was apparent in articles such as one titled, 'What Makes It Last?', published in *Arena Three* in 1964. K.H. from NSW observed that 'because there are relationships between women which have lasted literally until death, and others which are still flourishing after many decades, it's worth looking for clues'. K.H. emphasized that lesbians were not alone in facing the breakdown of relationships, arguing: 'Hundreds of thousands of relationships of all kinds go bust every year for hundreds of thousands of reasons. As many, or more, endure for a lifetime. And in this – the question of success or failure, you and I aren't "different from the rest" at all.' However, she suggested, the absence of social recognition did place an added pressure on lesbian relationships, which lacked 'the security of acceptance, and established usage'.[18]

The desire for committed, long-lasting relationships was voiced most clearly by women who lived in rural or remote areas or were not part of a wider lesbian social network. For these women, a relationship frequently provided not only intimacy and companionship, but also the women's only contact with another lesbian and its loss was proportionately devastating. Many personal testimonies of both Australian and British lesbians in the 1950s and 1960s include poignant accounts of women whose relationships ended, leaving them, in the short-term, without emotional support for the breakdown of the relationship, and, in the longer-term, completely isolated and without hope of locating other women like themselves. Envisaging their relationships in terms of marriage provided women in these circumstances, in particular, with a framework in which they could declare love and commitment as well as affording a sense of security in the permanence of their relationship. Wedding ceremonies provided women with an opportunity to express their commitment to a monogamous, life-long partnership, and make a declaration of romantic love for one another. L.B. from Warwickshire, writing to thank *Sappho* magazine for introducing her to her new partner, J.W., declared of their relationship:

> This is, in fact, a marriage of two people, both mature (in body, but not completely in mind!) who feel reasonably certain of having a lasting partnership; in fact, we are firm believers in a line from a gay wedding service we attended, that we'll be together 'as long as love remains' – and it will – with understanding and give-and-take on both sides.[19]

Post-war wedding ceremonies

Throughout the post-war period, Australian and British women in same-sex partnerships took part in marriage-like ceremonies or exchanged rings as a sign of their commitment and intention to forge a life-long relationship. Responding to a request for information from a lesbian couple in Bendigo, Victoria, who wished to marry in the late 1970s, a member of CAMP NSW, wrote:

> Homosexual couples do occasionally go through the form of marriage but these are private arrangements which cannot be registered as legal contracts. The majority of homosexual couples live together in what amounts to de facto marriage. The fact that they live together and are known to live together is usually sufficient for them. Some however feel the need to make their commitment to each other in a more public way. This is a human-enough wish on the part of people who love each other and are proud of their relationship. Some couples in this situation arrange ceremonies of their own, inventing a ritual if they like that kind of thing and want the occasion to be as symbolic as possible. Others simply hold a party and announce that they intend to live together as partners. The need for ceremony seems to be one stronger in some people than in others but is nonetheless as old as humanity.[20]

As this writer suggested, personal accounts indicate a wide range of different wedding ceremonies. Andrée described her marriage ceremony with her partner, Grace, in 1954. The couple travelled from Essex to Gretna Green with their friend, Dorothy Dyke, in order to get married. It was an epic journey, involving several car breakdowns and a night spent sleeping rough on Ilkley Moor, but the trio ultimately arrived in Gretna Green, where they were married at the anvil. Dorothy officiated, saying a few suitable words and then asking Andrée and Grace, 'Do you take this woman to be your wife?' The couple exchanged rings before the wedding party retired to a local hotel for a few days' honeymoon.[21] Andrée and Grace's choice of Gretna Green as a location for their wedding suggests a desire to draw on a dissident marriage tradition historically espoused by couples seeking a legal marriage outside of the typical social conventions of their local community. In Australia, British-born nurses Paddy and Robbie Byrnes used more traditional forms in the celebration of their wedding. Paddy recalled: 'I had my name changed to Robbie's. On 17 March 1956 we became as one in a wee church, after lighting two candles and exchanging wedding rings inscribed "Keep Faith".'[22] In the 1970s, Helen and Jackie took part in a Romany wedding in Newcastle, England. Helen explained that the two women had been having 'an affair', but 'I think we wanted society to accept us, to know that two women could make it. At the time we both needed security', so when Jackie suggested they marry, Helen agreed. She recalled: 'We had a fire and jumped the brush, exchanged gold wedding rings, cut one of our wrists. Quite painful. I've still got the scar actually.'[23]

While private and informal ceremonies such as these were not uncommon in this period, a small number of women sought 'legal' marriage as a means of formalizing their relationship. When prison reform activist, Wendy Bacon, gave *Mejane* an interview in 1971 about the eight days she had spent in a Sydney women's prison, she described a culture of same-sex couples. She recalled:

> There was allegedly one married couple in there who got married in a registry office and she was very butch and pulled the long pants that they wear [in prison] … down below her dress so she sort of looked like a male, and she was married to one of the women.[24]

In Britain, the *Sheffield Morning Telegraph* reported the case of two women who had appeared before a Sheffield court in 1966 on a charge of 'making for the purpose of being inserted in the register of marriage for the City of Sheffield, a false statement'. The groom was fined a total of £30, the bride, £10 and a civil court declared the marriage a nullity.[25] A similar case came to court in Manchester in 1971, when Rosalyn Atta, aged 21, pleaded guilty to having posed as a groom in order to marry 22-year-old Doreen Wimbleton, who also pleaded guilty to making a false declaration.[26] Tracing press reports of female husbands in Britain through the twentieth century, Alison Oram has suggested that women passed as grooms in wedding ceremonies for a variety of reasons, including the economic benefits of living as a man; the desire to cement a same-sex relationship through marriage; and the expression of a trans identity. In the post-war period, she argues, newspapers were increasingly likely to consider the possibility of a sexual relationship between women involved in such cases and to pathologize lesbian desire, suggesting that by this period, couples who married in these circumstances were more likely to be doing so as a means of formalizing a lesbian relationship.[27]

Debating relationship recognition in the 1960s

Calls for state recognition of same-sex relationships and officially sanctioned gay marriage began to be articulated with the emergence of non-commercial lesbian communities in the mid-1960s. *Arena Three* regularly included comments on the question of marriage which readers had written in. Opinions varied, between those who regarded same-sex marriage as a dream for a more tolerant future society and those who questioned the appropriateness of applying heterosexual marital structures to relationships between women. In December 1967, A.K. wrote in, imagining: 'The lesbian scene, 1987. I have often wondered what it would be like if, in twenty years time, we became acceptable to society …. Who knows, lesbian weddings might be taken for granted. The couple could join surnames, (for example, "Jones-Smyth"), be married in Church or Registry Office, and work out their own domestic arrangements.'[28] The following year, C.C. declared: 'I would also like more than anything for it to be legal for two girls to get married in a church or registry office.'[29] In November 1965, J.D. from Washington sparked a debate about monogamy and life-long commitment when she wrote:

> What is so utterly essential, all-important and goal-of-all-goals about Lasting Relationships? Admittedly, for people who strongly need someone, they can serve quite a useful function and result in a great deal of continued happiness. But basically monogamy, 'straight' or 'gay', is not en rapport with the emotional needs of most people. Monogamy tends to be a stifling dull pattern with time, and raising children seems the only valid excuse for insisting (societally) that two persons enter a relationship intended to be permanent. For most others, however, the 'lasting relationship' is impractical except as an emotional crutch for the lonely/insecure.[30]

Her letter apparently 'provoked a pleasing amount of controversy' and Wendy from Staffordshire retorted: 'JD's resigned cynicism savours rather of a sixth-former reading an overdose of Durrell than of "maturity".' For her, 'There is no purpose in any attachment whatsoever unless one can have faith, from the outset, in its sincerity.'[31] I.S. from Yorkshire also declared fidelity to be a fundamental requirement in a meaningful, lasting relationship. She argued:

> In a relationship based on fidelity there is a genuine, continuous awareness of another person and their need, a necessary sacrificing of one's own needs if it better serves the life which is the life of both. In return there is the reward of the companionship of someone who knows, understands and, where need be, supports against the inevitable injuries of everyday life. There is also the certainty of belonging, of having roots in an otherwise shifting world … Few of these factors can be present in, and none can be demanded from, a relationship which is transitory. For this is the very stuff of love, the material from which is woven a life which has value in itself, and a worth beyond that which it would have possessed if it had not been shared.[32]

The role of Christianity in promoting marriage was also the subject of debate. In a January 1966 article on a 'Christian View of Lesbians', Miss D.F. of Kensington wrote that Christian objections against a sexual relationship between two women might be resolved by homosexual marriage. She reflected:

> 'Do you want to get married? Could you keep the promises a Christian couple, marrying in church will keep?' If Christians feel that God accepts and blesses such unions, this would be the logical outcome of such a conviction. It would be backed by the consideration that God wills that all mankind should, through love of Him and each other, come to the fullness of human stature as joyful, creative members of his family, the church. For most, this would be heterosexual union and the raising of a family. For the few it would be life with another, but of a non-procreative type – analogous with the marriages of the elderly.[33]

However, Miss D.F.'s view of a Christian homosexual marriage was not shared by all, and in the following issue, Margot Whitehead challenged her assumption that Christians have the right to pass judgement on homosexuals or to exhort them to celibacy or marriage. She argued: 'to my mind, heterosexual marriage is an attempt to render mystical what is essentially a business relationship. Is not a married couple a sort of limited company for the production of infants?'[34] Writing into the magazine in 1968, C.C. from Essex agreed that marriage was not an appropriate model on which to structure same-sex relationships, although for her, the stumbling block was in the roles assigned to each party. She observed:

> I am of the opinion that the whole western conception of conjugal love is basically wrong ... Most homosexuals are, however, so steeped in this western conception that they tend to imitate a basically wrong situation, and they consider the perfect relationship to be one where partner A is aggressive, vagrant and sovereign, and partner B submissive, fixed and subordinate. There is irony too, for the physiological gap [which exists between men and women] does not exist between homosexual consorts, and great pains are taken to create it artificially. The very beauty of such a union is debased into something rather less and erroneous.[35]

The question of equality and the subservient role traditionally assigned to women in marriage was increasingly raised in the late 1960s, reflecting feminist critiques of marriage and the nuclear family which emerged at this time. In December 1968, A.H. from Herts wrote into *Arena Three* observing:

> I wonder just how many people have given thought to the utter nonentity of the married woman. First, she is expected to change her own surname to that of the male she marries, then she loses her own first name so that having married, for example, George Frederick Longbottom – her letters are then addressed to Mrs G.F. Longbottom. This, I think, is an atrocity of such sick-making subservience that I feel I must point this out to the married colleagues with whom I work, and most agree! I blame the women. They must actually enjoy being an appendage to the male they are legally in bondage to! Having subjected herself to the bondage, she is also expected to give up her career, and live wherever his work happens to be.[36]

Feminist and gay activist approaches to marriage

With the emergence of the Women's Liberation and Gay Liberation Movements in the late 1960s and early 1970s, a powerful critique of marriage and the nuclear family began to be articulated in activist circles. Feminist and gay literature, magazines and newsletters were filled with passionate accounts of the nuclear family as a heteropatriarchal institution which crippled its individual members, oppressed women and promoted compulsory heterosexuality. The marriage relationship at the heart of the nuclear family, feminists argued, was particularly oppressive and divisive for women. Reflecting on the different experiences of marriage for British men and women, *Spare Rib* argued: 'The power is in his hands. He may choose to treat you well. If not – if he doesn't give you enough for the housekeeping, or if he starts to beat you up – then nobody will intervene unless you admit that your marriage has irretrievably broken down and institute divorce or separation proceedings.'[37] Marriage was therefore an unequal institution in which women were placed in a subservient role, forced into unpaid drudgery, and isolated from the support of other women. In the social revolution which was to come, it was hoped new relational models would emerge to challenge and replace marriage and the nuclear family.

Same-sex relationships seemed to offer an opportunity for women to explore these new, more equal, forms of relationship. In an interview with *Shrew*, Gerlin, a youth worker from London, reflected: '[I]n most relationships there is a dominant partner. There's one person who's always making the decisions or being the boss, and this is what part of GLF is trying to say, look, we don't want to transfer the heterosexual relationship to the homosexual relationship. It should be more on an equal level.'[38] In their manifesto, written in June 1973, the Melbourne Radicalesbians similarly rejected marriage and heterosexual relationships as a model for lesbians, asserting: 'We recognise the institutions which oppress us, and will not set up copies of marriage, of role playing, of power dominance … We do not condone any manifestation of the ideals of monogamy or the nuclear family within our own relationships.'[39] In contrast to heterosexual marriage, lesbian relationships were presented by many lesbian feminists as inherently equal and loving. In consciousness-raising groups and at conferences, women began to work out new patterns for intimate relationships, rejecting the monogamous, committed couple as a model which inhibited self-expression and resulted in a loss of independence and individuality for women. As an alternative, women explored the possibilities of non-monogamy, regarding sexual intimacy simply as one means among many of expressing love and affection for other women.[40]

While many of those involved in feminist or lesbian and gay activism in the 1970s embraced these ideas and attempted to practise them in their personal lives, it was also recognized that the development of a vocal lesbian and gay rights movement enabled the issue of same-sex relationships to be put firmly on the political agenda. Campaigning groups such as the Campaign Against Moral Persecution (CAMP) in Australia, and the Albany Trust and Campaign for Homosexual Equality (CHE) in Britain raised the difficulties faced by same-sex couples in the absence of relationship recognition as part of their demands and argued for marriage equality. In 1977, Vivienne Cass, Clinical Psychologist and member of CAMP WA, made a submission to the Royal Commission on Human Relationships, outlining the ways in which she felt homosexuals were discriminated against in Australian society. She noted:

> At present a homosexual couple holds no status either legally or socially in Australian society … In practical terms, this means they are not considered next of kin, which in turn leads to disadvantage in areas such as inheritance, superannuation and pension benefits, visiting rights in hospitals, housing loans, passports, to name a few. Legally a homosexual is considered to be of single status and so his/her parents are taken as next of kin rather than their homosexual partner … The solution to these most oppressive problems is obviously some form of 'contract of responsibility' similar to a marriage contract in that it recognises the homosexual relationship as a legal one.[41]

In his influential book *Homosexual: Oppression and Liberation*, gay liberation activist and theorist, Dennis Altman, had made similar points, before reflecting on the less tangible ways in which a lack of recognition impacted on same-sex relationships. He argued: 'It is impossible to know to what extent love is strengthened by being public, yet romantic ideals of secret love not-withstanding, I suspect that after a time lovers have a psychological need for the support that comes from being recognised as such.'[42]

While the ending of economic and legal discrimination against same-sex couples fit relatively neatly into the rights-based approach of some lesbian and gay activism in the 1970s, activists also recognized the desire of a certain homosexual constituency for access to the institution of marriage itself. Vivienne Cass, in her submission to the Royal Commission on Human Relationships, continued:

> It's probable that most homosexual people – certainly most homosexual rights campaigners – are against the concept of holy matrimony as it exists. So if this argument seems to become a little impersonal, it is because we are arguing in favour of something we wouldn't care to try ourselves. Nevertheless, there are many people who have a deep, intimate and lasting relationship with a member of their own sex and who would like to solemnize the relationship in formal marriage. For practical purposes this is not possible, and it seems to us that thousands of people are being deprived of something they consider valuable. Furthermore, their sacrifice is not balanced with a corresponding benefit to society at large. In our view, the argument that the introduction of homosexual marriage would debase and corrupt the concept of marriage is a very shaky one indeed. The crucial tests would seem to be love, and an attempt to make something last.[43]

Addressing a Royal Commission, the 'formal marriage' Cass envisaged was presumably a legal contract endorsed by the state, but others also noted the desire of some same-sex couples for their marriages to be recognized by the Church. In 1971, the *Guardian* newspaper reported on a call by the Albany Trust for church leaders to 'consider sympathetically' the question of homosexual marriage. Writing in the Albany Trust's magazine, *Man and Society*, Sebastien Helmore had argued that: 'some homosexuals sincerely desired to enter into a binding union. Many a homosexual is aware that among his homosexual friends are some who have been able to build lasting unions, and if these are few, then there are many more homosexuals who frequently express the hope of attaining such a relationship.' *The Guardian* reported:

> In outward appearance such unions could well have much of the character of heterosexual marriage. The two would live together and depend on each other to varying extents: 'financially, psychologically, socially, emotionally, and presumably also sexually ... The commitment of such homosexuals to one another is a total one; it is exclusive, it is intended to endure through all difficulties, and they see themselves as one flesh.'[44]

These Church-sanctioned unions would therefore closely reflect the character of heterosexual marriage, being monogamous and binding for life.

Throughout the 1970s, these two perspectives on same-sex marriage were debated in the pages of British lesbian magazine, *Sappho*. The discussion was initiated in the very first issue in a short story by Elsa Beckett, titled 'Holy Matrimony', which portrayed a lesbian couple who decided that one of the women should cross-dress in order for them to participate in a church wedding. Charis and Alwyn were celebrating their fifth anniversary when Alwyn suggested the idea, complaining: 'It's a bore ... Here we are, married five years, a model marriage, and we have not had a single wedding present. No engagement presents – nothing ... and no congratulations. Just because we aren't legally married. AND that's not OUR fault. We're willing but they won't let us.'[45] Although Beckett raised the issue in a humorous way, other readers took the debate seriously. Concerned that some readers might try to emulate Charis and Alwyn and risk fines or imprisonment in the process, Scrivener from Glasgow objected to the story. She went on:

> It is easy to understand why sincere partners should wish to put, as it were, the seal of permanence on their union. But, surely, two girls, certain beyond doubt that they wish to marry, will find their own way to solemnise and seal the contract. I dislike the thought of a legally binding document or anything as soulless. I should hope an exchange of vows, possibly to be renewed with each anniversary would be sufficient for most of us. I wish I knew from personal experience – unfortunately I don't.[46]

Her views were echoed by 'Sister Chauvinism', who expressed herself to be 'very dubious about the proposal that gays should be allowed to marry each other. What on earth for?' she asked. 'Do you really want or need legal recognition of a "right" to your own lover?'[47] In a subsequent issue, Elsa Beckett responded to Scrivener, disputing her representation of marriage. She argued:

> Marriage is not soulless contract making, it is above all a public declaration of love which some lesbian couples may wish to make. It is not compulsory for heterosexuals – they can choose to marry or not. Why should not homosexuals have the choice too? Some form of recognition of homosexual marriages may be an important part of integrating homosexuality into the pattern of social behaviour.[48]

This debate reflected a growing divergence between different perspectives on the social significance of lesbian relationships. Scrivener and Sister Chauvinism characterized same-sex relationships as inherently private affairs, with Sister Chauvinism drawing on feminist critiques to challenge the notion of 'ownership' in relationships and posit lesbian intimacy as an opportunity to explore new relational models. Beckett, however, understood marriage as both a romantic affair between two individuals, which would be strengthened by public recognition, and a public indicator of social acceptance of lesbianism. In emphasizing the importance of a 'public declaration', Beckett reflected a shift in lesbian wedding practice which began in the 1970s, away from private ceremonies between the couple concerned, towards larger, more public events witnessed by family and friends.

The church and same-sex marriage

Church blessings were amongst the first forms of this wider social recognition of same-sex relationships, becoming increasingly common from the early 1970s. In his study of blessings of same-sex unions in the United States, Mark Jordan makes a clear distinction between legal and Church marriage, arguing that, although often encompassed in the same ceremony, the legal and religious aspects of these unions perform different functions. Recognizing this distinction, he argues, allows us to acknowledge both the participation of members of faith groups in homosexual activism dating back to the 1950s and 1960s and the historical practice of Church blessings of same-sex unions.[49] The post-war period witnessed a gradual shift in attitudes towards homosexuality in the Church, particularly in Britain, with the Church of England advocating law reform for male homosexuals in 1954, while still arguing that homosexuality was sinful.[50] The influence of this process of liberalization amongst British churches was felt in Australia in the late 1960s and early 1970s. In 1967, the Presbyterian Church issued a call for law reform, making a similar distinction between sin and crime in its characterization of homosexuality and in the early 1970s a series of Anglican committees recommended a change in the law.[51] In the context of this growing discussion of homosexuality, a number of Christian denominations began to reflect on the nature of homosexual relationships and the appropriate attitude of Churches towards them. In *Towards a Quaker View of Sex*, published in Britain in 1964, homosexual relationships were represented as typically short-lived, jealous and shallow in nature. However, the possibility of more committed and socially positive homosexual relationships was acknowledged, and the authors argued that these relational forms should be encouraged as preferable to promiscuity. This was a key motivation for religious ceremonies in the 1970s and later and Max Denton argues that Churches were a crucial site for carving out an alternative discourse on same-sex relationships in this period, drawing on the post-war idealization of love and companionate marriage to justify long-term, committed same-sex relationships. Theologian Norman Pittenger's 1967 book, *Time for Consent: A Christian's Approach to Homosexuality*, was influential in this context and Denton argues:

> To Pittenger, love was the only Christian ethical absolute. This simple theological frame allowed him to reconcile companionate-styled same-sex relationships with adherence to Christian moral faith and community … It also drew heavily on popular ideals of companionate marriage that had become prominent aspects of marital discourse and debate in the post-war era. The emphasis of mutual affection and sexual pleasure harkened back to the Christian ideals of companionate marriage articulated by Herbert Gray and the National Marriage Guidance Council, emphasising romantic love, mutuality and sexuality as the basis of companionate long-term relationships.[52]

Lesbian and gay Christian groups built on these ideas in the ensuing decade. In September 1978, the British Gay Christian Movement held a conference in Bristol to discuss homosexual marriages, in the context of a growing number of ceremonies taking place between Christians of all denominations. The Rev Martin Preston, a Baptist minister and member of the movement, explained that the movement 'wanted to counteract, among other things, the idea that gay relationships were impermanent. Many held to the ideal of life-long commitment.'[53] Following the conference, the movement reported that it had devised a service to bless same-sex unions, in which the priest was to ask the couple: 'Will you swear to remain faithful to each other, never allowing any other relationship to come before the one you are now to affirm?' The couple would then vow to 'love, honour and cherish you all the days of my life, until death divides us.'[54]

Although occasionally reported in the press or recorded in published literature, these debates about the appropriateness of religious blessings of same-sex unions tended to take place on the margins of Christian circles in this period. Despite its influence, *Towards a Quaker View of Sex* did not have the status of an official statement and, in the 1960s and 1970s, the possibility of church recognition or blessings of same-sex relationships was typically raised by individual clergy rather than in official reports. Ann, a member of the Australasian Lesbian Movement, explained to the *Sunday Observer* in 1970:

> I went to my vicar and told him I was in love with a woman and we would be living together so I'd be leaving the parish. He, as an individual, not as a spokesperson for the Church, said he believed this was okay and that he would rather I was with somebody rather than be a frustrated old maid. He said there were too many frustrated old maids in the parish.[55]

In 1976, an Adelaide clergyman told *Forum* magazine that homosexual relationships were no different to heterosexual ones and should be granted state and church recognition:

> I believe the time has come for the Church and State to make possible a ceremony similar to the marriage ceremony for heterosexual couples and that certain legal rights should be granted them … Like his heterosexual fellow, the homosexual longs eagerly to be in a relationship with another of commitment, mutual in giving and receiving, experiencing tenderness, loyalty, hopeful expectancy and union. This alone can bring the fulfilment he needs.[56]

Nevertheless, this statement was framed as an expression of personal belief and the clergyman who wrote it gave neither his name nor denomination, suggesting that he felt his views were at odds with, or might be censured by his church.

With the formation of homophile groups in the late 1950s and the rise of lesbian and gay activism in the early 1970s, a dialogue was established between some individual members of the clergy and homosexual groups, which enabled the discussion of homosexual relationships among other issues. In this context, the possibility of religious ceremonies recognizing same-sex relationships was increasingly discussed and Christian homosexuals came to be seen as having a particular need for weddings. Responding to a letter of inquiry about marriage ceremonies between women, a CAMP

NSW member wrote: 'Religious people have special needs in this context. They want to express the spiritual basis of their relationship and to make their promises before God as well as in front of their friends.' Directing the letter writer to a sympathetic pastor who could conduct such a ceremony, he continued: 'If you are a devout person you will feel the promises you make in this ceremony are as binding as they are in a marriage ceremony but remember, legally they have no status.'[57] Jo McVay-Abbott, secretary of the London group, Fellowship in Christ the Liberator, echoed this notion of the twin purpose of religious ceremonies in 1973 when she claimed that a Christian gay wedding was 'an expression of a couple's commitment to each other and to God'.[58] Similarly, Sydney lesbian couple, Maria and Jeanette, explained that they wanted to have their ceremony in the late 1980s 'performed in a church by a member of the clergy' because they wanted to have a marriage 'in the eyes of God'.[59]

Religious wedding ceremonies between same-sex couples were widely reported as a novelty in the mainstream press in Britain and Australia in the 1970s. In 1973, Australian newspapers reported that the Reverend Mario Schoenmaker, a Congregational minister, had conducted a marriage ceremony between two women at the CAMP clubrooms in West Perth. The Covenant of Love ceremony involved an exchange of rings and Elizabeth and Agnes 'took vows to love, comfort, honour and keep one another in sickness and in health. They also promised to be faithful to one another'. Rev Schoenmaker told the *Age* newspaper that 'although the ceremony took a different form from the normal wedding … It was still a church-sanctioned marriage, and was binding in conscience on the women'.[60] Emphasizing the importance of love as the basis of the union, Rev Schoenmaker commented: 'Theirs was a love I have rarely come across … theirs was a devotion to one another which to my way of thinking is purely divine … for LOVE, any love must always have a divine origin.'[61] In Britain, the early 1970s witnessed a number of clergymen agreeing to hold marriage or blessing ceremonies in church for same-sex couples. In March 1975, the *Sunday People* reported that Rev George Nairn-Briggs, vicar in the Surrey village of Salfords, had performed blessing ceremonies for several homosexual and lesbian couples. He told the paper he had 'no objection to blessing other gay "marriages" – provided the couples are in love and want a permanent relationship … "First of all, I will ask them to promise before God that they will care for each other and then I ask the Lord to bless their relationship"'.[62]

The arrival of the Metropolitan Community Church (MCC) in Britain and Australia in 1973 offered same-sex couples the opportunity to marry in a lesbian and gay church and the performance of same-sex weddings became a key focus of the MCC's mission. The Rev Arthur Ramirez of the MCC explained that although the church could not perform legally binding weddings for lesbian and gay couples, 'we are ready to give a formal Christian blessing to a homosexual couple, male or female, who convince us they have chosen to live together permanently and irreversibly'.[63] While Max Denton suggests that the MCC struggled to gain a strong foothold in Britain, where many gay Christians preferred to work within their existing denominations to change attitudes towards homosexuality, in Australia, the MCC established a thriving mission, in which same-sex weddings were a key element.[64] During the 1970s, the MCC opened branches across regional Australia, reflecting a demand from Christian lesbians and gay men outside of the cities. In 1976, a branch of MCC was established in Newcastle, NSW by two women, Breck and Ellen, who held the meetings in their home. The following year, another woman, Vicki, trained to be a minister and the church continued there until 1978, providing, amongst other services, counselling prior to gay marriages and conducting commitment ceremonies.[65] In the 1980s and 1990s, the MCC established themselves as key providers of same-sex wedding ceremonies in Australia and Britain, reaching out beyond their congregations in performing this service. In 1996, British couple, Dawn and Lisa, were married by a member of MCC 'after searching for months' for a 'church happy to bless our union'. *The People* newspaper reported:

> Dawn and pregnant Lisa were married five weeks ago in a ceremony held by Pam Haynes, a member of the Metropolitan Community Church. The Christian sect believes that lesbians and homosexuals are equal to heterosexuals in the eyes of God. The service took place at the Bridge pub in Peterborough. After saying prayers together, Dawn and Lisa were handcuffed to each other by friends.[66]

A few years earlier, Juliana and Sandie, from Victoria, were married by an MCC Reverend and *Labrys* explained:

> It was Sandie's idea to get married, and when Juliana decided that she also wanted to, she rang WIRE to find out how they could do it. WIRE gave them the Reverend Ben Bannen's phone number. The Rev performed a marriage ceremony in Juliana's backyard, with the usual entourage of witnesses, confetti … and the exchanging of vows … Their certificate says they 'were joined together in the rite of the Holy Union according to the church of Jesus, the Christ.' Sandie and Juliana are not religious, and do not go to church, but they felt it was right to do it that way: 'it's a holy union, not a marriage, it doesn't have any legal credibility, but it is a religious thing.'[67]

By the 1990s, there was also increasing debate in Australian Jewish circles about rituals of union. In 1993, Sydney lesbian Jewish activist Dawn Cohen argued in favour of lesbian and gay marriages and Jill Jones argues that this reflected a wider trend, claiming in 2001: 'Judaism appears to be the most receptive of religious traditions to the concept of lesbian and gay rituals of union'.[68] In 1998, Kerryn Phelps and Jackie Stricker became Australia's most well-known lesbian couple after their wedding, performed by Rabbi Ari Fridkis in New York, was the subject of intense media coverage.[69]

Activism on relationship recognition

Although some religious lesbian and gay networks afforded a space in which same-sex marriage could be debated and advocated for throughout the 1970s and 1980s, marriage continued to be regarded with suspicion or hostility in wider feminist and lesbian and gay activist circles in Britain and Australia in the 1980s and 1990s. Many activists asserted the potential of same-sex relationships to experiment with new, more creative forms of intimacy and feminist critiques of marriage as an oppressive institution for women continued to resonate until the end of the century and beyond. As Sydney journalist, Kirsty Machon, asked *LOTL* readers in 1996: 'So do lesbians and gay men need to waste valuable time and dollars barracking for a goal at best dubious, at worst, spurious? ... The concept of marriage can, for lesbians, be read as politically regressive. Its legacy comes encumbered with various odious baggage, not least of which is that it has historically signalled men's "ownership" of women.'[70] Lesbian theologian, Liz Stuart, made similar arguments in British magazine, *Diva*, in 1995. Reflecting on her own long-term relationship, she claimed:

> In the thirteen years we have been together, we have always resisted defining our relationship in terms of marriage. We would certainly like our partnership recognised and protected by law and by the Church, but we do not want to be associated with or incorporated into an institution laden with social expectations. We define our relationship in terms of friendship because this emphasises the equality and mutuality we strive for and is quite different from the privatised world of heterosexual coupledom.[71]

Although lesbian magazines and other publications provided a space for these views to be widely articulated, it is difficult to assess the extent to which they reflected the attitudes of less politically engaged lesbians and those who lived in regional or rural areas. Reflecting on forums held in Sydney to canvas community views on options for relationship recognition, Sally Cameron, co-convenor of the Legal Rights Service, told journalist Frances Rand: 'in researching what the community wants "the further we got out of Sydney the more people wanted marriage".'[72]

Even in urban and activist circles, the couple model of relationships saw a resurgence in the 1980s and 1990s and lesbian feminist critiques of the couple as a restrictive and regressive form of intimacy were gradually superseded by references to serial monogamy as the typical lesbian relationship pattern. In a 1993 issue of Australian lesbian and gay magazine, *PanDA*, Tanya Dale and Claire Hodgkinson debated the pros and cons of monogamy vs polygamy and Dale claimed: 'Lesbians are fairly famous for their serial monogamy.'[73] Emma Healey's article, 'The Curse of Coupledom', published under the by-line, 'Lesbians are coupledom junkies' in the June 1994 issue of *Diva*, began with the question: 'Where does a lesbian go on her second date? Answer: on honeymoon.' Healey argued:

> And yet not only do lesbians seem to fall into couple relationships immensely quickly but also with immense intensity. And though as recent research has shown, lesbian relationships do not in fact last longer ... lesbians will in fact move from one monogamous relationship to another with startling regularity ... We never mean to drift into these relationships, of course. It is just so much easier than always running out of underwear and making complicated arrangements to feed the cat.[74]

Three years later, Rachel Giese reflected on lesbian coupledom with less irony, beginning: 'Snuggling with my girlfriend each morning before we get up for work is one of my greatest pleasures. I love the daily-ness of our relationship: the morning coffee, mid-afternoon phone calls from work, doing the shopping together, the familiarity of her touch.'[75] While lesbian magazines and literature increasingly represented the couple as a ubiquitous form of lesbian intimacy, long-standing anxieties about commitment and longevity in lesbian relationships persisted alongside more recent feminist critiques of monogamy. Beverley Kemp asked: 'We've all heard the jokes about lesbian couples making a serious commitment two weeks after meeting. But do lesbian relationships last? What is the secret formula for staying together?'[76] Essex couple, Collette and Diane, quoted in her article, had been in a committed relationship for nine years but did not consider sexual fidelity to be crucial to their relationship. Collette reflected:

> [I]t would be totally unrealistic to expect that neither of us would never [sic] get tempted at some stage ... Diane could go out and get pissed one night and end up in bed with someone. Does that mean that nine years would completely go down the pan? It wouldn't for me. I know she would tell me herself and that it wouldn't mean anything ... The key part is that we trust each other and believe that we are meant to be together forever.[77]

While Collette felt that lifelong commitment was more important than monogamy, Nine Nada, also quoted by Beverley Kemp, questioned the value of long-term commitment, claiming: 'The fact is that relationships can also get boring after a time.'

Mirroring debates about the nature of lesbian intimacy and the value of the couple, the need for some form of legal protection or recognition of same-sex relationships continued to be articulated in Australia throughout this period. When the Australian Broadcasting Corporation announced in 1984 that it had decided to extend entitlements offered to heterosexual de facto couples, such as bereavement leave and the payment of removal costs, to same-sex couples, Melbourne lesbian activist, Helen Pausacker, wrote to commend them for their 'bravery' in taking this 'important and progressive step towards the acceptance of gays as equal to our heterosexual counterparts'.[78] Debate about relationship recognition gained momentum in Australia in the late 1980s and early 1990s. Lobbying by the Gay and Lesbian Immigration Task Force during the 1980s was effective in securing legal recognition of same-sex relationships in new Federal government regulations on immigration in 1991.[79] The following year, the NSW Gay and Lesbian Rights Lobby (GLRL) held a forum on 'Lesbian and Gay Relationships and the Law', which marked the beginning of an ongoing campaign around legal recognition of same-sex relationships. *Lesbians on the Loose* reported that the forum 'was packed. It became clear that many lesbians and gay men are interested in the question of legal recognition of their relationships.'[80] In 1993 and 1994, GLRL published a discussion paper on various possible approaches to relationship recognition, *The Bride Wore Pink*, and conducted a consultation exercise to canvas community opinion, before launching a campaign for amendment of existing de facto relationship legislation to include same-sex couples.[81] In the mid-1990s, activism in this area began to have an impact, with the

ACT enacting legislation in 1994 based on a broad concept of domestic relationships. NSW was the first state to introduce comprehensive legislative reform giving legal rights to same-sex couples with the passage of the Property (Relationships) Legislation Amendment Act 1999 (NSW) and other states passed comparable legislation in the subsequent five years.[82]

In Britain, relationship recognition received much less attention from activists and lobbying groups in the 1980s and 1990s. Weeks, Heaphy and Donovan found, in their research into same-sex intimacies in the mid-1990s, that the majority of lesbians and gay men they interviewed were suspicious of or hostile to the formalization of same-sex unions.[83] However, Weeks suggests that this did not indicate a lack of concern regarding the absence of legal protections for same-sex relationships and families, arguing that the experiences of lesbian mothers and the impact of the AIDS crisis had heightened awareness of the lack of legal protections. For Weeks, the absence of lobbying around relationship recognition in Britain reflected instead a pragmatic perception that: 'Under Conservative administrations same sex unions were too far away from a morally conservative agenda to be even contemplated.'[84] The enactment by Margaret Thatcher's Conservative government of Section 28 of the Local Government Act 1988, which prohibited local authorities from 'promoting homosexuality' and state-funded schools from teaching 'the acceptability of homosexuality as a pretended family relationship', exemplified the refusal to acknowledge lesbian and gay family formations, which was a key element of Conservative family values. The lobbying group, Stonewall, was established in 1989 by a group of activists campaigning against Section 28 and this remained a key focus of activism throughout the 1990s, counteracting the erasure of lesbian and gay families rather than advocating for legal equality in the sphere of intimate life.[85]

Wedding ceremonies in the 1980s and 1990s

Despite the lack of legal recognition, lesbian weddings or other forms of commitment ceremony continued to be popular during the 1980s and received increasing coverage in lesbian media and culture, pointing to a wider constituency, outside urban activist circles, for whom marriage was important. By the 1990s, the practice was beginning to spread to urban lesbian communities. Jill Jones argues: 'The "commitment ceremony" came into vogue [in Sydney in the 1990s] and by the mid 1990s had reached the stage of having jokes told about it by stand-up lesbian and gay comics.'[86] Unlike the private ceremonies of the immediate post-war decades, lesbian weddings in this later period became more public affairs, taking place in front of larger groups of friends and, increasingly, family. Influenced by the growing political and cultural visibility of lesbian identity from the 1970s onwards, personal accounts of lesbian weddings increasingly justified the importance of the ceremony as a public declaration of commitment. Jane explained to *Labrys* in 1991 that her marriage to Franca 'was a statement of reciprocal commitment, and of pleasure – "It's like having a nice painting – I felt I was so lucky I wanted to make it very public and have other people see it".'[87] Similarly Sara explained that she and her lover, Lindi-anne, wanted to 'tell each other and the world that we cannot imagine not being together and plan to stay with each other for as long as we possibly can (hopefully 'til death do us part)'.[88] Mirroring this motivation, wedding ceremonies often took place in public spaces. Environmental factors were significant in defining cultural traditions around ceremonies. Sydneysiders, Sonia and Lyn, planned to hold their commitment ceremony at Lane Cove National Park and Kim and Joanne had theirs in Centennial Park, while British couple, Dawn and Lisa, held their wedding in a Peterborough pub.[89]

The continued influence of feminist and gay political critiques of marriage in the 1980s was apparent in the terms some women adopted to describe their ceremonies. When Jane Clements reported on the weddings of three Sydney lesbian couples for *Lesbians on the Loose*, Kim and Joanne referred to their 1985 ceremony as an 'Alliance Day', not a marriage, and Sonia and Lyn called theirs a 'Commitment ceremony'.[90] Some women also sought to challenge conventional models of heterosexual weddings in the organization of their ceremony. In 1991, a member of the *Labrys* collective urged readers: 'If we as lesbians (and there seems a desire for it) want to publicly commit ourselves to one another in a relationship why don't we invent/make up our own ceremonies!'[91] Five years later, *LOTL* journalist, Elin O'Connell, reported on the Fijian wedding of Sydneysiders, Michelle and Vanessa, who, she claimed, 'opted for some of the frills of a conventional heterosexual wedding, but with that unique quality that makes lesbian events different'. Describing their wedding, which took place at a resort on the Coral Coast of Fiji during an organized holiday for lesbians promoted by Silke's Travel agency, Elin observed:

> The wedding party was suitably unorthodox. [Resort manager] David, dressed in stunning lurex drag, was 'Mother of the Bride'. [David's partner] Philly, presumably 'Father', looked a little bemused in a dress suit. The 'Flower Girl' was Warren, a drag hairdresser from Suva who prepared Michelle's elaborate hairdo and later taught her to hula. Silke's Travel agent Michelle was 'Best Man' … The Reverend, affectionately known as Reverend Paw Paw, attends ceremonies in the absence of the regular minister.[92]

While explicitly challenging gendered roles and presentation in the choreographing of the ceremony, Michelle and Vanessa's event nevertheless followed recognizable heterosexual wedding traditions in their choice of their own outfits and setting.

Other couples drew more directly on models of conventional heterosexual weddings in their choice of clothes and event organization. Sue Evans and Tracy Gardner told British women's magazine, *Bella*, in 1991 about their life together in a blended family with their children from previous heterosexual relationships. Tracy proposed to Sue 'on one knee with a bunch of red roses' during a shopping trip and the couple subsequently married:

> The date was fixed for 19 May in a Blackpool hotel. A friend made a two-tier pink and white wedding cake. Sue chose a silky aqua and white trouser suit and dresses of the same colour for her daughters. Tracy bought new black trousers, a white shirt and black tie and matching outfits with bow ties for the two boys, Dean

and Daniel. On the day itself, Tracy and Sue travelled in a blue Volvo decorated with ribbons and wedding bells. Then, before a woman lay preacher and watched by close friends and family, they vowed to be loyal to each other to the end of their days. Tracy recalls, 'We were both scared stiff, yet so happy. I'd never been married before, I thought I'd faint I was so nervous, mainly because my 71-year-old grandma, who means the world to me, was there. I didn't want her to be at all offended. Fortunately she's broad-minded!'[93]

Lou in Canberra described her similarly large commitment ceremony, performed by a civil celebrant in front of family and friends. She recalled:

We did have a big old commitment ceremony, in my mum's garden actually and ... [my dad] had this lime green Charger ... That was our wedding car and he drove ... So we went around the block a couple of times and then he drove up the driveway. Kaye was waiting for me in the back of the garden with the arch and it was all so romantic. So, and my mum, all my brothers and sisters, nieces and nephews were there, all our friends. There was about 200 people. Then we just went to the pub, so it was all lovely. Half the pub came ... Mum did everything, absolutely everything for it. Yeah. She said it was the cheapest, easiest wedding I've ever had to put together ... everything was purple ... Mum even planted purple pansies.

Lou's family, with whom she was very close, had played a central role in helping to plan and organize the event, while her partner, Kaye's family, had less involvement. Kaye's father had died but 'her mother was there. She was 70-something. She had no idea what was going on. She just couldn't work it out. So she said here's a plant because I'm not real sure how this works so here's a plant.'[94] Lou's account points to the ongoing tensions in lesbian weddings and commitment ceremonies in this period, between a growing social and cultural visibility and acceptance of same-sex couple relationships and an ongoing absence of legal recognition. In this context, many couples and their loved ones celebrated their love and commitment in a variety of ways, using language which included 'marriage' amongst other terms. Others, however, struggled, like Kaye's mother, to make sense of a ceremony which lacked the legal status of a marriage but referenced, through its visual imagery, a heterosexual ceremony, while centring on love and desire between two women.

Conclusion

The continuous tradition of lesbian weddings in both Britain and Australia throughout the second half of the twentieth century points to a persistent felt need, on the part of some couples, to make a formal commitment to their relationship. In the early post-war decades, these ceremonies were typically small and private, while the impact of a politics of lesbian visibility from the 1970s onwards resulted in increasingly large and public weddings by the end of the century. The benefits of social, legal or religious recognition of same-sex relationships were debated in lesbian organizations and publications from the 1960s onwards and these discussions point to a much more diverse range of views than has been acknowledged in accounts of the marriage equality debate. In part this reflects the diversity of lesbian experience in Britain and Australia: while those in urban and activist communities may have strongly articulated critiques of marriage as a model for lesbian intimacy, women who were more socially or geographically isolated and those with religious faith were more likely to value marriage as a means of expressing love and commitment.

Part Two

4

Lesbians and the nuclear family

In the opening issue of British lesbian magazine, *Arena Three*, 'Hilary Benno' described to readers her efforts at 'Scouting for … The Public Image'. Her search to understand how the British public envisaged lesbians led Benno to talk to a wide variety of people in different occupations, including:

> A male night telephone operator (the father of two) [who] told me cheerfully: 'Oh, we quite often hear them chatting on the line to one another. Married women, y'know, husband gone off for the weekend up North or somewhere … so they promptly get on the line to the old girl-friend, y'know, and pass on the glad news the coast's clear.'[1]

In characterizing the 'typical lesbian' as a married woman, engaging in discreet lesbian affairs alongside her marriage, the telephone operator interviewed by Benno reflected an aspect of lesbian experience in the post-war decades which has been largely erased in subsequent histories. The social pressures on women to marry in the 1950s and 1960s, and the lack of awareness of same-sex desire as a possibility for women, meant that significant numbers of women, who were attracted to other women or who later identified as lesbian, married men and had children with them in the post-war decades. While heterosexual marriage represented a stage in the life course for some women, before they openly declared a lesbian identity, others remained isolated in marriages, pursuing discreet affairs or maintaining silence about their desire for other women. Married lesbians were a significant and visible presence in the lesbian communities of the 1960s and 1970s, but the difficulties of reconciling this history with post-1970 narratives of lesbian autonomy and openly declared sexual identities have obscured their place in lesbian histories of the post-war decades.

When British lesbian organization, Minorities Research Group (MRG), began publication of its magazine, *Arena Three*, in 1964, married lesbians wrote in in large numbers. Following a *News of the World* article about the group that December, *Arena Three* editor, Esme Langley, observed:

> Astonishing, the letters that have been pouring in these last four weeks – one day we may find time to count them all more exactly. But a rough count just before Christmas was arrived at by sorting them into three piles: a) single women

b) married women (including divorced, widowed, or separated women) c) men. Even at that date, the b) pile contained more than 150 letters, all received since the N.o.W article … on December 13. Many of these married women had the same thing to tell us:

> Dear Miss Langley, At last I have found someone who will be able to understand. I got married when I was 20, in the hope it would 'change' me, but it made not a scrap of difference … I have never been able to speak to anyone about this before. Thank you for just being there to listen to me. Mrs …[2]

Six years later, in a report on the findings of a 1970 readership survey, *Arena Three* noted that, of the fifty readers who had completed the questionnaire, thirteen were married and seven divorced.[3] Although the lack of Australian lesbian magazines or organizations in the 1960s prevented Australian women in these circumstances from sharing their experiences with others, oral history accounts suggest that, as in Britain, a significant number of women who identified as lesbian were or had been married and had children. These women became more visible in the 1970s and Elizabeth recalled that, when lesbian social groups such as Clover were formed in Sydney in the early 1970s, married lesbians enjoyed a strong presence there. She said: 'There seemed to be quite a few married women, not, I didn't meet any that were living with their husbands at the time, they were divorced or separated or things like that, but they had been married and there were children around quite a bit.'[4] Western Australian lesbian magazine, *Lesbianon*, also reported in 1975 that their group, Lesbians Anon, included 'many married lesbians' with children.[5]

In her study of married lesbians in post-war America, Lauren Jae Gutterman has argued that many women who later identified as lesbian regarded marriage as 'inescapable'.[6] As in the United States, the decades after the Second World War witnessed a marriage boom in both Britain and Australia. Jane Lewis notes that, in Britain: 'After the Second World War, women married for the first time at increasingly younger ages and marriage became virtually universal in the 1960s'.[7] Between the 1940s and 1970s, marriage rates rose steadily in Britain, reaching a peak in 1971, when first marriages occurred at a rate of 98 per thousand single women over the age of 16.[8] A similar pattern occurred in Australia, where marriage rates were almost universal from the outbreak of the Second World War until the early 1970s; by 1971, 94 per cent of Australian women were married before their thirty-fifth birthday, and most in their early twenties.[9] Gordon Carmichael explains this trend in the immediate post-war decades as a result of social shifts in intergenerational relationships that encouraged young Australians to regard marriage as a vehicle through which to assert independence. One aspect of this was the growing acceptability of contraceptive use within marriage. He notes:

> After the deprivations of wartime, marrying and having children were appealingly normal prospects; to the extent that women in particular held these views, the marriage market was tailor made. Women were encouraged through the media, at home, at school, and by the Church to seek fulfillment in becoming the best

possible wives and mothers. The attitudes that held sway, when placed alongside growing confidence that one had the right and the ability to control one's fertility, clearly favored earlier marriage and undoubtedly contributed to more universal marriage as well.[10]

These attitudes were further bolstered in Australia by post-war prosperity, which provided young couples with available mortgages, low interest rates and high levels of employment, undermining older practices of delaying marriage until the acquisition of financial stability. Significantly higher wages than the pre-war levels had a similar effect in Britain, although post-war housing shortages complicated this picture.[11] In both Australia and Britain, younger marriage rates were also driven by the increased practise of pre-marital sex which resulted in 'shotgun' weddings, at a time when childbirth outside marriage was widely considered taboo.

Women's investment in marriage reflected both its centrality as a social institution and its specific social and cultural meanings for individual women in the 1950s and 1960s. Frank Bongiorno argues that by the 1960s, 'marriage had become virtually synonymous with full and responsible citizenship' and, in both Australia and Britain, its crucial role in social cohesion was reflected in the extent to which it was shored up by legislative and economic frameworks, scientific expertise and Christian morality.[12] Janet Finch and Penny Summerfield claim: 'Central to the aims of the post-war social reconstruction was the desire to consolidate family life after the disruptive effects of war and to build a future in which marriage and the home would be the foundations of a better life.'[13] The importance accorded to marriage by post-war British policymakers was indicated by the establishment of the Royal Commission on Marriage and Divorce, whose 1956 report asserted: 'It is obvious that life-long marriage is the basis of a secure and stable family life and that to ensure their well-being children must have that background.'[14] The authors of the growing number of sociological surveys agreed.[15]

Against this backdrop, individual women married for a variety of reasons including, according to Claire Langhamer, the desire for sexual or emotional intimacy, the establishment of a home, the 'quest for security and self-determination', and in order to conceive and raise children.[16] While many of these were longer-standing motivations for matrimony, the precise promise of marriage was undergoing significant change in the post-war period. Both contemporary observers and historians agree that a shift was occurring from notions of marriage as an institution to marriage as a relationship in the mid-twentieth century, with spouses increasingly expecting a more intimate connection with each other.[17] As Finch and Summerfield have demonstrated, the concept of the 'companionate marriage' gained wide currency in Britain after the war, 'being used to summarize a set of ideas about marriage which ranged from the notion that there should be greater companionship between partners whose roles essentially were different, through the idea of marriage as "teamwork", to the concept of marriage based on "sharing" implying the breakdown of clearly demarcated roles'.[18] In the first Australian sociological study of marriage and the family, published in 1957, A.P. Elkin noted the beginnings of a shift towards a more 'democratic partnership' model, which enabled the emergence of a new primary function of marriage: that of the 'provision of an emotionally satisfying centre' for personal development and health.[19]

An increasingly important component of this newfound intimacy was sex. Frank Bongiorno suggests: 'Sexual compatibility and mutual pleasure were essential to a successful union ... Couples, and especially women, were increasingly likely to recognise sexual fulfilment as a means of deepening the love between a husband and wife.'[20] At the same time, the growing influence of psychological notions of selfhood resulted in a prioritization of self-reflection and personal fulfilment over older notions of character and self-control and this had a profound impact on attitudes towards marriage from the mid-century onwards. Claire Langhamer has identified an increasing emphasis on love as the justification for and basis of marriage in the post-war period. She argues:

> Romantic love seemed to offer a way of binding modern self-actualizing individuals to the social contract of marriage. It promised an emotional connectivity which would improve those involved by creating something more than the sum of its parts: the co-actualizing heterosexual couple. Because of this, love was increasingly valued above all other factors in the making of legal commitment at a time when marriage was experiencing a 'golden age.'[21]

Women were encouraged to regard the pursuit of love and marriage as a journey towards personal growth and self-fulfilment. Marriage based on romantic love was a 'transformative' experience, building on longer-standing notions of marriage as the gateway to maturity: 'For women especially, becoming an adult was virtually synonymous with getting married.'[22]

Given the powerful influence of these post-war discourses idealizing heterosexual romantic love and marriage, it is not surprising that many women did not recognize or chose to suppress or ignore same-sex desires and marry men in this period. Some did so consciously, feeling that marriage offered them social acceptability or greater economic security, while others did not make a clearly articulated choice between lesbianism and marriage. Throughout the 1960s and 1970s, correspondence in *Arena Three* and its successor, *Sappho*, as well as letters to Australian gay and feminist publications in the 1970s, provide an indication of the motivations and experiences of married lesbians. In May 1974, E.V. from Surrey wrote to *Sappho* magazine to explain:

> I married young, totally ignorant in all aspects of marriage. I think why I married was not out of love but of a sense of duty, family pressure, it was the right thing to do – and it was expected of me. For years I tried to conform to be what every women's magazine said a young wife should be. God was I miserable! After a disastrous love? life and several miscarriages, I adopted two children. From then on my life was theirs. I at last had someone to love and I love them dearly. Three years ago I realized that I was not as other married women ... Soon I fell passionately for someone who of course was not gay and would have been horrified if I'd had the courage to declare myself.[23]

E.V.'s account of a sense of dislocation from married life, finally explained by a gradual awareness that she was attracted to other women, was echoed by many women in this period, who had married in response to social expectation and family pressure. Claudia, who founded Melbourne lesbian social group, Claudia's Group, in the early 1970s, told *Cleo* magazine: 'Most of the women who ring up are or have been married ... It is only recently that young women have been exposed to information about lesbianism and therefore know about it while in their teens. The majority of women had never heard the word until recently. They got married never quite knowing what was wrong.'[24] The pervasive discourse of marriage and heterosexuality was experienced by many women as so strong that they did not coherently consider any alternative. Megan recalled that, at university in 1959: 'In bed at night I fantasised about women, but it was boys I went out with.'[25] Despite her same-sex sexual fantasies, Megan felt that the overwhelming emphasis on marriage and motherhood as the goal for women in post-war Australia prevented her from clearly articulating the significance of her feelings for women, even to herself. She explained:

> Sexuality meant boys and, in spite of a non-permissive society, sex was what we were all groping towards. The double-think of the early 1960s involved never acknowledging what you were really doing, even with the opposite sex. There was a price to be paid for petting beyond the point of respectability. We went round singing 'It's Now or Never', but fending the boys off, preserving our virginity (technically, at any rate) for that never-never land of the future ... Possibly, it was the very distancing of male sexuality and companionship that made it seem the ultimate goal. To be home on a Saturday night, or to have to go out with the girls, was a personal failure. I became a man's woman, with a vengeance.[26]

Megan married in 1963 and had three children, before divorcing her husband in the later 1970s.

While many women, like Megan, did not make a conscious choice between same-sex desires and marriage, others were aware of their same-sex desires, but hoped that conforming to social expectations would help them to suppress those feelings. Liz told Australian lesbian and gay newspaper, *Campaign*, in 1981 that she had married her husband, John, thirteen years before for:

> Lots of reasons. I had a boring job. I thought I could become a housewife. I liked him – he was good company. I thought maybe it would 'cure' me. Financial and emotional security. Status, desirability as a woman, all of those reasons. After all, I thought, everyone gets married, has kids and lives happily ever after in the suburbs. That's all there was.[27]

Although she had known she was a lesbian since she was fourteen years old, Liz 'wanted to be normal' and hoped that marriage would help her achieve this. Other women told similar stories. One anonymous *Sappho* correspondent had 'enjoyed every minute of being around my own sex' during a period of service in the WRNS. However, when rumours began to circulate that she was a lesbian, she became frightened and pursued a relationship with a sailor. 'When my fiancé asked me to marry', she recalled, 'I accepted. Marriage, I thought, would soon straighten me out and it would be nice to have a family.'[28] Sue in Melbourne described a similar experience in the mid-1960s.

After having a number of affairs with women when she was a teenager, she gave in to family and social pressure and married at nineteen. She went on to have four children before her marriage began to break down and she re-joined the lesbian social and political scene as a lesbian mother in the early 1970s.[29]

Many women who married for these reasons concealed their previous desires or relationships with women from their future husbands. H.P. wrote to MRG in 1967:

> I only wish I had the courage to become a member of MRG. But as I am to be married shortly, I could never explain to my future husband my reasons for wishing to become a member … I would also like to offer you for your Library about a dozen paperback novels dealing with Lesbian themes – the possession of which I could not explain to my future husband.[30]

Others, however, were completely open with their husbands to be. Rae met her husband on the Sydney camp scene in the 1960s and he proposed to her knowing that she identified as a lesbian. She recalled:

> Well, so many of my generation actually married, some openly. My wedding was funny, the only straight person there was the groom. He was a bag hag in reverse, a lovely man, don't get me wrong … Oh God, yes [he knew I was a lesbian]. A couple of my exes and everybody – all at the wedding. No, Tony knew. In fact, he proposed to me at a gay ball. I just told him to shut up and sit down but the queens went out the next day and organised the wedding.

Rae struggled to articulate her reasons for marrying, presenting herself almost as a bystander in the process. She explained:

> I just did it because the queens went out and booked a church. Tony was a good bloke, he really was. I was in between relationships and it was going to be one of those things, I'll get married and then finish off, you know. Well, it didn't. I had two daughters, two lovely daughters. But we were friends, Tony and I were friends. Then when I was 40, I met this young woman and that was it. Tony and I split up and parted ways. We were friends.[31]

Although vague on her motivations for and experience of marriage, Rae ultimately presented her marriage as an interlude in her lesbian life, which she recalled fondly because it had given her 'two lovely daughters' and the friendship of a 'good bloke'.

Marriage as a disappointment

For women who entered marriage in the hope that it would provide a sense of fulfilment, the growing awareness that they were attracted to other women, or that marriage had not 'cured' them of previously acknowledged same-sex desires brought disillusionment. Reflecting on her life as a married woman in Gilgandra, NSW in the 1960s, Megan recalled:

> I won't go into the disappointment and loneliness of that relationship – they are the story of many housewives, both straight and gay. Once the pleasures of a regular supply of sex had lost their first excitement, I began to think about women again. When my husband had sex with me, I imagined it was a woman's body against my own. We were living in Gilgandra at that time, last bastion of the heterosexual imperative, where even electric plugs and sockets have male and female parts. Stickers on cars and fridges proclaimed: 'I'm a mountain man. I love mountin' women'. My imaginings were a secret life.[32]

As Megan noted, this narrative of disappointment in marriage was not confined to women who experienced same-sex desire after marrying. The growing cultural emphasis on romantic love and self-fulfilment as integral to a successful marriage meant that women who felt their marital relationship did not reach these ideals often experienced an acute sense of failure. Many post-war commentators, such as Herbert Gray, Chair of the Marriage Guidance Council in Britain, argued that love was essential to a successful marriage:

> The only sufficient reason for marrying is that you have come to love somebody of the other sex. Life must always have troubles in it. Married life has its own peculiar trials, for men are queer creatures, and so are women. It needs love, needs strong and loyal love, to carry a couple through. Love can solve a hundred petty problems, and make light of larger ones.[33]

However, romantic love proved an unstable basis on which to build a lifelong commitment and rising divorce rates, together with growing pressure to make divorce more accessible, prompted widespread concern about a potential 'crisis' in marriage. One difficulty, as Claire Langhamer notes, was that 'love' was an inherently slippery concept and many people articulated anxieties about how to know, with certainty, whether the emotion they felt for their future spouse was the true romantic love they sought.[34] This uncertainty was apparent in many of the accounts from married lesbians in the 1960s and 1970s, who described a realization after marriage that the emotion they felt for their husband was not of the transformative and fulfilling quality they had been led to expect. I.N. in Hampshire, who had had a love affair with another woman before they both conformed to family expectation and married, asked *Sappho* readers in 1975: 'How were we to tell that the same sort of feeling wouldn't develop for our men in marriage. I know now, of course, that they couldn't.'[35] Mrs R from Sussex wrote to *Arena Three* in 1969, asking to hear from 'other married readers … as to how they cope with the problems they inevitably must have if, like me, they only discovered their innate homosexuality after several years of marriage and children, and then realised all that their relationship with their husband lacked'.[36] Often, as in Mrs R's case, this realization crystalized only after experiencing love or desire for another woman. Lisa explained that it was only when she fell in love with a woman friend that she came to an understanding of the potential of romantic love. She told a journalist from *Cleo* magazine in 1974 that, when she kissed her lover Angie for the first time after years of marriage, 'that was the kiss which was the way books said it should be'.[37]

The post-war cultural emphasis on a mutually satisfying sex life as an essential component of a happy, loving, marriage posed a particular obstacle for women who realized their same-sex desires after marriage. Liz, who had her first affair with a woman after marriage and described it as 'fantastic. My first orgasm. It was incredible', told *Campaign* that sex with her husband was: 'Very disappointing. It didn't turn me straight! He's always tried hard to please me. He's been under a lot of stress at work so he's usually too tired to do anything but fall asleep. Thank goodness! When he does make love to me, I fake it.'[38] Mrs H.M. from Essex found the sexual aspect of her marriage particularly challenging, telling *Arena Three*:

> My biggest problem is that I just can't bear my husband making love to me. It absolutely revolts me, I am bruised where I pinch myself to stop myself screaming 'No!' when he's making love. But he is very touchy about this particular aspect of our married life – I suppose it is his male pride, and I just don't dare tell him how I feel.[39]

The continued influence of older concepts of marriage as an institution based on duty and commitment meant that many women felt obliged to remain married having once made their wedding vows. The influence of a newer discourse of love and selfhood, however, challenged this model of marriage. 'Love', Claire Langhamer claims, 'had the potential to destabilize, not least because people could fall out of love as readily as they could fall in love … Love, in fact, had a habit of escaping the bounds of marriage. Claims to an emotional authenticity that only the lover could judge provided powerful self-justification for transgression as well as commitment.'[40] Married women who desired other women emphasized this tension between their roles and emotional commitments as wives and mothers and their wish to express their sexuality and authentic self. This was often articulated as a sense of being torn between two choices: attempting to suppress their feelings for women and continuing to maintain the outward appearance of a happy married life or leaving their husband to begin a new life as a lesbian, which might also entail leaving or losing their children. In the 1950s and 1960s, many women chose to stay in their marriages, suppressing their desires or seeking a compromise between their attraction for women and sense of marital duty. From the 1970s onwards, however, an increasing number of women made the decision to leave marriages and embark on a new life in which they embraced a lesbian identity.

Choosing to stay

The social stigma surrounding divorce and single motherhood in the 1950s and 1960s, and the economic difficulties of attempting to support children as a single mother, meant that many women in this situation felt that maintaining the appearance of a happily married life was the only reasonable option open to them. Although there is limited contemporary evidence of these women's experience, it is clear that many married women in this period decided to remain in their marriages and conceal their same-sex desires from those around them. Pam spoke for these women when she declared to *Arena Three* in 1965:

> How right you are when you say 'they suffer in silence'. I am probably one of the types you had in mind. I am married, two children, quite attractive and, on the surface, quite happy. No one would guess and only I know that I have strong lesbian tendencies. How I often wish that I had someone whom I could only talk to about it. My constant fear is that I will do something that will give me away. Just to read about you made me feel better, so wishing you success.[41]

As Pam's account suggested, women in this situation often strove to maintain an appearance of happy married life and neither spoke about nor acted on their same-sex desires. Their stories typically only emerged much later and many others were never told. In 1975, M.J. wrote to *Lesbianon*, explaining:

> I think I should tell you, first of all that I am married, and 62 years old. So the realisation that there are many who feel the way as I have since about the age of fifteen is rather late. The fact that I had always been attracted to other girls, in that day and age, and in my circumstances, in a way never mattered, if you know what I mean ... From time to time I would meet someone, to whom I would be extremely attracted, but as they were all, I guess straight, it wasn't until I was in my forties, and had begun to read about Lesbian relationships, did I realize just what it was all about. Now of course, it is rather late, but if your magazine and advice can help other lesbians to find true fulfilment and lasting happiness, you will have done a wonderful thing.[42]

While M.J. felt that, at the age of sixty-two, it was 'rather late' to act on her sense of herself as a lesbian, her letter expressed a hope that the fulfilment she had failed to find might be achieved by younger lesbians. In Britain, a reader wrote to *Arena Three* expressing a similar hope. Offering advice to another married lesbian, she reflected on her own experience of remaining in a marriage in the post-war decades. Explaining that she had fallen in love with another woman during the war, just after marrying at the age of eighteen, the writer reflected that she should have left her husband then. By choosing to stay, she explained: 'I did us both a great wrong. Although I managed to repress my lesbian feelings most of the time, and now have a grown-up family, our marriage has not been a happy one – how could it be? We have not shared a bed for many years; now in middle age we are both frustrated and unhappy.'[43] Many of these accounts emphasize that, although the couple preserved the outward appearance of marriage, their relationship with each other did not live up to the emerging ideal of a sexually satisfying, companionate marriage.[44] Women in these circumstances dwelt on intense feelings of isolation and the 'tremendous sense of relief' they felt in locating a lesbian magazine or community.[45] T.O. from Kent told *Sappho*: 'Living in a village I daren't give even a hint of being gay and believe me there's nothing so isolated as a married gay in the country – especially when you don't know any others in the area.'[46]

An uneasy relationship with the lesbian community

This isolation prompted some married lesbians to seek out friendship or a lesbian community with whom they could share their feelings. In Britain, *Arena Three* and *Sappho* provided a focus for such women's hopes from the mid-1960s onwards and a number of women contacted these magazines in an attempt to reach out to other women. B.G. in Devon wrote to *Arena Three* in 1966 proposing:

> How about a Correspondence Club for homebound married members? If only six members wrote one letter a month for circulation, it would form the basis of a Married Women's Correspondence Magazine, which could be posted each month from one to another. I could design a cover, with names and addresses in order for mailing on to the next name on the list. Inside the cover could be pockets to hold snaps, or cuttings of interest, family news. Problems or worries could be discussed.[47]

While B.G. and others specifically sought a community of married lesbians with whom to share experiences, some women hoped that *Arena Three* might provide opportunities for them to put aside their identities as wives and mothers for a while and express their authentic selves. J.C. from Manchester wrote:

> As a 'Mrs' I think it would be a bad thing to start sorting ourselves out into 'Miss' and 'Mrs' groups. After all, our common denominator is that we are all Lesbians. I personally find it a lot more relaxing to sit in a roomful of 'Butches', having a drink and talk about music, books, etc than I ever would sitting with proud Mums, talking about our brilliant offspring … If this is what you want, you can do it with school meetings, etc. NO … What I want is to be ME, my own true self, with other 'butches' – married, or single.[48]

Letters such as these appeared regularly in *Arena Three* in the 1960s, indicating that married women frequently contacted the magazine in search of support or community. Indeed, editor, Esme Langley, wrote to US lesbian activist, Barbara Gittings, in late 1964, complaining: 'The enormous no. of unhappy married women who want to join MRG and *relax* from the strains of a miserable "home" life' … was causing the organisation a 'major headache.'[49] However, these isolated calls for friendship do not appear to have resulted in the establishment of support networks for married lesbians in the 1960s. In December 1966, when Mrs Thomas wrote to *Arena Three* asking of married members: 'Where the heck are they all? Do they exist? And do they not feel the need for friends to talk to', Esme Langley responded that previous calls from married members had received no replies.[50]

Attempts by married lesbians to seek community through this means were hampered by the ambivalent position adopted by the MRG in relation to married women. Despite the visibility of married women in the magazine, the group's membership rules effectively excluded many married women from joining, as wives were required to seek their husband's signed permission before subscribing to the magazine. Diana Chapman, one of the founders of MRG, recalled that this rule emerged in response both to warnings from Antony Grey, secretary of the homophile lobbying group, Homosexual Law Reform Society, that MRG might be prosecuted for obscene libel and the group's own fears that they might be at risk of legal action from husbands on the grounds of alienation of affection.[51] A number of married women wrote to *Arena Three* noting that they were excluded from membership by this rule. In March 1965, Pam, who had read about MRG in an article in the *Daily Mail*, wrote:

> After reading about your group I felt I had to write and offer my best wishes. I don't think you will ever succeed in overcoming public ignorance about us, but it is a comfort to me just to know that a society such as yours exists. I only wish I could join and help openly but I see I would be barred by your rules. You require a husband's signature, and that I could never ask for.[52]

While Pam explained that she could not ask for her husband's signature, presumably because he was not aware of her lesbianism, Mrs B.B. in Devon suggested that her husband would refuse: 'You will understand why I haven't got my husband's signature. He is not the type to begin to understand my difficulties, though I've tried to tell him many times. He just won't accept.'[53] Although it is possible that some married women found ways around the rule, others observed it scrupulously.[54]

For those married women who did find ways to subscribe to *Arena Three*, despite the rule, the community they joined was not unanimously welcoming. While Esme Langley and other readers were generally quite sympathetic to the plight of married lesbians, some readers expressed open hostility towards them. In 1969, D.S. from Essex wrote a scathing response to Mrs R's request to hear more from other married lesbians like herself. D.S. declared:

> As for Mrs R., well words fail me, for after so many years of marriage she finds out now that she has Lesbian tendencies? Never in this world can I believe that piffle, all true Lesbians must feel the same about that letter of hers, I would advise her to think again and ponder on just what a real Lesbian is, looks like, feels like and acts like, then perhaps she will perhaps, tuck the kids in bed as usual and sleep happily with her husband, knowing that she just hasn't got what it takes to qualify for the title LESBIAN.[55]

D.S. was not alone in questioning whether married women could call themselves 'lesbian' or claim a place in the lesbian community and these tensions continued to flare up periodically over the following decade in the letters' pages of *Arena Three* and *Sappho*. In 1978, Phoenix sparked a debate in *Sappho* by referring to married women who had affairs with other women as 'bisexual' and claiming that they were despised by homosexuals because they sought to 'preserve their marriage and "respectability" relegating their lesbian lover to an emotional outlet of a sort'.[56] While one married respondent seemed to accept a variety of identity categories, referring to herself as 'a married lesbian (bisexual if you prefer)', several others vehemently rejected the term. M.B. from Lincs wrote: 'Phoenix "How dare you assume I'm bisexual?" Married lesbians do not need their sexuality defined for them', while B.R. from Milton Keynes reflected more mildly:

> Do I qualify as bisexual? I suppose I do considering that I live with my husband and children. But to be a true bisexual, as I've always understood it to mean, is that one is sexually attracted to both sexes. I can truthfully say that I am never remotely attracted to men. It's always women, emotionally and physically.[57]

As Phoenix's comments reflected, distrust of married lesbians was exacerbated by a perception that such women would not commit to a lesbian relationship and that unmarried women who became involved with them risked being exploited and abandoned. The painful consequences which might arise occasionally emerged in letters such as one written by Mrs K.K. in London in 1965:

> Dear Miss Langley, I am dreadfully worried about a Miss G. and wish you could do something to help her. You see, we met at the [MRG social meeting at the] Bull's Head some while ago and started an affair but although it was only meant lightly she has now grown much too fond of me and wants me to leave my husband and children and go away with her. I hate to hurt her but this I cannot possibly do and I thought perhaps you could do something to help her as she is very lonely and unhappy. I never meant to upset her and believe me I have learnt my lesson now.[58]

Mrs K.K.'s contrition points to an awareness that readers of the magazine might hold her responsible, as a married woman, for the distress of her lover. Nearly a decade later, this issue remained a point of contention and in 1974, R.L. from Bedfordshire attempted to counter some of the negative portrayals of married lesbians by arguing:

> I'd just like to stress that not all of us married gays are out looking for a quick affair or one night stands to relieve the boredom of marriage or to have 'the best of both worlds'. A certain percentage may, but not all of us. For my own personal opinion, and not wanting to sound too old fashioned, I still believe in love and respect. If I am fortunate enough to meet 'the one', nothing on this earth, be it marriage, children, hell or high water, will ever prevent me from being with her.[59]

Same-sex desire and the marital home

Although letters in *Arena Three* point to the tensions around married lesbians' involvement with other women, it is clear that many women in this position did embark on lesbian affairs. In her work on lesbian desire, marriage and the household in post-war America, Lauren Jae Gutterman has documented what she describes as 'the remarkable extent to which wives were able to create space for lesbian desires within their homes and marriages in the 1950s and 1960s'. She argues that the marital home functioned as a lesbian space for many married women and that it not only 'served as the center of family life, yet it allowed access to lesbian communities and sheltered lesbian affairs'.[60] There is certainly evidence of some Australian and British women conducting lesbian affairs alongside marriage in the post-war period. Margaret Cranch described having an affair with a married woman who lived next door to her family home in mid-1950s Plymouth.[61] Mrs V.L. from Essex wrote to *Arena Three* in 1969 with an account of her long-term lesbian affair in the 1950s and 1960s. She explained:

> I had been married nearly 10 years when I met a friend I'd known when single. She was also married with two children, like myself. We had parted years ago thinking our affection for each other was 'wrong'. Now, even more keenly aware of the difference in our feelings towards each other and our husbands, we couldn't say goodbye a second time. We decided to manage somehow without hurting anyone.

Although the affair began in secret, it shifted to an open relationship and Mrs V.L. described how this lesbian intimacy was integrated into her marital life:

> Inevitably, the husbands found out. There were rows and threats … but we refused to part, and they didn't want divorce, so eventually we all settled down. Our families became friends, the children didn't mind an extra 'Auntie'. For the next 15 years we found some happiness – also much heartache.[62]

Mrs V.L.'s account suggests that some women were indeed able to turn their marital homes into a 'lesbian space' as Gutterman suggests. Other narratives point to similar possibilities. In 1974, journalist Kirsten Blanch interviewed two Australian women, Angie and Lisa, who were in a relationship with each other. Angie was twice divorced with three children and Lisa was married. Lisa explained:

> I had met Angie … and I liked her a lot. One night at my place we all got a bit drunk; my husband was there. In the bedroom Angie suddenly kissed me … We had to get well and truly sloshed before we could actually go on and make love the next time but ever since then it's been just us. I still live with John, who doesn't really know. I'm trying not to hurt him and I'm also afraid he may get vicious if he finds out.[63]

However, many women in these circumstances emphasized the constraints imposed on their relationship by the domestic context in which they were living. Liz told *Campaign* newspaper in 1981 that there was 'never enough' time to spend with her lover Pat, whom she had met at a women's group two years earlier. She explained: 'I get a day off every two weeks. [My husband] John works some weekends. His sister minds Mark. Naturally, nights with her are out.'[64]

Single women having affairs with married women often characterized their experience as one of loneliness and isolation in which they felt unable to form a fulfilling relationship with their lover. In 1967, Miss W.K. from London wrote to *Arena Three* to complain of this plight:

> A date can only be made on the infrequent occasions when the husband is out. Meetings have to be cancelled at the shortest notice owing to one of the children being ill, or for some other family reason. Mostly it is not possible even to ring up, when a few words on the telephone would restore equilibrium or help over a bout of depression. The weekends are completely taboo, because the Lord and Master is at home. In fact, one is lonelier than lonely, tolerated marginally if one is lucky and with the modest hopes of a few hours of the inestimable comfort of being together constantly being frustrated.[65]

Single women in this position described also feeling disconnected from lesbian community and support. Miss S.E. from Lancashire wrote to Esme Langley in 1965:

> Much as I would like to become a member of your organisation I'm afraid to join. My parents and friends would be horrified if they once knew how things were. I have been in love for many years with someone who is married, so that we can't go away together. Have you any helpful suggestions to make? Thank you for letting me have someone to write to about all this.[66]

Her letter suggested that the problem of limited contact with her married lover was exacerbated by her own isolation from a wider lesbian community, leaving her without a confidante with whom to share her difficulties. The emotional strain caused by conducting a relationship in these circumstances was not confined to unmarried women partners, however, and accounts also point to the distress married lesbians experienced in these situations. In 1966, Miss H.B. wrote to *Arena Three* requesting that copies of the magazine no longer be sent to her friend, Mrs X's house, as Mrs X had just made a serious suicide attempt following the news of Miss H.B.'s engagement. Miss H.B. was concerned that Mrs X's nineteen-year-old daughter would find out about Miss H.B. and Mrs X's relationship, rendering the situation even more difficult.[67] Relationships between two married women also posed challenges. In 1974, a married lesbian wrote to *Sappho*, describing the frustrations of her relationship with another married lesbian. She explained:

> My friend and I find ourselves trying to do our duty by our families; wanting to be together all the time and yet feel unable to leave our children. This gives us endless problems. The time we can spare together is brief ... by the time housework, meals etc are dealt with, we actually find ourselves with an hour, if we're lucky to relax together ... We are fortunate to have met, to have found one another; to be near enough to see each other every day, but the strain placed on us of being apart at the very time we need to be together is very great.[68]

An 'open' marriage?

The emotional strain caused by concealment meant that throughout the 1960s and 1970s, many married women opted to tell their husbands about their same-sex desires, hoping that it would be possible to openly pursue lesbian relationships alongside marriage. This could be a risky strategy for women who hoped to maintain an amicable relationship with their husbands and an active role in their children's lives. A letter from a married man to the *Evening Argus* newspaper in Brighton, in 1969, indicates the hostility and anger with which some husbands reacted to any disclosure of same-sex desire. The writer, Mr.V., explained:

> I am [a] married man of 28 and my wife, whom I love very much, is 26. We have a two-year-old daughter. Until recently we have always been very happy indeed, but recently my wife confessed something that she said had been preying on her mind for years. It was that when she was a student she had a brief 'affair' with an older colleague who was a lesbian. I simply cannot forget this, and at the moment I want nothing to do with her. I feel she must be abnormal, and I am wondering if I should leave her and take our little girl with me.[69]

While some husbands reacted unsympathetically, others attempted to be supportive and understanding out of concern for their wives or in the interests of keeping their family together. One contributor to *Sappho* wrote in October 1973:

> Life has been a little difficult recently as I finally told my husband all. This came as something of a shock to him, although he had suspected the dreadful truth for about a couple of years. After the initial shock which hit him for about five days, he has been very understanding, thank goodness and applied no pressure. I value his friendship very much and would hate to lose it. My children are happy and well adjusted and I do not feel justified in breaking up this family as long as it seems to be the best thing for them.[70]

Others were happy to ignore lesbian affairs in exchange for their wives' tolerance of their own extra-marital activity. Sheena, who was a member of the Manchester gay wives and mothers' group, told *Spare Rib* in 1975 that her husband was 'fully aware of [her] homosexuality ... I love Brian as a person and he doesn't seem to mind about me. He has his girlfriends – sometimes I fancy them too'.[71] The extent of social disapproval of lesbianism rendered some husbands willing to tolerate their wife's lesbianism to avoid the potential repercussions of it being known more widely. Fearful that they would be ostracized from their social circle, or lose the chance of promotion at work, some husbands agreed to keep their wife's secret.[72]

Occasional letters to lesbian organizations in the 1960s and 1970s suggest that some married couples considered it possible to accommodate a wife's same-sex desires within a successful marriage. In December 1964, Mr and Mrs B from Northampton wrote to *Arena Three* together asking 'Are there any other young married couples among MRG members who'd like to correspond with us, perhaps meet and share notes?'[73] In instances where both partners to the marriage were attracted to their own sex, this open model could be beneficial for the husband and wife. Elizabeth Wilson described the home of a married gay man and lesbian as a social hub in the early 1960s:

> In a flat just off that main road north of [Regent's] Park I remember parties where hectic scenes of rivalry were played out. Our hosts, a married couple, were a gay man and a lesbian. They organised a little coterie around themselves, entertaining us in a room with black walls and a harpsichord. He told the Tarot cards with obsessional and compelling attention to detail, while she regaled us with wild tales of pick-ups in the British Museum Reading Room.[74]

Similarly, Rae, whose husband had known she was a lesbian when she married him, was able to maintain a social life with friends from Sydney's camp scene: 'I still kept up my friendships with everybody and everybody would come to our house for dinner and for dinner parties and stuff like that.'[75]

A growing cultural understanding of lesbianism as an identity category in the post-war years is apparent in the response of some husbands to their wives' revelations, shaping their approach to accommodating lesbianism within marriage. Doris Brown told *Sappho* readers:

> I am and always have been lesbian. After over twenty years of marriage my husband has discovered the fact. He is a great guy and a very understanding person. Though the discovery threw him badly, he has taken it very well. Oddly enough his forgiveness is harder to take than his condemnation would have been … My husband and I have talked the whole thing over and he has agreed to give me a little elbow room. I'm now going to Friend (London). It helps to talk to others who understand. But he doesn't understand – how could he? – that I desperately need a woman.[76]

Doris' letter seems to indicate that her husband considered her lesbianism as an identity which could be expressed through membership of a lesbian or gay group, but did not regard it as an emotional desire for intimacy with another woman. A letter from an MRG member's husband in 1965 similarly points to the limits of such attempts at compromise. Mr W. wrote to *Arena Three*:

> Thank you for your very prompt reply to my letter. In retrospect I must admit that I wrote it partially in a mood of anger resulting from certain incidents connected with my wife's recently developed friendship with a local member of MRG. I realise now, after considerable discussion of the matter with my wife, that I may have misjudged the precise nature of this very rapidly matured friendship. Nevertheless, my view on the activities and function of your Group remain unaltered, and I do not wish my wife to continue her membership. She tells me that she had in any event decided not

to renew her membership owing to pressure of other work, and I understand that she is intending to write and return her card to you in the next few days.[77]

As Mr.W's letter suggests, while some husbands were prepared to contemplate their wives' exploration of a lesbian identity in the abstract, the wife's need for a loving relationship with another woman was often considered too great a threat to the family unit.

Where discretion was an important factor in husband's attitudes, married women might find themselves able to pursue discreet relationships with other women, with their husband's knowledge. In 1975, Rhonda appealed to Melbourne gay and lesbian group, Society Five, to put her in touch with other lesbians. A twenty-five-year-old married woman with a two-and-a-half-year-old daughter, Rhonda had recently moved to Melbourne from the country town of Albury and was struggling to find her place in the city. She explained:

> My husband understands my need to be with another woman (thank God). I was involved with someone at home but my husband's job has taken me away from her (of whom I miss terribly). But I find myself very lonely and lost. Melbourne can be a very very cold place. And it frightens me to think we're here for good. And I really need someone. Maybe someone like myself, lonely and in need of another woman.[78]

Her letter suggests that, while her husband was willing to condone a same-sex affair, their compromise was based on an agreement that his career must be a priority for them both. When his work required them to move and brought her relationship to an end, she accepted and responded to the resulting isolation on her own.

The gradual shift in attitudes towards extra-marital sexuality which occurred in some circles in the 1960s provided a few women with an opportunity to openly have casual sexual relationships with other women whilst married. Researching her November 1970 article on lesbianism for *The Times*, Victoria Brittain interviewed members of lesbian group, the Minorities Research Trust, one of whom described her experience in an open marriage. Brittain claimed:

> A few women successfully combine overt lesbianism with having a family and claim 'the best of both worlds'. Sheila Whyment-Lester is 29, the editor of Curious, a sex education magazine for adults, the new editor of Arena 3 and the mother of two little girls. She has always been a lesbian but was married happily for 10 years. 'I had my female relationships and he had his mistresses. It all broke up when he took one of my girls – I couldn't take it.' One night last week in Mrs Lester's flat in Soho her husband was cheerfully babysitting as she prepared to go out with a girlfriend she has known for seven years.[79]

The arrangement Sheila Whyment-Lester was able to agree with her husband was mirrored by other women in both Britain and Australia who took advantage of the emergence of a culture of sexual liberalization to explore same-sex desires. In December 1976, Ms R.T. from Melbourne wrote to sex magazine, *Forum*: 'I am a married woman who enjoys making love with another woman and whose life is happier and richer now that I can act out those feelings.' Explaining that she married due to social pressure, she nevertheless commented that she was 'lucky to find an understanding and very kind husband – my marriage and life could have been one big mess.'[80]

Such attitudes remained in a minority, however, in both Britain and Australia in this period and for most women, combining open lesbian relationships with marriage required much difficult and painful compromise or culminated in marital breakdown. When Sydneysider, Jan, told her husband about her same-sex desires in the early 1970s, they agreed to maintain their marriage alongside extra-marital affairs. Ultimately both Jan's husband and she herself moved their respective lovers into the marital home, and Jan recalled: 'we ended up with [this] extraordinary household where he had a relationship with one of his [students] …. [and] she moved in and my girlfriend … then moved in as well. To the slight amazement of the neighbourhood.' For Jan, this attempt to reconstruct the marital home as a space of lesbian and heterosexual extra-marital desire was not a success. Within a short time both her marriage and her lesbian relationship had broken down under the pressure and Jan moved on to start a new life as an independent lesbian.[81] Megan similarly described having affairs and attending occasional orgies in Sydney in the early 1970s, with her husband's knowledge and sometimes while he was sleeping in the same bed.[82] However, when Megan's affair with another woman prompted her to discontinue sexual relations with her husband, his acceptance came to an end. She explained: 'At first, Peter was tolerant and excited by the whole idea [of the affair with Kate] – so long as I kept sleeping with him too. These were the swinging 1970s. He was prepared to babysit once a week while I spent the night with Kate.' However, when Kate asked Megan to stop having sex with Peter:

> That was when the trouble began. I moved a double mattress into the spare room and Kate came over whenever Peter went out on the town, which was often. If he didn't score, he'd be home beating on my door, shouting 'What about my conjugals?' We would cower there, mattress pressed against the door, wondering whether he'd take an axe to the pair of us.
> 'Bloody lezzos', he'd shout. 'You don't know what real sex is, anyway' …
> I stayed on, in a marriage-in-name-only, for six years. They were years of violence, of sexual harassment, of being sent to Coventry by outraged in-laws.[83]

Her account of a gradual disintegration of the marital relationship was typical of many women who ultimately left their marriages in search of a new life.

Personal accounts and publications describing the experiences of married lesbians and lesbian mothers in the 1970s and 1980s frequently referred to the bitterness and distrust and high levels of physical, sexual and psychological abuse experienced by married women whose husbands became aware of their lesbianism. In their 1986 advice book, *Lesbian Mothers' Legal Handbook*, British activist group, Rights of Women, claimed:

In a survey we did on the experience of lesbian mothers in custody disputes four women had to leave home without the children because of their husbands' violence towards them once they discovered their wives were lesbians. Three women had to get ouster injunctions to get the man out of the shared home because of his violence. Ten out of 36 lesbian mothers had experienced violence towards them or their lovers/friends in some form.[84]

Lynne recalled that when her husband found out about her affair with another woman in mid-1970s Plymouth, she was forced to leave the family home because of her husband's violence. She explained: 'My ex husband was threatening me as well that he would swing for us and "Anytime you are out with that Sandy up at Harry's [gay bar] I'll be there, you just keep looking over your shoulder" … it was horrible and me and Sandy were scared to go out. He said that he would kill her.'[85] Similarly, Joan, who married in 1965 at the age of nineteen, and began an affair with a woman she met at a meeting of Melbourne lesbian and gay group, Society Five, in the early 1970s, described leaving her husband when he discovered the relationship and became violent.[86]

Deciding whether to leave

Whether or not violence was involved, for many women, the decision to leave their marriages was taken gradually, over an extended period of time and after considerable soul-searching and reflection. Despite the growing influence of companionate models of marriage which emphasized romantic love and personal fulfilment, longer-standing notions of duty and commitment continued to shape women's attitudes to marriage. Letters to lesbian magazines from married lesbians frequently referenced a sense of responsibility to honour the commitment they had made to their husbands and children. In 1978, B.R. from Milton Keynes invited unmarried lesbians to:

> Try and imagine the emotional turmoil when one discovers one's Sapphic tendencies when married to a kind decent man with the added responsibility of children. Telling your husband can be hell, when you are aware of how much hurt and distress your revelation will cause. My husband was not at all of the opinion that it was 'only women'. Rather I think he saw my feelings as a threat to his beloved family and it took a great deal of understanding to keep our home together for the children we both adore. Some may be of the opinion that I should up and away, but I accept full responsibility for the situation. After all, it was of my own making, so how can I gripe that life has been unfair?[87]

Women who were in the process of deciding whether or not to leave their marriages frequently framed this decision in terms of a conflict between duty and the pursuit of fulfilment or an authentic self. As Doris Brown phrased it in her 'cry from the heart' to *Sappho* magazine: 'should I walk out on my good husband and my sons and find myself a mate? Or should I crawl back into my hole and continue to throw my real self away?'[88] Some women described an attempt to stay out of a sense of duty, which ultimately proved unsustainable. In 1976, a 28-year-old mother of two from Victoria wrote to *Cleo* magazine describing her difficult family circumstances. For the past year, she had been sharing a bungalow in the garden of her marital home with her new girlfriend, while her husband and children lived in the house: a compromise which she and her husband had reached in order to maintain shared parenting of their children. However, she found the situation to be increasingly intolerable and was considering leaving the children with her husband as the best compromise between fulfilling her sense of responsibility and enabling her to express a lesbian selfhood.[89]

In some women's view, it was occasionally possible to fulfil both a sense of obligation and a need for personal fulfilment by leaving. An older married woman, offering advice to another married reader of *Arena Three* on the question of whether or not to leave her husband, tried to resolve the potential conflict by suggesting that divorce would enable both wife and husband to achieve fulfilment. She wrote:

> Surely the question to ask is: How deep are her lesbian feelings, and how old is she? If she is a young woman and finds married life intolerable the only solution is to leave her husband now, while he is still young enough to find someone with whom he can have a whole marriage. And she herself will at least not have to go through life living a lie …
>
> Take heart, dear housewife. I am sure there are hundreds, if not thousands who find themselves in the same dilemma. But if you are young enough and have the courage, make the break now, and at least be yourself.[90]

Speaking as someone who had not left her husband and felt that she had trapped both herself and her husband in a frustrating and unhappy situation, this letter writer suggested that breaking up the marriage would be best for all concerned.

Women who planned to leave their marriages also confronted a range of material obstacles. Prior to the radical reform of divorce law in Britain in 1969 and in Australia in 1975, obtaining a divorce could be problematic. In Britain, the case of Gardner v Gardner in 1947 established the principle that a wife's 'unnatural sexual relations with other women' could constitute a basis for divorce on the grounds of cruelty if persisted in against the expressed wishes of the husband and proven to have had an injurious impact on his physical or mental health.[91] In the subsequent decade, however, courts remained reluctant to define a relationship between two women as sexual without clear evidence and cases were also dismissed if a husband appeared to have tolerated or condoned the relationship. Married lesbians considering leaving their husbands also faced financial difficulties with, at best, a probable reduction in standard of living. Although a growing number of married women undertook paid employment in the post-war decades, most worked in part-time and lower skilled jobs, reflecting a persistent cultural belief that the husband was the primary breadwinner for the family.[92] Leaving a marriage typically brought significant financial consequences for women, who had not had the opportunity to gain skills or build a career in order to support themselves or children. Liz, who had been married to her husband, John, for thirteen years, told *Campaign* in July 1981:

> I've been thinking about telling him because of [my lover] Pat. I know I'm going to have to. I'm scared. He'll probably be devastated, the fragile male ego in regards to sex. He might get violent. He might do anything. It's going to be a big step when I do leave. I've got no training – only minimal training.[93]

When Lynne left her husband in Plymouth in the mid-1970s, she was working part-time in the Clarks shoe factory and did not have sufficient income to obtain suitable accommodation for her children. She recalled: 'in the end I actually left the children in the home with him, which has always been my biggest guilt, but the flat I did eventually find was horrible and [when] I brought my children there to see it, they said no.'[94]

The presence of children was typically the most significant concern for women considering leaving their marriages. The impact on children of marital breakdown was a worry for married lesbians as for many people contemplating divorce in this period, but lesbian mothers faced the additional fear that courts might not grant them custody of or access to their children. London Lesbian Line reportedly received several hundred calls a year from lesbians in the early 1980s who felt unable to leave their marriages and believed it necessary to conceal the fact that they were lesbians for fear of what would happen to their children.[95] Many women either chose to remain in unhappy marriages or delayed leaving by several years for fear of losing their children. Megan Forrest, who married and had three children in Melbourne before meeting and falling in love with another woman in the late 1970s, explained her decision to remain in her marriage until her children were grown up with the comment: 'there was the constant shadow of a court case and loss of the children altogether'.[96] Husbands could exploit those fears and, in the atmosphere of anger and recrimination which often followed a woman's admission to her husband that she was attracted to women, many men threatened to take the children away from their mother. One anonymous *Sappho* contributor explained: 'Since my children were born, my husband found out my secrets ... My husband is bitter towards me and who can blame him? He has told me if I leave him I will never see my children again.'[97] For women who delayed leaving, those years could be difficult ones. Tina described her experience of this situation in an article in *Sappho* in 1973, which recounted her gradual realization, during ten years of marriage, that she was a lesbian and the powerlessness she felt in the face of her husband's threats to prevent her from seeing her children. She recalled:

> The shame I feel, when my husband realizes that I have loved and shared many happy moments with a woman in a way never shared with him, is I suppose part of my punishment, as well as the guilt of knowing that one day this silly farce called a marriage will come to an end and deprive the children of a mother – or a father ... When I've been out, I have to put up with his routine questions: Whom have I met in secret? ... I expect and accept his suspicions and have become hardened to them ... Knowing that the law is on my husband's side, scares me.

> If I ever do leave and ruin his chances of promotion he can and would make sure that I lose any chance of getting the custody of my children. He says that the children will grow up to know only of homosexual relationships if they live with me. The fact that I am a good mother doesn't come into it. In the eyes of society I am unsuitable.[98]

In their 1982 book on lesbian motherhood, *Rocking the Cradle*, Gillian Hanscombe and Jackie Forster observed that many married lesbians endured psychological and physical abuse from their husbands rather than risk losing their children:

> The idea that lesbianism per se is accepted as grounds for deciding that a woman is an unfit mother has caused extreme distress for many lesbians and their children and is a principal reason for the fear lesbian mothers have that their children might be taken away from them if their lesbian sexuality becomes common knowledge. Consequently, they try to keep their sexuality secret, or, when angry husbands find out about it, allow themselves to be blackmailed and threatened and even abused, so long as they feel they have some chance of keeping their children.[99]

The fear of losing custody or access to their children which emerged vividly from the letters and oral histories of married lesbian mothers in this period was grounded both in the threats issued by angry husbands and the reported outcomes of child custody disputes involving lesbian mothers.

Child custody disputes

Cultural assumptions about the nuclear family and the respective roles of mothers and fathers were reproduced and reinforced in the courts in the context of child custody disputes in the 1970s and 1980s. Such cases rarely came to court prior to the 1970s as lesbian mothers would have been very unlikely to publicly admit to being in a same-sex relationship. Ruth Ford's analysis of a rare 1962 Australian case, involving a Victorian woman whose husband successfully sued for divorce and child custody on the grounds of her 'lesbian association' with another woman, demonstrates the hostile attitudes of courts in this period.[100] By the 1970s, custody cases involving lesbian mothers prompted increasing debate in the Australian and British courts and, in most cases, known lesbian mothers lost custody of their children. In Australia, the Family Law Act 1975, which created the Family Law Court, established the principle of the welfare of the child as the sole factor in determining child custody, officially replacing earlier fault-based criteria which considered the behaviour of each party to the marriage.[101] While this could theoretically improve the chances of lesbian mothers in winning custody, contemporary commentators differed regarding the impact of the Act. In an article on lesbian custody cases, Sydney activist Robyn Plaister claimed: 'Before the introduction of the Family Law Act in 1975, custody of children involved in divorce proceedings was usually given to the natural mother; the courts took the view that only she could provide those innate qualities of maternal love and affection.' However, following the

Act, she suggested, Family Law Court counsellors reported that children were being given to parents of either sex equally.[102] The mother's lesbianism was still explored in depth in many cases, considered as a factor in determining the child's welfare with regard to the environment in which the child was raised and the impact of the mother's sexuality on the child's psychosexual development. Lesbian mothers lost custody as a result of their sexuality in a significant proportion of cases in Australia between the early 1970s and mid 1980s, although it was possible for mothers to win, particularly if the father was considered unsuitable or older children expressed a wish to live with their mother.[103]

In Britain, contemporary reports suggest the legal context was even more hostile to lesbian mothers. Legislative changes through the twentieth century had gradually shifted the balance of parenting rights between mothers and fathers, moving away from the nineteenth-century presumption that legitimate children were the property of the father. The Guardianship of Infants Act 1925 established the principle of the welfare of the child as the paramount concern in custody cases and equalized parents' rights to custody. However, mothers' legal authority was still limited as, unless granted individual rights by a court, mothers needed to seek the consent of the father to any major decision affecting the child. This did not change until the Guardianship of Minors Act 1973 gave each parent authority to act alone. The rights of unmarried fathers also increased after 1959 when the Legitimacy Act gave such men the right to apply for access and custody.[104] Despite the interwar introduction of the welfare of the child principle, British courts continued to consider women's sexual behaviour a factor in their parenting ability. Adultery by the woman was typically regarded by the courts as a bar to custody until the late 1960s, on the basis that making a home for her husband constituted part of the role of a good mother. After 1969, this attitude was gradually overturned by decisions in the Appeal Court which considered that this principle was less important than the need for young children to be with their mother.[105] In the case of B v B, the judge asserted that 'unless there was some really good reason [otherwise] children of this age (under 6) should be with their mother. That was the social norm'. The following year, in the case of Re K, Sir John Pennycuik reasserted this principle, claiming that a mother, 'not as a matter of law but in the ordinary course of nature is the right person to have charge of young children', and that the mother is 'the natural guardian, protector and comforter of the very young'.[106] As a result of these broader assumptions about the roles of parents, throughout the 1970s and 1980s, courts typically awarded custody, particularly of younger children, to their mothers.

However, lesbian mothers were considered an exception to this principle and a mother's lesbian sexuality was frequently interpreted as impacting negatively on her ability to parent. In a 1982 case in the Appeal Court, Lord Justice Watkins ruled that parents who became homosexual following a marriage breakdown should not be allowed to keep the children of that marriage unless no other acceptable form of custody was available.[107] Few cases involving lesbian mothers were reported in Britain in the 1970s and early 1980s but contemporary analysis seemed to suggest that known lesbian mothers were very unlikely to win custody cases in Britain at this time.[108] In her 1976 article on lesbian mothers and child custody for *Spare Rib*, Eleanor Stephens claimed: 'When a woman who is a lesbian is unlucky enough to have to go to court to fight for custody she has at the moment no chance of winning. The judge always awards custody to the father.'[109] In 1978, Cohen et al. analysed the available British child custody cases involving lesbian mothers and reported that all but three mothers lost custody of their children, and Brophy's 1979 study of four cases noted that the mothers lost custody in all cases, despite their quality of care and proposed accommodation being at least equal to that of the father.[110] By the early 1980s, the possibility of lesbian mothers winning custody gradually began to increase and, when the activist group, Rights of Women Lesbian Custody Project, conducted a postal survey of British lesbian mothers in 1984, they found that of twenty-nine respondents who had been involved in disputes over access and custody between 1976 and 1984, thirteen had lost or given up care and control of their children, while sixteen had gained either joint or sole custody.[111]

Judgements in both Britain and Australia typically reflected and reinforced wider cultural assumptions that lesbianism and motherhood were incompatible. Despite the pronouncements of some judges that social attitudes towards lesbianism were changing and that being a lesbian was no longer considered a barrier to parenting, rulings nevertheless weighed up a woman's mothering abilities against her sexuality as if the two were oppositional. In the case of Campbell v Campbell in Adelaide in 1974, Justice Bright granted custody to the mother on the basis that her maternal instincts and love appeared to outweigh her homosexuality. He concluded:

> In the end, however, I am influenced most by my strong belief in the applicant's very great love for her children. I believe that herein lies the best safeguard for the children against any improper contamination ... I believe that if ill-effects become apparent from the applicant's homosexual activities she will find a way to desist from them rather than lose the affection and respect of her children.[112]

These presumptions of the incompatibility of lesbianism and motherhood were frequently used to justify removing children from their mothers' care. In a profile of Adelaide lesbian couple, Barb and Helen, for gay newspaper, *Campaign*, Tony James described the stereotypes of lesbians the women had encountered during their unsuccessful fight for custody of Barb's children. James observed:

> These homosexual stereotypes are particularly evident as one sifts through the bulky pages of the court transcripts ... One that came up two or three times in the court-room context was the implication that Barb's ability as a housekeeper and mother must surely have faded away now that she had assumed a homosexual lifestyle.[113]

Judges typically evaluated a lesbian mother's custody claim on the basis of a combination of material and developmental factors. As in all custody claims, the suitability and quality of accommodation each parent offered the child or children was taken into consideration and mothers, who often possessed fewer employment skills and a reduced earning capacity in comparison to their ex-husbands, having left the workforce early to raise the children, were typically disadvantaged in this regard.

Concerns about the impact on children's gender and sexual development of being raised outside of a nuclear family were a particular focus of cases involving lesbian mothers. A number of studies were undertaken between 1976 and 1983 assessing the nature and extent of this impact. Two US studies, by Martha Kirkpatrick and Richard Green, found that children raised by lesbian mothers were no more likely than other children to become homosexual or to adopt atypical gender roles.[114] In 1983, the results of a British study by Susan Golombok and others, comparing children in lesbian and single-parent households, were published, finding no difference in the gender identity, sex role behaviour or sexual orientation of the children.[115] As arguments regarding psychosexual development began to hold less weight in the later 1980s in the wake of these studies, judges increasingly emphasized concerns about the social 'embarrassment' resulting to the child from having a lesbian mother and a potentially increased risk of being ridiculed or bullied by friends and peers as a result of their mother's sexuality.

Lesbian mothers who became involved in custody cases encountered these attitudes in their interactions with a whole range of legal and court officials, from their own and their ex-husbands' solicitors and barristers, to the court welfare officers who visited their homes to prepare a report on their parenting skills and the quality of their relationship with their children for the court.[116] Gillian Butler, who acted as legal counsel for a significant number of lesbian mothers in the 1980s, emphasized the traumatic experience of the court process for lesbian mothers, recalling in 1991:

> Most of the cases that I've dealt with, women have actually retained custody but it's what they've gone through. I mean it's the humiliating questioning by some of these judges – not so much now. I've had judges ask women if they make a noise when they have sex. I've had judges say: 'It's not natural, animals don't do it.' You get disgusting things.[117]

Lesbian mothers' activist groups sought to challenge these views from the late 1970s and began to have some impact on the outcomes of cases in the 1980s. Robyn Plaister, founder of the Sydney Lesbian Mothers Group, published several articles in the lesbian and feminist press in the late 1970s, outlining the key issues facing lesbian mothers in custody cases and, in WA, Vivienne Cass provided published and individual advice for lesbian mothers.[118] In 1976, British group, Action for Lesbian Parents was established following a meeting with Maureen Colquhoun MP and began by lobbying the Lord Chancellor in relation to recent custody cases which demonstrated judicial prejudice.[119] In 1982, British feminist legal group, the Rights of Women, established a Lesbian Custody Project, using funding from the Greater London Council's Women's Committee, which published research and provided advice to lesbian mothers.[120] Groups such as Rights of Women, and individual lesbian mothers sharing their stories in the feminist and lesbian press, emphasized the importance of identifying a sympathetic solicitor and ensuring that they were well-informed on the issues and latest research.[121] Detailed legal guidance and advice was published in handbooks such as the Lesbian Custody Project's *Lesbian Mothers' Legal Handbook*.

The work of these activist groups in building up a knowledge base of how to approach custody cases and identifying sympathetic and experienced lawyers began to have an impact on the outcome of cases in the 1980s. Attitudes towards lesbian mothers and child development more broadly also began to shift, assisted in part by psychological and sociological studies such as that undertaken by Golombok. As a result, it became increasingly possible for lesbian mothers to obtain custody of their children, even in cases where a hostile ex-husband contested. In other cases, husbands did not contest custody, leaving the care of children to their former wives. D.J. from Lancashire shared her positive experience of gaining custody with *Sappho* readers in 1975:

> I was Mrs Average with two daughters when I met the one person I wanted to spend my life with. After much soul-searching during the following months I told my husband. The outcome was that I took my children immediately to live with my very dear friend. I then applied to the courts for custody and maintenance which I got without any trouble at all. I cannot express adequately the feeling of release and freedom to be myself. I wasn't being fair to my husband. I wasn't the person he thought I was … My children are quite happy. They see Daddy six times a year. Anyone tied by guilt feelings in a marriage or not – give yourself a chance to live your own life. After all children won't always be dependent on you. And then what?[122]

Conclusion

In the immediate post-war decades, extremely high rates of marriage in Britain and Australia prompted many women to marry despite, or without being conscious of, their desires for other women. Although the experiences of these women typically went unrecognized both at the time and in historical accounts of the period, the desires and relationships of married lesbians helped shape lesbian networks and communities in the 1960s and 1970s, as well as prompting us to rethink our understanding of the post-war nuclear family. By the 1980s, the growing cultural visibility of same-sex desire, together with an increased awareness of alternative routes into motherhood for lesbians, prompted fewer women who desired other women to marry and made it less difficult for those who did marry to leave marriages when they chose.

5

Creating a family

In 1978, a media scandal surrounding lesbians' use of artificial insemination by donor (AID) to conceive babies prompted Jackie Forster, editor of British lesbian magazine, *Sappho*, to declare to readers:

> The uproar over Lesbian couples and AID babies is just another aspect in the long struggle for A Woman's Right to Choose. It seems that lesbians are in the forefront in realizing that a fulfilled emotional and physical relationship is something quite apart from automatic reproduction as is the case in heterosexual unions. We are living proof of this. Our sexual relationship *does not cause an unwanted child*. Our loving relationship *selects a wanted child* [emphasis mine].[1]

Four years later, Australian lesbian and gay newspaper, *Campaign*, contrasted the experience of Sydney doctor, Louise and her psychologist partner, Judy, who conceived their two children together by artificial insemination, with that of single lesbian mother, Helen, whose child was the result of heterosex. While Louise and Judy were described as 'happily living together' and 'settled into a stable, loving relationship' before deciding to embark on parenthood, 'In Helen's case things were not so well planned. Her pregnancy was accidental after an unfortunate liaison with a married man.'[2] In her analysis of Australian discourses of lesbian motherhood in the 1980s and 2000, Barbara Baird has claimed that the adoption of similar narratives of lesbian parenting in media representations constituted a 'liberal assimilationist discourse'. In contrast to more pragmatic and ambivalent feminist approaches to mothering in the 1980s, she argues: 'The repeated claims that the children of lesbian families are (very) loved and (very) wanted also partook in a normalising liberal discourse' which emerged in the Australian media in 2000 at a time when prime minister, John Howard, was implementing policies aimed at bolstering the heterosexual nuclear family.[3] However, as the above quotation indicates, the discourse of lesbian parenting as both a rational process of careful evaluation and a supreme act of maternal love and commitment has a much longer history, emerging from earlier narratives of motherhood and choice in both countries. In the lesbian press, personal narratives, the mainstream media and lesbian activism, lesbians themselves and sympathetic commentators have sought to represent lesbian mothers as uniquely characterized by the rational choices they have made about motherhood, the careful planning with which they have approached these decisions and, consequently, the notable love and devotion they feel for their children. While this discourse gathered momentum from the late 1970s onwards, when lesbian-identified women began to use a variety of techniques to conceive outside of the context of a heterosexual relationship, its origins can also be seen in the earlier post-war conceptualization of lesbianism as a choice *not* to be a mother.

In the context of ongoing attacks on lesbians' right to conceive or parent children throughout the post-war period, the discourse of the much-wanted child has served a clear political purpose, but its pervasiveness has obscured the diversity of women's experiences of lesbian motherhood. As Damien Riggs has noted in his analysis of the 'discourse of love' as used in recent Australian queer parenting rights activism, claims for recognition as 'good parents' on the basis of 'love' accept and reinforce the exclusion of other parents who have not been recognized as 'good' by the state.[4] In an Australian context, Riggs suggests, these exclusions might encompass the historic experience of the Stolen Generations and ongoing attacks on Indigenous families and parenting practices, in addition to more recent political discourses around race, parenting and immigration. These insights could also be applied to a post-war British context in which, as Wendy Webster and others have demonstrated, black migrant women were frequently constructed as 'bad' mothers by the state, social welfare workers and sociologists because of their perceived failure to exhibit 'mother-love'.[5] It is not simply the notion of a loved or wanted child which has historically worked to exclude certain experiences of motherhood, however. The discourse of lesbian motherhood as the result of careful consideration and planning also re-inscribes certain class and racial assumptions. Such narratives assume both an economic capacity for forward-planning and a choice-based approach to life which privilege dominant white, middle-class narratives of family formation and life trajectory.[6] This discourse of choice and planning also contains an implicit assumption that the capacity to express love and devotion to a child is in direct proportion to the extent to which the child was planned for. Thus the 'wanted' children of lesbian mothers who had planned their pregnancies through self or artificial insemination were contrasted with the 'unwanted' – and presumably 'unloved' – offspring of a heterosexual sexual encounter whose culmination in pregnancy had not been intended or foreseen. In mapping out the key changes in lesbian practices of conception through the post-war period, this chapter will therefore pay close attention to the ways in which these shifts were accompanied by evolving narratives of choice and devotion.

As discussed in Chapter 4, the dominant experience of lesbian parenting in Britain and Australia up to and including the 1970s was that of the woman who had conceived her child(ren) in the context of heterosexual marriage, but this gradually gave way in the final quarter of the twentieth century to the use of other techniques of family formation in the context of pre-existing lesbian identities and relationships. From the 1970s onwards, self-identified lesbians began to explore a range of routes into motherhood, including fostering and adoption, AID, self-insemination and casual heterosex. These methods were utilized unevenly throughout the period and in each country and many would-be mothers considered a variety of options depending on factors such as legal and financial constraints and accessibility. As the notion of the 'lesbian mother' gained cultural traction in the 1970s, social hostility towards lesbians conceiving and raising children became more clearly and widely articulated and continued throughout the 1980s and 1990s. Both the possibilities and experience of different routes into lesbian motherhood were shaped by distinct patterns of hostile media attention; lobbying by Christian and right-wing family values groups; legislative and local government frameworks; and medical and other social policy guidelines and practices. A range of lesbian activist groups formed at distinct moments between the 1970s and 1990s to lobby around issues such as lesbian mothers' custody rights; access to clinical insemination; and lesbian and gay fostering and adoption and this activism also shaped the context in which lesbian motherhood was both understood and made possible.

Lesbian motherhood in the 1950s and 1960s

In the 1950s and 1960s, the cultural framing of lesbianism and motherhood as incompatible meant that women who recognized their same-sex desires early in life often felt that they faced a choice between their sexuality and motherhood and some consciously chose marriage in order to have children. In doing so they insisted on an understanding of lesbian identity as a choice to reject marriage and motherhood. This remained a powerful discourse until the late 1970s, when the emergence of feminist and lesbian activism around lesbian child custody cases began to open up a discursive space for the possibility of lesbian motherhood. The explicit rejection of marriage and motherhood, understood as fundamentally connected, is a common theme in lesbian narratives of the post-war period, utilized by narrators to support an account of a developing lesbian identity.[7] Sharyn, who was born in Victoria in 1951, observed that 'I never had a desire to get married, have children, any of that ... I'd never felt particularly maternal.'[8] In her discussion of what she terms hetero- and homo-domesticity as features of lesbian personal narrative, Amy Tooth Murphy has noted the rupture that discussion of hetero-domesticity represented in the oral history interviews she conducted with self-defined lesbians. Those who had never been heterosexually married typically made clear assertions of their rejection of marriage with comments such as 'I just knew I, I was not wanting to get married and all that kind've involvement' and 'you would be dying inside if you followed that path.'[9] In contrast, Murphy observed clear signs of disjunction in the narratives of those who had experienced heterosexual marriage but who struggled to incorporate this aspect of their lives into composed lesbian narratives, with one narrator initially failing to mention her marriage at all.[10]

The conceptualization of a lesbian identity as a childless one was also strongly articulated in contemporary accounts, which typically framed lesbian childlessness as a positive choice. In 1970 novelist Mary Renault equated lesbianism with childlessness in a letter to *Arena Three*. She observed that lesbians are:

> Nature's kindly answer to the population explosion instead of plagues and bombs, a perfectly natural bit of evolution – or sometimes the instinctive reflex of the artist who needs his main creative energies for his work; sometimes, perhaps, a

wise provision against our handing on recessive genes about which nature knows more than we.[11]

Renault's argument that the decision to be a lesbian and not have children represented a positive response to over-population was echoed by a number of women in the 1960s and 1970s, at a time when over-population was increasingly being represented as a threat to the environment and the survival of the human race.[12] In 1970, Miss J.I. from Berkshire berated as 'irresponsible' a lesbian couple whose decision to conceive and raise a child together had been reported in the media and observed: 'We are, in a small way, keeping the population down. Why should these two go out of their way to add to it?'[13]

Others presented pregnancy and motherhood as inherently heterosexual and feminine and therefore anathema to 'real' lesbians. In 1965, a contributor to *Arena Three* expressed this opinion in an analysis of British journalist, Bryan Magee's representation of lesbians in the *New Statesman*. Citing a claim by 'Mother Magee' that 'The deliberate avoidance of having children is itself severely disturbing for most women, Lesbian or otherwise', the author countered: 'This is merely a popular belief upheld by centuries of social convention. My own opinion and experience is that for a Lesbian having children could quite easily set up severe emotional disturbance.'[14] A decade later, L.G. from Belfast similarly suggested that the experience of motherhood was intrinsically heterosexual, in her response to letters from lesbian mothers printed in *Sappho*. She claimed:

> Surely the most slavishly submissive and ultra-feminine role any woman can play with a man is to allow him to impregnate her, suffer nine months of what appears to be pretty average mis-shapen biological hell, then settle down to suckling and nappies and pram-pushing in the park while Daddy struts and preens.[15]

Such debates in the lesbian media both constructed and sought to make sense of a notion of lesbian identity as incompatible with motherhood, reinforcing a widely held view that lesbianism represented a choice to avoid motherhood.[16] Instead, pets were frequently cited, both in cultural references and in personal narratives, as a more appropriate expression of lesbian family formation. Rene Sawyer, who was part of a network of butch/femme lesbians centred around the London lesbian venue, the Robin Hood club, in the late 1950s, described pets as central to butch/femme forms of domesticity in this period: 'Of course, we didn't have any children: I don't know about any lesbians that I knew at the time that had children. So, consequently, it was usually a little dog or a cat that one had in the family and that was their little baby.'[17] Marion Paull recalled similar attitudes in the Canberra Women's Liberation Movement in the early 1970s. Reflecting on her decision, with her partner, to explore the possibility of lesbian motherhood, she claimed that their feminist friends were dismissive: 'Straight sisters in the movement said we were once again aping heterosexual behaviour. Lesbians were heard to say it was disgusting and why couldn't we have dogs like everyone else.'[18]

While some women found this assumed choice between a lesbian identity and parenthood a relatively straightforward decision as they had no desire for children, others experienced considerable pain and conflict over the issue. Margaret recalled that, although she had never wanted children, her partner's desire for them ultimately brought about the end of their relationship. She remembered: 'My mother did say to me one time, "Don't you ever feel you'd like to have a little baby? Hold a little baby's hand in yours?" "No I don't. No and I have never felt like that."' Margaret met Iris, 'the love of [her] life', in Coventry in the 1950s, and the two women were together for fifteen years. However, as Margaret explained: '[Iris] wanted to have a little family. At the beginning of our relationship after about three or four years she wanted these children. She didn't like it that we weren't married and we couldn't be married.' Margaret tried to find a solution to this problem but could not and, after this, the couple avoided discussion of children, until one day, Iris told Margaret:

'[It's] the end of our relationship. Because I want to be married and I want to have a family life.' So I was ... devastated ... Because I did love her ... Sometimes when we'd been very close, making love, ... she'd cry sometimes afterwards because she wanted a baby and she knew there was nothing that could come of it.[19]

For women like Iris who wanted to have children in the 1950s and 1960s, whether or not they had previously recognized or acted upon lesbian desires, heterosexual marriage was the only socially acceptable route into motherhood. Single women who conceived or attempted to raise children in this period faced significant obstacles, from forced adoption of their babies to social ostracism and extreme social and economic hardship.[20] In 1996, Mary told *Lesbians on the Loose* magazine how, as a teenager, she had been forced by parental rejection and lack of access to state benefits, to give her baby up for adoption in NSW in 1965.[21] In the context of the Stolen Generations, Indigenous babies and children were systematically taken from their families and placed with white foster families between the 1920s and 1970s. When Betty fell pregnant in Sydney in 1970 and was abandoned by the father of the child, she was forced to enter an unmarried mothers' hostel. She recalled:

The Matron tried very hard to get my baby from me. I had only two months to go. Matron said to me, 'We have a lovely family who'd like to have your baby. They really want an Aboriginal baby'. I said, 'Oh no, you're not havin' this baby.' Matron got the doctor to me one night to give me an injection. When I became drowsy, they tried to force me to sign the adoption papers.[22]

Despite such intense pressure, some women – like Betty – did manage to defy social conventions and conceive or parent children outside of marriage. Betty kept her son while in a variety of jobs and living situations, and conceived a daughter nine years later, whom she raised while in a relationship with another woman. Racism and financial need impacted significantly on Betty's options as a mother, but some women's single parenting was enabled by better economic circumstances. Liz Naylor recalled the unconventional family structure of her aunt, whom she visited every summer in the Lake District in the early 1970s:

> She had an illegitimate child and my aunty Barbara was a very suss person. She had lots of 'female friends' like 'Erica' and they were really, I mean she was a big Dusty Springfield fan, you know lived on her own, she chose to have a child and bring it up. She was great and probably, I think, if not bi, you know I think her sexuality was somewhat questionable. She never had any male friends, she just had all these female friends.[23]

Liz's Aunty Barbara was a teacher and therefore might hope to be reasonably comfortable, financially, but many other lone mothers in this period struggled to afford housing and other necessities in the context of low average wages for women and the difficulties of combining employment with childcare.

Artificial insemination

Cultural resistance to the notion of lesbian motherhood as a coherent identity gradually shifted in the 1970s and 1980s as a small number of women began to conceive children in the context of a lesbian identity or relationship and thus challenged understandings of the lesbian mother. Although women pursuing a range of routes into lesbian motherhood contributed to this shift, AID attracted the most intense media, activist and legislative attention at the beginning of the period and was thus influential in framing the debate about lesbian motherhood in the 1970s and 1980s. Particularly in the early stages of this shift, transnational connections between Australia and Britain, and elsewhere in Europe, were crucial in determining access to information about the potential application of artificial insemination to lesbian parenting, while individual women's experiences were shaped by legal and ethical frameworks around reproductive technologies. Insemination of a woman with donor sperm had been developed as a technique for addressing fertility issues in the late nineteenth century and was debated and practised in Australia, Britain and elsewhere throughout the twentieth century.[24] Britain was one of very few countries in the early 1970s to allow unmarried women access to medically controlled artificial insemination and this is reflected in the differential development of the practice by lesbians in Britain and Australia. While the first cases of lesbian mothers conceiving by AID in Britain occurred at the beginning of the decade, the first verifiable cases in Australia date from the later 1970s.[25] Moreover, whereas clinic-based AID was used, or at least considered, relatively widely in Britain, being both legal and potentially accessible on the NHS, informal, self-insemination was the norm in Australia, where the legal situation was more restricted.

A small number of lesbian couples achieved pregnancies through AID in Britain in the early 1970s. Janice Hetherington claimed to have been the first lesbian in Britain to have a child by artificial insemination with the help of a doctor in Middlesex, after being inseminated in 1971. She explained that 'she had decided when she was in her teens that she was a lesbian and if she ever wanted to have children it would have to be by AID'. She began the process in her mid-twenties, after she had lived with her lover, Judy, for two years. The doctor himself was the donor and Janice paid a small fee for the treatment, which resulted in the birth of her son, Nicky.[26] However, it was not until later the following year that the potential application of reproductive technologies for lesbians began to be more widely discussed by British lesbians, after an Australian lesbian couple raised the issue at a Sappho meeting in London. Katharine and Marion had travelled to Britain in 1972 after being told by their local GP in Canberra that they were 'ahead of [their] time' and would require a husband's signature to obtain treatment. On arrival in London, the couple identified a sympathetic GP through *Time Out* magazine and Katharine was referred to a Belgravia gynaecologist, Dr David Sopher.[27]

Not long after the couple's arrival in London, lesbian organization, Sappho organized a meeting to explore different routes into motherhood. The discussion focused on marriage; fostering and adoption; and, at Katharine and Marion's suggestion, AID, which was previously unknown to Sappho members.[28] A report of the meeting in *Sappho* magazine provides an indication of the attitudes of British medical and social work professionals at this time. Various 'expert' guests, including a child psychiatrist and representatives of adoption agencies, were invited but only Dr Sopher attended. Discussing AID, Dr Sopher told the group that he had not considered the possibility of providing AID to lesbians before being approached by Katharine and Marion and that he had contacted the Chairman of the British Medical Association's Ethical Committee for advice. He reported:

> I asked if anything of this nature had ever been discussed or had there been any literature about it? They had never come across anything like this. They had never considered homosexual couples. Legally there is nothing to prevent artificial insemination for homosexual couples, but the ultimate power in the BMA is respectability and you may create more problems by forcing the issues.[29]

As his comment indicated, British doctors were not legally prohibited from providing AID to lesbians, but individual doctors were free to refuse the service on moral or other grounds, creating regional variations in access to clinic-based AID. Certainly, the response of the medical profession was a cause of concern for many lesbians considering AID and *Sappho* reported that the women who participated in the meeting were reluctant to make use of AID as an alternative to heterosex on the grounds that the medical profession was strongly opposed and they 'fear[ed] that society would never accept the situation of homosexual couples giving birth and bringing up their own children'.[30] This impression of the attitudes of the medical profession generally was supported by Janice Hetherington's experience, when she had sought AID a few years earlier. She and her partner faced some discouragement from doctors and she recalled:

> They all thought I was a crank. I eventually found a sympathetic one, who agreed to help if I underwent psychiatric tests … But most psychiatrists I approached thought I was mad. They seemed to think it would have been acceptable for me to have heterosexual sex with any Tom, Dick or Harry and then have a child, but not to do it this way.[31]

Katharine and Marion's gynaecologist, Dr Sopher, proved more sympathetic and became an important point of contact for would-be lesbian mothers in Britain in the 1970s, providing AID to several lesbian couples over the course of the decade.

This service was provided discreetly, from Dr Sopher's practice in Belgravia, following referrals from *Sappho* editor, Jackie Forster.[32] In 1978, journalist Joanna Patyna reported in detail on the treatment provided by the gynaecologist to would-be lesbian mothers, explaining that she and a colleague attended a consultation with Dr Sopher in which he: 'asked us how long we'd been living together, and when I replied, "three years," [he] commented that it indicated "a stable enough relationship." The only other question he asked related to the regularity of my menstrual cycle, from which he then calculated a suitable date for the artificial insemination to take place'. While Sopher apparently considered it important to verify the stability of the relationship, Patyna emphasized that the consultation had not included any medical examination, which Sopher claimed to be unnecessary, given that most women did not undergo such an exam before becoming pregnant. He did, however, assure her that full tests were carried out on the donor. The women were told that, although Dr Sopher would source the donor semen and make a room available in the clinic, he would not be carrying out the insemination himself. This task would be left to the women, to ensure that Joanna was relaxed and in a more 'receptive state'. The fee for the treatment was £12 per insemination, half of which was paid to the donor. Noting that these rates were extremely low in comparison to the £150 fee frequently charged by Harley Street doctors treating infertile heterosexual couples, Dr Sopher explained that he 'believed he was providing a worthwhile service on the grounds ... that the alternative of indulging in a casual heterosexual relationship would be abhorrent to women like us'.[33]

Sappho magazine reported enthusiastically on the progress of those couples seeking children through AID throughout the 1970s, generating a discourse around lesbian motherhood which drew on spiritual and feminist language to present this form of conception as women-centred and chaste. The birth of Katharine and Marion's first child, Benjamin, in May 1974 was announced under the headline 'Easter '74 A.I.D. A.D.' and Babs Todd, Jackie Forster's partner, enthused:

> I'm very grateful that I saw him on the day he was born. I don't think I have ever been so profoundly moved. It is not as if the miracle of birth is a new thing to me. I have two children of my own ... [But] here he was – is – a Virgin Birth made possible by science. And I was allowed to hold him in my arms, and felt very proud and very humble.[34]

Sappho was a key driving force in developing AID networks in Britain and transnationally in the 1970s. Editor, Jackie Forster, was co-mother to her partner, Babs Todd's two daughters, conceived in the context of a previous marriage, and was motivated by her personal experience to include lesbian mothers in the community and to explore alternative forms of conception to marriage. In addition to promoting discussion in the magazine and organizing debates around lesbian motherhood, Forster acted as a point of contact and source of information for women interested in AID and put would-be lesbian mothers in touch with others who had already conceived children.[35]

In Australia, the much more restrictive framework governing use of reproductive technologies created a very different pattern of lesbian motherhood in the 1970s. In the context of the difficulties in accessing AID, the first lesbian conceptions by this method do not appear to have occurred until the later 1970s. Sydney couple, Louise and Judy, had two children by artificial insemination in 1978 and 1980, at the Royal Prince Alfred clinic, after recruiting a pool of donors from among their male friends.[36] In 1982, Melbourne lesbian feminist, Barbara Wishart, presented a paper at the Third Women and Labour conference in which she described her own decision to become pregnant by AID, which resulted in the birth of her daughter in 1980. She recalled: 'In my own case I took the step to become a mother in 1978 with rather mixed feelings, and I felt very much alone.'[37] Barbara Wishart's experience appears to have occurred during what Deborah Dempsey describes as 'a very small window of opportunity for Victorian lesbians to obtain clinical donor insemination' between the late 1970s and early 1980s.[38] In October 1981, Australian gay newspaper, *Campaign*, reported that Melbourne's Queen Victoria Hospital was 'the only hospital in Australia that will provide [artificial insemination] to lesbians'. Interviewing Dr Flowers, director of medical services at another Melbourne hospital, the Royal Women's Hospital, *Campaign* reported that most hospitals would 'under no condition … provide artificial insemination to single women'. Dr Flowers explained:

> This is because the doctors and social workers at the unit felt single parents carried many problems in this society. The rate of battered babies among single mothers is an example … and with regard to lesbian couples, the hospital would have to take into account its role as a public institution. As a public institution we would have to reflect public opinion. Of course you could argue that public opinion is changing towards homosexuals, but we must remember that we are in the public eye.[39]

Throughout the 1980s and 1990s, the lesbian and gay press and literature on lesbian parenting reported widespread reluctance on the part of medical professionals to provide artificial insemination to single women or lesbians. In a 1997 report written by Jenni Millbank, the Coalition of Activist Lesbians noted that anecdotal evidence suggested that public hospitals across Australia routinely denied lesbians and single women access to publicly funded donor insemination services.[40] In July 1993, the Northern Territory minister for health, Mike Reed, told parliament that 'NT medical facilities will never be available to enable lesbian women to have children'. He explained: 'I cannot, under any circumstances, believe that allowing homosexual couples to have custody of children is anything [but] prejudicial to the interests of the children and the community in general.'[41]

Legal and policy frameworks also prevented lesbians from accessing donor insemination through the public health system in various states across Australia. In New South Wales, Queensland, Tasmania, the Australian Capital Territory and the Northern Territory ethical guidelines established by the Fertility Society of Australia and the National Health and Medical Research Council limited provision, while in Victoria, the Infertility (Medical Procedures) Act 1984 confined access to donor insemination and other reproductive technologies to married couples.[42] Deborah Dempsey has argued that NSW was 'historically, the most liberal jurisdiction with regard to clinical eligibility criteria for donor insemination' and that 'Lesbians and unpartnered heterosexual women have been an acceptable client group to some Sydney-based and regional New South Wales clinics since at least the mid-1980s.'[43] Some lesbians therefore travelled from other states (especially Victoria) to NSW clinics in order to receive treatment. Nevertheless, the NSW lesbian and gay press continued to report that medical practitioners were refusing fertility treatment to all but married, heterosexual couples throughout this period and, by the early 1990s, activists were beginning to urge lesbians to seek legal redress. Sydney lesbian magazine, *Lesbians on the Loose*, asked readers in 1993, 'So if you think you have been denied donor insemination services because you are single or a lesbian, what can you do? The answer is, of course, complain. The NSW Anti-Discrimination Act 1977 makes it unlawful to refuse someone a service on the grounds of their homosexuality ... or of their marital status.'[44] However, it was not until later in the decade that any legal challenges were launched. In 1996, a single woman, Gail Pearce, from Adelaide successfully challenged South Australia's Reproductive Technology Act 1988 arguing that limiting provision to married or de facto couples breached the Commonwealth's Sex Discrimination Act.[45]

Private clinics were less likely to deny access to lesbians. In 1991, *Labrys Newspaper* reported, 'There are Doctors that are willing to inseminate lesbians ... It is a matter of asking around or going to see different doctors until you find one that is willing to assist you with insemination.'[46] Maxine described how she and her partner, Jane, had conceived their first child through clinic-based donor insemination in Perth in the late 1990s. She explained:

> I wrote my own GP, said to him: 'John, this is what we want to do' and he said, 'No problems, I'll give you a refer to a specialist who's linked to a clinic.' We went to see this specialist and he was uncomfortable but didn't refuse us. We were referred to the fertility clinic and he just progressed us through the artificial insemination by the anonymous donor process and Janey got pregnant on the second cycle.[47]

Nevertheless, in the context of difficulties in accessing AID treatment, medical reproductive technologies remained a minority route into motherhood for lesbians in Australia until the early 2000s. In 2002, McNair, Dempsey, Wise and Perlesz reported that, in their study of 115 children of lesbian parents, only 8 per cent had been conceived by clinic-based insemination (and a further 6 per cent by IVF or GIFT).[48]

In Britain, however, AID played an important role in defining concepts of lesbian motherhood from the late 1970s onwards, both for would-be lesbian mothers themselves and in wider society. In early 1978, an exposé by tabloid newspaper, the *Evening News*, prompted largely hostile discussion of the practice in the media and parliament and brought the concept of lesbian motherhood into public debate in Britain for the first time. On Thursday, 5 January 1978, undercover reporter, Joanna Patyna, revealed how she had posed as a lesbian 'mother-to-be' in order to uncover the secret practice of lesbian AID. Under the dramatic headline, 'Dr Strangelove', Patyna described how she had joined Sappho, pretending to be in a lesbian relationship and asked to be referred to a doctor who provided AID to lesbians.[49] Joanna Patyna's story created a media sensation and dominated the press throughout the UK and Ireland for several weeks. Questions were raised in Parliament and Tory shadow minister, Rhodes Boyson, called for legislation outlawing the practice, declaring: 'To bring children into this world without a natural father is evil and selfish. This evil must stop for the sake of the potential children and society, which both have enough problems without the extension of this horrific practice.'[50] In the initial media frenzy, Dr David Sopher went into hiding and activists protested at the offices of the London *Evening News*.[51]

Two discourses around lesbian motherhood emerged from the scandal which dominated discussion of lesbian mothers in Britain throughout the 1980s and 1990s. The first was the notion of motherhood as a right, which some lesbians and their allies laid claim to and critics disputed. The second was the argument that the children of lesbian mothers were uniquely 'wanted' and that this demonstrative desire to be a mother against all obstacles was evidence of lesbians' worth, if not superiority, as mothers. The concept of motherhood as a right to which all women could stake a claim emerged strongly from feminist and lesbian and gay activist interventions in the 1978 scandal and subsequent campaigning. When activists invaded the London *Evening News* offices, they reportedly chanted: 'Our bodies, our lives, the right to decide ... Every woman's right to have a baby ... Lesbian mothers unite.'[52] Following this action, the *Evening News* agreed to publish a response from lesbian mothers in which the women complained that the paper 'continually suggests that lesbians are freaks with no right to bear children'.[53] Claims centred on a woman's right to bear children were also a key aspect of the black women's movement in this period, in response to women's experience of forced sterilization and contraceptive experimentation, but there is no evidence that white lesbian activists in the 1978 scandal connected these campaigns.[54] In the public debate around the scandal, commentators frequently countered these claims with assertions of the rights of the child, suggesting that these were not only in conflict with the rights of women, but superseded them. The emphasis on children's rights drew on discourses of child-centred parenting which had been dominant in medical and social work literature on parenting and child development in the post-war decades.[55] Dismissing the suggestion that 'two women living together in a stable lesbian relationship have a right to the fulfilment and satisfaction of raising a family', Frederick Whitehead told readers of the *Birmingham Post*: 'Children should not be conceived in the belief that they are proper indulgencies for adults like two-car garages, hi-fi stereos or holidays on the Costa whatever. Conformist majorities have rights as well as aberrant minorities and the former are better able to judge the rights of an unborn child than the emotionally involved few, however vociferous.'[56] This theme of the need for the community to give voice to the rights of children whose interests would otherwise be neglected was echoed in numerous responses to the debate.[57]

Although media coverage of the issue was initially dominated by sensationalist reporting and critiques of lesbian motherhood, some journalists and, increasingly, readers expressed sympathy and support for the situation of lesbian mothers. In later stages of coverage, a discourse of lesbian mothers' children as uniquely 'wanted' began to emerge, which stressed the hurdles that would-be lesbian mothers faced in conceiving as evidence of their considerable investment in motherhood. Lesbian mothers who gave interviews to the media during the scandal framed their accounts through this narrative of a wanted and hard-won child. On 6 January, the London *Evening News* included a piece entitled, 'The most remarkable family in Britain', which told the story of a '*Sappho*' family who had unknowingly assisted undercover journalist, Joanna Patyna, by sharing their experiences of lesbian motherhood with her. The article explained that student 'Helen' had conceived her son 'Michael', by AID, over two years earlier, after some period of deliberation. Helen shared her London home with her lover, Julie, and Julie's other lover, Alison. After some years of living together in a three-way relationship, Helen 'suddenly became aware of a very pressing need to have a child – a tremendous urge to have a baby of her own.' Julie recalled: 'And one day she came home very excited because she'd heard about a doctor who would inseminate lesbians. Well, we didn't take advantage of the service immediately. In fact we agonised about it for a year, wondering whether we'd be doing the right thing.' Julie explained that the women discussed a number of concerns they had, including what the donor would be like, whether they could trust the doctor, and whether their child would be rejected by society, before ultimately taking the decision to go ahead with AID.[58] Another lesbian couple also emphasized the considerable thought and effort which had gone into planning their child in an interview published in the *Liverpool Echo* the following week. Lesley and Christine claimed to have spent three years 'thoroughly thrash[ing] out the pros and cons' of conceiving a baby by AID and the women expressed many of the concerns voiced by Michael's parents.[59]

Journalist, Lucy Orgill, similarly deployed this discourse in the *Derby Evening Telegraph*, emphasizing that the most important aspect of lesbian mothers was that their children were wanted. She argued:

> But what really counts with a child is the feeling of love, security and being wanted. And whatever else the children of gay women may suffer, they're wanted all right. Why else would a gay woman go through the preliminary hell which precipitates conceiving a child? …
>
> Weigh up her strong maternal instincts against that of the promiscuous typist, the prostitute who came unstuck, even the career woman who manages to fit in a quick pregnancy before going off again to pursue her career, leaving her child for somebody else to bring up from the age of six months, and it's not difficult to sort out the good mothers from the indifferent.[60]

Suggesting that the degree of commitment to conceiving equated unproblematically with the degree to which a child would be loved and wanted, Orgill proposed a hierarchy of modern forms of motherhood, in which lesbian mothers came closer to the conventional ideal by virtue of their presumed dedication to their role. The decoupling of lesbian reproduction from sexuality was also an important, if largely implicit, theme in this discourse, allowing lesbian mothers to be compared favourably to unmarried mothers whose children might be presumed to be the product of uncontrolled heterosexual sexuality. Letters to *Sappho* during the scandal repeatedly invoked an image of heterosexual promiscuity and child neglect in support of lesbians' rights to parent. J.C. from Yorkshire wrote: 'I work with "disturbed and delinquent" kids and feel if one is going to start vetting AID recipients, one might as well start banning quite a few heterosexual couples from having kids, as some of them are a lot more damaged than I would imagine the young lad is mentioned in the Observer.'[61] F.F. from London similarly claimed:

> In the old days children were brought up by maiden aunts. Some now live in children's homes. There is wife beating, child battering and all kinds of unsatisfactory environments that children get born into. But the human race still survives. I think it's a very good idea for lesbian couples to have children. I'm sure they'll make a very good job of bringing them up. There is no doubt the children will be as happy and well adjusted as anyone else.[62]

Such responses point to underlying assumptions about the (middle-class and coupled) nature of lesbian mothers, which Barbara Baird has noted as a feature of a similar discourse in Australia in 2000.[63]

Despite the widespread condemnation of the practice in the British press in early 1978, AID continued to be available to British lesbians in subsequent decades. No legislation was passed to restrict its availability in the wake of the scandal and the British Medical Association resisted attempts to interfere in its jurisdiction, determining in late 1978 that the decision whether or not to provide treatment to lesbian couples should be an ethical one left to individual practitioners to decide for themselves.[64] Ironically, the scandal was instrumental in promoting the practice of lesbian motherhood in Britain in the late 1970s and early 1980s. The extensive media coverage drew the practical possibility of lesbian motherhood to the attention of many lesbians for the first time and several women referred to it as a catalyst in their personal decision to conceive a child. Al, who was active in feminist politics in Leeds in the late 1970s, recalled the press coverage of lesbian mothers and AID. As a regular contributor to local radio programmes, offering a feminist perspective on numerous issues, Al found herself asked to comment on the scandal and later recalled it as part of the context in which she reached a decision to try to conceive a child of her own.[65] Clare, in London, reflected that one of the repercussions of the scandal was to 'just let everybody know that if you want to have children, you went to Sappho'. 'So', she recalled, 'we did that and they referred us to a doctor in South Kensington who was happy to do it for lesbians.'[66] Australian feminist journals also reported on the story, although its impact on would-be lesbian mothers in Australia is less clear.[67]

Nevertheless, despite the importance of the scandal in increasing awareness of the possibilities of lesbian motherhood, the numbers of lesbians actually making use of clinic-based donor insemination in Britain in the 1970s and 1980s may have remained relatively low. Although Sappho was instrumental in promoting the possibilities of AID to this London-based community and the magazine's more widely distributed readers, access to gynaecologists willing and able to perform the procedure in the early and mid-1970s was less reliable outside of London. A letter to *Sappho* from P & J in Wales illustrates this difficulty. P wrote:

I've just read about the birth of the little boy. I'm so pleased for the couple that I must write to congratulate them. I'm still exhilarated by the birth of our own little boy three months ago ... After years of talking about the ideality of AID, but not knowing how to go about using the method, my partner and I decided that I would have to get pregnant in the usual way.[68]

This couple had found the travel costs to London to visit Dr Sopher beyond their financial reach and, after two unsuccessful visits to the gynaecologist, had decided that P must have a casual sexual encounter with a man in order to conceive. Christine told the *Liverpool Echo* that the process of seeking out AID treatment was relatively straightforward but again medical provision was limited outside London. She explained: 'I went and saw my GP in Liverpool and asked about AID. She said there was no shortage of donors, and she didn't even question the fact that I was single. She tried to get me an appointment with a gynaecologist in Liverpool, but she was too booked up so now she's fixing for me to see one in London.'[69] Although Christine claimed she encountered no reluctance to provide her with treatment in principle, her account also suggests that there were practical obstacles to finding a gynaecologist outside of London. Al, who took the decision to try to conceive in Leeds in 1979, dismissed the possibility of artificial insemination as too expensive and largely unavailable:

Well I was aware of the Dr Sopher in Harley Street thing but there was no way I had the money for Harley Street so it didn't really appeal ... but certainly, during the 70s, you couldn't get insemination on the NHS or even through private medicine for lesbians in those days. Or indeed, I mean the whole science of it was in its infancy.[70]

Despite Al's impression, artificial insemination was, theoretically at least, available to lesbians on the NHS during the 1970s and 1980s. However, newspaper reports suggest that only a small number of clinics provided the service in the early 1980s. The weekly magazine, *Love Affair*, told a lesbian couple who enquired about getting pregnant in 1982 that there was an eighteen-month waiting list for AI, while the *Mirror* newspaper claimed that, although AID was available free on the NHS, there were only thirty centres nationally which could provide the service and women had to wait up to two years for treatment.[71] By the early 1980s, the British Pregnancy Advisory Service had established itself as the leading provider of AID and claimed to inseminate about 200 women a year by AID through six centres.[72]

Despite ongoing controversy around the provision of reproductive technologies to lesbians in the 1980s, no further restrictions were enacted. Media and parliamentary pressure led to the appointment of a Royal Commission into the medical, social and ethical implications of reproductive technologies but, when the Warnock Report was published in 1984, its recommendations included continued provision to single women and lesbians. However, by the end of the decade, in the context of a more powerful political assertion of conservative family values, a last-minute amendment to the Human Fertility and Embryology Act 1990 did begin to restrict British lesbians' access to clinic-based AI. A change to the 'welfare principle' required clinics and other treatment providers to take account of 'the welfare of any child who may be born as a result of the treatment, and of any child who may be affected by the birth, including the need of that child for a father' in determining whether or not to assist any woman in conceiving.[73] The Human Fertilisation and Embryology Authority, which licensed clinics providing fertility treatment, left individual doctors and clinics to interpret the legal requirement as they considered appropriate and some continued to offer treatment to lesbians, drawing on the notion of a 'wanted' child to justify that position.[74] By the early 1990s, however, lesbians' access to clinic-based donor insemination nationwide was significantly constrained and London-based campaigning groups, the Campaign for Access to DI and the Stop the Amendment Campaign, told *Rouge* journal in the summer of 1990, 'At present only two clinics in Britain provide access to DI for lesbians.'[75]

Feminist approaches to lesbian motherhood

Reproductive technologies contributed to a growing openness to the possibility of separating motherhood from marriage in the 1970s. As small numbers of women began to consider conceiving children while in a lesbian relationship or identifying as lesbian, the concept of lesbian motherhood as a potential choice gradually emerged, alongside a broader cultural shift towards parenting outside marriage. This shift occurred slowly, throughout the 1970s and into the 1980s. To some extent, the slow pace of change in attitudes was due to ambivalent attitudes towards motherhood in feminist theory and networks, an important arena for the exploration of lesbian identities and sexuality in this period. In Britain, motherhood was a key area of divergence between black and white feminist activism. Black women challenged racist characterizations of their families as 'problem families' and fought for their right to be mothers in a context of coerced abortion, forced sterilization and loss of child custody. Moreover, as Tracey Reynolds has argued, mothering, more broadly, played a central role in collective organizing for black feminists, who mobilized as mothers against educational exclusion, academic underachievement, police oppression of black youth, poor housing and many other forms of oppression in a racist society.[76] Black feminist theorists and activists in the 1980s theorized state attempts to control their fertility as evidence of long-standing economic and racial discrimination. In her 1984 article for *Feminist Review*, Amina Mama claimed:

> The limiting of Black female reproduction, in stark contrast to the slavery period, is a recent phenomenon. It would be unrealistic to divorce this from the world economic situation … Pressure is put on Black women, particularly young, single ones to have abortions and both start and continue using the pill. Disturbing evidence about the long-acting contraceptive, depo-provera has provoked campaign action and protests from Black women, and even cries of 'genocide' from some quarters. Childcare is another site at which our contemporary reproductive relation to the state must be considered. Inferior housing and financial situations, coupled with racist evaluation of Black homes and mothers, go some way to

accounting for the high proportion of Black children in care. Financial difficulties and inadequate childcare facilities particularly affect the Black single mother. Recent legislation has further weakened the position of parents in relation to the social services and foster agencies. Unfamiliarity with the legal intricacies involved in retrieving children from the state agencies, and the racism of officials involved in disputes that arise, give cause for concern, as do the problems that arise out of transracial adoption and fostering in a racist society.[77]

In Australia, Indigenous women similarly understood motherhood as a basis for activism against racism, organizing as mothers to protect the integrity of families and the survival of their children and communities.[78]

In contrast, many white feminist theorists and activists focused on women's biological and social roles as mothers as a central cause of women's subordination, alongside broader critiques of the nuclear family. Early radical and socialist feminist literature typically argued for a re-imagining of women's parenting role, which would liberate women from their current dependence on men. Simone de Beauvoir's classic, *The Second Sex*, represented pregnancy and motherhood as the objectification of women, while Shulamith Firestone's influential work, *The Dialectic of Sex*, argued that women's reproductive function as the bearers of children, combined with the lengthy mother-infant dependency in humans, had produced an imbalanced power relationship between men and women.[79] Firestone was widely read and cited by Australian radical feminists. Pam Stein began her essay on 'Women's Oppression' by summarizing Firestone's argument and later asserted: 'Central to the liberation of women is the provision of alternatives to the present pattern of child-bearing and housekeeping, which results in women bearing the entire responsibility for the socialization of children and housework while men are forced to be "breadwinners".'[80] In her 1974 critique of Jill Johnston's *Lesbian Nation*, published in Hobart-based radical feminist journal, *Liberaction*, Linda Freeland also claimed that the cultural emphasis on reproduction was at the root of women's subordinate social position. She argued: 'Because our society tends to see sex in terms of procreation only … men and women are restricted to roles based on extensions of their reproductive functions. And this is the basis of sexism.'[81] By the later 1980s, however, both radical and poststructuralist feminists were beginning to re-evaluate motherhood, offering new ways of reading the body and suggesting that motherhood as a biological experience could be separated from the constraining social institution of motherhood.[82]

The greater influence of socialist feminist approaches on British feminism meant that such ideas were less dominant in British feminist circles and discussion of motherhood in feminist publications was largely limited to a focus on childcare and removing the practical obstacles to women's independence posed by parenthood.[83] Although the question of whether or not women should be mothers was rarely considered, the strong emphasis on women's right to contraception and abortion implicitly framed motherhood as a limiting role for women. A small number of British lesbian feminist publications, however, did provide a forum for discussion of motherhood as a compulsory role for women and several contributors advocated a rejection of motherhood. In 1986, an article in *Gossip* asserted:

> In the heteropatriarchy, Motherhood is the only activity that gives heterosexual women the **illusion** of exercising power, of existing autonomously, of being independently significant. The reason: Men can't give birth; only women can produce offspring; therefore the 'power' of women resides in our reproductive function. They ignore the fact that this particular heteropatriarchal lie is the **foundation** of male superiority, male dominance, male control. They ignore the fact that Motherhood is the justification for female inferiority, weakness, and subjugation to men. Such 'feminists' have traded the difficulty of radical struggle for the illusion of safety, and the consequences for WLM have been destructive.[84]

The author particularly criticized lesbians for choosing to become mothers, arguing that the 'rebirth' of motherhood amongst white lesbians represented 'the exercise of economic privilege to further one's own vanity and egotism' and emphasized the financial and emotional costs of motherhood.[85] In British journal, *Spinster*, US-born feminist, Sheila Shulman recounted how she had struggled for many years in the late 1950s and 1960s with her own investment in the cultural notion that a woman who was not a mother was not a 'real' woman. Having embraced both feminism and her own lesbianism in London in the 1970s, she argued:

> One of the joys, one of the wonders of being a lesbian feminist would be, if only I could do it, being able to put the whole question of children, of motherhood, away, behind me. One of the joys would be to acknowledge finally once and for all that having them is no part of my being a woman, and that I am nevertheless a whole woman and a real one.[86]

Shulman understood the rejection of motherhood by lesbian feminists to be a radical and creative choice which would enable all women ultimately to be freed from the expectation of motherhood. She explained:

> The world has never been confronted with thousands, maybe hundreds of thousands, of untied women, responsible only to themselves, each other and a common vision. Who knows what that kind of energy could do? … I want to be with my peers, my friends, to try to think in new tracks, if we can find them, to do things I've never done, to imagine new worlds, to create durable bonds with no biological imperatives to cement them, to be a woman in unheard-of ways, to play, goddamit, to learn to work together.[87]

Motherhood, for Shulman and many other feminists, directed women's energy and nurturing capacity towards children and away from each other and the feminist revolution; the choice to reject it was central to her understanding of lesbian feminism.

Such debates impacted on individual women's decisions about motherhood. Barbara Wishart, an activist in Melbourne in the 1970s, claimed in 1982 that, for much of the preceding decade:

> The enthusiastic rejection of stereotype femininity threw the baby (and the mother) out with the dirty bathwater, and we entered into an anti-motherhood phase which seems to have lasted some seven or eight years. During this time motherhood was out. Mothers felt unsupported by the women's movement, child care became an unimportant goal, feminists who chose to have children were criticised for seeking personal solutions or letting down the cause and being ideologically unsound, and the lively debate about the experience of motherhood and the care of children which characterised the first few years disappeared, replaced by other issues seemingly more important and more radical.[88]

As a young lesbian, Barbara therefore 'tacitly accept[ed] an ideology which seemed to be saying that motherhood could not be an acceptable part of any self-respecting feminist's vision of liberation, for wasn't this after all one of the key ways men had oppressed and controlled women in the first place?' Those women who already had children, she suggested, 'had to cope by themselves as best they could with all the conflicting feelings about their own mothering raised by the feminist critique of women's traditional roles' and many simply left the movement.[89] Janet Ree similarly claimed that many of the early demands of the British Women's Liberation Movement 'sprang from … beliefs that mothering oppressed women – and children too'.[90] She vividly recalled eagerly attending a meeting of her local women's group in Arsenal, a few days after giving birth to her daughter, excited to see her friends and share her experience:

> I arrived, late, at the meeting. Nobody looked up. I sat down, and I realised nobody was going to say anything to me about having Becky. I couldn't believe it, because these were good friends. After about three quarters of an hour, when nobody had said anything to me at all, I found myself crying, tears dropping onto the page, and I got up and went home.[91]

Her friends' failure to resolve the tension between a theoretical questioning of motherhood as a social ideal and her individual experience and need for emotional support engendered a sense of isolation which many other feminist mothers also described.

If mothering in general tended to be downplayed in feminist circles, lesbian motherhood was still regarded by many British and Australian feminists as impossible for much of the 1970s. When Australian feminist journal, *Scarlet Woman*, interviewed three lesbian mothers for their lesbian special issue in 1976, the women all commented that feminists typically assumed that they could not be mothers and lesbians. Chris referred to 'the confrontations you get with people who say, "you've got a kid, but you're a lesbian!" They can't think of that together.'[92] Pauline recalled, 'Someone said I must be bisexual because I've had a child I couldn't possibly be lesbian.'[93] Barbara Wishart also found that motherhood was considered both politically incorrect and impossible for a lesbian feminist in 1970s Melbourne. She explained:

> I had ... started having relationships with women, and in coming to terms with my lesbian identity and lifestyle the possibility of having a child or of acknowledging publicly that I still had a longing to have a child, seemed even more remote ... [M]any of us in those days, on the surface at least, accepted the prevailing patriarchal definition of a lesbian as a woman who did not want, did not have, perhaps even did not like children – one who chose a life not only largely independent from men but also free of children and maternal responsibilities and therefore it was painfully difficult to confront the question of having a child for this meant questioning your sexuality (was I a *real* lesbian if I wanted a child?)'[94]

The question of whether or not it was appropriate to parent a boy child was the focus of particularly heated debate in some feminist circles. The influence of separatist practices on feminist communities in Britain and Australia meant that investing love and energy into men (of any age) was widely regarded as problematic and the widespread use of women-only spaces for lesbian activism and socializing created difficulties for the mothers of boys. Katinka Strom articulated this argument forcefully in her letter to *Gossip* in 1986:

> I am alarmed and sickened by the thought of lesbians being burdened with boys/men, forced into taking care of and nurturing their oppressors once again, men/boys filling the lesbian community, and the danger this presents to girls (incest, verbal and physical violence, boys taking all energy and attention) and mothers. What happens to girls' rights, to women-only space, etc. if many lesbians have become loyal to boys instead?[95]

A small number of women were motivated by separatist ideological perspectives to relinquish existing sons, while a preference to conceive a girl was much more widely expressed. P&J from Wales, who in 1974 responded with delight to the news that a Sappho member had given birth to a baby boy and told readers about their three-month-old son, concluded: 'I was even more reassured when I knew that their baby was a boy too. (My partner reminds me he is a person first and a boy second.)'[96] In 1984, Jessica Wood responded to Sheila Shulman's critique of lesbian motherhood with a defence of the practice, explaining why she was 'seriously considering it' herself. In her imaginary picture of her own life with a baby in it, she claimed: 'I still feel I've enough time to have a baby and I don't see why she won't get in the way of absolutely everything I do ... Of course ... I do find myself assuming that out of lesbian wombs come girls. Mmmmm.'[97] Strategies for selecting the sex of a baby were widely discussed in British and Australian feminist debates on motherhood from the 1970s to the 1990s and Janet Dixon voiced the experience of a number of would-be mothers when she recalled: 'Although I did what I could to try to conceive a girl, I couldn't be sure that I had.'[98]

Despite feminist critiques of motherhood, by the late 1970s, some women in lesbian feminist circles in both Australia and Britain began to consider the ideological and practical possibility of conceiving children as lesbians. The issue of how to ensure the continuity of feminist communities into the future had been a point of discussion in some separatist communities in the United States and elsewhere throughout the 1970s. Greta Rensenbrink has traced the development of an interest in parthenogenesis in US lesbian feminist communities through the 1970s and early 1980s.[99] Scientific interest in the possibility of spontaneous human conception as a result of an ovum splitting, rather than through impregnation by sperm, emerged in the 1950s alongside the development of reproductive technologies. The possibility of women conceiving and raising children independently of men appealed to a number of lesbian feminists in the early 1970s, who were excited by the potential of scientific research in this area, but feminist critiques of science soon rendered the idea of parthenogenesis problematic. In the later 1970s, following the emergence of cultural feminism and a growing enthusiasm for building a lesbian separatist culture, parthenogenesis – as a method of ensuring the reproduction of daughters without male involvement – had renewed appeal. While increasingly suspicious of reproductive technologies and science more broadly as instruments of the patriarchy, Rensenbrink argues that some lesbian feminists adopted core scientific ideas such as the theory that spontaneous conception could be triggered by a physical shock and merged them with feminist and mystical concepts of women's bodies and culture. Such ideas were debated and shared in the United States through publications such as the periodical, *Daughter Visions*, but reached a wider audience, including readers in Britain, where they fed into a growing perception that feminist lesbians could contemplate parenthood.[100] Separatist communities provided an ideal space for imagining and attempting to realize these visions as proponents of parthenogenesis emphasized the importance of purifying the would-be mother's body of the poisons of patriarchal culture, as well as the catalytic effect of shared female energy and rituals in inducing conception. Few women seriously attempted parthenogenesis, however and, by the mid-1980s, the failure of attempts to develop a clear understanding of how to perform parthenogenesis in practice led to disillusionment with the idea. While women increasingly turned to alternative means of conception, debates about parthenogenesis had contributed to opening up a space for discussion of lesbian motherhood.

Casual heterosexual encounters

Many women in this period took the decision that, despite their pre-existing self-identification as lesbians, the only viable way in which they could conceive a child was through heterosexual intercourse. Janet Dixon, a London-based lesbian separatist in the early 1970s, reflected:

> In the spring of 1976 I decided to act on a need I had felt for a very long time. I wanted a child. By June, after one attempt at conception, I was pregnant. (This, in the days before widespread artificial insemination, meant a public climb down from separatism.) My separatist friends said I was selling out, and taking on the role of mother was just doing what the patriarchy had trained me for. In any case they would never sanction sex with a man for whatever reason, not to mention

taking the risk of giving birth to a male child. Women who I had attacked for bringing up boy children wanted to know if it had been an immaculate conception or simply parthenogenesis, and what was I going to do with it if it were a boy?[101]

Janet's account focused on the political implications of her decision both to have sex with a man and to conceive a child and highlighted the impact this had on her social and support networks. In Janet's white, lesbian separatist circles, heterosex was ideologically condemned, but other lesbians considered it preferable to insemination. In her write-up of the Lesbian Mothers' Conference, held in Leeds in 1986, Angela reported that, of the nine women who attended the workshop for Black/Women of Colour lesbian mothers, five mothers and two would-be mothers 'said that they would sleep with a man in order to have a child. The reasons given for this were because we felt that AID was an unnatural way of having children, and also felt it would be unfair on the children, who may react badly to being told they were produced in this way'.[102]

Other women described the experience as emotionally difficult on an individual level. Both Lucy and Ann, who recounted their experiences in a pamphlet produced by the London Feminist Self Insemination Group, had initially decided to try to conceive by means of a casual sexual encounter with a stranger. However, they each claimed to have found this process to be much more emotionally demanding than they had anticipated. Lucy recalled:

> The actual mechanics of getting pregnant I never really considered. I would meet someone in a bar, sleep with him once, emerge unscathed and that would be that ... In fact, I got pregnant in much the same way as I fantasised. It wasn't quite so painless. The picking up of the men was degrading. For a while no one paid me the slightest attention and I remembered how when I was younger, I had felt ugly and inadequate if a man didn't find me attractive, and beautiful only if he did. That evening I had to keep rushing into the toilets to check in the mirror that I still did like the way I looked; to check that I still did 'exist'.[103]

Ann also envisaged a quick and painless process but found the reality much more emotionally difficult and abandoned the attempt after one cycle. She recalled:

> I began trying to get pregnant in August 1978. I went to bars, clubs, the British Museum, a punk rock concert, art galleries and to Piccadilly Circus. I even sat through a meeting on the crisis in British capitalism. Sometimes I went on my own, sometimes with Lucy. But everywhere it was impossible to fulfil my fantasies of a cool, quick pick-up. I had sex with three men – and left another in bed, fearing he was going to stick his very sharp knife in me because he was unable to get an erection. The physical sex was painful, unpleasant and degrading and so was the selling myself beforehand.
>
> I became an emotional wreck and by the time I decided ovulation must be over, I was in tiny pieces. I burst into tears whenever I thought about it; it felt like an eternal punishment. And at the end of the month when my period came, I knew that I couldn't go through all that again.[104]

Not all conceptions by heterosex were planned in the ways these accounts suggest, however. Many women moved between lesbian and heterosexual relationships and sexual encounters for considerable periods of their lives and even those who identified as lesbian and whose relationships were almost entirely with other women occasionally had sexual encounters or affairs with men. Chloe, who had identified as a lesbian since moving to Queensland in the mid-1960s, had a brief sexual affair with a male doctor in Sydney in the early 1970s, which resulted in her pregnancy. She recalled that she had been working as a nurse and living with a friend who was undergoing transition to become a woman when the affair took place:

> I think what happened, looking back, I was … 27, 28 years old – it's illogical, but a Saturn Return. It's a big change period in your life – Saturn Return, 28. I think that because I was living with my friend who was taking oestrogen – to keep her boobs and to be a woman – I think that oestrogen [which] was just floating in the air around the whole house affected me and I had a fling for three weeks with a doctor which ended up with me being pregnant …
>
> I was never going to have children. I [had] already been a lesbian for years. I was never going to have kids … I didn't want to bring another child into this dreadful world … and I wasn't interested in kids. But I did, I did have this fling with a doctor who I worked with. I liked him because he was very democratic. He was different from the others. He was a pretty down to earth sort of fellow and I liked him … He used to flirt with me, which very few men ever did because I looked so obviously like a dyke. Anyway, one day when we were all too drunk, I said, are you all talk or is there any action in your flirting? So I ended up pregnant and I went to have an abortion [but] they were so horrible to me. They were so judgemental and awful I didn't follow through.[105]

The number and variety of explanations Chloe gave in her account of her heterosexual affair and subsequent pregnancy point to the difficulty she experienced in fitting this aspect of her life story into her narrative of lesbian feminist identity and sense of gendered selfhood. Others, however, described casual heterosexual encounters in ways which suggested a more fluid sense of lesbian identity. In 1978, lesbian couple, Lesley and Christine, told the *Liverpool Echo* that their two sons, Jamie and Peter, had been born as a result of 'casual relationships' Lesley had had with men in her early 20s. Now that the boys were eight and six years old, Christine was considering conceiving a baby by AI.[106]

While AID was typically framed as a planned choice for motherhood, class and racial assumptions often underpinned the ways in which heterosex as a form of conception was interpreted by others. In her account of Lesley and Christine's experience, journalist Anne Robinson implied that class differences between the two women had shaped their different patterns of sexual behaviour and approaches to conception. 'Extrovert' Lesley, she claimed, who had conceived the boys by 'two different fathers, whom the children had never known', had been 'on the dole, living in a grotty bedsit with a one-year-old baby and a three-year-old' when she met Christine. Robinson reported that Lesley had been aware of her same-sex desires from the age of twelve and had a sexual affair with a 'much older woman' at fifteen before the casual heterosexual relationships which led to her pregnancies took place. Christine, by contrast, was described as being 'from a middle-class background' with 'happily married' parents; 'much quieter [and] far less self-assured' than Lesley, began sexual relationships at a much later age and found the idea of sex with a man abhorrent.[107] Lesley's conceptions by heterosex were implicitly presented as unplanned and irresponsible acts, evidence of a lack of self-control, while Christine's decision to utilize AID was linked to her middle-class upbringing, sexual continence and stable family background. Attitudes to race also shaped reactions to conceptions by heterosex. When Betty's affair with an Indigenous man in NSW resulted in her pregnancy in 1970, she found that the hostile responses of those around her were shaped by their attitudes towards her as an Indigenous woman. After studying at a missionary training college and then working as a nurse, Betty had found support from the Salvation Army and some white foster parents, but all rejected her when she fell pregnant. Like many Indigenous women in her situation during the period of the Stolen Generations, Betty found that when she sought refuge in an unmarried mothers' hostel, the Matron pressured her to give up her baby for adoption and tried to coerce her into giving her baby to white adoptive parents. Escaping from the hostel before her due date, she was obliged to undergo intrusive questioning about her sexual experiences from a male Welfare Officer in the Child Welfare Department in order to obtain social welfare.[108] Long-standing cultural stereotypes which framed working-class and women of colour as sexually promiscuous impacted on the ways in which some women's routes into pregnancy were interpreted by others, reinforcing a hierarchy between white, middle-class lesbians who 'chose' motherhood through planned artificial or self-insemination and working-class or women of colour whose 'unplanned' pregnancies through heterosex were read as evidence of immorality or irresponsibility. This was apparent in press coverage of a lesbian couple from Manchester who featured repeatedly in the British media in the early 1990s as they married, conceived a child, sought joint residence through the courts and ultimately broke up. Much of the coverage framed the two women as irresponsible parents, emphasizing the youth and unemployed status of both women, the birth mother's pre-existing two children and the fact that the biological father of their child (conceived by heterosex) was serving a prison sentence. The women pushed back against this narrative, however, drawing on the discourse of a wanted child to claim: 'We planned the baby and we had a stable relationship so I thought it would be easy to get legal recognition.'[109]

As awareness of the risks of HIV transmission increased in the early 1980s, many women began to regard casual heterosex as an unacceptably dangerous route into conception. In her account of the journey she and her partner, Louise Wakeling, went on to conceive a child together in the 1980s, Margaret Bradstock mapped the impact of a growing awareness of AIDS. When the couple first considered the possibility in the late 1970s, Bradstock recalled that, in their Sydney circles, 'at that stage heterosexual copulation was the only known way to get a baby'. The couple delayed until the youngest of Margaret's three children from a previous heterosexual marriage had reached high school and then, in 1983, decided that Louise would attempt to conceive by a casual heterosexual encounter. Margaret recalled:

> In 1983 we went on holiday to Bali with the girls, now aged fifteen and nineteen, and the plan was that Louise should have a brief 'affair' with someone cute and come back pregnant. (Yes, the girls were in on the act, and approved). A lot of time was spent spotting potential fathers, and she finally decided on one who was pursuing her avidly at Sanih Beach ... So, she encouraged him. Unfortunately, by the time he plucked up the courage to come calling, Louise was in the throes of an attack of 'Bali Belly' and nearly threw up in his face as he hovered uncertainly on the doorstep. That was the end of that.[110]

The potential risks of HIV infection do not appear to have occurred to Margaret or Louise at this point, but not long after, they were confronted with the dangers. They began to hear about other lesbians conceiving through self-insemination, using a pool of donors, and decided to try this method. Three potential donors were selected, but the women only proceeded with two of them. As Margaret explained:

> We finally ended up with Paul and Gary, and another willing donor whom, fortuitously as it turned out, I fought bitterly with over other issues so that his contribution to the scheme was abandoned. Fortuitous because he had AIDS at the time and no one knew, though I think he was beginning to suspect. Some ten months later, he was dead. Had we gone ahead with his donation, Louise would probably be dead now too, not to mention the baby. I regret the quarrel, but maybe it was fated.[111]

Margaret's account implies that, although the impact of AIDS was beginning to be felt in the gay male community from which they drew their pool of donors, they may not have discussed the issue with their donors or taken any precautions. By 1993, however, when Prue Borthwick and Barbara Bloch published their booklet on lesbian parenting in Australia, they were explicitly advising lesbians who wished to get pregnant to consider the risks of HIV transmission and to avoid casual heterosexual encounters as a method of conception for this reason:

> [N]one of us should give in to the idea that it might be easier to go to the pub and pick up a good looking stranger. As all the research into HIV/AIDS prevention tells us, it is impossible to work out whether someone is infected with the HIV virus, simply by looking at them or asking about their sexual history. This is why straight and gay people everywhere are encouraged to have only safe sex unless they are absolutely certain that their partner is not infected. It's well to remember that what is needed for conception is the exact opposite of safe sex.[112]

The AIDS Council of NSW, while acknowledging the possibility that some lesbians might conceive through sex with a man, focused on 'alternative insemination' as a route into pregnancy and framed clinics as the safest option in the context of AIDS.[113]

Self-insemination

Self-insemination began to be discussed as a route into lesbian motherhood in Britain and Australia in the late 1970s, although there is some evidence of women using this technique earlier in the decade. In London, the Feminist Self Insemination Group was established in October 1978 when a small group of lesbian feminists who wished to have children responded to an announcement in the *London Women's Liberation Newsletter*. The women who came together to form the group all shared a lesbian feminist politics and approached the issue from a perspective of wishing to avoid heterosexual intercourse and feeling a level of discomfort with the involvement of medical professionals in the process of conception. Emphasizing 'choice' as a central concern, they described the technique they developed as 'a woman-controlled method of conception' and claimed:

> Self insemination has political significance because it widens the choice women have about how to conceive, and gives women more choice about the type of relationship they have with a biological father. It challenges the idea of biological links as the basis for a relationship between the adult and child. It separates conception and reproduction from a sexual relationship, allowing us the choice to have a child and the freedom to have the sexual relationships we choose.[114]

This conceptualization of self insemination as 'woman-controlled' emerged at a time when the risk of lesbian mothers losing custody of children they had conceived in a heterosexual context was being widely debated in lesbian and feminist circles, as well as in the context of broader feminist discussions of women's reproductive and bodily rights. The perception that lesbian mothers faced considerable risks in relation to the integrity of their families and that women in general were vulnerable to patriarchal social structures which prioritized the rights of men generated a desire to explore means by which women could form family structures independently of men. The emphasis on choice (echoing the language of a woman's right to choose, which was fundamental to developing feminist discourse) also emerged from an incipient discomfort with the involvement of male medical professionals in processes such as AID. By the early 1980s, this had developed into a vocal international movement of radical feminists, who articulated a powerful critique of reproductive technologies, as an attempt by patriarchal doctors and scientists to seize control of reproduction and render women powerless or obsolete. The Feminist International Network of Resistance to Reproductive and Genetic Engineering (FINNRAGE) provided a focal point for activism and some feminists, such as Jalna Hanmer in Britain and Rebecca Albury and Robyn Rowland in Australia, entered into lively debates on the issue in the radical feminist press.[115]

While not necessarily critical of reproductive technologies per se, feminist self insemination networks regarded women's autonomy as central to the process they were exploring. Drawing on their knowledge, contacts and shared experience, the women in London Feminist Self Insemination Group collaborated to determine the best techniques for collecting and transporting sperm and inseminating themselves.

One member of the group, Clare, was a pharmacist and a member of the feminist Women in Science group and the women also read and conducted research into reproductive issues.[116] In around 1980, they produced a booklet, *Self Insemination*, setting out the practical knowledge they had acquired alongside individual women's accounts of their experience. The first of a number of British guides to self-insemination in this period, it was followed in 1987 by Lisa Saffron's book, *Getting Pregnant Our Own Way* and her 1994 book, *Challenging Conceptions: Planning a Family by Self Insemination*.[117] Other networks sprang up around Britain in the early 1980s and Miriam claimed that 'Leeds was one of the first places to have a really strong and organised movement for lesbians to have babies ... my friend was one of the first, I think, to have an AI baby, and I think she had her son in 1984.'[118]

In Australia, Women's Health Centres were a major source of information on self insemination techniques, some of which were producing guidance leaflets by the early 1990s. Although the first Australian book on lesbian parenting and methods of conception was not published until 1993, British and US literature was available through feminist bookstores in the 1980s and relevant information on charting ovulation was produced by the Family Planning Association and the Catholic Church.[119] In January 1981, *Campaign* newspaper reported on the publication of a booklet, *Artificial Insemination – An Alternative Conception*, from San Francisco. Summarizing the contents of the booklet for Australian readers, the author advised that insemination could be carried out using a needleless syringe, a glass eye dropper or a turkey baster (described for the benefit of those unfamiliar with this utensil). Lesbians were advised to collect the sperm in a jar and inseminate within two hours.[120] Self insemination became the most widely practised form of non-traditional conception for lesbians in Australia in the late 1980s and 1990s, when clinic or hospital-based artificial insemination was often difficult or impossible to access and many women preferred the degree of control over the process which self insemination offered. Research carried out with 136 Victorian women for the Lesbian and Gay Families Project, published in 2002, found that 28 per cent of existing parents had conceived by self insemination, as opposed to 52 per cent by heterosexual intercourse.[121]

The insemination techniques adopted by women using this method varied to some extent. Much of the literature focused on the importance of women charting their menstrual cycle and changes in body temperature in order to identify when they were ovulating and therefore most likely to conceive. For a few days around the period of ovulation, women would seek to obtain sperm and inseminate themselves with it. The London Feminist Self Insemination group advised:

> The practicalities are simple. The men ejaculate into a clean, small glass or plastic container a short while before we arrive, or while we wait in another room. We aim to keep the sperm at just below body temperature and the donors often keep the room warm in cold weather for this reason. Then we draw the sperm into a needleless syringe, lie down and put the syringe into our vaginas. In the privacy of the room it was possible to remain lying down for half an hour or so and to think positive and welcoming thoughts about the sperm![122]

In Australia, women often used a diaphragm to assist in the process of inserting and retaining the sperm in the vagina. Maura, a registered nurse who lived in Sydney, took the decision to try to conceive by alternative insemination in 1974 and recalled:

> My problem was mechanical – how to get egg and sperm together. I believed I had the knowledge and personal resources to overcome this mechanical problem. Leichhardt Women's Health Centre told me about using a Dutch Cap (diaphragm) to hold the sperm against the cervix. I adapted their advice to suit my needs and limits of personal dexterity.[123]

The location of the insemination process and the means by which women obtained the sperm on each occasion was largely determined by the decisions women had taken about their intended relationship with the donor. Some women were happy to know and be known by their donors, while others felt strongly that they wished to remain anonymous to the donor and therefore used a go-between to collect the sperm. Others wished the precise donor to remain unknown to all and obtained sperm from a pool of men who would be asked to arrange amongst themselves which of them would make the donation on any particular occasion. The London Self Insemination Group decided that they did not wish to know which donor's sperm had resulted in a pregnancy. A friend of two women in the group had identified a network of gay men who were willing to act as donors and, after an initial meeting to obtain the donors' medical histories and discuss the basis on which the arrangement would proceed, 'they tried to make sure that different men provided the sperm on each day we inseminated ourselves in one month.' The process by which the sperm was collected changed over time:

> At the beginning, meetings to collect sperm were as anonymous as possible, a telephone number to ring, and then 'Karen' would meet 'David' at an agreed place, say, a tube station. Particularly for the women who had not been at the first meetings [with the donors] these times were awkward and anxious. After a very short time the donors suggested we used a room in one of their houses. This was the arrangement that we continued with. It quickly became quite easy to relax in the pleasant rooms we used. We could be completely private and use the sperm in a much shorter space of time than when we had taken it to our own homes.[124]

For other women, carrying out the insemination in the donor's home was not an option, but the journey home was considered too far, so a less private place had to be used. Manja described the process she adopted in the early 1980s, based on her desire to maintain anonymity between herself and the donor. She had decided that she wished to conceive and raise a child collectively with a number of women and all four women therefore embarked on the journey to obtain the sperm. One of the women, Tess, had found the potential donors, but was apparently not familiar with the neighbourhood in which the men lived. Manja described how the four women set out in Tess's van, named Susanne, on an hour-long journey from central Melbourne: 'In the van now, driving out to the extremities of suburbia. Anni is navigating from the newly furnished back of the van, where she sits on cushions with me and the dogs. Iluwka sits in the front seat, keeping company with Tess, who drives.'[125] When the women reached their destination and found the correct house, Manja and Iluwka remained in the van while Tess and Anni went to the house. Recounting the experience, Manja explained: 'Tess is donning her urban guerrilla disguise, she and I have chosen to maintain our anonymity. Anni doesn't care about it, doesn't feel threatened by them at all. "Tess, you look amazing!" She is transformed in her shoulder-length black curly wig and a touch of red lipstick.'[126] Manja was to inseminate herself in the van and, earlier that day, had prepared a suitable environment in the back of the vehicle: 'Curtains hung up on all the windows. The carpet cleaned and piled with cushions. One large potted fern with many out-stretched fronds and a few little ones still furled up into themselves – just like babes in the womb.'[127] When the women returned with the sperm, she drew the curtains and attempted to draw the surprisingly small quantity of white fluid into her syringe. Unable to achieve this, as the syringe was too short for the clean jar she had brought, she finally used her fingers. Insemination completed, the women drank coffee and port in the back of the van, while Manja '[attempted] to do a shoulder stand in the van with my knees bent against the roof.'[128]

Donors

Identifying and negotiating the relationship with a donor was a crucial first step in the self-insemination process. Many women asked male friends to act as donors. British lesbian, Linda, asked her friend, a photographer, and he agreed.[129] Following an unsuccessful attempt to participate in a self-insemination group, another couple, Clare and Linda, asked a number of left-wing, heterosexual friends if their male partners would act as donors.[130] However, as Borthwick and Bloch observed in their Australian book: 'For some lesbians finding a donor can be the hardest part of the self-insemination. Many of us socialise principally with other women.'[131] Personal accounts suggest women often drew on wider friendship networks to identify donors. In 1982, London's *Time Out* magazine reported on the situation of 'would-be lesbian mothers' and described the experience of Patsy, 'a 31-year-old lesbian', who had been introduced to Wang, 'a 20-year-old Oriental' by a mutual lesbian friend for whom Wang had previously acted as a donor. Patsy and Wang met in a West London restaurant to exchange £10 for the sperm (which Wang had produced after retreating to the restaurant toilet for ten minutes).[132] Other women placed or answered advertisements in the gay or alternative press. In April 1993, *Gay Times* carried an advertisement stating: 'Lesbian who wants to have child seeks gay man who wants to be father.'[133] Some men also instigated contact. In 1983, a group of 'radical young men' in Leeds and Bradford advertised their services as sperm donors in the *Lone Plains Drifter*, a newsletter for 'anti-sexist men'.[134] *The Independent* newspaper reported in April 1993 that Peter Tatchell and other men in the activist group, Outrage!, were 'discussing how such introductions [between lesbians and donors] can be effected more formally' and lesbians seeking sperm donors were encouraged to contact them directly.[135]

Many donors during this period were gay or radical men who were either known to the lesbian mothers or to their wider friendship networks. Typically, agreements were made that the donors would not be involved as a parent to the child and, in some cases, would not be known to the child at all. Natalie Barney and her partner, Denise Wilson, told British morning television programme, Good Morning, in 1994 that Natalie had conceived with the help of a gay donor, who was to remain anonymous. 'A friend had pointed him out [at a gay nightclub] as someone who would make "a lovely sperm donor", she said ... A legally binding document between the couple and the gay donor bars him access to the child and prevents them from claiming maintenance payments.'[136] In the 1970s and 1980s, men who acted as donors frequently articulated their decision to do so as a political act.[137] The London Feminist Self Insemination Group framed their donors' attitudes in these terms:

> Their contribution to our self-insemination group came from a strong political motivation, they never wanted to be fathers, but felt that lesbians who wanted to should be able to be parents. On this basis they were contributing to the disempowering of one of the basic rights claimed by patriarchy – that biological fathering gives men power over women and children.[138]

The Melbourne support group for lesbians who wanted to have children, Lesbian Litters, made a similar point in the early 1990s. The members had compiled a list of men willing to donate their sperm and a group member, Claire, noted that only one man on the list had requested involvement with a potential child and most wanted complete anonymity: 'They are doing it because they believe that lesbians should be able to have children if they want to have children, that they don't make any better or worse mothers or parents than anybody else. So they are doing it from a political belief.'[139] Other men made a personal decision to be a donor as an act of friendship to a particular woman. David told *The Guardian* journalist, Heather Welford, in 1994: 'I knew Helen wanted her child to be aware of who its father was and I knew she was happy for me to have some contact with the child after the birth, but this was always her baby, not mine ... I felt that I could support Helen as a friend.'[140] By the 1990s, shifting notions of fatherhood and masculinity and a growing discourse of gay male parenthood resulted in an increasing number of lesbian mothers and donors envisaging a more active role for donors from the outset.[141] Literature on lesbian motherhood encouraged would-be lesbian mothers to reflect carefully and engage in detailed, open discussion with their donors about the roles they each expected to play following the birth of the child, cautioning that feelings and attitudes might change over time. Much of the literature regarding lesbian family formation in this period recognized an (often implicit) desire on the part of would-be lesbian mothers to restrict the legal rights of the donor in response to a pervasive sense of fear at the vulnerability of their family forms to external intervention or threat. In her 1994 book, *Challenging Conceptions*, Lisa Saffron claimed: 'Most women do self-insemination in order not to share parental responsibility with the child's biological father. The possibility of a donor acquiring parental responsibility equal to the mother's and more than that of a co-parent is very threatening' and went on to advise readers on how they could 'protect themselves from [this] risk'.[142]

Nevertheless, some women felt strongly that the involvement of the donor or father in raising the child was important for the child's well-being and development. Marcia Eubank, who was raising her five-year-old son, Marcus, with her partner Claudette Simpson, told black British newspaper, the *Weekly Journal* in 1994:

> I think it is every woman's right to have a child and as long as you can give them a stable environment, the parents' sexuality is not important. The only warning I give other lesbians thinking of having children is to make sure the father has some involvement with the child's upbringing, although I know many who have children strictly on the basis that the father will have no involvement. I don't agree with that; it's not good for the child to isolate the father. Marcus sees his father and he's happy for it.[143]

Sydney lesbian television presenter, Julie McCrossin, made a similar argument in 1998, telling *LOTL*: 'I feel there's some real ethical issues about consciously eliminating a father.'[144]

By the 1990s, a gradual shift had also occurred, both in Britain and Australia, in the attitudes of some gay men, in particular, towards sperm donation. Damien Riggs claimed in 2008:

> Ensuing decades, however, have seen moves toward increasing numbers of gay men focusing upon their own reproductive needs. At the same time, and perhaps not unrelatedly, there has been increased attention paid, both within Australia and internationally, to voices from the ever growing men's movement and its focus upon securing the rights of men as parents. Men's rights groups that emphasise the rights of fathers typically utilise the notion that 'all children need a father' and that men are more than simply sperm donors in order to legitimate their rights claims.[145]

Prevailing legal frameworks around concepts of fatherhood or parenthood as rights (such as access, residency and decision-making) and responsibilities (particularly financial) in the UK and different states in Australia impacted on these decisions. Throughout the period, laws regarding fertility treatment in all Australian states assumed that women users of these services would be heterosexual and therefore recognized the husband or male de facto partner of the woman as the legal father, rather than the donor. A similar situation applied to clinic-based insemination in the UK but, under the Children Act 1989, donors outside of a clinic setting could apply to the courts for parental responsibility for a child and, under the Child Support Act 1993, could be required to pay child maintenance.

Many women suggested that choices regarding donors were based initially on availability of men willing to accept the role, followed by discussions around medical background. However, the physical profile of donors was also a factor for some women. In their 1993 book, Borthwick and Bloch suggested that, in contrast to clinic-based insemination, where the donor pool was often limited to medical students who were likely to be from Anglo backgrounds, self-insemination gave women the opportunity to 'select someone on their known characteristics such as looks and personality'.[146] Quoted in their book, Kristin, a health worker in a community health centre, commented: 'Some women want a donor that looks a bit like them or is taller and has the same colour eyes and same colour hair. I guess if you want those things in a donor that's okay.'[147] The London Self Insemination group, in contrast, acknowledged that unexamined assumptions about race may have shaped their attitudes towards donors. The group informed readers of their pamphlet that 'we are all white, middle-class lesbian-feminists' and that 'Our group of donors were all white'. Reflecting on the implications of this, they noted: 'We do not know if any of their black friends considered being donors. We did not at that time think through the implications of having black donors, as we were not presented with the possibility. We acknowledge that this lack of thought is in itself a covert form of racism.' One member of the group had apparently asked for a 'white donor' on the grounds that 'she didn't feel she could assure her ability to present another cultural background', amongst other issues. The pamphlet proposed further debate with black feminists on this issue and quoted a Puerto Rican feminist who had challenged this line of argument on the basis that many lesbian mothers lived in 'Third World neighbourhoods' where they were surrounded by different cultures.[148] However, some would-be lesbian mothers who sought black donors noted a difficulty in finding men willing to donate sperm. Pat noted that there were no black men in the donor group she knew and that BPAS only had three men of colour on their donor list, who were heavily in demand. As black lesbians who strongly wanted black donors, she and a friend contacted a black gay men's group at Gay's the Word bookshop in London and recalled: 'They had a big meeting about it, but they said no way. They thought it was disgusting that we had the nerve to ask them to be donors.'[149] The impact of historic racism and cultural assumptions of 'whiteness' could also result in the erasure of donors' ethnicity. Linda described how, many decades after she and her partner had conceived three children by self insemination, her family had discovered that one of their donors had Indigenous heritage. The donor's own mother had (unbeknownst to him) been a member of the Stolen Generations and had been taken from her Indigenous community to be raised by adoptive parents as a white child. When her Indigenous family attended her funeral, he was made aware of his family history and passed this information on to the children conceived using his donor sperm.[150]

Fostering and adoption

Many of the narratives which characterized debates about lesbian motherhood from the 1970s to the 1990s were reproduced or given new inflections in discussions of whether lesbians should foster or adopt children. Although adoption was not officially open to lesbian couples in this period, there is evidence of some unmarried women who managed to adopt. When Katharine wrote to her parents in the early 1970s to inform them that she was having a baby with her female partner, the correspondence referenced two women, 'Miss P- and Miss C-', who had adopted two boys and a girl together in Canberra during Katharine's childhood.[151] The Adoption Act 1958 (UK) and the Adoption of Children Act 1958 (Australia) allowed applications from married couples or single people, thereby enabling unmarried women to apply individually. From the 1970s, British and Australian lesbians began to advocate for change to enable joint applications from unmarried (lesbian) couples. In November 1972, Australian lesbians, Caroline Ainsley and Madeline Peterson, sent an open letter to sexologist Frank Caprio, responding to his recent book, *The Lesbian*. Complaining that he provided a misrepresentative image of lesbians, focused on a 'minority of a minority', they suggested that, if he wished to explore permissiveness and sensationalism, he should look to heterosexual relationships. Long-term, committed lesbian couples, they argued, would in the future provide a solution to the problems caused by the 'perversities, deviations and the unchaste actualities of today's heterosexual norms':

> Many orphaned, neglected, battered children already, or yet to be, brought to existence, can and shall we vow, one day find every form of social welfare, discipline, freedom of religious persuasion, and tutored upbringing, in most lesbian homes! Homes, sir, that are no less equivalent in value, warmth nor security and love, than any heterosexually-founded homes today![152]

Their argument made explicit a suggestion which was implicit in many of the claims made by advocates of lesbian motherhood in the British press in the 1970s: that in a moral hierarchy which demonized casual relationships, extra-marital pregnancy and certain forms of working motherhood, (white, middle-class) lesbian couples might offer a stable and financially secure home which more closely fit social ideals of parenthood. The shift in parenting advice in the 1950s and 1960s towards a child-centred approach, which urged mothers to be guided by their child's individual requirements and to make their interactions with their child fun and stimulating, placed an increased burden on mothers and parents who failed to meet these demands were increasingly accused of risking psychological damage to their child.[153] In this context, a middle-class lesbian couple with the financial resources to offer a child full-time consistent care-giving might appear preferable to a mother with competing demands on her time and attention.

Arguments in favour of lesbian adoption in this period typically relied upon two parallel hierarchies: that of the ideal mother, in which a white, middle-class lesbian mother would sit below that of the married, heterosexual mother, but potentially above the single or working mother, teenage mother, black mother and neglectful or harmful mother; and that of the child, in which children in need of foster care or adoption were ranked by age, race, dis/ability and other criteria. Such assumptions underpinned the repeated suggestion in the British lesbian press in the 1970s that lesbians should be allowed to adopt 'difficult to place' children. In February 1973, *Sappho* reported on a recent Campaign for Homosexual Equality (CHE) forum called 'New Ghettos for Old? The homophile movement in a straight society', in which panellists had discussed gay parenting. Lesbian author, Maureen Duffy, had advocated lesbian adoption, arguing that many homosexual couples wanted to adopt and had no 'hostility towards children', but Chad Vara of the Samaritans had countered that there weren't enough children available for adoption as there was high demand for babies. In response, *Sappho* claimed, Duffy: 'shot back she didn't mean white skinned, blue-eyed parent-matching babies, but older children inurred [sic] in institutions up and down the country.'[154] Her implicit suggestion that white babies were considered 'ideal' candidates for adoption and were therefore quickly placed with 'ideal' married, white parents were echoed by a correspondent to *Sappho* in the same issue. GRB from East Sussex claimed:

> Certainly, I can see no reason why [lesbian] couples, if their relationship is sufficiently stable, should be prohibited from bringing up a family. It seems particularly relevant to bring up the question of handicapped, half-caste and other 'difficult to place' children. Gay couples who have overcome the problems besetting a socially unacceptable minority group, to make a lasting, stable relationship, would be particularly well equipped to look after these children – having far more understanding, from their personal experience to help them cope with their own difficulties.[155]

In staking a claim for lesbians' aptness to parent socially marginalized children, such advocates implicitly drew on narrative tropes about the 'wanted' child. Language such as 'difficult to place' framed disabled and black children as 'unwanted' and positioned white, middle-class lesbian couples as a solution to the social problem these children apparently posed. The wider structural context – in which racist attitudes towards black mothers made them vulnerable to having their children taken away from them and lack of financial and social support forced many single mothers to relinquish their children – was not acknowledged.

Such arguments were framed in a context in which many individual social workers and adoption agencies were resistant to placing children with lesbian and gay parents. When Sappho held their November 1972 meeting on routes into motherhood, adoption and fostering were chosen as one of the three possible options to consider. The report on the meeting, published subsequently in *Sappho* magazine, indicates that much of the discussion focused on the attitudes of adoption agencies towards lesbian applicants, which were assumed to be a significant hurdle in achieving lesbian adoption. The Sappho Public Relations officer had contacted several adoption agencies to invite them to attend the meeting but '[t]heir disgusted refusals broke her nerve.'[156] This seemed to exemplify the attitudes of agencies and a number of members of the group reinforced this from their own experience. One couple, who had adopted an older child, criticized the attitudes they had encountered from agencies and another woman reported: 'Two girls I know in this country, one French and one English, tried many adoption societies in England and France and got nowhere.' Ultimately, these women had successfully adopted two Indian children through an international adoption society.[157] The hostility of agencies was explained by one participant in the discussion as a result of religious belief, observing: 'Most Adoption Agencies are church dominated and the churches promote the belief that homosexuals are corrupters of children.'[158] Religious faith was also a barrier to lesbian adoption in Australia, where adoption was typically administered by a combination of state and private organizations, including

Christian groups such as Barnado's. In 1989, a dispute arose in Melbourne when four social workers resigned from North West Foster Care agency in Brunswick, run by the Anglican Church, in protest at the organization's decision to adopt more stringent screening of gay applicants. The CEO of the agency claimed that its religious ethos had helped shape this policy decision, noting: 'The Anglican church has traditionally supported the sanctity of marriage between a man and a woman and not promoted homosexuality as a preferred option. We have to bear this in mind.'[159]

Concerns about the stability of lesbian relationships may also have been a factor in the attitudes of agencies. At the 1972 Sappho meeting, the adoption group's discussion of the 'rigidity of questions' asked by societies focused in some detail on the question of the desired length of relationship between a couple to demonstrate their ability to give children a stable home.[160] This issue came up repeatedly in letters to *Sappho* which were published in the eighteen months following the meeting report. In May 1973, S.W. from London, a 'gay social worker', outlined the various reasons they strongly objected to adoption by gay couples, which included the risk to the children of being known by their peers to have 'different' parents; the lack of heterosexual and appropriately gendered role models and being placed 'in a potentially stressful position which has a far greater likelihood of breakdown of the parental relationship'.[161] D.C., who wrote in in March 1974, describing her and her partner's attempts to adopt, encountered a similar attitude from Westminster City Council, to whom they had submitted a long-term fostering application two years previously. She explained that, although the first social worker they met had been unconcerned by the fact that they were two women, problems had emerged when their case was referred to the wider committee. Summarizing the arguments made on each side, D.C. noted that the social worker had reported back:

> 'The Committee has decided such a relationship is not stable.' We asked if any enquiries had been made into our friendship, e.g. asking the referees how long we'd known each other (eight years), whether we appeared likely to split up etc?
>
> Oh no, such a relationship is not stable.
>
> What could we do with such uncomprehending opposition? She told us of all the supposed advantages of a child remaining in a Home ... and informed us that no other London Council would consider us. All of this without the notion of lesbianism ever being mentioned! We have a modern flat approved for child minding purposes. We have a mortgage which must indicate, at least, an intention of staying together. One of us works at home so the child need never be unattended or farmed out unless one of us became gravely ill or died. We were reasonably young (27) but not too young not to know our own minds. Neither of us saw herself as a pretend father with the resultant confusion for the child. The only objection – or at least the only one given – was that we were two women.'[162]

As this account suggests, the possibility of being approved for fostering or adoption as a lesbian or lesbian couple varied, according to the views of individual social workers and adoption panels, and the policies of agencies. Some social workers were clearly strongly opposed to lesbian fostering and adoption, such as S.W. from London, noted above, while others took a more pragmatic approach of evaluating lesbians on a case-by-case basis without explicitly acknowledging their sexuality. Tensions occasionally arose between social workers and members of adoption panels or agency directors, when placements initially approved on a case basis by individual social workers were vetoed by panels on the grounds of principle. There is evidence, however, that lesbians were sometimes able to foster and adopt children as single applicants at least from the 1970s, assisted by an informal 'don't ask, don't tell' policy operated by some social workers and agencies. Judith Weeks told the *Daily Telegraph* in 1993 that, alongside her partner, Pat Romans, she had fostered fifty-two children and adopted one between the mid-1970s and mid-1990s. She had initially worked in childcare in Plymouth, with responsibility for fostering out children, and claimed that, as a social worker: 'She would often foster children to single women, with no thought of whether or not they were lesbian, "simply whether they were good." Nor was it an issue when she first applied to foster children herself. "Nobody talked about, or thought much about, lesbianism then."' When Judith applied to adopt her daughter, Katie, her lesbianism was again disregarded in the application process. Judith had already provided foster care to Katie but, when she was a year old, Judith wrote to Katie's birth mother and offered to adopt her: 'I said that if she stayed with us she obviously wouldn't have a father, and that must be considered, but that no one could love her more.' The mother telephoned her agreement the next day. Judith recalled: 'Every time the social worker came we were prepared for her to ask us about our relationship, but she never did. I'm sure she knew. In the way that all social workers who had placed children with us knew, but never mentioned it.'[163]

Wider attitudes towards lesbian and gay adoption fluctuated throughout the period. In October 1989, Virginia Chadwick, NSW Minister of Family and Community Services, announced that applications to foster would no longer be accepted from lesbians and gay men on the grounds that they could not provide children with a positive role model, overturning the situation under a previous state Labor government, in which a number of gay men and lesbians had successfully applied to be foster parents.[164] Helen Campbell, solicitor for the Women's Legal Resources Centre in Sydney, claimed in 1991 that 'applicants for fostering or adoption of children face very extensive "suitability testing". Gay and lesbian applicants at present face overwhelming discrimination and have virtually no chance of being considered on their merits.'[165] The Lesbian and Gay Foster and Adoptive Parents group was founded in response to Virginia Chadwick's 1989 announcement and, supported by the Anti-Discrimination Board and the Lesbian and Gay Rights Lobby, lobbied on issues relating to lesbian and gay fostering and adoption through this period.[166] In the UK, lesbian and gay fostering and adoption became a flashpoint for tensions between Labour local councils and right-wing politicians and media from the mid-1980s to the mid-1990s. In 1985, Hackney borough council sparked a lively debate in the local media when they commissioned and considered a report on whether they should encourage fostering and adoption applications from lesbians and gay men as part of wider policy attempts to end discrimination against lesbians and gay men in the borough.[167] Other London boroughs, including Lewisham and Ealing, similarly moved to allow lesbian and gay fostering and adoption, while, in November 1986, Birmingham announced plans to allow lesbians to act as foster parents as part of a charter for female rights.[168]

In the early 1990s, gay fostering was the focus of intensified adverse media attention, which revealed and exacerbated tensions within councils' social services departments.[169] Following negative media coverage of a decision by Wandsworth Social Services to place an eighteen-year-old boy, 'suspected of prostitution', in the care of a homosexual couple, the Director, Mike Rundle, sent a memo to all staff stating that applications from gay and lesbian candidates should 'not be entertained'. Local government union, Nalgo, challenged the suggestion that gay men and lesbians should be disqualified as potential foster parents and threatened to take strike action over the issue.[170] In December 1992, Hampshire County Council told journalists, reporting on the fact that they were considering a fostering application from an openly lesbian couple, that none of their eight hundred current foster carers were lesbian or gay.[171] The lesbian couple, whose application to foster under-fives was under consideration, had been encouraged by social workers, but when the case was referred to Hampshire County Council, their application was rejected. A spokesman for the council claimed that they had not been rejected due to their lesbianism, but a Labour Party councillor, advocating for the couple, claimed the minutes of a committee meeting suggested otherwise.[172]

During the 1980s and 1990s, the impact of lesbian claims that certain lesbian parents might be suitable carers for 'difficult to place' children began to be reflected in the attitudes of social workers and government agencies. In February 1982, a lesbian couple wrote into the British weekly journal, *Love Affair*, asking if it was possible for them to adopt a child legally and were advised:

> I doubt whether any British adoption society would be prepared to accept a gay couple on their already long waiting list ... However, if you feel you could give a home to a 'special child' – one who, because of handicap or age, isn't so easily adoptable as a little baby – then get in touch with the Association of British Adoption and Fostering Agencies.[173]

Similarly when, in March 1993, a lesbian couple became the first in Australia to openly adopt a child through official channels, it was following their application to adopt a 'special needs' baby. Only one of the women applied to legally adopt the child, as NSW law only allowed heterosexual couples or single people to adopt, however the NSW Department of Community Services were aware that the woman was in a long-term relationship with another woman and put both women through a detailed selection process.[174] In the same year, when a row broke out in Britain over the publication of a government White Paper on adoption, Health Secretary, Virginia Bottomley, justified her decision not to ban gay adoption on the same grounds. The *Daily Telegraph* reported: 'One senior source said Mrs Bottomley had rejected a specific ban because she was unwilling totally to close the door on homosexuals being allowed to adopt severely handicapped or problem children whom no other potential parents would take.'[175] This stark claim demonstrates the extent to which hierarchies of adoptive parents and children in need of placement were gaining traction in the debate over lesbian and gay adoption: although regarded as far from ideal, certain lesbian parents might provide a potential solution to the social problem of 'unwanted' children.

Conclusion

As potential routes into lesbian parenthood shifted, from marriage and motherhood in the 1950s and 1960s, to new possibilities offered by artificial and self-insemination from the 1970s onwards, new discourses of lesbian motherhood emerged. In the post-war decades, lesbianism and motherhood were widely understood to be incompatible and an explicit rejection of motherhood as a choice formed an element of cultural constructions of lesbianism. As the experience of women who sought to leave heterosexual marriages to begin a new life as a lesbian began to be discussed in family law courts in the 1970s, the figure of the 'lesbian mother' gradually emerged. Debates about whether and how lesbians should utilise new reproductive technologies to become mothers outside of the context of heterosexual marriage reframed the narrative trope of 'choice' in the 1970s, with proponents of lesbian motherhood arguing that, for a lesbian, the decision to parent represented a carefully planned choice for a much desired and loved child. Repeatedly recurring both in lesbian constructions of parenthood and wider cultural debate, the discourse of choice and the wanted child relied heavily on notions of white, middle-class, coupled parenthood which implicitly and explicitly reproduced existing hierarchies of class, race and family structure.

6

Parenting

The implications of lesbian parenting, both for the individual children concerned and for society more widely, have been one of the most contested aspects of lesbian experience in the later twentieth century. Both in lesbian and feminist communities and literature and in wider British and Australian society, lesbian motherhood has sparked radically opposed claims. In his study of Australian sexual history, Frank Bongiorno asserts that 'the growing number of lesbians opting for motherhood ... poses a powerful challenge to widely held assumptions concerning gender roles and the naturalness of the patriarchal family'.[1] Barbara Baird concludes that 'the consensus view in the feminist, popular and academic literature by the end of the 1990s' was that 'lesbian families are reinventing the family, redefining family values, and transforming the meaning of parenting'.[2] The ways in which lesbian parent families do and have done this are a point of debate, however. Gillian Dunne argues that planned lesbian families enable the construction of 'more self reflexive, egalitarian' approaches to childcare, while Suzanne Slater claims that the lack of cultural scripts of lesbian motherhood results in lesbian couples negotiating their roles from a 'clean slate'. Sandra Segal-Sklar suggests that as both parents in lesbian parent families are women, their roles and the distribution of power transcend conventional gender divides.

However, much of this analysis is underpinned by an assumption that all lesbian mothers (influenced by feminist and leftist commitments to egalitarianism and anti-capitalism) have sought to challenge existing family models in their own parenting practice and a presumption that gender difference is not a factor in a lesbian relationships. As Jacqui Gabb notes in her work on British lesbian parent families, 'An egalitarian model is not typical of *all* lesbian parent families and contrarieties among lesbian parent families need to be acknowledged as part of family diversity.'[3] Building on Lisa Duggan's notion of homonormativity, Baird has argued that the lesbian mothers who were represented in the Australian mainstream and lesbian press in 2000 were far from radical: they were, in fact, 'affluent lesbian mothers in stable relationships, who would not be a drain on the state, [and] did little to challenge the heteronormative discourses that excluded so many parents in non-normative settings nor those whose sexual identity and parenting arrangements underwent change'. The discourse of lesbian motherhood which had emerged in Australia by the late twentieth century, in Baird's view, 'aligned itself closely with neoliberal and neoconservative versions of the good citizen'.[4]

This chapter will explore the experiences of a wide variety of lesbian mothers raising children across the second half of the twentieth century. As Gabb and Baird's insights suggest, British and Australian lesbian mothers were not a homogenous group in this period: each individual parent brought a different set of attitudes and experiences to their role; class, race, regional and gendered identities, educational background and socio-economic circumstances all shaped women's notions and practice of parenting, while the absence of lesbian mother role models for most, if not all of this period meant that women who took on lesbian parenting often did so in isolation and in a spirit of treading new ground. As a result, lesbian parenting practices varied enormously, from the experiences of some urban lesbian feminists in the 1980s who aimed to radically reinvent notions of the family and gender, to those of some married lesbian mothers who believed the heterosexual nuclear family represented the best environment in which to raise their child. Nevertheless, no one parented in a cultural vacuum. Deeply embedded, if elastic, notions of the ideal nuclear family shaped the ways in which lesbians understood their parenting throughout this period, acting as an explicit or implicit framework or providing a model they wished to contest. Tracing the ways in which approaches towards and attitudes about lesbian parenting shifted through this period, this chapter will demonstrate how the nuclear family model was not only interwoven with, but also radically changed by, cultural debates about lesbian parent families from the 1970s to the 1990s.

Post-war discourses of parenting and child development

In 1973, Dr Clair Isbister, Consultant Paediatrician at Sydney's Royal North Shore Hospital, told delegates at the International Council of Women regional conference in Sydney:

> There can be no doubt as I can support with a multitude of references that the most satisfactory arrangements for rearing children are still to have a father and mother committed to their long term care and that love, tenderness, unselfishness, loyalty, and mutual trust and concern for the welfare of others and constructive discipline and self control provide the best environment in which to live.[5]

Her claims drew on a considerable body of psychological and sociological literature which had emerged in the post-war decades, supporting the widely held cultural assumption that mothers were naturally fitted to play the dominant role in childcare, but that fathers were equally necessary in certain key ways. In her study of motherhood in post-war Britain, Angela Davis has claimed that, in the 1950s, 'The ideal mother figure ... was a full-time homemaker dependent upon her breadwinner husband, with two, three or four children, living within a nuclear family' and similar attitudes were promoted by women's magazines and other cultural commentators in Australia.[6] Although rising rates of divorce and the increasing practice of cohabitation impacted on this ideal over the second half of the twentieth century, research suggests that many women in both countries echoed Isbister's view and remained committed to an ideal family consisting of a mother and father and more than one child into the 1970s and beyond. British psychologist John Bowlby's influential work on mother-child attachment had contributed to a gradual shift in concepts of mothering since earlier in the century, emphasizing the importance of the emotional bond between mother and child in addition to the mother's traditional role in the more mundane practical tasks of parenting. His claim that mothers who left their babies and young children with anyone except the father or close relatives endangered their child, helped to shape a growing belief in the psychological importance for children of the close emotional and physical bond between mother and child.[7] As psychoanalyst, Donald Winnicott argued, maternal deprivation could lead to juvenile delinquency and Dolly Smith Wilson has claimed that, in Britain, Winnicott's views were extremely influential in shaping the attitudes of national policy makers and local officials such as magistrates, police officers and social workers towards juvenile crime and working mothers.[8] A 1965 public opinion poll, which found that 80 per cent of respondents believed women with young children should stay at home, suggests that these views also had a significant impact on public attitudes.[9]

The role of the father was less visible in this literature, but he was nevertheless regarded as essential as a support for the mother and a companion and guide for older children. As Isbister explained:

> For the first three years of life mother controls the child's nutrition and the emotional environment. As Bowlby has shown she shows the child the meaning of love in the way she meets his everyday needs and the child needs a constant mother figure if he is to develop normal attachment and the ability to love ... The mother needs a man – a constant male protector and sustainer; does the child need a father? ... [Sir James] Spence showed that though mother was the main factor in preserving her child's health in the first 10 years, father was more significantly related to the adolescent's ability to adjust to society.[10]

While Isbister implied that the need for fathers was open to question in the post-war period, notions of fatherhood had nevertheless shifted and expanded through the twentieth century. Nineteenth and early twentieth-century approaches to fatherhood had emphasized the twin roles of the father as provider and ultimate authority in the family, but the father's role gradually extended in the mid-twentieth century to encompass a psychological role in child development as well. As Laura King has argued in her study of fatherhood and masculinity in mid-twentieth-century Britain, entertaining and guiding children and assisting mothers were increasingly incorporated into concepts of fatherhood.[11] While the continued importance of the provider role meant that men were not expected to be in frequent or constant contact with their children, the father came to be characterized as the 'fun parent', who took pleasure in sharing some part of his leisure time with his children, a role encouraged by popular psychologists. Assisting children with homework and ensuring their moral development were also considered important, building on Victorian notions that religious instruction and the oversight of children's education were the responsibility of the middle-class father.[12]

Child development became an increasing focus of attention in the post-war decades, as the role of the state expanded to intervene more closely in the daily lives of its citizens.[13] In Britain, the establishment of the Welfare State led to the appointment of an army of social welfare professionals, from healthcare professionals and teachers to social workers and child welfare officers, who increasingly monitored and intervened in the home lives and development of children. This attention was particularly directed towards working-class and migrant families, who were the subject of a growing discourse on 'problem families' in the 1950s and 1960s.[14] In Australia, the promotion of an increasingly scientific approach to motherhood resulted in a significant increase in advice aimed towards, and monitoring of, mothers and their children.[15] As both countries worked towards the establishment of a social democratic state, children increasingly came to be regarded as future citizens, whose development into healthy and responsible adults was crucial to the functioning of society. The heterosexual nuclear family was understood to be the only environment in which this development could occur. Concepts of child development in the period up to the 1970s were dominated by two schools of thought – psychoanalysis and social learning theory – both of which emphasized the importance of the nuclear family environment in shaping children's healthy development. Psychoanalytic theories, popularized in Britain by well-known figures such as Winnicott and agony aunt, Clare Raynor, regarded the desire for motherhood as part of the normal psychic development of women and argued that girls unconsciously internalized maternal values and behaviour from their mothers. Social learning theory, proposed in many post-war sociological studies, suggested that girls learned adult female roles in a practical way by observing the work of the women around them and by being praised when they imitated their mothers' behaviour.[16] Both schools of thought therefore considered 'normal' female development to be possible only in an environment in which a mother-figure was present and modelling normative values of heterosexual femininity and motherhood. For boys, both psychoanalytic and social learning theories similarly emphasized the importance of being able to identify with and imitate a same-sex parent in early childhood, rendering the presence of a father or father-figure in the household crucial to the establishment of a masculine gender role.[17]

Despite the strong social and cultural emphasis on the nuclear family as the ideal environment in which to raise children, in reality other familial models existed throughout the post-war period. Tanya Evans has claimed that a lack of statistics and neglect of the subject by historians has meant that 'the numbers of unmarried mothers prior to the 1970s have been seriously underestimated'.[18] In the 1950s and 1960s, the majority of these women were co-habiting with the father or another man or later married. Lower wages for women, the absence of financial support for lone mothers and social disapproval of motherhood outside of marriage, in both Britain and Australia, made it difficult for women to raise children alone and those without the support of fathers or their families were often forced to give children up for adoption.[19] Motherhood was linked to marriage and cultural and social attitudes framed both as women's ultimate role in this period. By the 1970s, attitudes towards working mothers and expectations of marriage were beginning to shift, opening up some new possibilities for reimagining motherhood. Dolly Smith Wilson has suggested that working mothers were challenging child deprivation theories as early as the 1950s in Britain, articulating an alternative discourse which emphasized the benefits to children of a mother's wage, in the form of better nutrition, housing and educational opportunities. In some areas, this was not an insignificant proportion of mothers: by the early 1960s, 42 per cent of women in London with children under 5 were in paid employment outside of the home.[20] Numbers of single parents gradually increased, reaching 19 per cent of all families with children in Britain in 1990 and 15 per cent in Australia.[21] Although no clear statistics exist from this period, a proportion of these numbers would have been lesbian mothers. The absence of a widely understood concept of the 'lesbian mother' meant that many mothers with female lovers or co-parents were assumed to be 'lone mothers' at least until the late 1970s, if not beyond. As attitudes towards unmarried mothers shifted through the period, such assumptions could provide a means for lesbian mothers of escaping censure for defying heterosexual norms or be the cause of more negative evaluations as a parent lacking a stable relationship.

Motherhood and the married lesbian in the post-war decades

The cultural emphasis on the nuclear family shaped the attitudes of many lesbian mothers in the post-war period, impacting on the decisions they took about the environment in which they wanted their children to be raised. As discussed in Chapter 4, the social and economic constraints on women's independence in the 1940s, 1950s and early 1960s, combined with powerful social taboos against lesbianism, meant that women in this era who had married and had children were extremely unlikely to openly express lesbian desires or leave their husbands for a female lover, opting instead to maintain the outward appearance of marital respectability. Although such women left few archival traces, by the 1970s, the gradual opening up of discussion about lesbianism enabled some married lesbian mothers to speak of their experience. Many of these women reinforced wider social attitudes that the nuclear family represented the ideal environment in which to raise children. J.G. from Somerset spoke for a number of her fellow lesbian mothers in 1973 when she wrote to lesbian magazine, *Sappho*, about a television play she had recently watched depicting a wife and mother who fell in love with another woman and considered leaving her family. She declared:

> What was the result? Just what one would expect – that the mother's love proved to be stronger than the sudden new attraction of lesbian love. Speaking as a mother myself, I can only say 'I should hope so too!' Would I be considered unliberated and old fashioned if I suggested that any relationship which breaks up a marriage, and robs a child of its mother and the security of two parents, is wrong and that any woman who embarks on such a course is selfish and unnatural?[22]

Five years later, another *Sappho* correspondent made a similar point, noting that, although she felt a coward in opting to stay married rather than pursue her lesbian desires, 'I comfort myself with the thought that at least [my two children] are leading a lifestyle that society decrees, and that hopefully at some future date will be useful citizens and will thank dear Mum and Dad that they are what society now calls normal.'[23] Both women emphasized their belief in the importance of their role as nurturers of their children and the centrality of the nuclear family to children's development into responsible and well-adjusted citizens. For these women, and many others, this strong sense of duty dictated their decision to remain in a heterosexual marriage as the ideal environment in which to raise their children.

Unmarried lesbian mothers

Despite the cultural emphasis on the nuclear family, however, some women did raise their children either alone or with a female lover in the post-war decades. The need for discretion meant that the women who did so in the 1940s and 1950s left very little historical trace of their experiences, but their existence is recorded in the recollections of a later generation. Correspondence between an Australian lesbian couple, who had conceived a child by AID in the early 1970s, and their parents, provides one such example. The parents of one of the women referred to a family they had known in the 1940s and 1950s in which children had been raised by unmarried women in their local area of Melbourne:

> The only instance we know of children being brought up by two women is the two P-boys, and then the little girl, who was adopted by Miss P- and Miss C-. There has never been the slightest overt indication of lesbianism there, whatever the private relationship is, but the problems both for the two women and for the boys in particular were severe, as you well know.[24]

Their comments suggest that the women maintained a discreet silence regarding the exact nature of their family relationship, but that, in this case, this was not sufficient to deflect either criticism of them as unmarried mothers, or suspicions of their lesbianism. In other cases, however, social attitudes towards families and parenting appear to have been sufficiently flexible to allow some space for alternative family structures. In their summary of the history of lesbian motherhood in Britain written in the late 1980s, Sue Allen and Lynne Harne claimed: 'Growing up in the fifties and sixties … some of us can remember children being brought up by two "aunties", women who we realized later to be lesbians.'[25] The strong belief in women's natural maternal instinct in this period meant that women were typically seen as the ideal carers of children, regardless of their marital status or biological relationship to the child. Andrée recalled that she and her lover, Grace, who ran a kennels together in Essex in the early 1950s, were widely accepted by their local community as two unmarried women who were well-placed to make a variety of contributions to society. One night, Andrée recalled that the local policeman had called unexpectedly at their home with a baby. He had apparently just arrested the baby's mother on a minor charge and needed someone to care for it until the mother had appeared before the magistrate the following day: this pair of respectable, local women seemed an obvious choice, despite their lack of experience of childcare, and he simply left the baby with them until the mother was released and in a position to collect it.[26] The assumptions which accounts such as this reveal suggest that, in some circumstances, women caring for or raising children in situations outside of the nuclear family norm could be accepted, if not regarded as ideal.

Lesbian mothers in the 1950s and 1960s adopted a variety of strategies to deflect potential social disapproval of their family structures. Some couples who lived together with their children presented themselves as friends who, left to raise their children alone after the termination of a marriage, had banded together for mutual support. Others, like Mrs M.D. from Bromley, who had been left with five children after the end of her marriage, established a home with a gay male friend, providing them both with cover for their homosexuality. She explained:

> I was lucky enough to become friendly with a gay boy ten years my junior who has been my helpmate ever since I divorced my husband. Although the eldest children understand the position, as I think they should, we maintain an outward appearance of 'normal' family life for the sake of the children.[27]

Paul Bathurst recalled that his mother concealed her sexuality from him and his younger brother when she left her marriage to move in with her lover, Margaret, in the mid-1960s. He explained: 'I grew up among gay women yet, as my mother held that children don't like being different, I had no idea she was gay.' While this proved an effective strategy with the two boys, who were both under five when their mother moved in with Margaret, the couple nevertheless experienced hostility from neighbours: 'We were … seen as different, though I was too young to notice. Neighbours in our council flats gummed up our front door. The driver of a dumper truck, seeing Margaret's dress and manner [short hair, shirts and ties], mounted the pavement and deliberately drove into her. Her recovery took months.'[28] Others, however, were able to live openly as a couple, without apparent social censure. In 1974, seventeen-year-old S.S. from Devon wrote to *Sappho* to say that she had lived openly, for the past ten years, with her mother and her mother's lover and had not encountered any difficulties. S.S. explained:

> I know when I used to be at school I was sometimes asked by my friends, why did my mother live with a woman who looked like a man? and I used to say that was her way of life, and left it up to them to sort it out for themselves. I have NEVER lost any friends because of this, I have even brought my boyfriends home and they have never packed me up because of my mother and her butch.
>
> The three of us were granted a council flat in Devon knowing what my mother and her friend were.[29]

Her account suggested that both the sexual and gender identities of her mother and her mother's lover had raised comment but she did not feel that this recognition had resulted in any adverse consequences.

Child custody disputes and the nuclear family

In the 1970s and 1980s, cultural assumptions about the nature of the ideal family and the respective roles of mothers and fathers were examined, reproduced and reinforced in the courts in the context of child custody disputes involving lesbian mothers. Reported judgments in both Britain and Australia demonstrate the importance placed by the courts on the heterosexual nuclear family as the ideal environment in which to raise a child. Evaluating the Australian cases to date in 1982, Robyn Plaister concluded:

> The nuclear family situation is looked upon favourably by the courts, and if a man intends to marry soon after divorce his custody application is seen in a positive light. The lesbian mother can be discriminated against because she does not have an adult male in her family environment, which the courts seem to find necessary. Thus, a nuclear family will be preferred to either a single woman or one living with another woman.[30]

Similarly, in Britain, the potential of the father to provide a conventional nuclear family environment, particularly if he had or intended to begin a new heterosexual relationship, was considered a significant benefit by the courts. Ben Griffin argues that the legal concept of the welfare of the child emerged in late nineteenth-century-parliamentary attempts to preserve the principle of paternal authority in the face of growing recognition of the role of mothers and mid to late twentieth-century courts continued to utilize this flexible concept to maintain normative ideas of the family.[31] In 1980, the judge in G v D declared that 'the long term interests of the children would be better served by being brought up in an ordinary household with a father and mother (or mother-substitute) rather than in a household which consisted of two women living together in the way that the mother and (Ms C) were'.[32] Prevailing theories of child development underpinned assumptions that children, and particularly boys, needed to live with a male role model in order to develop conventional gender roles. In a 1976 British case, a psychiatrist called by the husband argued:

> John [the child]'s mother practices statistically abnormal sexual acts which can be looked upon either as a deviation from normal or frankly perverted. I have no evidence before me to state that this environment will not affect John's future emotional and psychological development. In the absence of a father or father-figure, male identification is not possible unless a substitute father is provided and this, within the setting of a homosexual environment, would not be satisfactory.[33]

The judge, in awarding custody to the father, concluded that the boy needed to live with his father in order to 'develop along strong normal masculine lines.'[34] The danger to girls of growing up in a lesbian household, particularly if this was a feminist environment, was also stressed in court rulings. In an early 1970s British case reported by Eleanor Stephens, the mother was accused of 'exposing her children to "an exotic atmosphere in which intellectual opinions expressing themselves as an eagerness for total feminine freedom, sexual and otherwise, will have a marked influence."' The judge denied custody to the mother on the grounds that 'her "passionate interest in the women's liberation movement" was likely to mean that her daughters would grow up with "little or no respect for the ordinary obligations of family life" and "be exposed to propaganda about sexual morality which could expose them to quite extraordinary risks in adolescence"'.[35]

Lesbian mothers involved in custody cases responded to these assumptions in a variety of ways. Some sought to minimize the difference of their home environments from the ideal heterosexual nuclear family, dressing and presenting themselves in accordance with normative notions of femininity, avoiding involvement with feminist or lesbian activism and attempting to raise their children along established gender lines.[36] Others asserted the radical difference and potential advantages of being raised in a lesbian household and affirmed their efforts to challenge normative gender roles in their children.[37] The perceived risk that children of either sex, raised in a lesbian household, might themselves become homosexual was also raised in many cases and this posed a further dilemma for lesbian mothers who were often required to adopt a position on whether they hoped that their children would grow up to be homosexual or heterosexual in adulthood.[38]

Concerns about the impact on children's psychosexual development of witnessing lesbian affection or relationships resulted in the courts indicating a strong view that discretion was necessary to protect the children of lesbian mothers from harm. In roughly half of the reported Australian cases, conditions were imposed upon the mothers' custody or access, prohibiting them from the open expression of their sexuality. In the case of Campbell v Campbell in 1974, Justice Bright awarded custody to the mother but required her to give an undertaking

> to the effect that she will not sleep in Linda's bedroom with Linda over night or allow Linda to sleep in her bedroom with her over night, [and] that she will not engage in or permit any acts of a sexual nature with Linda in the presence of the children or of other persons who might report those acts to the children.[39]

Similar conditions were imposed in the cases of Spry, Brook and Schmidt, and in the case of Cartwright, heard in Melbourne in 1977, Justice Smithers required the mother to 'refrain from any act or word which would reasonably be calculated to suggest to any of the children that she or any friend of hers is a lesbian.'[40] Reflecting on her own experience of fighting for custody of her son, Kate Harrison told readers of Australian feminist journal, *Refractory Girl*, in 1980:

> A myth which seems to be continuing at full strength is one which sees homosexuals as being sexually irresponsible. Sex is somehow a greater part of our lives and our conduct is consequently suspect. Unlike heterosexual women, lesbians cannot be trusted to keep their sexual urges under control in front of children. This seems to be the implication of questions asked about my behaviour in front of my child. How, I was asked, did I kiss my lover? In the normal fashion of people in an ordinary relationship? Was it passionate or not? Similarly my friend was asked by the judge how we behaved at parties, whether as two heterosexual lovers would who were newly in love or some other way? ... Whatever the actual

sexual habits, lesbianism was obviously a thing to be hidden. It was suggested that the fact that my son was aware that my friend and I shared the same bed was 'pushing' homosexuality on him.[41]

For Kate, the court's excessive concern with her sexual behaviour reflected both an assumption that lesbians generally were hypersexual and a fear that witnessing any form of homosexual behaviour was liable to result in a child becoming homosexual themselves. Similar concerns were demonstrated by British courts, which frequently imposed restrictions on mothers' access and custody, preventing mothers from living with, or showing affection towards, lovers in the presence of their children.[42]

This emphasis on discretion was also intended to protect children from the social disapproval and teasing which it was assumed they would experience if their mothers' lesbianism were widely known. In Cartwright v Cartwright, Justice Smithers declared: 'There is no doubt that conventional morality frowns on homosexuality which clearly has a strong potential for causing estrangement from family and friends and associates of young and teenage children.'[43] Justice Murray made a similar point in the case of Spry, arguing: 'Community attitudes towards homosexuality have, fortunately, changed over recent years, but not, I venture to say, to such a degree as to ensure that the children will have freedom from spiteful comment from their peer group who may be influenced by the attitudes of their parents.'[44] British judges made similar assumptions and lesbian mothers' activist group, Rights of Women, reported one 1976 case in which the judge 'stated that the boy should live in a house which he could describe as "normal" to his friends and that he would be less likely to be teased if he had a normal background. Further, that if he lived with his father, no one need ever know of his mother's lesbianism.'[45] These arguments were used to justify both removing children from the custody of their mothers altogether and imposing restrictions on mothers' ability to express affection towards lovers or be open about their lesbianism in public.

A culture of fear and concealment

During the 1970s and early 1980s, British and Australian courts rarely awarded custody to known lesbian mothers and, for those women who lost custody of their children, the experience was often devastating. Rights of Women reported the words of one woman who lost custody and had told them:

> When I lost custody of my child I felt completely destroyed. I lost my job and got evicted from my house. It was a very hard time, but I have survived and recovered. Although they could stop me living with my child, they could not stop the love between us, in fact it has grown stronger.[46]

Kate Harrison described the impact of the court hearing itself as damaging for lesbian mothers and their lovers. Reflecting on the way in which the judge summed up her own and her lover's personalities, she observed:

So I, for example, was intelligent, unemotional and apparently not warm towards my son or any other person. My lover, after 90 minutes cross examination, was summed up as an aggressive, unattractive personality who presumably would influence my emotional decisions … What incalculable damage is done to women and men by being dismissed as 'unattractive', 'unpleasant', etc by one of society's most powerful institutions?[47]

The numbers of openly lesbian women who sought custody of their children through the courts and lost were probably relatively small, but the wider impact of court attitudes was much greater and helped shape approaches to lesbian parenting for decades. The threat of losing custody of their children was a constant danger in the minds of many British and Australian lesbian mothers in the post-war period, prompting women with children to conceal their lesbianism and to adopt a variety of strategies to conform to normative family models as closely as they were able. Major cases were reported in the tabloid and broadsheet press, often reproducing negative stereotypes of lesbian mothers, and individual husbands regularly used the threat of 'taking the children away' as a means of controlling the actions of their wives or ex-wives. From the mid-1970s onwards, the experience of lesbian mothers who had faced custody cases was increasingly widely reported in the feminist and lesbian and gay press and became the focus of workshops and papers at feminist conferences.[48] Many lesbian mothers, who were involved in feminist or lesbian networks in this period, knew or were aware of women who had lost custody or access to their children following the breakdown of a former heterosexual relationship and this further contributed to the climate of fear.[49] In their 1984 booklet, *Lesbian Mothers on Trial*, the Rights of Women Lesbian Custody Group claimed that 'many lesbian mothers, or lesbians caring for children always live with the fear at the worst of having their children removed, or at the least of being put under surveillance by the welfare authorities'.[50]

This constant underlying sense of threat impacted on the lives of lesbian mothers, prompting many to conceal their sexuality from family, neighbours, schools and wider social networks. Reports suggested that, if a woman's sexuality became known, former husbands were more likely to contest custody, either because they believed their ex-wives would not provide a suitable environment for the children, or out of a desire to punish them for the perceived insult or emotional injury of being married to a lesbian. Where possible, therefore, women who were separated from their ex-husbands often chose to conceal their lesbianism from children or from society more broadly, to minimize the risk of discovery. The Rights of Women Lesbian Custody Group reported:

Another woman who had always denied her lesbianism to her ex-husband stated that she felt she had to stay 'firmly in the closet', to her two younger children who were between the ages of 4 and 6 as they were too young to keep silent, although she had tried to tell her older child. She feared her ex-husband would go for custody if he found out about her lesbianism. She felt, however, that it was a great strain to have to conceal such an important part of her life.[51]

Many women described the difficulties and anxieties which resulted from attempting to conceal their lesbian relationships from their children and former husbands. Delphine from Maroochydore in Queensland wrote to *Campaign* magazine in the late 1970s, seeking advice on how to resolve this issue. She explained:

> I live with my girlfriend and I have two little children, a boy aged four and a girl aged two. When my girlfriend moved into my house we had an agreement we would stay in the closet and not show affection in front of the children ... My ex-husband takes the kids every second weekend, enabling us to go away by car down the coast, and he pays me generous maintenance, and my parents, who are well-off, are very good to me and the kids. All this would change if any of them knew about my homosexuality – they would be shocked to the core and might try to take the children away from me. After 18 months of putting up a front, only inviting my parents at set times, and making sure Judy is out of the way when Matt comes to pick up the kids, I'm getting sick of it, and feel there would be little to lose by taking them into our confidence.[52]

Although frightened that exposure could result in the loss of her children, Delphine was finding the stress of concealing her relationship increasingly intolerable and sought advice on whether she should tell her children and family. Her girlfriend, she noted, insisted they should continue the concealment as 'she says our whole family's happiness depends on discretion and tact'. Jane, *Campaign*'s agony aunt, agreed, commenting that Delphine would 'be crazy to rock the boat at this juncture'. Painting a depressing picture of the poverty, social ostracism and loss of child custody which Delphine would likely experience if her lesbianism became known, she advised concealment at least until the children reached the age of eleven and preferably until the death of Delphine's parents and an imagined future in which Delphine's ex-husband remarried and moved to Western Australia, losing interest in the children.

As Delphine's account indicates, former husbands were not the only figures who were perceived as threatening a woman's right to parent her child. Grandparents or other family members could apply for third party custody if they felt strongly about a mother's lesbianism and social workers or other representatives of local authorities and the state were considered a potential threat in some cases. One British woman told delegates at a lesbian mothers' conference that she had been 'quietly living in her own home with her three children and her lover' when they 'inadvertently ... came under the scrutiny of the Social Services. When they discovered the homosexual relationship they instituted an Ex Partie judgement and whipped all three children in care'.[53] Attitudes towards race and class further complicated the experience of some lesbian mothers, making them more vulnerable to state intervention in their parenting. In a discussion of the experience of being a Black lesbian, published in British feminist journal, *Feminist Review*, in 1984, Gail commented on 'the whole threat about your children being taken away from you, or the feeling that you somehow should not have children, the internalized stuff. Not only because of the threat that they might be taken away from you, but you partially believe that perhaps they do need a nuclear family'.[54] Ellen, a British Muslim woman of Turkish Cypriot origin, who began a relationship with another woman after her husband deserted her in mid-1970s London, recalled:

> I think, after 3 months I felt really guilty that I was actually having this relationship with a woman. I felt that if they ever found out, you know, I'd be a disgrace and if my, if the social workers ever found, or if anybody found out, my kids would be taken away and I felt really guilty that my kids might discover it, so I told this woman that I wasn't a lesbian now, that I was just, I could be bisexual, but I wasn't a lesbian because I'd been married and I told her to go.[55]

Ellen's account suggested that both the religious values she had been raised with and her experience of the racism of British authorities combined to create a sense of guilt and fear about the potential consequences for her children of her lesbian relationship. She ended her relationship after a few months and was celibate for another five years before she felt able to explore and express her desires for women again.

For those lesbian mothers who were in relationships with other women, the need for concealment could pose a number of practical and emotional difficulties. Angela, who had a seven-and-a-half-year relationship with a lesbian mother in London between 1964 and the early 1970s, recalled that the climate of fear around child custody impacted on their social lives and living arrangements:

> There was quite a lot of trouble at the end of the 60s with lesbian mothers losing their kids. I wasn't out, neither of us were out on the actual scene in those days. I came out on the scene after I'd broken up with [Jean] because I wouldn't come out on the scene while I was with her because of what could happen to the kids. Because the kids could have been taken away and put in a home.

She explained that she did not socialize with other lesbians while she was living with Jean and ultimately the couple also decided to live apart:

> We did live together at one time and then ended up having separate flats … Had to be very careful … Because as I say, when they were little we did live together but when they started school and that it was easier to live separately again because of what people would say and it coming back on the kids.[56]

As Angela's account suggests, the steps lesbian mothers and their partners felt necessary to guard against loss of child custody could prevent lesbian couples from living together and isolate them both from each other and the wider lesbian community. Marit, who made similar compromises when she began a relationship with a married lesbian mother in Melbourne in the 1980s, presented these precautions as a difficult but reasonable response to the threat. She explained:

> I remember [Sally] particularly wanting to be careful because of the laws at that time around – we had lesbian friends who had lost custody of their children, access to their children, simply because of being lesbian. The ex-husbands had taken it to

court and declared them as unfit mothers because of that. So [Sally] was – there was no way she was going to let that happen to her. So for a while until financial settlement and custody and all that stuff had been sorted out, it was very important to her that it was not public knowledge … it was difficult but I accepted it.[57]

For Marit, although the secrecy which she and Sally maintained in the early years of their relationship was difficult, she was able to make sense of it in the context of the climate of fear around child custody. Nevertheless, measures such as these placed considerable stress on many women's relationships and lesbian mothers and their partners frequently referred to the tensions they experienced as a result. Delphine from Maroochydore noted in her letter to *Campaign* that the situation she had described was 'causing rows between us and spoiling our normally smooth relationship'.[58]

The pressure to conceal lesbian relationships from children, either imposed by court restrictions or by an attempt to avoid contested custody, was also a source of anxiety for lesbian mothers in this period. Many women considered being open with their children about their sexuality to be an important aspect of good parenting and therefore experienced conflict and guilt if forced to conceal their lesbianism. One lesbian mother, who contacted Vivienne Cass, a psychology PhD student specializing in homosexual parenting and a member of activist group, CAMP WA, believed the risk was one which must be taken. She explained: 'Although I am aware of the risks, I could not live with myself if I were dishonest and this is not a principle that I wish to pass onto my children.'[59] For her, coming out was not just important individually in building a personal lesbian identity, it was also central to her sense of self-respect as a good parent and role model for her children. Similarly, for the lesbian mothers who attended British lesbian group, Sappho's meeting on lesbian motherhood in 1972, honesty with children was also regarded as important. Although they reported that 'the greatest anguish' in their situation was the 'GUILT about taking our children out of straight society', they agreed: 'When the children ask questions about the relationship, they should be given the straight answer that the two women love each other … whatever the age and whenever any question was asked by the child it must be answered immediately, honestly and naturally.'[60] If a court imposed restrictions on a mother's expression of affection to an existing partner, this could also pose emotional difficulties for the children. Eleanor Stephens reported that 'a [British] couple who, out of fear of losing what little they had, followed this injunction [to secrecy] found that the children were upset by the change. They assumed their mother and lover had quarrelled and that something was wrong for them to be more distant.'[61] Other women, who had told their children about their lesbianism, but needed their co-operation in concealing the fact from the father, expressed concerns about the pressure this placed on their children. The Rights of Women Lesbian Custody Group reported:

> One woman, who was divorced before she came out as a lesbian, said: 'My daughter's father doesn't know I'm a lesbian. I don't know what his attitude would be, and I'm not going to ask him, but the fear of what he could do controls a lot of my life and her life too. She goes to stay with him regularly and she has to keep a careful silence on our activities.'[62]

Many lesbian mothers like this one described being compelled either by court orders or by the fear of loss of custody, to parent in ways which conformed as closely as possible with normative family ideals. Openly challenging the nuclear family model by presenting alternative family structures in positive terms could pose a considerable risk to a woman's ability to have access to or custody of her children.

Awareness of the problems lesbian mothers were facing in child custody cases provided renewed impetus for the formation of lesbian mothers' support groups in Britain and Australia from the mid-1970s onwards. In addition to supporting lesbian mothers, many of these groups aimed to change the attitudes of both the courts and wider society with regard to lesbian mothers, making more accurate information about lesbian mothers and their children widely available and highlighting the discrimination faced by lesbian mothers in custody hearings. These sometimes conflicting aims resulted in the development of an ambiguous discourse on lesbian motherhood which presented lesbian parenting as both subversive and no different from heterosexual parenting, simultaneously encouraging lesbian mothers to conform to conventional social norms while assuming that they wished to challenge them. In addition to holding symposiums and giving lectures, activists contributed to the production of plays, documentaries and films exploring the experiences of lesbian mothers and child custody. The US documentary, 'In the Best Interests of the Children', was widely discussed and aired in Australia and Britain.[63] However, Susan Hemmings, reviewing the film in *Spare Rib*, complained that 'its main aim is to raise the issue of lesbian custody cases under the banner, "lesbian moms are just like you and me"', rather than challenging the nuclear family and gender roles. British and Australian cultural productions took a more critical approach to these issues, highlighting the potential for lesbian mothers to create new family structures and break down normative ideas of gender. Alison Lyssa's play, 'Pinball', which premiered at the Nimrod Theatre in Sydney in 1981, described a custody battle between Theenie and her ex-husband Sylvester and highlighted the differences between the upbringing their child Alabastar would receive in his parents' respective households. While his father offered a private-school education, an affluent suburban upbringing and 'the love and role model of a father as well as a mother', his mother hoped to raise a sensitive, feminist boy outside of the violent, 'macho' mainstream values represented by her ex-husband and his male relatives.[64] As Margaret Bradstock noted in a review for *Gay Information*, 'The custody case emerges finally as an aspect of the larger struggle against sexism, heterosexism and conservatism'.[65] British Gay Sweatshop Theatre Company's women's group, whose first play, 'Care and Control' (1977), explored lesbian custody cases, aimed to emphasize that such cases were an aspect of a broader fight against the patriarchy in which all women were involved. The programme for the play, which opened at Action Space and toured for three months, stated:

> Single mothers, lesbian and heterosexual, face the same kind of prejudice when they come before the judicial system. A woman is suspect in the eyes of the State when she asserts her right to live independently of men. She is seen as a direct challenge to family life and the traditional sexual roles which the court uphold.

It is against these attitudes and assumptions, which deny all of us the right to decide the most basic and intimate matters of our lives, that women are organising to fight the custody battle. It is a dramatic development – one which the women of Gay Sweatshop wished to explore, not only for the sake of representing the struggle, but to advance it![66]

Lesbian mother activism in this period also highlighted financial insecurity and poverty as factors which impacted on lesbians' ability to parent their children. British chapters of the international movements, Wages for Housework and Wages due Lesbians, were formed in London in 1975 and campaigned for women to be paid for their domestic labour and care work in the family. At a lobby at the House of Commons in March 1978, Rachel Smith of Black Women for Wages for Housework and Wages due Lesbians delivered a speech in which she argued:

I am a lesbian mother and an immigrant [and] … I'd like to say that lesbian women like all women are under attack by the government taking away our Child Benefits … we are always short of money. We have to depend on the Social Security pittance, low housekeeping money and low women's wages, and there's always a risk of losing our jobs if we are lesbians, or not getting them if we are Black or immigrant.

Black and immigrant women when we come to this country, we often lose custody of our children … Because we don't have the money to bring our children here or because the British consuls keep them out, they have effectively taken them from us.[67]

For Smith and others in the movement, economic disadvantage and social deprivation were interlinked with overt discrimination against lesbian mothers, trapping women in marriages they wanted to leave, forcing them to raise their children in poor living conditions or preventing them from having custody of their children altogether.[68]

Feminist approaches to parenting

Feminist and lesbian and gay theorizing and activism was productive of radical new approaches to parenting in the 1970s and 1980s. Many women considered feminist parenting to be an opportunity to challenge gender role stereotyping in children. Linda recalled that the feminist mother's group she and her co-mother were involved in in London in the late 1970s and early 1980s had 'lots of discussion around gender and behaviour and those kind of things around the boys and the girls in that group'.[69] The extent to which these ideas were widely circulating in British feminist circles in the 1970s and 1980s is apparent from the advice literature produced for lesbian mothers in relation to child custody. In a section of their *Lesbian Mothers Legal Handbook*, dealing with how to prepare for a home visit from a court welfare officer, the Rights of Women group suggested that mothers should: 'Think about clothes the children wear, toys they are playing with. Your probation officer may be into traditional stereotypes of what boys and girls wear, toys they should play with, and the sort of role models they are getting.'[70] While implicitly advocating that lesbian mothers ensure their children conform to normative gender roles in the presence of a court welfare officer, the advice also points to an assumption that, in daily life, lesbian mothers would likely be challenging these roles. Lynne recalled that challenging gender roles was an important part of the philosophy at the lesbian feminist crèche she was involved with in London in the early 1970s.[71] She explained: 'we aimed to challenge what we then called sex roles with the children, which we did … they had dressing up things and you know boys could wear dresses and the girls – well, the girls would wear trousers anyway, we didn't put them in skirts, but we did have skirts in the dressing up box.' Although Lynne felt that this endeavour had been successful and the children 'didn't have concepts of boys being superior to girls and they just didn't have that concept at all of male privilege and male superiority', this was undermined when the children began to attend a more formalized nursery at the age of four or five. There, the 'nursery workers were reinforcing [normative gender] values and [the children were directed towards] girls' toys and boys' toys and so on.'[72]

Once children reached school age, feminist mothers in Britain and Australia increasingly expressed their frustrations in the undermining of their values by mainstream schooling and some mothers took the decision to seek alternative educational environments. Megg home-schooled the child in her care in early 1980s Queensland because:

> We didn't want her to have a patriarchal education. She got extremely well educated in Ancient Greek goddesses and other things. As well as a very old fashioned but very solid education in reading, writing, maths and recorder and all sorts of – how to swim and all of those kinds of things.

Megg shared this role with her lover, Radda, drawing on a middle-class education which later enabled her to work as a teacher. Chloe tried a number of different alternatives to mainstream schooling for her daughter in the late 1970s. She recalled: 'I went to the women's lands [in Northern NSW] when my daughter was about to start school, because I thought I didn't want her to go to a patriarchal school.' There were a number of other children who were part of the community and the children were home schooled. However, following a police raid on the lands, in which a child welfare officer insisted that it was not a suitable environment for children, Chloe felt that her continued presence with her daughter would bring the other women unwanted attention from the authorities. She took the decision to relocate back to Sydney, where she enrolled her daughter in a Rudolph Steiner school.[73]

In addition to breaking down gender roles more broadly, some feminist lesbian mothers also emphasized the importance of challenging hierarchical power structures embedded in patriarchal society. Age was an important power differential which some sought to challenge, encouraging open conversations with their children and attempting to displace the barriers of secrecy and power between adults and children.[74] The different implications of sexism, depending on the sex of the child, were also widely discussed. Empowerment was considered important for girls, who needed encouragement to have confidence to resist oppression in a patriarchal society, while boys needed to be taught to have respect for women's autonomy and not simply to accept the privilege which society would give them. Jean, whose son and daughter were approaching their early teens when she became involved in feminist activism in Melbourne in the 1970s, recalled:

> I was well aware as a female myself that my daughter was not going to inherit the world in the same way my son was. There was no way that she was going to have as easy a time of it as he would automatically do as a male. So she wouldn't get as much pay – you know, the whole caboodle, and so it proved – you know, that's how it is. She's had to struggle in a way that he hasn't and totally unfair, you see, in this society. So I wanted to protect my daughter as much as make sure my son understood that. You know, you have to encourage your daughters and make sure your sons know that they have to respect women's spaces.[75]

Linda made a similar point in an article for *Spare Rib*, calling on all women to provide more space in feminist circles for the discussion of child raising. She asked:

> Do we raise children to fit into the patriarchal mould, or do we raise them to be fully aware of women's position in society, of discrimination, and of the choices that could be open to them in a feminist society? … Children are the future now, and I feel should be made aware of the valueless, subordinate position women have been assigned over the years. They should be told about lesbian discrimination, racism, classism etc. What better place than within the women's movement?[76]

However, some lesbian mothers recalled feeling under pressure to meet high expectations from other women in the movement with regard to breaking down gender roles in their children. This sense of being judged or failing to live up to their own and others' feminist ideals was most often expressed by mothers of boy children. One Australian lesbian mother, who took part in a joint discussion with other feminist lesbian mothers for *Scarlet Woman* in 1976, complained: 'Living in an antagonistic lesbian household was to a certain extent destructive, because it really undermined my confidence about the way I related to [my two-year-old son]. He'd play with a hammer and it'd be seen as sex role conditioning. Everything was picked up.'[77]

Feminist attempts to undermine gender roles explicitly challenged post-war medical and sociological concepts of child development, reimagining the lesbian family as a site in which normative gender roles and social structures could be critiqued and deconstructed. This tension between feminist challenges to the nuclear family and normative social attitudes, policed through family courts and social welfare provision, framed the language in which lesbian parenting was debated in this period. Feminist psychological research, such as Golombok, Spencer and Rutter's comparative study of the psychosexual development of children raised by single and lesbian mothers, responded to this conflict by seeking to prove that being raised by lesbian mothers did not impact on a child's normative gender and sexual development.[78] Individual lesbian mothers, pursuing custody, access and other rights with regard to their children in the courts between the 1970s and 1990s often similarly downplayed the radical potential of lesbian parenting and sought to show how their families could provide an environment modelled on normative understandings of child development. In media interviews following her and her partner's successful application for a joint residence order in relation to their 22-month-old son, 'Miss B' was typical of many such mothers when she claimed: 'He goes to a nursery and we have heterosexual male friends and so he will have male role models … He is a wonderful, boyish boy. We won't be doing anything to change that.'[79] The tension between feminist and normative approaches to parenting and child development also impacted on the children of lesbian mothers. Clare and Linda felt it was very important to raise their three children to challenge sexism and conventional gender roles but Clare reflected that, as the children of lesbian mothers in the late 1970s and 1980s, 'our children had a lot of pressure to be perfect and I think Tom, particularly – well, probably the girls too – but Tom now is acknowledging a lot of difficulties to be the most non-sexist, non-racist, non-boy. He's fine and he's lovely but he's trying to work through quite a lot of that.'[80] Gipsy Hosking and Margie Ripper have argued that the construction of the discourse of 'the best interests of the child', deployed by Australian courts, psychiatrists and social workers as well as opponents and advocates of lesbian and gay parenting, has both silenced and produced considerable pressure on the children of lesbian and gay parents. Characterized as vulnerable, innocent but abstract figures, children of lesbian and gay parents have not been afforded the opportunity to offer their own opinions or experiences in this debate but have found themselves at the centre of a contest between social attitudes and their family experience which has required them to 'prove' that lesbian and gay parents can and do produce 'well-adjusted' children.[81] Recognizing this tension, the provision of space for the children of lesbian mothers to voice their own experience and political views was regarded by some as an important aspect of feminist parenting in the 1980s and 1990s. Linda urged readers of *Spare Rib* in 1987: 'Older children, especially girls and pre-adolescent boys, often have much of value to contribute in workshops and meetings and their experiences as children of lesbian mothers are valid. The women's movement should not need to be told that children need space to be heard.'[82] At the third national lesbian parenting conference in Canberra in 1998, this need was also recognized with a panel of six children of lesbian parents speaking and answering questions about their experience and views.[83]

Feminism and family structures

Feminist ideology also impacted on the approaches of some lesbian mothers to parenting roles in the 1970s and 1980s. Feminist and lesbian and gay activists articulated powerful critiques of the nuclear family, constructing it as oppressive and damaging both to women and children. In addition to linking women's social subordination to the institution of the family, lesbian and gay and feminist critiques also stressed the indoctrination of children which occurred within the nuclear family. As Clare explained in Australian feminist journal, *Vashti's Voice*, 'The nuclear family takes on the values of the society which are warped and destructive, and foists them on the child(ren), thus ensuring the continuation of the status quo.'[84] In particular, the family was considered the primary context for the performance of adult gendered roles and the socialization of children into normative roles, which were oppressive of both women and homosexuals. In their submission to the Australian Royal Commission on Human Relationships (1975), CAMP NSW therefore argued:

> The fundamental way in which nuclear families perform their function as socialising agents is by conditioning their members into adopting certain sex roles. This means that certain roles are assigned to people according to their gender, regardless of their individual personality. These roles serve to uphold the power structure of this patriarchal society by striving to ensure that men take on roles of power and women those of weakness … The expectation, produced and fostered by society in families, that all its members will be heterosexual, marry and establish nuclear families, has severe effects on families from which a homosexual comes, and on homosexuals themselves.[85]

Critiques of the nuclear family and the struggle to liberate women from the constraints of patriarchal society and enhance women's autonomy fostered the development of ideas of collective parenting. The influence of the hippy movement and broader counter-cultural experiments in new ways of living had also been important in the early 1970s in encouraging women to live collectively, while Indigenous women in Australia and many migrant women in Britain drew on longer-standing cultural practices of shared childcare. In Australia, many of those involved in urban feminist or lesbian and gay activism lived in shared houses, which increasingly became women-only by the mid-1970s and, in London and other British cities, women lived in squats or collective houses in housing association properties. This provided a material context in which it was possible to explore new family structures. Al was involved in raising two children who lived in a collective house with her and three women in Leeds in the 1970s. When her daughter, Shelley, was born in 1977, they continued to live in the collective house for a few years, with parenting shared between the women in the household.

Collective parenting was felt to offer many advantages, both for parents and children. The model freed women from the constraints of mother-child dependency and enabled biological mothers to pursue other activities outside of childcare. Lynne reflected: 'Autonomy and independence was also very important to us … [B]ecause of the oppression of the nuclear family we didn't want to live as families, we wanted to have our own independence ourselves.' She and her daughter lived in lesbian feminist collective houses and squats in London for a number of years in the early and mid-1970s and were involved in several collective childcare situations. She explained:

> I certainly did not want to be a full time mother and very few of us did. And we didn't have that pressure on us to, like mothers do now, to spend all your time with your children. I mean although there was ideological pressure coming from Bowlby and so on, we thought we would do it differently and we would be able to work and care for children by having this collective childcare and having nurseries and so on.

This approach sought to challenge the views of child psychologists, such as John Bowlby, who had emphasized the strength of the bond between the biological mother and her child. Instead, as Lynne explained: 'We believed that … our children … could get the appropriate care and attention from anyone, it didn't have to be the biological parent, yeah provided that they got that attention, then it would be okay.'[86] Collective parenting was also considered to be beneficial for children in offering them the focused attention of a variety of adults and the opportunity to develop close relationships with adults and children outside of their biological family. Shelley, who spent her early years in a collective house in Leeds in the late 1970s and early 1980s, recalled: 'I had four people interested in my wellbeing: reading bedtime stories, taking me swimming. It meant the adults who were looking after us were fresh and not tired.'[87] Lynne explained that the opportunity for her daughter, who was a only child, to develop close relationships with other children was one of her motivations in participating in a collective crèche. She recalled that she and other lesbian mothers she knew believed:

> It was good for our children to have sisters and brothers and that these children in the crèche would be their sisters and brothers and in fact they were because they grew up and although they changed they all kept in contact with each other and my daughter's still in contact with one of the boys that she was close to in the crèche, and one of the girls.

Chris made a similar argument about the benefits of collective parenting from her experience in Sydney in the 1970s and 1980s. She explained:

> I have lived in a situation where a group of children was co-parented by a group of adults. Those children are now extremely well adjusted young adults themselves and are still nurtured by the warmth of having a bigger gaggle of caring aunties than most of their peers who come from the limitations of nuclear families.[88]

Explicitly challenging the notion that a nuclear family represented the ideal environment in which to raise a child, Chris utilized the language of child development to claim that alternative families could produce 'well adjusted' children.

Individual women became involved in caring for or parenting non-biological children for a variety of reasons, because they were lovers or friends of lesbian mothers or they enjoyed spending time with children, but also as an act of solidarity with other women. Appeals for support for lesbian mothers, combined with the feminist emphasis on collective parenting, encouraged women to take on these roles. In the early 1980s, an article in British radical feminist journal, *Trouble and Strife*, represented shared childcare as a feminist duty which would help to undermine the perceived threat posed by fathers to feminist parenting. In the context of patriarchal power hierarchies, the involvement of fathers in childcare, the author claimed, 'can only mean a transmission and reinforcement of those values that as feminists we are working so hard to get rid of,' but lesbian mothers could not break free from fathers' involvement unless alternative childcare was forthcoming from feminist communities.[89] Women in both Britain and Australia became involved in feminist childcare in a variety of circumstances and for different periods of time. Megg became involved in co-parenting Jade, the daughter of a heroin addict, when Jade's mother was sentenced to three years in prison in Sydney.

Megg's friend Radda, who had known Jade's mother, agreed to take Jade in and, when Megg came to live with her, the women shared parenting Jade with other women they knew on the Sydney Rape Crisis Centre collective. Megg recalled:

> Jade became the Rape Crisis child, if you like. So she was also on roster … Somebody pick up Jade … so all of these women would turn up at the school to pick Jade up. These teachers were forever looking, just going, 'Oh, you're the mother?' We'd go, 'no', completely unhelpfully, and then disappear.

Decisions about how to parent Jade were also taken as a result of discussions by the women in the Rape Crisis Centre collective, although with Radda and Megg as the primary care-givers. When Jade's biological mother was released from prison after three years, Jade returned to live with her and Megg and Radda travelled to Queensland and lived there. They remained in contact with Jade, however, and Jade subsequently joined them for a further period when she felt unable to live with her biological mother.[90] Clare and Linda spent their weekends caring for a little girl who was the daughter of a young single mother they knew in London in the mid-1970s. Linda recalled: 'We used to have her for the whole weekend. And [we learnt] that we worked well together, looking after a child. And that we both found it interesting and fascinating and lovely. She was the most gorgeous child.' She remembered this as a 'wonderful experience' but, when the mother rang one day from a train station to say that she was moving to Glasgow with the child, the two women were 'heartbroken'.[91]

Despite radical attempts to challenge long-standing notions of the primacy of biological parents in relation to their children in the 1970s, assumptions about the superior rights or ultimate authority of the biological mother persisted through many of these collective parenting endeavours. Clare and Linda were not alone in expressing 'heartache' when their relationship with the young girl they had cared for was abruptly brought to an end by the biological mother's decision to relocate. In 1985, Jean Freer wrote to *Trouble and Strife*, complaining of the lack of rights enjoyed by women who participated in the childcare of non-biological children. She explained:

> Having taken this politic [of the feminist ethics of collective childcare] to heart in the early 1970s, I some time later became involved in co-parenting, with all the good times, hard work, confusion, distress etc, that involves. However, when the biological mother had had enough of the difficulties of co-parenting, and [received] more offers of help from other women, I was left without rights and without access (except for one hour, once a year on the child's birthday) …
>
> The calls for involvement by childless women with mothers must be realistic if we are going to raise our children with humane values and compassion. What kind of society are we really trying to create? Many of us have experienced much more pain – exclusion, denial, invalidation, ridicule, rip-off and general abuse – from women than we ever imagined possible.[92]

The extent to which women, such as Jean, maintained relationships with children they had cared for often depended on the attitude of the biological mother and, at times, on the child themselves. Megg retained life-long, if sporadic, contact with Jade and, when Jade had her own daughter, reflected: 'I do feel like I've got a granddaughter.'[93] Lynne described how a woman who had been her lover for a period during her daughter's childhood became a co-mother:

> It ended up me sharing childcare with my lover and then when we split up, she looked after my daughter ... and so became a sort of non-biological mother because she shared looking after my daughter equally after and we did live in the same house, the same squatted house, she had the part downstairs and I had upstairs.

Although Lynne and her ex-lover subsequently moved into different houses, this woman remained involved in parenting Lynne's biological daughter.[94] This was also the case with other collective family structures which were created in the 1970s. Most of these collective households did not survive beyond the mid-1980s, due to the impact of urban regeneration programmes on the availability of suitable housing and the difficulties of maintaining long-term commitments to shared living on the part of the adults. Reflecting on the break-up of her collective household in Leeds in the early 1980s, Al explained:

> There were various reasons it didn't work out and one of them was, when there's a lot of hostility which we had from young men on the street, it tends to make you implode on yourselves ... It was also that it's difficult enough to get on living with one person for years and years and years, let alone four of us. And it was also that feminist politics were going through quite a turbulent time in terms of the rise of revolutionary feminism versus socialist feminism, radical feminism and that was splitting the movement ... I think as well, ... I was the oldest – when I had Shelley I was 31, the others were in their twenties ... so they were still at that stage in their lives when they would do something for a bit and then think 'Oh, I'll go do something else'. So it's all a bit more fluid when you're at that stage of life I think.[95]

Nevertheless, many of the women and children who established collective family structures maintained their relationships over the long-term. As a thirty-year-old adult, Shelley noted that 'I see all my mums to this day – apart from Rose, because she died last year' and her mother, Al, described similarly maintaining her relationships with the other women and children in their collective household.[96] When the first mother and child moved away from their household, the boy would come to stay regularly for weekends – 'a bit like an access arrangement' – and when the second child and mother moved, they maintained a close relationship for several years and the child came back to live with Al and Shelley for two years while studying for her A' Levels. Al reflected: 'There isn't a word for it really. They could say I was a co-parent in their early years, but there isn't a word for my relationship with them, which is – I mean I'm not their mother. Maia says, "She's my sort of mother". So, yeah, we all stay very close and there's a bond.'[97]

Redefining motherhood?

These varied attempts at collective parenting sparked debates about the nature and definition of mothering which both informed and were influenced by wider social shifts in attitudes to parenting in the decades after the 1970s. During 1985 and 1986, letters and articles published in *Trouble and Strife* debated what it meant to be a mother in the context of the lived experiences of the contributors in caring for children. In 'Thicker than water?', Ruth Wallsgrove wrote as a feminist who had chosen not to be a biological mother, but had had several experiences of non-biological parenting, including 'tak[ing] on two children full time' at a period of 'crisis' in the biological mother's life. Exploring the conceptual differences between 'mothers' and 'non-mothers', Wallsgrove suggested:

> Those of us who get involved with children in ways other than giving birth to them have the freedom to be irresponsible, to leave, to cause trouble by going on about the right-on-ness of sharing and of mothers giving up certain things without understanding that lectures do not instantly alter feelings – and that the mother only has their word that they'll keep their side of the bargain.[98]

If non-mothering constituted the freedom to leave, conversely mothering meant 'sole responsibility for a child every day'.[99] This, she suggested, was an issue of control, which simultaneously brought responsibilities and power, both socially and individually, over the child. Women who chose to be biological mothers, she argued:

> Want [the child] to know they are its mother; to be identified as mothers socially; yes, even to be the one who has to get up in the middle of the night. If that sounds crazy to some non-mothers, it doesn't to me ... I know something about what you get back for doing that; and part of what I know is that you get a sense of power, strangely. Not just over the child ... but also in relation to other adults.[100]

Motherhood, ultimately, she suggested, gave women 'some area of life, childcare, where they'll have the last word, where the importance of their position – as one and only Mum – is assured'.[101] Vinty Hawkes, however, disagreed profoundly. As someone who had been 'living with my lover and her two children' for the last five years, Hawkes emphatically denied that mothering was about 'power and control'. For a mother, she argued:

> Her children are not objects over which power and control may be wilfully asserted – she is their carer in the most intimate and tender sense, she has been bound up with their lives physically, mentally, emotionally, she wants life *with* and *for* her children.[102]

Motherhood, for Hawkes, was not necessarily a biological relationship: women could become mothers by giving birth, by adopting children or 'by having a child given over to our care by a mother who wishes us to assume her caring'.¹⁰³ It was, rather, a qualitative relationship. Mothers were those who were 'Ultimately ... responsible' and who had 'their [children's] interests *unequivocally* at heart'.¹⁰⁴ This role had to be understood in a specific contemporary context in which mothers – and particularly single, Black and lesbian mothers – were continually under threat of losing their children. While Hawkes and Wallsgrove conceived the role of motherhood in very different ways, both agreed that, at the time of writing, a child could only have one mother and shared mothering, as opposed to shared caring, could only occur 'when there is an enormous and profound change in our society and an enormous and profound trust between the adults concerned, not mixed up in questions of power and control'.¹⁰⁵

As women began to conceive children in the context of lesbian relationships, the profound changes referred to by Hawkes were set in motion. Many of the women who conceived children in these new circumstances envisaged alternative models of family structure and, in the 1970s and early 1980s, these structures were often, but not always, shaped by feminist and counter-cultural ideas about collective parenting. During the 1978 British media scandal around the use of AID by lesbians, the *London Evening News* printed an interview with three middle-class, professional women, Helen, Julie and Alison, who were collectively raising a child they had planned together and conceived by donor insemination. Describing their family structure, the women explained that, although Helen gave birth to their son and was called 'Mummy' by him:

> The word Mummy doesn't have all that much meaning for Michael. To him, it's just like any other name ... like Julie or Alison. For most children the person they call 'Mummy' is the most important figure in their lives. I don't think Michael makes that distinction. There is no one central figure in his life – there are three.¹⁰⁶

The women described their family structure in terms of three co-mothers, a relationship which had been determined by the fact that 'We were all in on the decision that he would happen.' Although they believed it was important that their son had male role models and had encouraged Michael's relationships with his grandfather and a gay male friend, they were clear that, when asked, they would tell him that he did not have a father but had three mothers.

Family structures with multiple mothers were also established by some Australian lesbian mothers in the 1970s and 1980s. In 1984, Manja contributed a story to feminist journal, *Hecate*, describing the 'circle of wimin-cummers' in which she intended to conceive a child. She began by citing the dictionary definition of this 'obsolete' word:

CUMMER: KIMMER (two spellings, from the Scottish: Originally French 'commere' from Latin, 'com + mater')

1. A god-mother: A co-mother
2. A female intimate: A gossip
3. A woman, a female – applied like 'fellow' to a man, and specifically to a witch, wise-woman, mid-wife, etc.¹⁰⁷

The concept of 'cummering' as both a relationship between woman and child and an intimate relationship between women enabled Manja to describe the collective parenting endeavour she planned with her cummers, Anni and Tess, who would share 'the money issues and nappy washing and getting up in the night-type work that goes with the daily care of an infant' as well as 'the wider visions' and 'responsibility' of motherhood. With these women and their mothers and friends, Manja imagined that there would be 'many women, giving their thoughts and support and criticisms and energy, helping to unwind and redefine the role of wimin as mothers, as cummers, each unto herself and to each of the others'.[108] This new family model was envisaged as an act of liberation for women and children, creating 'an unsolitary mother with unharnessed offspring. Nuclear (family) disarmament'. Specifically, it was an act of liberation from men; a 'leap into powerful visions in a space where women and their children are out from under the thumbs of fathers'.[109]

The role of the co-mother

The emergence in this period of new family models in which two or more women claimed a parenting role for a particular child in their care posed a radical challenge to conventional models of the family, both in the decoupling of motherhood from a biological relationship with the child and – more profoundly – in the challenge they posed to the presumption that only one woman could mother a child at a time. This shift is most apparent in relation to the figure of the 'co-mother' or 'non-biological mother'. Co-mothers played an important role in lesbian parenting throughout the second half of the twentieth century, but key conceptual shifts began to take place in the ways both lesbians themselves and the wider community understood the role in the 1980s and 1990s.

In the immediate post-war decades, the psychological and sociological emphasis on the mother-child bond, combined with the invisibility of lesbian relationships, had rendered the role of the 'co-mother' or 'non-biological mother' in lesbian mother families extremely problematic. Children were assumed to need one mother – ideally the biological mother or, failing that, a mother-substitute – but the prevailing discourse allowed little space for the possibility of more than one mother. Chloe, who had a number of relationships with mothers, beginning with a three or four-year relationship with a woman who had a pre-school-aged daughter in Queensland in the mid-1960s, recalled the difficulties she experienced in making sense of her role. She explained:

> A lot of the time when I had relationships with women with children, these kids had a perfectly good mother and so I thought I had to take a father role. I thought I had to do that. My own father was not a very good role model, so all I knew was to be like my father, which was very critical. It took me many, many years to, and many relationships, and many fights with girlfriends, to realise that the way I related to children was not the best.[110]

However, when Chloe became a biological mother in the 1970s, she did not experience the same sense of conflict in her role, suggesting that it was the role of the non-biological mother which she found difficult to conceptualize, rather than parenting more broadly. Marion similarly made a distinction between different parenting roles. Describing a six-year relationship she had with a mother of five children in the 1960s, she made no comment on her relationship with the children, beyond the observation that 'some of [them] lived with us', suggesting that she did not consider her role with the children as significant. This was in contrast to her description of herself as a 'lesbian nonmother' in relation to the two boys she and her partner had through artificial insemination in the early 1970s.[111] Other women interpreted the non-biological parent role differently in the post-war decades. Elizabeth, who was in a butch/femme relationship with a divorced mother of two in Sydney from the late 1960s, commented that her role with the children was dictated by her role as the femme in her relationship with the children's mother. She recalled:

> Joy used to like me to wear long gowns, and I had long hair, and she liked that and I went along with it. And she wore three piece suits, but tailored ones, I mean they weren't, they were ones she had made specially for herself, and a gold watch fob and you know, all the trappings. And she was the mother of the two boys and I took the maternal role with the two boys and quite liked it actually.[112]

Elizabeth therefore separated the biological and social roles of the mother. Although continuing to distinguish between Joy as the 'mother' and herself, she described herself as taking the 'maternal role', which may have included cooking and cleaning for the family as well as potentially giving the boys emotional care and attention.

The conceptual difficulty of the co-mother was reinforced by her lack of legal standing or social recognition. Regardless of how involved a woman might be in parenting a child in the context of the home and private family life, she was typically excluded from formal interactions with schools, doctors and other representatives of authority. Lacking the legal standing of a parent, non-biological mothers did not have the authority to take major decisions about a child's health, education or place of residence and had no legal right to a continued relationship with the child beyond that which was permitted by the biological mother. This broader social context impacted on the ways in which women themselves understood lesbian parenting roles up to the 1970s. Lesbian couples tended to make a clear distinction between the biological mother, who had both the responsibility for and legal right to the child or children, and her lover, whose parenting role was typically conceived as supporting the mother and was not designated a 'mother' herself. Involvement in the children's lives often came to an end with the termination of a relationship. Chloe recalled that, after a three or four-year relationship with a lesbian mother: 'I came home from work one day and she had disappeared. She'd just gone and disappeared, vanished, gone off with a friend … I was totally devastated. I couldn't eat for a week. She changed towns, gone off with this other woman … I haven't seen her or the little girl much ever since.'[113]

As Chloe's account implies, although most lesbian couples in the post-war period appear to have accepted the wider social and legal assumption that lovers of lesbian mothers had no parenting rights or responsibilities, many co-parents nevertheless developed emotional bonds with the children in their care. Paul reflected powerfully on the relationship he enjoyed with his mother's lover, Margaret, during the two decades she and his mother were together:

> Margaret loved us. We had a ritual: on Monday evenings I could have her to myself, and in these precious hours she was like a father. She could make toy cars from a cotton reel, a candle and a rubber band, or build a playhouse in the garden. Sometimes we simply talked. She has been dead nearly a decade, and I miss her still.[114]

Although Paul's mother and Margaret remained lovers until Margaret's death, the lack of recognition of co-mothers left many women who formed bonds with non-biological children vulnerable in the event of a relationship breakdown. Yvonne Craig, who was raised by two women whom she later discovered were her biological mother, Greta and Greta's partner, Tina, recalled a painful scene when Tina left: 'When I was 11 [in 1947], I was on the beach with Tina one day at Worthing when she started crying. I learnt that someone wanted to marry her, but she couldn't choose between me and him. He then said he would take me as well, but Greta said no, she wanted to keep me.'[115] Yvonne's childhood memory points to the painful separations co-mothers could face in the event of a relationship breakdown, knowing that legal and social attitudes gave them no right to a continued relationship with children they had been parenting.

By the late 1970s, however, some lesbians were beginning to challenge notions of the primary relationship between the child and a single biological mother. As an increasing number of women planned and conceived children together in the context of a lesbian relationship, a growing belief emerged that both or all of the women involved in that process should be regarded as parents. Clare and Linda, who conceived their three children by self-insemination in London in the 1980s, before moving to Australia, understood themselves as active agents in promoting new ideas of motherhood and particularly lesbian motherhood, through their practice as partners and parents. Clare reflected that they considered themselves to be 'pushing the boundaries', 'leading another charge of the revolution'. One aspect of this was challenging social attitudes towards lesbian mothers and Clare recalled that, on the day after Linda had given birth to their first child, Tom, she, Clare, was 'nursing him, walking up and down the ward at the West London Hospital [and] I said to him – I leaned over and I said to this tiny baby, "We have got a job to do, Tom. We're going to show the world that I'm your mother"'. Clare and Linda went on to have two further children, conceived by Clare. As their children grew older, Clare and Linda worked hard to ensure that schools and the wider community recognized them both as equal parents of their children, participating actively in community social events. Clare explained: 'We got involved at the schools, did everything at the schools ... So we were accepted and we made sure the school contacted both of us always. But we made a point of doing that.'[116] While Clare emphasized that both she and her partner regarded themselves as joint mothers of their children, other women felt that they were creating new parenting roles in other ways. A lesbian social work student who wrote to the *Newham Recorder* in 1986 to complain about attitudes which would exclude her from fostering children claimed: 'I am in a stable and caring relationship, and my partner and I constantly examine how we relate to each other in order to overcome inequality or insecurity. Role-defined tasks attributed to mother or father are restrictive boundaries which uphold our unequal society. A child would benefit from parenting which strives to transcend those boundaries.'[117] Elizabeth Wilson also felt that lesbian parenting offered an opportunity to transcend existing parenting roles. Looking back to 1984, when her partner, Angela Mason, gave birth to their daughter, conceived by artificial insemination, she recalled:

> When Angela's child was born, some friend, I mean it was mostly straight ones I must say, all this thing, 'Oh what are you to it? You have to be something nameable to this baby. So are you her auntie?' And the same people said, 'Oh, you're like a father to her.' So there would always be an effort to sort of corral a unique relationship into something that's already existed, and I suppose it's a sort of human trait really.[118]

For Elizabeth, her relationship with the new baby was 'unique' and could not be named using pre-existing familial terms.

The conceptual challenge this practice posed to notions of parenthood began slowly to impact on legal and social frameworks in the 1990s. In Australia, co-mothers continued to lack legal status throughout the twentieth century. Helen Campbell, solicitor for the Women's Legal Resources Centre, told *LOTL* readers in 1991: 'The lesbian partner of the natural mother of the child, no matter how closely involved and no matter what arrangements are made between the women themselves, has no legally recognisable status and will not be regarded as a parent with the rights or duties of a parent.'[119] However, a 1996 NSW Supreme Court ruling pointed to the beginnings of a shift which gained more rapid ground in the early twenty-first century. The ruling found the former partner of a lesbian biological mother financially responsible for two children conceived by AID during the course of the women's relationship. As Barbara Guthrie and Andrea Malone noted in an article for *LOTL*, the decision suggested that lesbians 'may find ourselves with the financial obligations of a heterosexual parent without any of the rights attached to parenthood'.[120] In Britain, co-mothers gained some legal status in 1991, when the Children Act 1989 came into force. Prior to this, as Sue Lee told the 1986 Lesbian and Gay Parenting conference in London, regardless of whether a co-mother 'has equal care with the biological mother' of the child she planned with her lover by AID, 'She has no legal rights at all except testamentary guardianship [being named as the child's guardian in her lover's will].' This left Sue and others in her situation vulnerable to the biological mother's decision to 'walk out'; the 'right of the biological mother to share responsibility' with another person; and 'no right of abode' with the child.[121] However, the Children Act 1989 enabled legal recognition of non-biological parents for the first time, making it possible for mothers who were not the birth or adoptive mother to apply for joint residence orders and 'parental responsibility' for their children. Such orders allowed co-mothers to make decisions about a child's schooling or medical treatment and to retain parental responsibility in the event of the biological mother's death.[122]

The legal difficulties experienced by co-mothers for most of the period were exacerbated by social invisibility. Many lesbian mothers described the ways in which their role in their children's lives was erased or obscured by the misreading of their family. Mary Waterford, 'one of the mothers of a 4-year-old boy who was conceived by insemination in 1985', complained: 'Invisibility of lesbian mothers is hard – it's often assumed that I must be a deserted single parent.'[123] Katharine described a similar experience of being mistaken for a single parent of the two boys she co-parented with her partner in Canberra in the 1980s. Even when both parents were present, alternative interpretations might be put on their familial relationships.[124] Pearlie McNeill noted that with 'monotonous regularity', strangers would assume that her partner was her daughter and their child, her granddaughter. 'The invisibility of a lesbian lifestyle', she felt, 'makes it impossible for heterosexually defined people to consider that the close bond they see between two women could exist outside the bounds of the family structure'.[125]

Challenges of redefining motherhood

The tension between lesbian parenting and heteronormative notions of the family meant that, despite the commitment and efforts of many lesbian mothers to raise their children in new family structures, long-standing assumptions about the nature of motherhood, as well as material structures based on the norm of the heterosexual nuclear family, posed many obstacles. Widespread conceptualizations of motherhood as biologically based and instinctual proved difficult to overcome, both in terms of the attitudes of friends, family and wider society and within lesbian co-parenting relationships themselves. Pearlie McNeill and Marie McShea described the difficulties they experienced in co-parenting their daughter, Susannah, in Australia and Britain in the early 1980s. Pearlie and Marie agreed to co-parent both Pearlie's two biological sons from a previous relationship and their daughter, Susannah, whom Marie conceived in the context of their lesbian relationship, planning to 'share equally the responsibility, the workload and the fun'. However, the couple experienced many difficulties in sharing the parenting of Susannah, and ultimately their relationship as lovers broke down. Although exacerbated by many specific circumstances in their individual situation, they ascribed the tensions which arose more broadly to a combination of Marie's inability to relinquish her role as 'the mother' and Pearlie's difficulties in defining her role as a co-mother. Marie recalled that 'I wanted to be able to share the decision-making process, but felt on some deep irrational level that I knew best because, as society continually reinforced, I was the mother. I found it hard to hear and accept Pearlie's resolutions.'[126] Pearlie described her role as the co-mother as 'vague, unseen, without definition, unfocussed. I was not a father …, I was not a mother, but a sort of built in support system, something that could be described as lying between the roles of nanny and an Aunt'. This lack of definition in her role meant that Pearlie felt unable to 'validate myself and my experience in the face of the enormous emphasis placed on my partner's, the mother's experience'.[127] While undermined by her own self-doubt about the role, Pearlie also felt silenced by those around them, who continually deferred to Marie, 'the mother', on any issue concerning Susannah. Both women felt that social conditioning about the roles of mothers and fathers and their own lack of role models in a lesbian co-parenting situation made it very difficult for them to share parenting in the ways they had hoped.

Pearlie and Marie's experience was echoed by many other lesbian mothers in Britain and Australia in the 1980s and 1990s, who struggled against internalized assumptions and wider social attitudes to develop new roles as parents. Many women felt unprepared for the challenging emotions and communication difficulties which arose in their attempts to share parenting of their children. The lack of role models and often a physical and emotional distance from others with parenting experience meant that lesbian mothers often felt isolated in dealing with any difficulties which arose. Megg recalled that co-parenting a young girl with her lover, Radda, caused tensions in their relationship which they were unable to discuss or seek advice on. When the couple shared a remote house in Far North Queensland with Jade, sleeping arrangements became a source of jealousy. Megg explained:

> It was actually a hideously painful dynamic for me. Where Jade would get up first thing in the morning and say, 'Radda, can I sleep with you tonight?' Radda would go 'Yeah, sure.' (Because we had separate bedrooms. So that was part of that [feminist] culture as well – you didn't lose your independence. You had your own bedroom.) Really, to sleep with Radda, I would have had to get up at three o'clock in the morning. It was like competing with a three-year-old for the right to sleep with my girlfriend.
>
> Again, I spoke about that to mutual friends, who just thought it was insane that I was jealous of a child. We were young and nobody's got parenting skills and we've isolated ourselves from the people who have. Yeah, it was hideous. It was very hideous. Emotionally hideous.[128]

Clare recalled that, when she and Linda moved with their three children to Australia in the late 1980s, their division of roles proved a source of tension. Linda did not have a visa to work in Australia while Clare had a well-paid job, so she worked full time to support the family and

> We decided it would be good if Linda could be home most of the time so the children didn't have to go to day care or have anything. But actually, I think that certainly wasn't good for me because I was jealous of the time. Matilda was two when I started. I was able to make us a very good living but I found it very hard.[129]

Clare's experience of jealousy in finding herself deprived of time with her children because of her role as breadwinner was reflected in many women's struggle to challenge social structures which assumed that one parent would be the primary breadwinner while another was the primary caregiver.

Homonuclear families?

Not all lesbian mothers in the 1980s and 1990s framed their parenting roles and family structures as a critique of existing social norms. Some women felt that it was important to prioritize the rights and responsibilities of the biological mother, while others sought to deflect negative social attitudes towards their family by living discreetly. When Liverpool couple, Lesley and Christine, participated in an interview with Anne Robinson for the *Liverpool Echo* in 1978, they explained that they were currently raising Lesley's two sons from previous heterosexual relationships and that Christine was attempting to conceive a third child by AID. Although they described the two boys as having 'two parents of the same sex. One they call Mum and the other they call Christine', they emphasized Christine's primary relationship with the planned baby. Lesley explained: 'When the baby comes, I will play a much lesser role. Chris will be a mother and I will be there to support her. She might go back to work or not, it's her decision. If she stays at home, we will live on my income.'[130] Similarly, when Jenny and her partner Jakki's son were born in Canberra in 1998, they split their roles between Jenny, as the primary breadwinner, and Jakki, the birth mother, as primary carer. However, this division of roles was not successful and the couple's relationship broke down when their son was nine months old. In retrospect, Jenny realized that Jakki had been 'desperate to have me do more, and I suppose interact more, to give her a break'. The couple found, as did many other lesbian mothers, that the first year with a newborn baby was 'tough' and their agreed allocation of roles did not work well for them. Jenny recalled that Jakki would have liked her to:

> have him more so that she could have more of a break, and I guess give her some recognition that she was doing it tough, that she had him all day, every day while I was at work. But I was at work, working full-time supporting us, and would then try and take turns as much as I could in the evening hours.[131]

While the division between breadwinner and carer adopted by Jenny and Jakki drew on implicitly gendered normative parenting roles, other lesbian parents utilized explicitly gendered terms to differentiate their roles. In an interview with the *Derby Evening Telegraph* in 1978, Lesley, who lived with her partner, Pat and Pat's two children from a previous marriage, explained: 'They do tend to treat me as the father figure, though they're fully aware I'm a woman. But I'm the one who goes out to work, I tend to play with them more – so I'm the one they come to with their broken toys to mend.'[132] When Natalie Colley and Denise Wilson were expecting their child, conceived by self-insemination in 1994, Denise told a journalist: 'I do not see myself as a father figure, more as an uncle.'[133]

For women who did not envisage parallel, co-parenting roles in the structuring of their families, the role of the non-biological or 'other' parent continued to raise both challenges and opportunities between the late 1970s and 1990s. When Katharine and Marion were amongst the first lesbians to conceive their two sons by AID in

Britain in the early 1970s, they struggled to articulate their respective parenting roles and their relationship to each other as co-parents, a difficulty which they were unable to overcome. Katharine, as the birth mother, understood her role relatively unproblematically as 'the mother', but Marion's role remained ill-defined and a source of tension between them. Reflecting back on this period of her life, Marion said: 'I won't talk about the role of the lesbian nonmother, except to say that it is a difficult one.'[134] When the couple split up after eight years, Marion maintained regular contact with her sons and former lover, but Katharine increasingly considered herself a single parent.[135]

Maxine also described her co-parenting role in language which made a clear distinction between the biological mother and herself, but considered this an opportunity to think creatively about her parenting role. When her partner, Jane, gave birth to their son in Perth in the late 1990s, Maxine explained that, although she had always wanted to have children, she did not consider herself a mother:

> I just went into the whole thing, the other parent thing. It was probably a good thing 'cause I wasn't hustling to be mother. I knew that mother was a unique relationship, that was a unique role, that you can't have two. You have a mother and a parent and I'm the parent and I've got to find my way in the parent role and Jane is 150 per cent mother anyway, you know, I could never put a nappy on in front of her.

Maxine suggested that, although initially she found it difficult to identify her role, particularly during the infancy stage when she felt 'almost extraneous' to the bond between Jane and their son, ultimately she created a place for herself which developed from who she was as an individual:

> It's something that comes from your individual personal expression and mine is one of an active, outdoor person who builds things and does things … Either it's just the nature of the role that you're in, as the non-birthing parent you might also be the bread winner, where you've just got to find your place. You don't know as much about what's going on at this school because you're not going there every day.
>
> … So I suppose what I realise is that my role is to be comfortable being not Jane, not being the mother and to show the children other things that I think are part of the world ….
>
> So in a way what I've been able to be is the one who bursts the family out of the house to unfamiliar environments and shows them the world, and is not their mum.[136]

For Maxine, her parenting role was therefore defined simultaneously by not being 'the mother' and by being herself and drawing on her own interests and outlook to define her relationship with her children.

Community responses to lesbian mothers

Whether or not lesbian mothers sought to construct alternative models of the family and gender, their interactions with the wider community often demonstrated a perception that lesbian families posed a challenge to conventional notions of the family and assumptions of a unique mothering role. Many lesbian mothers and their children faced community disapproval from neighbours, schools and welfare authorities throughout the period while most made adjustments to their lives to avoid difficulties. In Britain, hostile social attitudes towards lesbian mothers were fostered by negative media attention which often represented lesbian mothers as unnatural and a drain on taxpayers' money. Headlines in the tabloid press such as 'How can a baby's father be her mother and be her father again? We tell you how … ' and 'Four Gay Parents "Are Bizarre and Abnormal"' presented lesbian families as incomprehensible and outside the norm.[137] In the context of wider debates about public spending and who constituted a worthy recipient of public benefits under successive Conservative governments, much of the media coverage portrayed lesbian mothers as an unreasonable financial burden on the state. In May 1997, the *Daily Mail* asked: 'Must we pay lesbians to conceive by pickle jar?' and in October 1996, extensive media coverage of two lesbian policewomen who had a daughter together through AID utilized headlines such as 'The lesbian parents playing happy families in a police house'.[138] Representations of lesbian families as abnormal or 'playing' at being families reflected the language used in Section 28 of the Local Government Act 1988, which described same-sex families as 'pretended family relationships' and prohibited the 'promotion' of homosexuality by local authorities.[139]

For lesbian mothers and their children, schools were a key arena in which social attitudes towards their family structures were encountered.[140] Of the thirty-six lesbian mothers who responded to Rights of Women Lesbian Custody Group's survey in 1984, ten stated that they had experienced problems with nurseries or schools, while a further three sought to conceal their lesbianism from their child's school. The report noted:

> The problems ranged from hostility from teachers, to mothers who had lost custody being refused access to the school; also lovers or friends being excluded from the school or from picking up the children.
>
> One mother said she was treated as a 'problem family' by the school, another said her daughter had become a school refuser, and the teachers blamed the mother's lesbianism rather than the other pupils' heterosexism. Two mothers said that the school was far more supportive to the father, because they were lesbians and feminist.[141]

Children's and lesbian mothers' difficulties at school could be determined by the attitudes of individual teachers or headteachers. Liz Baker, who spoke about her personal experience as a Black lesbian mother at the Lesbian and Gay Parenting Conference in London in 1986, explained that 'Her son is now going through problems with society's attitudes and pressures from outside … The children of one of

her friends go to a school where the head is lesbian – this makes things much easier.'¹⁴²
The demographic of the area in which they lived could also affect the school's attitude. Lynne recalled that her daughter experienced few problems at school in Hackney in the 1970s, where there were a high proportion of lone mothers and other alternative family structures.¹⁴³ However, in 1992, *Sydney Star Observer* reported the homophobic harassment a lesbian mother had experienced in Blackheath in the Blue Mountains. The headteacher was apparently unsupportive and told the mother: 'Blackheath wasn't ready for people like her.'¹⁴⁴ Sociological research by Yvette Taylor, Catherine Ann Nixon and others in the early 2000s noted that working-class lesbians' own experiences of marginalization at school shaped the ways in which they interacted with their children's schools and it is clear that racial and class identities also impacted on the experience of individual families between the 1970s and the 1990s.¹⁴⁵ Katharine was able to overcome difficulties with her son's school in Canberra in the early 1980s by drawing on her father's status on the school board. The headmaster of the local grammar school had expressed a reluctance to admit Katharine's son as a pupil on the grounds that he might experience difficulties during puberty arising from his family situation. However, Katharine asked her father, who was on the board of the local Society of Friends school, to speak to the headmaster and her son was subsequently accepted. Many lesbian mothers who did not have such social capital to draw upon simply responded to the experience or fear of conflict with the school by hiding their sexuality. Fiona told the *Glasgow Herald* in 1978 that 'because of the prejudice that exists we never tell anyone that we are lesbians, I have to consider the children above all else, and people always think that if lesbianism is involved it all smacks of dirt and filth.'¹⁴⁶

Conclusion

The late twentieth century witnessed major upheavals in British and Australian notions of motherhood and women's social roles more broadly. In the years after the Second World War, the vast majority of women parented in the context of a heterosexual marriage and regarded this role as their primary social contribution. By the end of the century, many more children were being born and raised in a variety of family circumstances and women considered motherhood a choice which could be combined with other personal aspirations or not taken at all. Lesbian mothers were both impacted by and instrumental in driving these profound social shifts, disrupting social norms and reshaping cultural approaches to motherhood and the family. As this chapter has demonstrated, even when lesbian parent families closely resembled an ideal white, affluent, middle-class nuclear family, any 'homonormativity' they sought to represent was fundamentally an illusion. Daniel Winunwe Rivers notes in his US study that lesbian mothers, gay fathers and their children 'call into question the belief that family is always heterosexual'.¹⁴⁷ By demonstrating that children could be raised outside of a context of a biological mother and a biological father, British and Australian lesbian mothers challenged the nuclear family ideal.

Lesbian motherhood was also socially disruptive, however, in subverting post-war notions of the single, biological mother. The figure of the lesbian co-mother, obscured and erased for much of the period by legal frameworks and social attitudes, nevertheless radically undermined the central belief that mothering was a unique, gendered role which could only be undertaken by one woman at a time. In creating families in which more than one woman actively raised a child at the same time, lesbian parents disrupted assumptions which were at the core of British and Australian notions of motherhood. This was a gradual process which occurred unevenly throughout the second half of the twentieth century; a process in which some lesbian parents actively participated but which others worked to minimize; and a process which was marked by considerable, ongoing resistance. As a result, it took place in fits and starts, manifesting in different ways at different historical moments and varying between individual women and between families. Nevertheless, lesbian parent families were instrumental in fundamentally shifting notions of the nuclear family and motherhood during this period, demonstrating by their existence that a child need not be raised by a heterosexual couple or 'mothered' by a unique, biologically related female parent.

7

Family, kinship and support

Recalling the evening, in the early 1970s, when she travelled to her mother's home in Sydney to tell her that she was leaving her husband and now identified as a lesbian, Robyn described how her mother had protested: 'Oh, you'll be lonely when you get old!' Robyn reflected:

> And I think it's very interesting because she actually told my two sisters and some of her close friends the next day [that I was a lesbian] … [and] one of her friends said: 'Oh, we'll send you The Well of Loneliness' and I thought that is the worst book that anyone could give someone, you'd think you end up suiciding or whatever else … and I think that's a general perception, that you'll be lonely in your own life, and yet in comparison to my two sisters, I have so many friends it's not funny. I've got a huge group … Whereas when you leave a marriage, you're just isolated in that minute family, usually. So I guess I'm very lucky, overall.[1]

Robyn's account highlights the widely held popular perception, which was current for much of the mid and later twentieth century, that lesbians and gay men were isolated figures, occupying the margins of society. Rejecting this interpretation of her life, she contrasted her own 'luck' in having 'a huge group' of friends, with both her sisters' experiences and with the constraints she believed heterosexual divorcees were confronted with in creating supportive and sociable networks.

In his study of queer domesticities in late nineteenth and twentieth-century Britain, Matt Cook confirms this assumption that 'after the Second World War … hetero/homo, gay/straight understandings of sexuality gained more general currency and family was imagined being more radically dissociated from homosexuality'.[2] Lesbian pulp fiction of the 1950s and 1960s typically presented lesbians as lonely figures, occupying a liminal space on the margins of society and excluded or distant from family. For Alison Oram, the public image of female homosexuality that was newly emerging in the British press in the 1950s was multi-layered, presenting lesbians as both an external and internal threat to the family. She concludes: 'The lesbian was not simply figured as urban, lonely and excluded from mainstream structures of femininity and the family. In the fifties, homosexuality was seen as a potential sexual hazard within the family, among wayward daughters, and particularly among unhappy wives in affectionless marriages.'[3] Kath Weston explains this distancing of homosexuals from the family as arising from two assumptions:

> For years, and in an amazing variety of contexts, claiming a lesbian or gay identity has been portrayed as a rejection of 'the family' and a departure from kinship ... Two presuppositions lend a dubious credence to such imagery: the belief that gay men and lesbians do not have children or establish lasting relationships, and the belief that they invariably alienate adoptive and blood kin once their sexual identities become known.[4]

Lesbians, according to these assumptions, were both estranged from their families of origin and unable to form families of their own.

In her study of homosexuality and kinship in post-war North America, however, Heather Murray has demonstrated how much more closely homosexuality and the family were interconnected in the decades after the Second World War. The increasing cultural focus on the psychology of the self not only prompted families to look inward, seeking a greater intimacy with and understanding of family members, but psychological literature on homosexuality centrally implicated the nuclear family in the homosexuality of its members. Dominant psychoanalytic explanations of homosexuality placed the blame squarely on the shoulders of parents, identifying the cause of homosexuality in over-bearing fathers and emotionally smothering mothers. For educated individuals, Murray argues:

> the immediate postwar period was a time of self-awareness about same-sex attractions, including what those attractions revealed about the nature of their true selves. In turn, these gays had to negotiate how, or even whether, they would give expression to this often hidden self in the family context. This dilemma was complicated by a sense of ambivalence and uncertainty that surrounded the family not just as a place of self-disclosure but as a place of mutual intimacy and affection between parents and children, where one central commonality between them was a presumed heterosexuality.[5]

Matt Cook similarly points to the possibility of unspoken intimacy with family in this period. Focusing on Rex Batten's various accounts of his domestic life as a gay man in the years after the war, Cook argues that Batten experienced his family home as a safe and supportive space for himself and his male lovers despite – or perhaps because – he never explicitly discussed his sexuality with his parents.[6] If homosexuals in the immediate post-war decades were likely to 'seek some form of integration' into the family, Murray charts a shift towards a more open confrontation of the family with homosexuality in the 1970s. Gay liberation urged a public declaration of sexuality and selfhood – whatever the attendant risks of familial rejection or estrangement – while lesbian feminism, she suggests, saw such openness as the basis for greater intergenerational intimacy and understanding between mothers and their lesbian daughters. Many British and Australian lesbians, influenced by these emerging political ideas, chose to 'come out' to their families in the 1970s and later, prompting a re-evaluation, or break, in their relationships with family of origin.

In Britain, a renewed articulation of lesbians as excluded from and a threat to the family emerged in political and cultural discourse in the 1980s. Long-standing media representations of homosexuals as a threat to children were fuelled in 1987 by scandals surrounding several children's books exploring homosexuality, including *Jenny Lives with Eric and Martin* and the evening screening of a lesbian short film, *How to Become a Lesbian in 35 Minutes*, by a lesbian community group in a school building.[7] Headlines such as 'Lesbian Plots to Pervert Nursery Tots' and 'A lesbian mother's terror rule' depicted lesbians as a threat to children and family life.[8] Conservative Prime Minister, Margaret Thatcher, expressed public support for such views, telling the Conservative Party conference in October 1987 that, as a result of the political views of 'hard left education authorities', 'Children who need to be taught to respect traditional moral values are being taught that they have the inalienable right to be gay.'[9] Later that year, her government supported an amendment which became Section 28 of the Local Government Act 1988, stating that: 'A local authority shall not promote the teaching in any maintained school of the acceptability of homosexuality as a pretended family relationship.' In the protests against the legislation by lesbian and gay activists throughout the late 1980s and 1990s, the suggestion that lesbians and gay men inhabited 'pretended family relationships' was repeatedly challenged. Following a protest against Princess Diana's speech to the Sixteenth International Congress for the Family in July 1990, lesbian activist, Danielle Ahrens, from the group Brighton Area Action against Section 28, explained that 'The delegates to this congress are trying to make people believe that lesbian mothers and gay men looking after children are not real families but are pretend family groups. We are not pretending and we have no lesser values than any other family.'[10] In Australia, the public events and debates generated by the International Year of the Family (IYF) in 1994 created a space for a variety of opinions on lesbians' relation to the family to be expressed. While a report by the National Council for IYF urged policy-makers to be inclusive of lesbian and gay families, Jennifer Connell in lesbian magazine *LOTL* argued that much of the debate assumed that lesbians had no place in a discussion about the family and a poll published in the *Sydney Morning Herald* found that almost 60 per cent of respondents did not believe lesbian and gay couples with children represented a family.[11]

As historians have explored the shifting cultural representations of homosexuals in relation to the family and the manner in which homosexuals maintained ties with their families of origin in the post-war decades, sociologists have noted the emergence, in the 1980s, of new forms of lesbian and gay family or kinship. In her work on lesbians, gay men and kinship in the San Francisco Bay Area in the 1980s, Kath Weston argued:

> At the height of gay liberation, activists had attempted to develop alternatives to 'the family,' whereas by the 1980s many lesbians and gay men were struggling to legitimate gay families as a form of kinship ... Gay or chosen families might incorporate friends, lovers, or children, in any combination. Organized through ideologies of love, choice, and creation, gay families have been defined through a contrast with what many gay men and lesbians in the Bay Area called 'straight,' 'biological,' or 'blood' family.[12]

Weston saw the 'families of choice' of the 1980s as a response both to an ideological rejection of the nuclear family and a need for alternative forms of support for lesbians and gay men. In contrast to the lack of autonomy and affection many lesbians experienced in their interactions with their families of origin, families of choice were characterized by the affirmative agency lesbians exercised in creating and sustaining them. By the mid-1990s, British sociologists, Weeks, Heaphy and Donovan, identified a further shift, enabled by changing social attitudes to same-sex intimacy and the family. While noting that this was a period of transition in concepts of the family more broadly, they found evidence of a broadening of notions of chosen family, to encompass a blend of friends and lovers with selected members of biological family.[13] Australian personal narratives point to a similar trend occurring amongst Australian lesbians. Sally described her family as 'people who I admire, respect and who are good people, positive influences', which, for her, included 'family related by blood [and] then there's the family of friends that we have who have been fantastic support'. From the late 1990s, Sally 'included the two different types of family in the same family celebrations'.[14] Rachel similarly considered her family to be a blend of friends, blood and adoptive family. She commented: 'my family was huge. My family was my friends, my women's group people, particularly you know different people within the Women's Network. Also my actual family and my extended family.'[15] In the context of these shifting notions of 'family', this chapter considers the extent and nature of Australian and British lesbians' interactions with their families of origin and 'chosen families', exploring the sources of practical and emotional support available to women at key moments in their life course.

Negotiation or estrangement: Relationships with families of origin

British and Australian lesbians' relationships with their families of origin varied considerably throughout the second half of the twentieth century. In the immediate post-war years, many women chose to conceal their same-sex desires and relationships from their families of origin, believing that their families would disapprove or not understand, or wishing to avoid hurting them. Virginia reflected that she kept her social life on the camp scene in Sydney secret in the early 1960s because: 'I was more worried about my parents. Like I didn't want my parents to be hurt or them to think any differently of me, that was probably my main motivation.'[16] Sandie also kept her lesbian relationship from her parents in 1960s Brighton, recalling the occasional nerve-wracking moments when the separate worlds of family and relationships nearly collided:

> My parents turned up in Brighton out of the blue. Oh, my God, that was terrifying! They rang me from Brighton seafront, from somewhere near the Aquarium, and I was so lucky because they couldn't find me. They couldn't find Grand Parade, they couldn't find where I was living with my girlfriend, so they rang to say, 'We're here, darling! But we can't find you.' Thank God for that! Oh! Because, I mean, they thought I'd moved down on my own, you see.

Sandie spent a panicked fifteen minutes removing all evidence of her girlfriend's presence from their home before meeting her parents at the seafront.[17] Similarly, when Margaret recognized her attraction to other women in 1950s' Sydney, she went to considerable lengths to conceal her lesbianism from her family, maintaining two separate flats to disguise her relationship with her lover and telling her parents stories of dates with men. Aware that her sexuality would conflict with their working-class Catholic moral views, Margaret never told them and reflected that, by the time she adopted a more open lesbian identity in the 1970s: 'Mother had died and father had died so I spared her that shame.'[18] For these women, and many others, keeping knowledge of their sexuality from their parents enabled them to maintain an ongoing relationship with families of origin.

However, discretion was not always an option and the revelation of lesbianism could be devastating to familial relationships. Laurie, who had her first sexual relationship with another girl at the age of eleven, was caught by her mother, kissing a girl. Her 'tomboyish' gender presentation was a further source of concern to her father, and when he found out about her attraction to girls, he sent her for medical treatment to 'cure' her of her lesbianism. At the age of sixteen, Laurie and her then girlfriend jumped on a train from the small rural town of Manjimup, WA, where she was raised, and ran away to Sydney. Although Laurie was able to maintain a good relationship with her mother, who visited her in Sydney, she remained estranged from the rest of her family.[19] Laurie's experience was not unusual when families became aware of a woman's lesbianism in this period and Francesca Curtis, one of the founding members of Australia's first lesbian organization, Australasian Lesbian Movement, recalled that the group was established to provide a point of contact for women who needed support after familial estrangement. One of the other founders, she explained, 'knew this young woman and when she told her parents that she was a lesbian they threw her out and wouldn't have anything to do with her and she committed suicide'.[20] Familial rejection was not inevitable, however, and some women described supportive relationships with their families of origin. When founders of British lesbian organization, Minorities Research Group, Julie Switsur and Cynthia Reid, began a relationship in the mid-1960s, their mothers came to MRG social meetings to help run the group's library service.[21]

Although discretion seemed the only or best strategy to many in the post-war decades, the emphasis on 'coming out' as a political act encouraged women who were involved in feminist or lesbian activism in the 1970s and 1980s to declare their sexuality to their parents and wider family. For some, this led to a breach with their families of origin. Margaret, who was active in lesbian and feminist political circles in the late 1960s and early 1970s, told her siblings about her sexuality in 1974. Her family reacted badly to the news and, over thirty years later, the pain was apparent in her account of this experience: 'There was a sister, an evil sister and an even more evil brother, who didn't take at all kindly to my being a lesbian ... My brother, who was a big red-neck pig of a man, was horrified by it. And I didn't have, haven't had any connection with either of them since then much at all.'[22] Later generations of British and Australian lesbians also experienced estrangement from families of origin. Melisa McLean recalled that, when she came out to her extended family in Haringey, their response was not positive:

> [W]hen I first came out, my mum was really cool. My sister was really great. But my extended family, my gran and my aunts and my uncles and all of that, they

found it really quite difficult. As a result, it crushed me. I was quite crushed by it. I was particularly crushed by one of my aunts because I told her first ... I told my aunt and I told her because I thought she would understand. But she didn't understand actually, and she was quite dismissive and pushed me away sort of thing. Not physically, but just mentally, psychologically. That really upset me. And then my gran, when I told my gran about it, she thought I had been possessed by the demons or something and that the young people, my friends had led me astray ... I just cut ties with them. And even though I made that decision to do that and it felt like a powerful decision and I felt like I was taking control, it was actually quite hard and it hurt me to do that.'[23]

While accounts of irrevocable breakdown in relationships and the pain this caused are apparent across the period, many women remained entangled in family networks to a greater or lesser degree, often with the topic of their sexuality remaining unspoken or ambiguous. Phyllis Papps, who was raised in a Greek family in Melbourne after the Second World War, described a period of some confusion with her family in relation to her sexuality. She recalled having had a 'long conversation' with her mother at the age of about twelve or thirteen, in which she tried to explain to her mother why she was not interested in men. When, following the death of her father in 1966, Phyllis's mother moved into a flat with Phyllis and Phyllis' lover, Robyn, Phyllis therefore assumed that her mother was aware of the nature of their relationship. However, her mother apparently understood the situation differently and claimed that it was not until 1970, when Phyllis, as a lesbian activist, took the decision to appear on television to talk explicitly about being a lesbian, that she became aware of her daughter's sexuality. Phyllis recalled that 'my mother for some years refused to have anything to do with me ... [and] took legal action to prevent me making claims on her estate'.[24] Angie Stone, who began having relationships with other women in London in the mid-1990s, suggested that, in her case, not explicitly acknowledging her sexuality to her mother opened up spaces of possibility for her mother to interact with her partners. She recalled:

Like with my mom, we didn't actually have the conversation of me being gay. Okay, it weren't even a thing of me having to say 'oh mummy I'm gay' whatever. It's like she knew. And she would meet my girlfriends, invite them round for dinner, I mean there'd be times when I'd be phoning up my girlfriend and saying 'Where are you?' and they'd say they're at my mom's, d'ya know I mean? And I'd say 'What you're doing there?' 'Oh I saw your mom so de de de whatever', you know. And when we split up my mom would ask me where they gone and I'd say 'They're mad.' And my mum would say she really liked her and I'd say 'She's mad, you know we can't have mad people in the house' ... and she'd be upset ... Cos my mum would do that, she would invite them back round to try to get us to talk ... so I had to tell my mum that they're mad and not allowed back in her house.[25]

Although Angie appeared confident that her mum 'knew' she was gay, and this may have been the case, her narrative also points to the layers of possible meaning in family interactions over sexual identity. The suggestion of confusion apparent in her account hints that there may have been some difference between what Angie 'knew' (that she was gay) and what her mum 'knew' (that these women were important to Angie but then inexplicably disappeared from Angie's life).

While levels of ambiguity in relation to sexuality enabled many women to maintain ties with their families of origin throughout the period, the nature of those relationships was nevertheless impacted by what was unspoken as much as by what was acknowledged. Heather Murray has noted the role of shared heterosexual experiences of marriage and parenthood in promoting emotional intimacy between post-war parents and their adult children and, in the absence of these points of reference women could feel emotionally distanced from families of origin.[26] In place of the emotional intimacy which Murray sees as central to notions of the ideal post-war family, Australian and British lesbian narratives point to the enduring importance of a sense of familial obligation in maintaining ties held together by caring responsibilities. As the NSW Gay and Lesbian Rights Lobby declared in their response to a discussion paper on the International Year of the Family in 1994:

> It is a ridiculous assumption that because we are homosexual we cease to be part of a family. Gay men and lesbians are sons and daughters, fathers and mothers, grandfathers and grandmothers, uncles and aunts, nephews and nieces. We appear at all levels of the family tree. With this belonging to a family comes a responsibility and commitment to caring for others in your family.[27]

Cultural assumptions that unmarried children, and especially unmarried daughters, would shoulder the primary responsibility of caring for elderly or infirm parents meant that lesbians and their families often maintained frequent contact or came together in times of crisis, regardless of tensions around a woman's lesbianism.[28] Barbara recalled two friends of hers from work, D and M, who maintained complete discretion about their relationship, while caring for D's mother:

> They always stood at opposite ends of any photograph or anything like that so no-one could possibly think they were a couple. D was very nervy and very frightened by that, having tried to train in the Anglican church as a Deaconess I think and things like that. She had still a lot of worry about that. But they lived together for 42 years and looked after D's mum, who was quite a cranky old lady etc etc. They were totally primary to each other.

Despite having been in a relationship with another woman for thirty years from the early 1960s onward, Barbara herself did not explicitly broach the topic of her sexuality with her mother until the 1990s, when she had moved into her mother's home to care for her. By this stage, her elderly mother was deaf and Barbara wrote her a note saying: 'Now between what you don't hear and what you don't want to hear, I want to be quite clear that I'm a gay person and I'm very happy about that.' Barbara offered to move out into her own flat, but, despite the fact that her mother 'never did like it', she asked Barbara to stay.[29] The theme of parents weighing up a desire for company and practical support against disapproval of a daughter's sexuality runs through many lesbian personal narratives throughout the period. Jean expressed this quite pragmatically in her account of coming out to her father in the 1970s:

> My mother had died by that stage. My father accepted it … My father, who would be perhaps the only one who might be a little bit thing about it – by this time I was in my 30s and I'd been my own person for a long, long time and I think he knew that if he rejected me I'd just have no trouble about cutting him out of my life, and he couldn't afford to do that really. So he had to accept me as I was or not at all, so I wasn't about to stand any nonsense from him and he was fine.[30]

Race, religion and biological family

The degree of openness with which women discussed their sexuality and relationships with biological family was shaped both by the nature of individual relationships and by a perception of the level of risk involved. For lesbians of colour, in particular, the support provided by families of origin could be considered too important to risk with an open declaration of lesbianism. In their 1993 book documenting the lives of Black lesbians in Britain, Valerie Mason-John and Ann Khambatta claimed:

> Many Black women see their communities as a safe space in which they are protected from the institutionalised and individual racism they experience in Britain. So for many Black lesbians, the support of their communities is of great importance … Since Coming Out can mean loss of family, friends, cultural bereavement, isolation, nervous breakdown, forced arranged marriage or fear for our lives, it is hardly surprising that some lesbians choose to lead a double life rather than lose the support and safety of their communities.[31]

As Mason-John and Khambatta suggested, for lesbians of colour, living in a racist society, the risk of losing contact with family and community was increased by the potential loss of support in coping with the daily challenges of racism. In a discussion with other black lesbians in *Feminist Review* in 1984, Gail had similarly argued that:

> The family! The family is very contradictory for us. There are emotional involvements, there are ties, the roots that it represents for us all as individuals in a fundamentally racist/sexist society. That's why Black people may decide not to come out as lesbians or gay for fear of being rejected by a group of people whom you not only love but who represent a real source of security, of foundation. That's a choice that has to be respected as a political choice, not just an individual one.[32]

Natalie Thomlinson argues that differing notions of the family were an important aspect of the alienation many Black women felt from the white women's movement in

Britain in the 1970s and 1980s. In contrast to white feminist theorizing of the nuclear family as a key site of women's oppression, 'Many Black feminists characterised the nuclear family not just as an oppressive institution, but also as a refuge from the racist state.'[33] Black feminist activism in the 1980s and 1990s theorized the family in different ways and familial models such as motherhood were central to forms of Black feminist activism.[34] The question of whether lesbians of colour were more likely to experience rejection from biological family if they came out was also raised in British lesbian and feminist discussions in this period. Shaila argued in 1984 that: 'The myth that Black families or people are more homophobic than whites should really be demolished, because really what is obvious is that the security links we need with our families/communities are stronger.'[35] For Shaila, it was the greater need Black lesbians had for family and community support which was at the root of the notion of Black homophobia. Others pointed to different explanations. Linda Bellos considered the view to be motivated purely by racism, arguing: 'Saying that homophobia is more prevalent in the Black community is like saying there are more Black men who rape.' Femi Otitoju agreed: 'It is a dirty, vicious lie that the Black community is more homophobic. This is racism. Go to any community with a strong religion or faith, and see how homophobic they are.'[36]

The impact of religious faith on the attitudes of families was raised by a number of women. Tokunbo Alijore, whose family originated in Nigeria, explained her decision to 'live two lives' in London in the 1980s and 1990s, in terms of her family's religious views:

> As an African, we don't talk about those things because they do not exist. Africans and Caribbeans are super under-the-carpet. It's not tolerated. Say you're gay, bisexual, lesbian, transgender, queer, non-binary, there's no understanding. It only got to what you did in bed, that's it. If you're gay, that's all you did. They didn't have an understanding because there was no education. You had the bible aspect of it, saying if you were this way inclined, you deserve to die.[37]

For Jeanette Winterson, who was raised by white Pentecostal adoptive parents in Lancashire in the 1960s and 1970s, her mother's discovery that she was having an affair with another girl resulted in an intervention by the whole church community. The pastor raised the issue and preached against the 'abominable sin' of lesbianism during the Sunday morning service and Jeanette's adoptive mother led an exorcism carried out by church elders. She recalled:

> There was going to be an exorcism ... it was my mother who let in the elders for the service of prayer and renunciation ... The demon is supposed to pop out and maybe set the curtains on fire or fly into the dog who will foam at the mouth and have to be strangled ...
>
> When I was locked in the parlour with the curtains closed and no food or heat for three days I was pretty sure I had no demon. After three days of being prayed over in shifts and not allowed to sleep for more than a few hours at a time, I was beginning to believe that I had all Hell in my heart.

> At the end of this ordeal, because I was still stubborn, I was beaten repeatedly by one of the elders.[38]

While Jeanette Winterson's mother drew on religious interventions to address what she considered to be sinful behaviour, other women recalled that their family's religious objections were expressed in different ways. Frances Mohan felt that her parents' negative reaction to the discovery that she was a lesbian was caused by their religious views, but prompted them to seek medical intervention:

> When I actually came out my Mum was away on holiday so I told my Dad. My Dad, like, he's a big, big time Christian and didn't take it very well, and when my Mum came back you know they I think they both sort of came to me and said: 'You have to go and see the doctor.' So I did go to the doctor, yeah. And the doctor referred me to a psychiatrist. Now of course you know in a West Indian family you just do what your parents say. You don't really question. So I went to the psychiatrist and had a chat and she just said, there's nothing wrong with you, go home.

Frances's ability to 'live her life' was assisted by the attitudes of her siblings, who reacted more positively to her sexuality. She recalled: 'I've got a younger brother and a younger sister and they were very, very supportive, really supportive you know which was really, really helpful for me.'[39] Active religious faith did not always lead families to reject lesbianism, however. Clare felt that her parents and siblings had been 'fine' when she told them she was a lesbian in early 1970s Sydney and recalled that her father 'wrote back straightaway and said, "We teach our children how to brush their hair and clean their teeth and tie their shoes. We teach them how to love. We don't teach them who to love." So they were good Catholics in that sense.'[40]

Practical family support

Kinship ties have been widely understood as a vital source of practical and emotional support at key moments in the life cycle and the quality of a woman's relationships with her family of origin could therefore have a significant impact on her access to support. In her analysis of kinship and sexuality, Judith Butler proposes:

> If we understand kinship as a set of practices that institutes relationships of various kinds which negotiate the reproduction of life and the demands of death, then kinship practices will be those that emerge to address fundamental forms of human dependency, which may include birth, child-rearing, relations of emotional dependency and support, generational ties, illness, dying, and death (to name a few).[41]

As Butler notes, in addition to general emotional support, kinship networks have the potential to provide practical assistance during childbirth and parenting and at times of illness and death or bereavement. While lesbian personal narratives point to the frequency with which women continued to fulfil these obligations towards their families of origin throughout the second half of the twentieth century, there is less evidence that women received this familial support in return. For those women who were estranged from their families or whose familial relationships were complicated by tensions around their sexuality, this practical and emotional support might not be forthcoming. As a result, women in both Australia and Britain described struggling in isolation through challenging periods in their lives or, at times, building and drawing upon lesbian and feminist networks of support.

British sociological studies of the family in the second half of the twentieth century emphasized the importance of practical support from extended family for women undertaking childbirth and parenting. In their early 1990s restudy of Young and Wilmott's classic study, *Family and Kinship in East London*, Geoff Dench, Kate Gavron and Michael Young emphasized that, for most people, a period of independence in early adulthood was followed by a reassertion of the importance of familial networks when they had children. They claimed: 'No one with children dependent on them can be independent of others. As they realize this, the mothers in our study rediscover that conventional families offer wide and durable networks, and are an effective basis for securing support.'[42] In her historical study of motherhood in Oxfordshire in the second half of the twentieth century, Angela Davis reinforces these assertions, although emphasizing some individual and regional nuance. She claims:

> Rather than recalling an institution in decline, many women throughout the period 1945–2000 reported the centrality of the extended family to their lives. In both traditional urban and rural areas the extended family network offered women company and entertainment, with families coming together to celebrate rites of passage such as engagements, weddings, christenings and funerals ... Women who were born in the 1950s and 1960s recalled how important the extended family had been during their childhood. Moreover they also referred to the importance of family connections when they raised their own children in the 1970s, 1980s and 1990s.[43]

Carla Pascoe Leahy similarly asserts the importance of familial support in her historical study of Australian motherhood, claiming that the mother's most significant relationship on the birth of a child, apart from that with their child, is the relationship with their own mother.[44] Pascoe Leahy offers a nuanced picture of the late twentieth century, charting a shift over time, from a more reticent culture of mothering in the immediate post-war decades, where new mothers were expected to resolve many of the physical and emotional challenges of motherhood in private, to a more open and collaborative approach in the 1970s and 1980s, emphasizing variations in individual experience which were shaped by where a mother lived and the proximity of her family. Nevertheless, the personal narratives on which her research draws consistently emphasize the centrality of familial support to women's experience of mothering, whether in its presence or absence, and regardless of the quality of that support.

In contrast to this picture of mothers as embedded in varying degrees in extended family support networks, lesbian narratives rarely make reference to familial support or the expectation of it, suggesting that practical and emotional assistance in parenting was typically contingent on a heterosexual identity. Women who conceived their children in the context of heterosexual marriages support this view in their accounts, indicating that the move from heterosexual marriage to a lesbian identity could be marked by a shift in relationships with extended family. Emily Struick, who began a relationship with another woman while married and pregnant in the late 1980s, recounted a 'rather traumatic' experience with her family just after her daughter's birth:

> When I went home from the hospital, I was getting frequent calls and visits from my girlfriend and my mother, who was there to help me, asked me about them. I decided that there was no point in lying to her, so I told her the truth. Her response was extremely negative and in the following period of time I received a lot of condemnation from my family. Comments such as 'Why didn't you decide that you were a lesbian before you became pregnant?' were common. My parents even went so far as to offer my husband financial support to get [my daughter] Rosemary away from me. His parents told him to simply take Rosemary and leave me.[45]

Other women went to considerable lengths to conceal their sexuality from their families, fearing that financial or practical support would be withdrawn. Delphine, a divorced lesbian mother from Maroochydore in Queensland, told *Campaign* magazine, in the late 1970s, that she feared the practical support she received from her parents, 'who are well-off [and] very good to me and the kids' would be withdrawn if they discovered she was in a relationship with another woman.[46]

In the 1970s and 1980s, as some women began to conceive children in the context of lesbian relationships, such forms of discretion became harder to maintain and tensions with extended family were made more explicit. In 1973, *Sappho* published the correspondence between an Australian lesbian couple living in England and their parents, announcing the expected arrival of their first child. In their reply to their daughter, A (the birth mother), A's parents explained that they were 'shattered and grieved' by the news and expressed their dismay that a child was being born into a lesbian relationship. Although confirming that they still loved their daughter and would like to have a relationship with their grandchild, A's parents warned that any practical support would be dependent on her leaving her lover and recognizing the harm they believed was caused by raising a child in a lesbian environment. They offered:

> <u>If at any time</u> you come to an acceptance of the point of view we hold about what would be best, and what would be worst, for your child, you can count on our support, both financially and in every other way, in pursuing a different form of life from your present, whether in England or elsewhere. You can count on one of us coming to you in need. We are sure that you can count on all the help that your sister and brothers can give you.[47]

A's parents' letter suggested a tension between a desire to have a relationship with their grandchild and a moral and social condemnation of the notion of lesbian motherhood.

As a respectable, middle-class couple who played an active role in their local community and church, they were also concerned about how their daughter's actions would be seen by others. They explained that they intended to tell extended family members that their 'very Women's Lib' daughter 'wanted a child but not a husband', thereby implying that the child had been conceived by a heterosexual encounter rather than AID in the context of a lesbian relationship.

Other families were more accepting of lesbian mothers and offered some practical support. Chloe noted that, when she gave birth to her daughter in 1970s' Sydney, conceived after a brief affair with a man, her mother stayed with her for two weeks to provide assistance.[48] When A's lover, B, told her mother that she and A were expecting a child, her mother wrote: 'This is a diabolical thing you girls have done', but offered to 'help you all through this terrible time'. The support she offered was both practical and the sort of intergenerational advice which comprised an important aspect of familial support in parenting:

> Should you decide to come home [to Australia] after the birth I'll expect you to come here. This is your home. I'm your mother and you shall have my bedroom and the balcony will be ideal for the baby and the gardens near by ... A will need all the love and attention we can give her and maybe she would like to tell her mother I'll look after her ... Please remind A to wear a bra <u>night</u> and day or she will have dropped bosoms. She must do so at once and until she has finished feeding; also to rub her tummy with oil or it will be covered in stretch marks and oil on her breasts until she has finished feeding. These sound like old wives tales, but I did them and look at me – your lovely mother ... No use spoiling her figure. That is why there are so many flabby figures about. As for you – take the greatest care of her.[49]

While B's mother offered help despite her disapproval of her daughter's actions, some families went further in their expression of acceptance. Clare found her family in Sydney to be 'very accepting' when she introduced them to her first child, whom her lover, Linda, had given birth to in London in the early 1980s. She recalled:

> My parents saw him as their grandchild. My mother was in hospital and she had leukaemia so you couldn't go into the room unless you were gowned up. So Linda was at the door with [baby] Tom and Mum said: 'Show me, let me see my grandson.' ... So Dad thought he was lovely, went out straightaway and bought him this huge Snoopy toy that Tom had forever. We were living with Dad.[50]

Her account of familial acceptance and enthusiasm was relatively unusual, however, and many lesbian mothers of this period raised their children with limited or no familial support.

Lesbian mothers and community in the post-war decades

In the immediate post-war decades, lack of familial support or contact could result in considerable isolation for lesbian mothers. Forming alternative support networks was often problematic in a period when it was difficult to locate other lesbians and women raising children outside of marriage faced widespread social disapproval. With no lesbian organizations in existence in either country until the 1960s and limited awareness that lesbians could be mothers for another decade, lesbian mothers were typically unable to identify other women in a similar position to themselves prior to the mid-1970s. Jean and Laura, who had been raising Jean's two children together since the early 1970s, told Australian lesbian group, Older Wiser Lesbians, in 1985: 'We spent so many years bringing up the children we became very socially isolated. We didn't have many friends and no friends who were lesbians.'[51] Those who were able to access gay and lesbian bars often found that they provided little support as there were no other lesbian mothers there. In 1973, J.G. from Lancashire wrote to *Sappho* explaining that she lived in a village with her friend, her five-year-old daughter and her friend's two children. The women were able to visit gay pubs in Burnley and Manchester but found themselves to be 'the odd ones out ... We have both been married. I am a widow and my friend is seeking a divorce. Others seem always to be single. We have children, if others have a child it often seems to be left with Grandma to be brought up.'[52]

From the late 1960s, a small number of lesbian mothers in urban areas began to be able to access support from other women in a similar position. As lesbian social groups formed in the late 1960s and early 1970s, such as those which emerged from *Arena Three* and *Sappho* magazines in Britain, or CAMP NSW, Clover and Claudia's Group in Sydney and Melbourne, lesbian mothers were sometimes able to reach out to others in these networks. Sydney lesbian social group, Clover, which was established in 1971 as a respectable alternative to the commercial bar scene, accommodated lesbian mothers. Elizabeth, who joined with her partner Joy, recalled that, like them, many of the Clover members found house parties more convenient as a means of combining socializing with childcare and would bring their children and put them to bed upstairs before socializing with their friends downstairs.[53] She explained:

> They ran dances occasionally but they had membership and you met at people's houses and you had bbqs and swimming nights and booze-ups basically and meet-people nights ... And of course a lot of these women had children too [which] made [the bar scene] more difficult ... It was easier to go to someone's house and ... we slapped the kids in bed.[54]

British lesbian group, Sappho, also had several lesbian mother members, including Babs Todd, lover of *Sappho* editor, Jackie Forster. In 1974, a Sappho Gay Wives and Mothers Group was formed. The first meeting, enthusiastically reported by 'Jacqui', included a six-hour discussion session followed by dinner and a disco and was attended by twenty-three women from across the UK who were living in a wide variety of circumstances. The group agreed to meet monthly and established an organizing collective and a newsletter.[55]

Activist networks often provided a basis for lesbian mothers' groups in the early and mid-1970s. A Camp Women's Association newsletter in 1973 commented that this Sydney lesbian political group now had four or five lesbian mothers amongst its twenty to thirty members. Lesbian mothers were encouraged to come along to the

Thursday evening coffee meetings with their children and plans for a future clubhouse included 'a children's room with playpen, cots, beds, toys'.[56] In 1976, Sydney activist, Robyn Plaister, established a lesbian mothers' group in Sydney after her involvement in the Campaign Against Moral Persecution (CAMP NSW) drew her attention to the issue of child custody. Robyn herself was active in campaigning on the issue for a number of years, but the group also performed an important function as a support group for lesbian mothers and their children.[57] In Melbourne, Judith Power started WACKIT (Women and Children in Transition) in 1978 when she lost custody of her five-year-old daughter and received 'very little support' from her 'straight W[omen's] L[iberation] sisters'. The group existed for five years as a 'support, resource and action group' for lesbian mothers and all women going through marriage breakdowns.[58] In Britain, 'a small group of gay wives and mothers', who were mostly members of the Campaign for Homosexual Equality (CHE)'s Women's Campaign Committee, met in Manchester in 1975 to discuss their experiences.[59] Regional lesbian mothers' groups formed across Britain in the 1970s and 1980s, many under the umbrella of CHE.[60] After CHE's Women's Campaign Committee organized a conference in Manchester, delegates such as Linda from Buckinghamshire were motivated to try to establish groups in their local areas.[61] Leeds also had an active Lesbian Mothers Group in the 1980s, which was connected to the wider community, receiving funding from the women's discos at the Dock Hill pub in Harehills.[62] Conferences were another important means of bringing isolated lesbian mothers together to share experiences. A lesbian mothers' 'get together' was organized as part of the Brent Women's Centre Summer Festival in 1978 and 150 Australian lesbian mothers met at the Bridge the Gap Forum in Melbourne in September 1984.[63]

Many of these groups emerged from lesbian or lesbian and gay activism, rather than feminist networks, reflecting the ambiguity of feminist theoretical approaches to motherhood and the family in this period and the mixed experiences of lesbian mothers in feminist spaces and networks in the 1970s and early 1980s. Despite repeated efforts to provide childcare at conferences and other women's events, lesbian mothers regularly complained of feeling isolated from feminist communities and excluded from events.[64] This sense of exclusion was a product both of an ideological ambivalence towards motherhood and structural issues which posed practical obstacles to lesbian mothers' participation. A number of lesbians expressed the view that the Australian women's movement was unwelcoming of mothers for much of the 1970s.[65] One woman told *Sydney Women's Liberation Newsletter*:

> We have all felt alienated from the women's movement at some stage of its/our development. This alienation can be most acute if you are a woman alone with a child ... Occasionally one has to confront feminists who dislike children and feel oppressed by their prescence [sic]. At these times one must beg for understanding and tolerance. Whilst such feelings are valid in general terms, they are contrary to feminist theory and lead to feelings of guilt in the mother. Since guilt is a tool commonly used to oppress, the intolerant become our oppressors, constricting the freedom of women with children and minimizing their role as valuable members of WLM.[66]

The type of feminist discomfort this woman described also caused practical obstacles for lesbian mothers. Lynne Harne reflected that, in London:

> As a lesbian through the seventies having a child was something I often kept quiet about in both the lesbian and feminist movements … When I had problems over childcare, or the school, or with the child's father it was not something I felt I could raise as a political issue or ask support for. I felt I had no right to ask for support, because I had stupidly brought it all on myself … being a mother was my own problem and politically un-right-on.[67]

The authors of a statement issued by Melbourne group, the Lesbianfeminists, in July 1975 similarly highlighted that practical hurdles perpetuated the exclusion of lesbian mothers from feminist circles. Lesbian mothers, they argued, faced particular obstacles to participating in the movement, because they often did not have husbands or family with whom they could leave children and were therefore forced to bring them to meetings.[68] Despite repeated assertions of the importance of providing childcare at feminist events, the complaints of mothers suggest that actual provision of adequate childcare may not have been consistent. Financial constraints could also work to exclude lesbian mothers disproportionately from other women. Frequently supporting themselves and their child or children on a single wage or benefit payment, lesbian mothers often struggled financially and were unable to fund travel to conferences or other feminist events.[69] Joan, who was involved with the Radicalesbians and other lesbian groups in Melbourne in the early 1970s, recalled that she was one of very few women in those circles with children. While she was able to ask gay male friends to babysit her three elder children, she took the baby with her to conferences and meetings. As a young, Aboriginal woman with four children, she found the Radicalesbians to be very white and middle-class and felt that they were able to live comfortably on the dole in the knowledge that their parents would support them if necessary, while she struggled to feed her children on a widow's pension and lived on porridge and lamb shank broth.[70]

Mothers of boy children found it particularly difficult to access feminist spaces as separatist ideas and the emphasis on women-only space often precluded the presence of boys. Linda and her partner, Clare, were living in the Seagull lesbian housing co-op in London in the early 1980s when Linda gave birth to their son, and she recalled that some of the other residents were so hostile that she felt she couldn't go out in case he cried on the stairs and someone shouted at her. She explained:

> There were a few women there who really thought … there shouldn't be a boy at all in that housing co-op … of any kind and actually came and talked to us and said we should give him away, we should give him, we should find some nice gay men, who, you know, they want boys so we should give him away. A couple of them were people I'd had reasonably close relationships with so it kind of really, you know it kind of surprised me … and people coming and saying those kind of things to you was really hard … There were also lots of people there who tried to protect us from them and did lovely things and came over and brought us meals and all that kind of thing so it wasn't the majority by any means but it made it really difficult to live there.[71]

During the 1980s, as more lesbians became parents, there was a growing recognition of the practical needs of lesbian mothers. Some lesbian feminist communities sought to establish systems of support for parents, while feminist publications increasingly discussed the issues faced by lesbian mothers. Victoria Golding notes that, in the lesbian community which formed in Todmorden in Lancashire in the 1980s, a babysitting rota was established for lesbian parents, allowing women to leave their children with another member of the community on a Saturday and participate in social events such as the women's disco or activism against Section 28.[72]

While the Todmorden babysitting rota continued for eight or nine years, many of the lesbian mothers' groups and initiatives were short-lived, compounding the isolation experienced by lesbian mothers.[73] With some lesbian mothers still married or concealing their sexuality and others struggling to raise children with little support and limited financial resources, there were many obstacles to collective organizing. Sylvia, who raised her younger sisters in Adelaide in the early 1970s, following the death of her mother, recalled that, although she had 'a lot of friends in the women's movement and, of course, they were all lesbians', she did her mothering without support:

> It wasn't easy, but I didn't have anybody to talk to. I didn't have any help, there was nobody – my brother was there, but he wouldn't help. He didn't do any babysitting … The whole thing was there was nobody in my age group had children of that age and people were not having babies … that all came later. So I didn't have anyone to talk to about it, but I never thought about it. What you don't have, you don't know and I just managed, I suppose.[74]

Throughout the 1980s and 1990s there continued to be periods and geographical areas where women felt isolated from communities of lesbian mothers. Katharine recalled that, when she was raising her sons in Canberra in the 1980s, she did not know any other lesbian mothers and she was not aware of any single parents at her boys' school either.[75] When Linda and Clare returned to Australia from London with their children in the mid-1980s, Linda tried hard to establish a lesbian mothers' group along the lines of the close feminist self-insemination group they had left behind in London. However, despite repeatedly advertising in the Sydney gay and feminist press, she did not receive much response and was unsuccessful in building a community of lesbian mothers.[76] Similarly, Sally, who left her marriage to begin a lesbian relationship in late 1980s Melbourne, reflected that 'As far as I knew [lesbian mothers' groups] didn't exist … So on an individual basis I shared experiences with other lesbian mums but it was few and far between.'[77]

The practical hurdles which lesbian mothers had faced in earlier decades continued to present an obstacle to lesbian mother's community formation into the 1990s. In 1998, Lyn Morgain, a sociologist and lesbian parent of three, who was due to give the keynote address at the National Lesbian Parenting Conference in Canberra, told *LOTL* magazine:

> Yes, I am saying it's harder to take part in gay and lesbian community life when you've got children. For me, that's not a big drama, but on a political level I completely appreciate and understand why there is a dialogue about inaccessibility

of night-time entertainment. For many lesbian parents, non-participation in events really calls into question their sense of being part of a community, or being a dyke at all.[78]

As Lyn Morgain suggested, the centrality of the commercial bar scene to lesbian and gay community spaces excluded children and made it difficult for their parents to attend. As wider social attitudes to single mothers and lesbians became more tolerant towards the end of the 1990s, lesbian mothers often found that much of their leisure time was spent at children's activities, prompting them to mix with the typically heterosexual parents of their children's friends. The difficulties of accessing lesbian communities were often greater for those lesbian parents who were not resident in cities or larger urban areas. When British actor Sophie Ward left her heterosexual marriage and began a new life with her lover and children in 1996, she lived in a small village. She reflected: 'For a long time, we were the only gay parents we knew.'[79]

Support in old age and times of crisis

In addition to the experience of reproduction and parenting, the need for physical care, financial assistance or other forms of practical support could emerge at different stages in women's lives, such as during periods of illness or unemployment or following the break-up of a relationship. It is difficult to gauge the extent to which these types of support were available to British and Australian lesbians, particularly in the immediate post-war decades, when many women were isolated from wider lesbian networks. Andrée, who lived with her partner, Grace, in Essex and then Cornwall between the 1950s and 1990s, recalled knowing a small number of other lesbians for whom she and Grace would occasionally provide support in times of crisis.[80] It seems likely that women who were part of communities centred on urban lesbian bars in the 1950s and 1960s may also have established mutual support networks to meet these needs. Recalling the lesbian social scene in Brighton in the 1950s and 1960s, Vicky suggested that these networks were close and self-sufficient, explicitly regarded as 'family' by their members: 'It was a very insular position really because you became part of a very close-knit family, if you like. And the outside world didn't really encroach on it.'[81] Sandie echoed this view, reflecting: 'In the sixties, there was more of a sort of family feeling. I don't know how else to express it. Because we used to say, then, "Oh, he's family or she's family." Even if you didn't know them. And that immediately gave you a feeling of closeness because being gay was being one of a minority group.'[82] Social and bar communities such as this sometimes provided assistance in times of crisis. Laura Jackson, who became part of a lesbian butch/femme bar community in Southampton, in the early 1970s, recalled:

> [D]espite violence in a lot of relationships, there was a great deal of love and caring in that community. Women would do anything for each other. If anyone was in

trouble, if anyone was going to get the sack for being 'queer', they would all support each other. They'd share money, they'd share their flats.[83]

Outside of bar communities, local neighbourhoods and housing networks also acted as a source of support for some women. Sandie recalled that, in her building in Brighton:

[T]here were two gay boys living on the ground floor, two gay girls living in the basement and us two on the second floor ... But the six of us gays, we were all desperately short of money and several of us were out of work and the money just used to run out because we were all trying to help one another out and help to keep one another.[84]

For young people, in particular, this type of support continued to be important and, at times, available, in later decades. Ley Anderson, who lived in a shared lesbian house in Peckham in the late 1980s, recalled:

There was more of tight knit-ness back then, and there were different kind of groups and networks. So if one didn't have one thing, another would help out ... some of us were students, some of us were in-between jobs as they say, some of us were downright just unemployed. Whatever it was, and I remember thinking, "Right, okay, I'm low on food." There were food banks and all that, that these days ... This was, you low on food, you go to your mate ... But it was all sorted. It was like, "Listen, well, yeah, take some bread, take some beans" ... Sometimes a bit of adversity helps cohesiveness and none of us didn't have ... We weren't living like lords, do you know what I mean? We were young, so there wasn't a lot of money, so we just left home ... and I think that I felt that people had my back a bit more, if that makes sense?[85]

Later in life and in times of illness, emotional and caring needs became more pressing for many women. In her 1994 review of gerontological research and its implications for the family and social networks of Australian older lesbians, Judith Davis argued that:

Family support is seen to be an important factor in healthy ageing, and in delaying admission to institutional care. For some lesbians, there is often a geographical and/or emotional distance from their families of origin. Social networks, and intimate relationships shift and move over time, and professional careers may add to this dilemma.[86]

It is difficult to assess the nature and degree of support British and Australian lesbians may have received during illness and old age, as women in these circumstances rarely had an opportunity to articulate or record their experiences. Monika Kehoe's 1980s survey of the experiences of lesbians over the age of sixty in the United States concluded that: 'We cannot help but notice the relatively low priority given to family members [amongst those from whom lesbians would seek help during serious ill health], whether because there aren't any or because, if they exist, they would not be supportive.'[87] It seems likely that Australian and British lesbians would similarly prefer to seek assistance from lovers or lesbian or gay friends. Occasionally, lesbian personal narratives refer to providing this type of support. Gill mentioned her role in caring for an older lesbian friend in Brighton in the 1960s, recalling:

> Laurie'd just come out of hospital and she was still in bed, in effect, at home. She was an old friend I'd met on my first visit to Pigott's. So I said, 'Well, I'll go and look after her and live with her till she's better.' She'd got a separate room so I moved in with her. She didn't seem to get any better. Anyway, one day the surgeon turned up and said she possibly only had three months left to live, so I decided I was going to devote all the time I could to making her last days happy. I started inviting people in to see her.[88]

More commonly, women in relationships received emotional and caring support from lovers. Eleanor met her lover, Doreen, at work in the British Civil Service in 1952 and the couple were together for thirty years before Doreen died. Eleanor recalled:

> Towards the end of her life [Doreen] became very ill, this was a very anxious time for us and as she got worse it became harder to maintain the old feelings for each other. She was ill for two years, I used to pick her up from the hospital on Saturday mornings and take her back on Sunday evenings so that she had some sort of home life from the hospital. I knew she would have done that for me.[89]

Women who were not in long-term committed relationships could be more vulnerable to isolation in their final years, however. Mairi, whose mother Babs Todd who had been in a relationship with *Sappho* editor, Jackie Forster, in the 1970s, recalled the final years of Jackie Forster's life in the late 1990s. Mairi and Jackie had lost touch when Babs's relationship with Jackie broke down in the late 1970s, but the pair met again coincidentally, when Mairi was an adult. Mairi explained:

> And then, when she realised who I was, she just ... after that, she always called me her 'almost daughter' and burst into tears, and was terribly proud of our relationship, and ... I actually was the person who notified, when she died, and looked after all the, you know, going to the Registry Office, and getting her papers together, and things, because she ... when she died, she died with nothing and no one, really.[90]

Mairi's account of Jackie Forster's final illness points to the isolation that even women who had previously been active members of wide lesbian networks could experience in periods of dependency or old age.

The risks faced by lesbians who needed care were addressed by some lesbian feminist communities in Britain and Australia in the 1980s and 1990s. As women who had formed networks through feminist activism in the 1970s and 1980s began to consider the implications of aging, some debated collective strategies they could employ to maintain their independence during illness and in old age. Jean, who became part of a strong lesbian feminist network in Melbourne from the 1970s, described the community response when her lover developed terminal cancer in the 1990s:

> We set up a Lesbian Cancer Support Group at that time, a few of us; I was in desperate need of something like that. The community rallied, they were very good, and I've been involved in many deaths over the years where we've rallied and supported each other ... people would come in and visit ... but we didn't need the 24-hour care, the roster that we've had for a lot of our friends over the time.

Jean made a distinction between the social and emotional support she and her lover needed in this instance and the wider range of practical assistance other women might require. She explained:

> A lot of members in our community are not with anybody so we've got to support each other and we have to have a back-up executor too ... We might not even – we don't see each other all the time but we know – I know certain women in the community, lesbians in the community, who would be here for me without any trouble whatsoever ... Even the ones that I'm not particularly fond of I know would be around ... In fact, I remember one lesbian years ago who wasn't particularly liked who didn't have many friends who chose to die at home rather than go into hospital. Boom, there was a whole roster, 24 hours, not a problem. We'd always talked in the Lesbian Cancer Support Group, it's all very well for those who are popular or who have many friends or have a partner. It's those women who don't have a partner and who don't have many friends, what happens to them? Well this woman was a case in point you know, that she just wanted to die at home and everybody rallied.[91]

Victoria Golding identified similar support networks based on a culture of collective care in her research into the lesbian community in Todmorden, Lancashire, in the 1980s and 1990s. Her interviewees noted that, in times of crisis such as serious illness and death, the lesbian community would work together to provide practical support such as cooking, cleaning and childcare for women they may not necessarily have been close to.[92]

Emotional support

If notions of lesbian kinship were important in providing a source of practical support to British and Australian lesbians in this period, these ties were a crucial source of emotional support for many in difficult periods of their lives. Theorists of queer emotion have noted that queer people may experience grief, loss or trauma not just in moments of bereavement or relationship breakdown, but in the mundane encounters of daily life which exclude them or produce discomfort or a sense of failure. As Sara Ahmed argues, these experiences of queer loss go unrecognized by heterosexual culture, which does not value what has been lost: 'the failure to recognise queer loss *as* loss is also a failure to recognise queer relationships as significant bonds, or that queer lives are worth living, or that queers are more than failed heterosexuals, heterosexuals who have failed "to be".[93] Lesbian personal narratives of the late twentieth century are full of accounts of unspoken grief and unrecognized loss. Diana Chapman recalled the sense of distance she felt as a lesbian in 1950s and 1960s London from work colleagues and friends with whom she could not discuss her emotional life:

> Can't talk about it. And of course another awful aspect of it is that if you're desperately upset because of your emotional life, and let's face it, a lot of us spend a hell of a lot of time being upset about our emotional lives, I mean if you're a straight woman you can come in and 'Oh my god, he's gone off with another woman, I feel so terrible!' and they'd all say. 'Oh you know, he's treating her so badly, the swine!' but you could be bleeding from the ears but you could say nothing. You couldn't say, 'I'm in love with a woman and she's gone off with another woman'. You had to keep quiet about everything![94]

This sense of isolation could be particularly acute when a lover was the only other lesbian a woman knew. Margaret, who had carefully concealed her relationship with her lover, Jann, in 1950s Sydney, described her extreme isolation when Jann decided to marry an American naval officer and move to the United States. She recalled:

> And there was I in Sydney feeling really very bad because this had happened and she'd really gone and I was alone and she was there and I was very sad and lost and depressed and angry and lots of other things. But we were writing all these happy letters because I didn't want her to know I was feeling as bad as I was, so I was writing these happy letters, 'How are you?', 'What fun it must be'. And not telling her how bad I was feeling.[95]

Decades later, Barbara in Melbourne described a similar experience. Reflecting on the break-up of her first, long-term relationship with another woman in the late 1980s, Barbara recalled that her loneliness was exacerbated by her isolation from lesbian networks. The two women had met at college in the early 1960s and, although her lover had gradually become 'much more aware and in touch with what was going on in lesbian things', Barbara's visual impairment meant that she 'had no way to find those things out'. Looking back on the period when their relationship broke up, Barbara remembered:

> But when she really went out of my life, that was a terrible time ... so I thought it'd be nicer to die, but of course you don't ... I had a very lonely time, because I really didn't know where I could go to find out anything. I don't, didn't read well enough to read the phonebook or anything even if there was anything in it, or magazines

or papers or anything. Finally, one of my friends let me know about the [lesbian] organisation called Lynx which was the most wonderful group …

Only one person, a colleague, who's a very straight, devoted Anglican woman, said 'Barb, whatever's wrong?' Nobody else as far as I know noticed or thought about it or – which is fine, I didn't want them to. So I told her, and again, she was quite troubled that this would be the case, but could see that it was the case, that this was a grief equal to any marriage breakup or anything else. In fact it's almost harder for us, because so much has had to be hidden. In a marriage breakup, everyone's allowed to be sympathetic, whereas we had to carry the lot, and all the previous pain.[96]

The inability to express or receive recognition of loss with the ending of a relationship could also be exacerbated by legal structures and cultural practices which denied the existence of that relationship. Barbara described the experience of her friend, M, whose partner, D, died after forty-two years of their being together. She explained:

That was a story in itself because M looked after [D] through awful blood cancer and bone cancer and things and terrible haemorrhages and, you know, ghastly things. Then, when D actually died, M wasn't allowed into the room in the hospital to say goodbye because she wasn't next of kin. It was just so grieving. M never really got over that.[97]

Londoner, Sharley McLean, was devastated when Georgina, her lover of over twenty years, died while on a visit to her family in 1977:

She went to her family for Christmas; they wanted her to come. She was saying she hadn't been feeling all that well; she'd been very busy with her school work. She took all these photographs and she was going to put them in an album. Then she hadn't phoned and she hadn't phoned and I kept waiting and by Boxing Day I thought, 'This is so unlike her'. And I phoned and I was told she had died, just like that, and then immediate hostility. They obviously found letters and photographs; they wouldn't even tell me where she was getting buried. I couldn't go to her funeral and they told me, 'You're wicked, you're evil, you led her astray'. They destroyed the photographs. I just walked around like a zombie.[98]

The hostility Sharley experienced from Georgina's family was echoed in Maxine's account of her lover, Izzi's sudden death in Perth in 1989. She recalled:

[S]he hadn't told her family that she was in a relationship with a woman and so it was messy, yeah, it was messy and complicated and very, very sad. So there were some people that understood, and those who stood beside me, and of course most people don't understand cause most people haven't been through it. That was just a lonely time. It was a three year relationship and there's all of that overlay of we weren't married, we weren't this, we weren't – you know, it's not as if I'm a widow … [I was living] in her house, so I had to find somewhere to live, and I went around to her place to pick up the bicycle – the one that I'd made her – because I didn't have any wheels and her parents called the police on me and didn't let me into the place until after the funeral and they let me go in for an hour to get my stuff and then I had to find somewhere to live.[99]

The very real possibility of being excluded from hospitals or funerals of loved ones by hostile family members or healthcare workers was an ongoing source of concern and debate in lesbian publications from the 1960s to the 1990s, which drove debates about relationship recognition.[100] Alice Petherbridge reflected on the problem of biological family excluding lesbian lovers and friends from funerals in an article in *Labrys Newspaper*, commenting that, in the event that 'the person who has died is a lesbian friend or lover … The family usually takes over, lesbian friends have no input into the service and often there is no mention of lesbianism or lesbian friends or lovers.'[101] The solution, she suggested, was to develop alternative lesbian forms of mourning, which were more relevant to the emotions and beliefs of those involved.

The particular experience of queer grief and loss meant that women who were part of lesbian kinship networks described looking to these relationships for sources of emotional support. Pavithra Prasad suggests that this urge to find solace in lesbian kinship reflects a shared understanding of the unique nature of queer loss:

> [A]s queer people, we know loss as an inevitable part of becoming queer. Queer kinship heals these wounds in ways that are immeasurable. We hold each other in relation not because we know the detailed contours of each other's pain, but because we see in them an interstitial quality that mirrors our own. Perhaps that is why, when we face loss and grief, our chosen family can grieve with us without having had the same attachments or traumas. I share with my queer family, forms of grief that remain veiled; forms of grief that are minoritized, not just because they are the lived realities of queer minorities, but because they are made minor to queer people themselves.[102]

For Prasad, queer kinship is crucial in providing solace in times of grief because only queer kin can appreciate the ways in which such grief is compounded over time and exacerbated by the daily experience of its denial and minimalization. For these reasons, many British and Australian lesbians turned by choice to lesbian friends and family for emotional support, even when alternative sources of support were available to them. Clare, whose relationship came to an end after more than two decades, recalled: 'when I split up with [Linda] and I was incredibly distraught for a long time, my sisters and brothers were terrific and wonderful but I wanted to be with other lesbians. So I have very close lesbian relationships.'[103] Jean similarly distinguished between her biological family of children and grandchildren, with whom she shared a strong, loving bond, and her lesbian kin who represented her source of emotional support: 'I'm very much involved with my biological family because of the grandchildren but my lesbian community is my support, my home base, and that's where I live most of the time.'[104]

Conclusion

British and Australian lesbian narratives point to shifting notions of kinship over the second half of the twentieth century. In the post-war period, when hostile social attitudes meant disclosure of same-sex desire could result in the breakdown of relationships, many women sought to maintain contact with families of origin by concealing their sexuality. As visibility became an increasingly important part of lesbian identity from the 1970s onwards, a gradual shift towards greater openness occurred, but ambiguity remained central to the ways in which many women negotiated their relationships with families of origin. Although avoiding a total breach with families of origin was important to most women, especially lesbians of colour, for whom family also represented a network of support against racism, the extent to which lesbians received practical or emotional support from families of origin varied. In its absence, some women, particularly in the post-war decades, described experiencing considerable isolation and precarity. However, for others, lesbian networks provided an important source of financial and caring support and lesbian and other queer friends and lovers offered a unique form of emotional sustenance which helped to redefine notions of family and kinship.

Conclusion

The diverse histories of lesbian intimacy explored in this book prompt a rethinking of established narratives in post-war British and Australian history. While it has long been accepted that both societies witnessed profound transformations in heterosexual practice, marriage patterns and notions of parenting in the second half of the twentieth century, the ways in which same-sex desire was implicated in this history has not been considered. Personal accounts demonstrate that women who desired other women were entangled in these shifts, both reacting to and, at times, driving change. Paying attention to these stories enriches our understanding of British and Australian lesbian history as well as reframing current narratives of family and intimate life more broadly.

Lesbian notions and practices of intimacy were shaped throughout the second half of the twentieth century by a cultural context in which desire between women was simultaneously silenced and vilified. Few cultural representations of lesbianism were available in either country before the late 1960s and this cultural silence was particularly profound in an Australian context. Novels, films and documentaries with lesbian characters or themes depicted intimate relationships between women as immature, warped or doomed to failure while media representations typically linked lesbianism with crime, divorce or antisocial behaviour. The concept of 'lesbian motherhood' as a possible identity category did not begin to acquire cultural meaning until the 1970s and thereafter became a focus of hostility in the media. While feminist and lesbian and gay communities and activism produced and encouraged a proliferation of more positive depictions of lesbian existence from the mid-1960s onwards, this was a gradual process, marked by setbacks and regional variations. Many women who desired, loved and built lives with other women therefore did so in a context of relative or complete social isolation throughout the period, with no cultural scripts on which to draw in imagining and structuring their relationships. Their practices of intimacy drew on and adapted dominant cultural models and ideals, including marriage, commitment and prescribed domestic roles. Others met lovers through communities located in lesbian subcultures or feminist networks and developed forms of lesbian intimacy collectively, forging alternative relational structures.

While the absence of cultural scripts posed conceptual challenges for women expressing intimacy and forming families with other women, the context of social hostility produced structural barriers. Gender inequalities in relation to mortgages and other contracts limited women's access to housing, while social hostility to overt lesbian relationships produced difficulties in securing rental accommodation and prevented women from expressing lesbian intimacy in family homes. The integrity of women's families was threatened for much of the period by a hostile legal environment in which courts and social welfare officials typically considered lesbians to be unfit mothers and legal frameworks constrained lesbians' access to a variety of routes into motherhood. Negative social attitudes expressed by friends, family and colleagues and articulated in the media impacted on women's choices and experiences throughout the period. Lesbians faced verbal and physical abuse, estrangement from family, hostility from neighbours and schools, and the economic disadvantages which arose from precarious employment and social dislocation.

Women who desired and forged intimate relationships with other women responded to this context in a variety of ways. Many forms of lesbian intimacy were characterized by discretion. Particularly in the early post-war decades, women often attempted to conceal their relationships with other women from those around them. This impetus shaped lesbian forms of domesticity, prompting lovers to live apart or to adapt the layout or presentation of their homes in order to mask the sexual or emotional nature of their relationships from others. While a desire for commitment was often more urgent in the context of social isolation and the cultural framing of lesbian relationships as fragile and short-lived, wedding ceremonies and other expressions of commitment were typically small, private affairs in the 1950s and 1960s. For women raising children throughout the period, discretion often seemed an imperative in the face of hostile legal and social frameworks in which known lesbian mothers risked losing custody of or access to their children in court or at the hands of social welfare officials.

Although the need to survive and to protect intimate relationships with women and children often required constant negotiation with levels of visibility and discretion, lesbians also responded to hostile social conditions by challenging social attitudes and oppressive social structures. Intimate relations were an ongoing focus of lesbian activism from the 1960s onwards in both Britain and Australia. Lesbians were advocating for same-sex marriage as part of a wider claim for relationship recognition and kinship rights throughout the period, insisting both on the need for next-of-kin recognition and pension and housing rights and on the emotional importance for some of religious ceremonies and public acknowledgement of their relationships. Parenting was a key site of lesbian activism after the 1970s, with a range of support and lobbying groups challenging family court rulings against lesbian mothers, protesting against legislation which asserted the primacy of nuclear family models and advocating for lesbian rights to foster, adopt and access reproductive technologies.

Both the need for discretion and the impetus to activism shaped lesbian forms of intimacy in unique ways in late twentieth-century Britain and Australia. In the early post-war decades intimate relationships between women were often structured around an assumption of the importance of roles. Women who forged same-sex relationships in isolation and lacked cultural scripts for lesbian intimacy described looking to their parents' marriages, or to wider social structures of intimacy as models for their relationships, while the impact of butch/femme relational forms on women who met lovers through lesbian subcultural communities produced a conceptual reliance on roles in different ways. The impact of feminist theorizing around the family and gendered roles prompted the emergence of new structures of intimacy from the 1960s onwards, however, with a growing emphasis on equality as an ideal in lesbian relationships. Approaches to sexual desire and intimacy similarly reflected these influences, with monogamy and commitment typically imagined as ideals in the immediate post-war decades, and alternative sexual cultures prioritizing non-monogamy and sexual and emotional independence emerging in the 1970s.

Feminist and lesbian and gay activism impacted on lesbian forms of intimacy in other ways too. The growth of visible lesbian communities from the 1970s onwards and the political emphasis on 'coming out' and declaring a lesbian identity produced shifts both in models of lesbian relationships and parenting practices and in wider social attitudes towards same-sex intimacy. Although some women openly expressed their desire for other women or structured their relationships around visible gendered roles in the 1950s and 1960s, from the 1970s onwards the goal of living openly in a lesbian relationship or raising children as a lesbian mother became an ideal which an increasing number of women sought to attain. Continued social hostility and the ongoing threat of consequences such as familial estrangement, loss of employment or child custody prompted women to make strategic decisions about visibility, choosing to be out at work but not to family or out to friends but not to ex-husbands. Nevertheless, the gradual shift away from concealment of lesbian practices of intimacy had a significant impact on cultural and social attitudes towards lesbian relationships and lesbian parenting. As a growing number of women took part in demonstrations for lesbian mothers' rights or told their stories of adoption or self-insemination to journalists, they generated a wider social awareness of the possibility of lesbian motherhood and demonstrated to teachers, neighbours, families and friends that there were alternative ways to be a parent outside of heterosexual marriage. Similarly, as more women chose to tell their friends and neighbours that the woman they lived with was their lover, or to invite their families to their lesbian wedding, they produced a discursive shift in how intimacy between women was understood in late twentieth-century Britain and Australia.

These shifts had implications beyond social and cultural attitudes to lesbianism. Lesbian practices of intimacy reshaped models of intimacy and family life across Australian and British society. As women involved in feminist theorizing and activism advocated equality as an ideal in intimate relationships, lesbian relationships provided a unique space for new forms of intimacy to be explored. Some women forged non-monogamous relations with multiple female lovers or aimed to structure their relationships around ideals of equality and autonomy. As their relational forms became more visible in the last decades of the twentieth century, they created new cultural scripts which suggested alternative models of intimacy to the traditional patriarchal marriage and helped drive a transformation in acceptable and ideal forms of intimacy. Lesbian parenting practices also challenged established concepts of the family, profoundly unsettling assumptions about the psychological and social importance for children of being parented by a singular, biological mother, supported by a biological father. These shifts were gradual and hard-won by generations of lesbian parents who struggled to maintain and build new forms of lesbian family in the face of media vitriol and a denial of their right to care for their children, but the implications have been profound. As my own children enter their teens at a time of renewed cultural anxiety around gender and sexuality, I am inexpressibly grateful for the life these previous generations made possible for me and conscious of the responsibility to keep struggling to make space for new forms of queer kinship and intimacy in the future.

Notes

Introduction

1. Jeska Rees, '"Are You a Lesbian?" Challenges in Recording and Analysing the Women's Liberation Movement in England', *History Workshop Journal* 69, no. 1 (2010): 177–87; Sally Newman, 'Sites of Desire: Reading the Lesbian Archive', *Australian Feminist Studies* 25, no. 64 (2010): 147–62.
2. For example, Nan Alamilla Boyd and Horacio N. Roque Ramírez, eds., *Bodies of Evidence: The Practice of Queer Oral History* (Oxford: Oxford University Press, 2012); Clare Summerskill, Amy Tooth Murphy and Emma Vickers, eds., *New Directions in Queer Oral History: Archives of Disruption* (London: Routledge, 2022).
3. Sherna Berger Gluck and Daphne Patai, *Women's Words: The Feminist Practice of Oral History* (London: Routledge, 2016); Michael Frisch, *A Shared Authority: Essays on the Craft and Meaning of Oral and Public History* (Albany: State University of New York Press, 1990).
4. Amy Tooth Murphy, 'Listening in, Listening Out: Intersubjectivity and the Impact of Insider and Outsider Status in Oral History Interviews', *Oral History* 48, no. 1 (2020): 35–44.
5. Dan Royles, '"Fuck the Gay Movement": Dissemblance and Desire in a Black AIDS Activist Oral History', in *New Directions*, ed. Summerskill et al.
6. Rebecca Jennings, '"It Was a Hot Climate and It Was a Hot Time": Lesbian Migration and Transnational Networks in the Mid-twentieth Century', *Australian Feminist Studies* 25, no. 63 (2010): 31–45; Rebecca Jennings and Liz Millward, '"A Fully Formed Blast from Abroad"? Australasian Lesbian Circuits of Mobility and the Transnational Exchange of Ideas in the 1960s and 1970s', *Journal of the History of Sexuality* 25, no. 3 (2016): 463–88; Rebecca Jennings, '"A Meeting of Different Tribes"? Travelling Women and Mobility between European and Australasian Women's Lands', *Women's History Review* 31, no. 1 (2022): 88–106.
7. Laura Doan, *Disturbing Practices: History, Sexuality, and Women's Experience of Modern War* (Chicago: University of Chicago Press, 2013), 139.
8. Judith M. Bennett, '"Lesbian like" and the Social History of Lesbianisms', *Journal of the History of Sexuality* 9, no. 1/2 (January–April 2000): 15.
9. Doan, *Disturbing Practices*; Heather Murray, '"This Is 1975, Not 1875": Despair and Longings in Women's Letters to Cambridge Lesbian Liberation and Daughters of Bilitis Counselor Julie Lee in the 1970s', *Journal of the History of Sexuality* 23, no. 1 (2014): 96–122.
10. Levi CR Hord, 'Specificity without Identity: Articulating Post-gender Sexuality through the "non-binary lesbian"', *Sexualities* 25, nos. 5–6 (2022): 632.
11. George Morris, 'Intimacy in Modern British History', *The Historical Journal* 64, no. 3 (2021): 796.
12. Ibid., 797.

13 Jan Plamper, William Reddy, Barbara Rosenwein and Peter Stearns, 'The History of Emotions: An Interview with William Reddy, Barbara Rosenwein and Peter Stearns', *History and Theory* 49, no. 2 (May 2010): 259.
14 William Reddy, *The Making of Romantic Love: Longing and Sexuality in Europe, South Asia and Japan, 900–1200 CE* (Chicago: Chicago University Press, 2012), 348.
15 Marcus Collins, *Modern Love: An Intimate History of Men and Women in Twentieth-Century Britain* (London: Atlantic Books, 2003).
16 Hera Cook, *The Long Sexual Revolution: English Women, Sex, and Contraception 1800–1975* (Oxford: Oxford University Press, 2004).
17 Alana Harris and Timothy Willem Jones, eds., *Love and Romance in Britain, 1918–1970* (London: Palgrave Macmillan, 2015).
18 Hsu-Ming Teo, 'The Americanisation of Romantic Love in Australia', in *Connected Worlds: History in Transnational Perspective*, ed. Ann Curthoys and Marilyn Lake (Canberra: ANU Press, 2006).
19 Anthony Giddens, *The Transformation of Intimacy: Sexuality, Love and Eroticism in Modern Societies* (Cambridge: Polity Press, 1992), 58.
20 Ibid., 61.
21 Gillian A. Dunne, *Lesbian Lifestyles: Women's Work and the Politics of Sexuality* (London: Macmillan Press Ltd, 1997); Jeffrey Weeks, Brian Heaphy and Catherine Donovan, *Same Sex Intimacies: Families of Choice and other Life Experiments* (London: Routledge, 2001).
22 Lynn Jamieson, 'Intimacy Transformed? A Critical Look at the "Pure Relationship"', *Sociology* 33, no. 3 (August 1999): 477–94.
23 Yvette Taylor, 'The Ties that Bind: Intimacy, Class and Sexuality', in *Mapping Intimacies: Relations, Exchanges, Affects*, ed. Tam Sanger and Yvette Taylor (London: Palgrave Macmillan, 2013), 16.
24 Jacqui Gabb, 'Querying the Discourses of Love: An Analysis of Contemporary Patterns of Love and the Stratification of Intimacy within Lesbian Families', *The European Journal of Women's Studies* 8, no. 3 (2001): 318.
25 Morris, 'Intimacy', 811.
26 Heather A. Murray, *Not in This Family: Gays and the Meaning of Kinship in Postwar North America* (University of Pennsylvania Press, 2010).
27 Eve Kosofsky Sedgwick, 'Shame, Theatricality, and Queer Performativity: Henry James's The Art of the Novel', in *Gay Shame*, ed. David M. Halperin and Valerie Traub (London: University of Chicago Press, 2009).
28 Ibid., 59–60.
29 See, for example, Halperin and Traub, eds., *Gay Shame*.
30 Heather Love, *Feeling Backward: Loss and the Politics of Queer History* (London: Harvard University Press, 2007), 20–1, 29.
31 Benno Gammerl, *Anders fühlen: Gay and Lesbian Life in the Federal Republic: A History of Emotions* (München: Carl Hanser, 2021).
32 Joanna Bourke, 'Fear and Anxiety: Writing about Emotion in Modern History', *History Workshop Journal* 55, no. 1 (2003): 111–33.
33 Love, *Feeling Backward*, 21.

Chapter 1

1. Interview with Chloe Bardsley, 1 May 2012.
2. National Sound Archive (NSA), Hall Carpenter Collection (HCC) (C456/32) Julie Switsur.
3. Interview with Jenny Pausacker, 23 May 2013.
4. NSA, HCC (C456/46/01-02), Ellen Noor.
5. Lillian Faderman, *Scotch Verdict: Pirie and Woods v. Dame Cumming Gordon* (New York: William Morrow, 1983); Lillian Faderman, *Surpassing the Love of Men: Romantic Friendship and Love between Women from the Renaissance to the Present* (London: The Women's Press, 1985); Carroll Smith-Rosenburg, 'The Female World of Love and Friendship', in *Disorderly Conduct: Visions of Gender in Victorian America*, ed. Carroll Smith-Rosenburg (New York: Knopf, 1985).
6. Martha Vicinus, *Intimate Friends: Women Who Loved Women, 1778–1928* (London: University of Chicago Press, 2004).
7. Sharon Marcus, *Between Women: Friendship, Desire, and Marriage in Victorian England* (Princeton: Princeton University Press, 2009).
8. Martha Vicinus, '"They Wonder to Which Sex I Belong": The Historical Roots of the Modern Lesbian Identity', *Feminist Studies* 18, no. 3 (Fall 1992): 472. See also Blanche Wiesen Cook, '"Women Alone Stir My Imagination": Lesbianism and the Cultural Tradition', *Signs: Journal of Women in Culture and Society* 4, no. 4 (1979): 718–39.
9. Jack Halberstam, *Female Masculinity* (Durham: Duke University Press, 1998), 56.
10. Lucy Bland and Laura Doan, eds., *Sexology in Culture: Labelling Bodies and Desires* (Cambridge: Polity, 1998); Lucy Bland, 'Trial by Sexology? Maud Allen, Salome and the Cult of the Clitoris Case', in *Sexology in Culture*, ed. Bland and Doan; Roy Porter and Lesley Hall, *The Facts of Life: The Creation of Sexual Knowledge in Britain 1659–1950* (London: Yale University Press, 1995); Harry Oosterhuis, *Stepchildren of Nature: Krafft-Ebing, Psychiatry and the Making of Sexual Identity* (Chicago: Chicago University Press, 2000); Roy Porter and Mikulas Teich, eds., *Sexual Knowledge, Sexual Science: The History of Attitudes towards Sexuality* (Cambridge: Cambridge University Press, 1994).
11. Nicole Moore, *The Censor's Library: Uncovering the Lost History of Australia's Banned Books* (St Lucia: University of Queensland Press, 2012).
12. Nan Alamilla Boyd, 'Talking about Sex: Cheryl Gonzales and Rikki Streicher Tell Their Stories', in *Bodies of Evidence: The Practice of Queer Oral History*, ed. Nan Alamilla Boyd and Horacio N. Roque Ramirez (Oxford: Oxford University Press, 2012), 111, 110.
13. Sally Newman, 'The Archival Traces of Desire: Vernon Lee's Failed Sexuality and the Interpretation of Letters in Lesbian History', *Journal of the History of Sexuality* 14, nos. 1/2 (January/April 2005): 59.
14. Halberstam, *Female Masculinity*, 56.
15. Valerie Traub, 'History in the Present Tense: Feminist Theories, Spatialized Epistemologies, and Early Modern Embodiment', *Representations* 33 (1991): 1–41; Jason S. Farr, 'Libertine Sexuality and Queer-Crip Embodiment in Eighteenth-Century Britain', *Journal for Early Modern Cultural Studies* 16, no. 4 (2016): 96–118.
16. Lisa Featherstone, *Let's Talk about Sex: Histories of Sexuality in Australia from Federation to the Pill* (Newcastle: Cambridge Scholars Publishing, 2011), 268.

17 Angela Davis, '"Oh No, Nothing, We Didn't Learn Anything": Sex Education and the Preparation of Girls for Motherhood, c.1930–1970', *History of Education* 37, no. 5 (September 2008): 667. See also Jane Pilcher, 'School Sex Education in England 1870–2000', *Sex Education* 5, no. 2 (2005): 157–74; Rachel Thomson, 'Moral Rhetoric and Public Pragmatism: The Recent Politics of Sex Education', *Feminist Review* 48 (1994): 40–60; Lesley Hall, 'Birds, Bees and General Embarrassment: Sex Education in Britain from Social Purity to Section 28', in *Public or Private Education?: Lessons from History*, ed. Richard Aldrich (London: Woburn Press, 2004).
18 D. Epstein and R. Johnson, 'On the Straight and Narrow: The Heterosexual Presumption, Homophobias and Schools', in *Challenging Lesbian and Gay Inequalities in Education*, ed. D. Epstein (Buckingham: Open University Press, 1994); D. Epstein and R. Johnson, *Schooling Sexualities* (Buckingham: Open University Press, 1998); Lynne Hillier and Anne Mitchell, '"It was as Useful as a Chocolate Kettle": Sex Education in the Lives of Same-Sex-Attracted Young People in Australia', *Sex Education* 8, no. 2 (2008): 211–24; Angela M. Salas, 'Power and Repression / Repression and Power: Homosexuality in Subversive Picture Books and Conservative Youth Novels', in *Sexual Pedagogies: Sex Education in Britain, Australia, and America, 1879–2000*, ed. Claudia Nelson and Michelle Martin (Basingstoke: Palgrave Macmillan, 2004).
19 'Nina Miller', in *Women Like Us*, ed. Suzanne Neild and Rosalind Pearson (London: Women's Press, 1992), 119.
20 Ibid., 121.
21 Bella, correspondence with the author.
22 NSA, HCC (C456/73), Margaret Cranch.
23 NSA, HCC (C456/15), Diana Chapman.
24 Interview with Margaret Jones, 31 August 2007.
25 'Sylvia', in *Women Like Us*, ed. Neild and Pearson, 64.
26 'Nina Miller', in *Women Like Us*, ed. Neild and Pearson, 122.
27 NSA, HCC (C456/46/01–02), Ellen Noor.
28 Interview with Susan Nicol, 25 November 2012.
29 Interview with 'Rachel', 19 May 2012.
30 Haringey Archive and Museum Service (HAMS), Haringey Vanguard (HV), Interview with Nakissa Campbell.
31 Interview with Maxine Drake, 22 January 2013.
32 Interview with 'Margaret', 28 October 2014.
33 Interview with Chloe Bardsley, 1 May 2012.
34 Interview with Megg Kelham, 27 February 2013.
35 Roxxy Bent, 'In Bed with … Sam and Wendy', *LOTL* 9, no. 7 (July 1998): 18.
36 Interview with Marit, 9 December 2012.
37 Interview with Jean Taylor, 22 September 2012.
38 Interview with 'Louise', 25 August 2012.
39 Kirsten Hearn, 'A Woman's Right to Cruise', *Trouble and Strife* 9 (Summer 1986): 26.
40 Albertine Winner, 'Homosexuality in Women', *The Medical Press and Circular*, 3 September 1947, 220.
41 Ibid., 219–20.
42 Eustace Chesser, *Odd Man Out: Homosexuality in Men and Women* (London: Victor Gollancz, 1959), 112–13.
43 Interview with Margaret Jones, 31 August 2007.
44 Sandra Willson, *Between Me and Myself: A Memoir of Murder, Desire and the Struggle to be Free*, ed. Rebecca Jennings (Melbourne: Text publishing, 2022), 53.

45 Bryan Magee, *One in Twenty: A Study of Homosexuality in Men and Women* (London: Secker & Warburg, 1966), 133-4. See also Bryan Magee, 'The Facts about Lesbianism: A Special Inquiry into a Neglected Problem', *New Statesman*, 26 March 1965, 491-2 and readers' letters in response in *New Statesman*, 2 April 1965, 530 and 9 April 1965, 570.
46 DMC, 'More Thoughts on the "Public Image"', *Arena Three* 1, no. 9 (September 1964): 7.
47 Virginia Ironside, 'Lesbianism', *19* 2, no. 6 (March 1969): 67-9; Nicola Thorne, 'Love without a Man', *Vanity Fair*, March 1970, 60-3.
48 Dilys Rowe, 'A Quick Look at the Lesbians', *Twentieth Century* (Winter 1962/63): 69-70.
49 'A Visit to the Doctor', *Boiled Sweets* 2, no. 1 (1973).
50 DMC, 'More Thoughts', 7-8.
51 Diana M. Chapman, 'What Is a Lesbian?', *Family Doctor* 8, no. 15 (August 1965): 474.
52 On homophile magazines, see Martin Meeker, *Contacts Desired: Gay and Lesbian Communications and Community, 1940- 1970s* (Chicago: University of Chicago Press, 2006); Julian Jackson, *Living in Arcadia: Homosexuality, Politics and Morality in France from the Liberation to AIDS* (Chicago: University of Chicago Press, 2009); David S. Churchill, 'Transnationalism and Homophile Political Culture in the Postwar Decades', *GLQ* 15, no. 1 (2008): 31-66; David Minto, 'Mr Grey Goes to Washington: The Homophile Internationalism of Britain's Homosexual Law Reform Society', in *British Queer History: New Approaches and Perspectives*, ed. Brian Lewis (Manchester: Manchester University Press, 2013). In the 1970s, Sappho continued this reluctance to discuss the erotic aspect of lesbianism. When an autobiographical article was published, describing a reader's first sexual experience, it prompted numerous complaints from readers. Cherry Pitcher, 'First Sex', *Sappho* 6, no. 5 (1978): 13.
53 Chesser, *Odd Man Out*, 92, 93.
54 D. J. West, *Homosexuality* (London: Penguin Books, 1968), 65.
55 Anthony Storr, *Sexual Deviation* (London: Penguin Books, 1964), 70, 71.
56 Barbara Creed, 'Public Myths versus Personal Identity', Papers and Proceedings: First National Homosexual Conference: Melbourne, 16-17 August 1975.
57 George Robb, 'Marriage and Reproduction', in *Palgrave Advances in the Modern History of Sexuality*, ed. H. G. Cocks and Matt Houlbrook (London: Palgrave Macmillan, 2006).
58 Alison M. Downham Moore, 'Victorian Medicine Was Not Responsible for Repressing the Clitoris: Rethinking Homology in the Long History of Women's Genital Anatomy', *Signs Journal of Women in Culture and Society* 44, no. 1 (2018): 55; Hera Cook, *The Long Sexual Revolution: English Women, Sex, and Contraception 1800-1975* (Oxford: Oxford University Press, 2004). Although feminists in both countries began to counter this narrative in the 1970s, Germaine Greer's strong defence of the vaginal orgasm drew on and maintained a longer Australian tradition. See Frank Bongiorno, *The Sex Lives of Australians: A History* (Collingwood, VIC: Black Inc, 2015), 238-9; Germaine Greer, *The Female Eunuch* (London: MacGibbon and Kee, 1970).
59 'A Visit to the Doctor'.
60 Barbara, 'Turning the Fan Around', paper delivered at the Radicalesbian Conference, Sorrento, Victoria, 6-8 July 1973.
61 Wendy Clark, 'The Dyke, The Feminist and the Devil', *Feminist Review* 11, Sexuality (Summer 1982): 36.

62 Joan Nestle, 'The Fem Question', in *Pleasure and Danger: Exploring Female Sexuality*, ed. Carole S. Vance (London: Routledge and Kegan Paul, 1984), 235.
63 Clark, 'The Dyke', 35.
64 Marion Paull, 'Letter from Australia', in *The Persistent Desire: A Femme-Butch Reader*, ed. Joan Nestle (Boston: Alyson Publications Inc, 1992), 176.
65 Yorick Smaal, 'Sex in the Sixties', in *The 1960s in Australia: People, Power and Politics*, ed. Shirleene Robinson and Julie Ustinoff (Newcastle: Cambridge Scholars Publishing, 2012), 86-7.
66 'Pat James', in *Women Like Us*, ed. Neild and Pearson, 60.
67 Smaal, 'Sex in the Sixties', 86.
68 'Pat James', in *Women Like Us*, ed. Neild and Pearson, 60.
69 Paull, 'A Letter from Australia', 176.
70 NSA, HCC (C456/32) Julie Switsur.
71 Barbara Bell, *Just Take Your Frock Off: A Lesbian Life* (Brighton: Ourstory Books, 1999), 92.
72 Ibid., 91.
73 Barbara, 'Turning the Fan Around'.
74 Interview with Laurene Kelly, 19 February 2013.
75 NSA, HCC (C456/97) Dorothy Cooper.
76 NSA, HCC (C456/105) Liz Kelly.
77 NSA, HCC (C456/40) Gilli Salvat.
78 Interview with Sylvia Kinder, 11 June 2012.
79 Kate Millett's *Flying* (New York: Alfred A. Knopf, 1974) advocated breaking down sexual possessiveness, which she understood as being at the core of patriarchy.
80 NSA, HCC (C456/83) Shirani Situnayake.
81 Sarah Lucia Hoagland, *Lesbian Ethics: Toward New Value* (Palo Alto: Institute of Lesbian Studies, 1988); Kathleen Martindale and Martha Saunders, 'Realizing Love and Justice: Lesbian Ethics in the Upper and Lower Case', *Hypatia* 7, no. 4 (Fall 1992): 148-71; Denise Thompson, 'Freedom for What? Lesbian Relationships and Responsibility' (1984), National Library of Australia.
82 Simone de Beauvoir, *The Second Sex* (London: Jonathan Cape, 1953 [1949]); Monique Wittig, *Les Guerilleres*, trans. David Le Vay (London: Owen, 1971).
83 See Beatrix Campbell, 'A Feminist Sexual Politics: Now You See It, Now You Don't', *Feminist Review* 5 (1980): 15.
84 Sue Roxon, 'To Be or Not to Be? Is that the Question?', *Sydney Women's Liberation Newsletter*, October 1975, 12.
85 David Halperin points to a similar emphasis on equality in gay male sexual culture in this period: David M. Halperin, *How to Be Gay* (London: Harvard University Press, 2012), 51-3.
86 Jan Smith, 'Lesbianism and Mental Health', *Broadsheet* 53 (October 1977): 19.
87 Valerie Mason-John and Ann Khambatta, *Lesbians Talk: Making Black Waves* (London: Scarlet Press, 1993), 30.
88 Smith, 'Lesbianism', 19.
89 Marilyn McLean, 'Letters', *Lesbian Newsletter* (September 1977), 2.
90 Interview with Laurene Kelly, 19 February 2013.
91 Interview with Sylvia Kinder, 11 June 2012.
92 'Lesbian Questions', *Gay Information* 3 (August-September 1980): 5.
93 Radicalesbians, 'The Woman-Identified Woman' [1970], in *The Second Wave: A Reader in Feminist Theory*, ed. Linda Nicholson (New York: Routledge, 1997).

94 Dana Shugar, *Separatism and Women's Community* (Lincoln, NE: University of Nebraska Press, 1995).
95 Interview with Sand Hall, 30 January 2017.
96 Jeska Rees, 'A Look Back at Anger: the Women's Liberation Movement in 1978', *Women's History Review* 19, no. 3 (2010): 337–56.
97 Leeds Revolutionary Feminist Group, 'Political Lesbianism', reprinted in *Love Your Enemy? The Debate between Heterosexual Feminism and Political Lesbian*, ed. Onlywomen Press (London: Onlywomen Press, 1981).
98 This issue was explored in a historical context by Lillian Faderman in *Surpassing the Love of Men* and Sheila Jeffreys, 'Does It Matter If They Did It?', *Trouble and Strife* 3 (Summer 1984): 25. See Lynne Segal, *Straight Sex: The Politics of Pleasure* (London: Virago, 1994).
99 Kimberley O'Sullivan, 'Dangerous Desire: Lesbianism as Sex or Politics', in *Sex in Public: Australian Sexual Culture*, ed. Jill Julius Matthews (Sydney: Allen & Unwin, 1997), 118. See also 'The Dildo Dilemma: Patriarchal Power Tool, Substitute Penis or Lesbian Sex Toy?', *Labrys* (August 1991), 4.
100 Susan Ardill and Sue O'Sullivan, 'Upsetting an Applecart: Difference, Desire and Lesbian Sadomasochism', *Feminist Review* 23 (Summer 1986): 41.
101 Sarah F. Green, *Urban Amazons: Lesbian Feminism and Beyond in the Gender, Sexuality and Identity Battles of London* (Basingstoke: Macmillan, 1997), 159–96.
102 From a Whisper to a Roar (FWTR) oral history collection, interview with Jennie Wilson. http://www.whisper2roar.org.uk/oral-history-archive/
103 See, for example, Janice G. Raymond, 'Putting the Politics Back into Lesbianism', *Journal of Australian Lesbian Feminist Studies* 1, no. 2 (December 1991): 7–21. See also NSA, HCC (C456/83) Shirani Situnayake and FWTR, Jamie Wildman for a personal discussion of this perspective.
104 'Plan to Open Lesbian Centre', *Sydney Star Observer* 188 (24 July 1992): 6.
105 Kimberley O'Sullivan, 'Sisters under the Skin', *Sydney Star Observer* 173 (27 December 1991): 12.
106 Kimberley O'Sullivan, 'Entertainment for the Adventurous Lesbian', *Campaign* 130 (October 1986): 37; Kimberley O'Sullivan, 'Touch Me There', *Campaign* 131 (November 1986): 42–4.
107 NSA, Sisterhood and after: the Women's Liberation Oral History Project (SAA) (C1420/40), Sue O'Sullivan.
108 Emma Healey, *Lesbian Sex Wars* (London: Virago, 1996), 140.
109 Kate Lloyd, 'Meet the lesbian punks who've been written out of London's history', *Time Out*, 25 April 2017.
110 FWTR, Jamie Wildman.
111 Lloyd, 'Meet the lesbian punks'.
112 Healey, *Lesbian Sex Wars*, 152–3; FWTR, Jamie Wildman.
113 O'Sullivan, 'Dangerous Desire', 122–3.
114 Kimberley O'Sullivan, 'Wicked Women', *Sydney Star Observer*, 29 April 1988, 13; Rosalie Woodruff, 'Ms Wicked in Heaven', *PanDa* 7 (May 1993): 5.
115 'Performance Art', *Labrys*, no. 8 (July 1991): 2.
116 C. Moore Hardy, 'Lesbian Erotica and Impossible Images', in *Sex in Public*, ed. Matthews, 133.
117 Mason-John and Khambatta, *Lesbians Talk*, 51.
118 See Boyd, 'Talking About Sex'.

119 David Bell, 'Pleasure and Danger: The Paradoxical Spaces of Sexual Citizenship', *Political Geography* 14, no. 2 (1995): 139–53; Chris White, 'The Spanner Trials and the Changing Law on Sadomasochism in the UK', *Journal of Homosexuality* 50, nos. 2–3 (2006): 167–87.
120 Letter to the Editor, *Lesbianon* 6 (1975), 8; Pablo Castel, 'Domestic Violence', *Wicked Women* 2, no. 9 (1993): 30–1; Frances Rand and Bronwyn Arns, 'Lesbian Rape: The Hate That Dare Not Speak Its Name', *PanDA* 2, no. 3 (March 1994): 8; NSA, HCC (C456/83) Shirani Situnayake.
121 For example, *Forum* 5, no. 11 (October 1977): 81.

Chapter 2

1 Claire Langhamer, 'The Meanings of Home in Postwar Britain', *Journal of Contemporary History* 40, no. 2 (April 2005); Martin Pugh, 'Domesticity and the Decline of Feminism, 1930–1950', in *British Feminism in the Twentieth Century*, ed. Harold L. Smith (Aldershot: Edward Elgar, 1990); Jane Lewis, *Women in Britain since 1945* (Oxford: Blackwell, 1992); Elizabeth Wilson, *Only Halfway to Paradise: Women in Post-war Britain 1945–1968* (London: Tavistock, 1980); John Murphy and Belinda Probert, '"Anything for the House": Recollections of Post-war Suburban Dreaming', *Australian Historical Studies* 36, no. 124 (2004): 275–93; Louise C. Johnston, ed., *Suburban Dreaming: An Interdisciplinary Approach to Australian Cities* (Geelong: Deakin University Press, 1994); Graeme Davison, Tony Dingle and Seamus O'Hanlon, eds., *The Cream Brick Frontier: Histories of Australian Suburbia* (Melbourne: Monash Publications in History No. 19, 1995); Roger Silverstone, ed., *Visions of Suburbia* (London: Routledge, 1997).
2 Betty Friedan, *The Feminine Mystique* (London: Gollancz, 1963); Hannah Gavron, *The Captive Wife: Conflicts of Housebound Mothers* (London: Routledge & Kegan Paul, 1966); Ann Oakley, *The Sociology of Housework* (New York: Pantheon Books, 1974).
3 Judy Giles, 'A Home of One's Own: Women and Domesticity in England 1918–1950', *Women's Studies International Forum* 16, no. 3 (1993): 239–53. See also Pat Thane, 'Family Life and "Normality" in Postwar Culture', in *Life after Death: Approaches to a Cultural and Social History of Europe during the 1940s and 1950s*, ed. Richard Bessell and Dirk Schumann (Cambridge: Cambridge University Press, 2003).
4 Wendy Webster, *Imagining Home: Gender, Race and National Identity 1945–64* (London: UCL Press, 1998), 92 and 149.
5 Matt Cook, 'Warm Homes in a Cold Climate: Rex Batten and the Queer Domestic', in *Queer 1950s: Rethinking Sexuality in the Postwar Years*, ed. Heike Bauer and Matt Cook (London: Springer, 2012), 115. On queer male domesticity in this period, see also Matt Houlbrook, *Queer London: Perils and Pleasures in the Sexual Metropolis, 1918–1957* (Chicago: University of Chicago Press, 2006), 114–18 and Martin Dines, 'Bringing the Boy Back Home: Queer Domesticity and Egalitarian Relationships in Postwar London Novels', *The Literary London Journal* 10, no. 2 (Autumn 2013).
6 For an earlier period, see Sharon Marcus, 'At Home with the Other Victorians', *South Atlantic Quarterly* 108, no. 1 (Winter 2009): 119–45.
7 See Amy Tooth Murphy, '"I Conformed; I Got Married. It Seemed Like a Good Idea at the Time": Domesticity in Postwar Lesbian Oral History', in *British Queer*

       History: New Approaches and Perspectives, ed. Brian Lewis (Manchester: Manchester University Press, 2013).
8   Rebecca Jennings, *Unnamed Desires: A Sydney Lesbian History* (Melbourne: Monash University Publishing, 2015).
9   Alison Blunt and Robyn Dowling, *Home* (London: Routledge, 2006), 22.
10 See Alice T. Friedman, 'Hiding in Plain Sight', *Home Cultures* 12, no. 2 (2015): 139–67.
11 Interview with Jennie Partington, 30 April 2012.
12 'The Young Homosexual', *Arena Three* 6, no. 5 (May 1969): 3.
13 'Thoughts of a Late-night Feminist', *Rouge* 8 (June/July 1980): 9.
14 'Towards a Christian View of Lesbians', *Arena Three* 3, no. 1 (January 1966): 19.
15 'Compact', *Arena Three* 4, no. 5 (May 67): 3–10.
16 Sandra Willson, *Between Me and Myself: A Memoir of Murder, Desire and the Struggle to Be Free*, ed. Rebecca Jennings (Melbourne: Text Publishing, 2022), 65.
17 'We Decided We Were in Love', *Sunday Times* colour supplement, 12 September 1965, 21.
18 Lennox Strong, 'The Marble Statue', *Arena Three* 2, no. 7 (July 1965): 5–6.
19 'Woman Set House on Fire after Girl Friend Left', *Kilburn Times*, 30 December 1966.
20 NSA, HCC (C456/14) Mabel Hills.
21 NSA, HCC (C456/68) Rene Sawyer.
22 *Arena Three* 2, no. 6 (June 1965), 11.
23 Interview with Margaret Jones, 12 September 2007.
24 Interview with Margaret Jones, 18 September 2007.
25 NSA, HCC (C456/33) Cynnie Reid.
26 Rebecca Jennings, 'The Gateways and the Emergence of a Post-Second World War Lesbian Subculture', *Social History* 31, no. 2 (2006): 206–25; Jill Gardiner, *From the Closet to the Screen: Women at the Gateways Club, 1945–85* (London: Rivers Oram Press, 2003); Rebecca Jennings, 'A Room Full of Women: Lesbian Bars and Social Spaces in Postwar Sydney', *Women's History Review* 21, no. 5 (November 2012): 813–30; Jennings, *Unnamed Desires*.
27 Marion Paull, 'A Letter from Australia', in *The Persistent Desire: A Butch Femme Reader*, ed. Joan Nestle (Boston: Alyson Publications Inc, 1995), 174. See Ruth Ford, '"The Man-Woman Murderer": Sex Fraud, Sexual Inversion and the Unmentionable "Article" in 1920s Australia', *Gender & History* 12, no. 1 (2000): 158–96 and Lucy Chesser, *Parting with My Sex: Cross-dressing, Inversion and Sexuality in Australian Cultural Life* (Sydney: Sydney University Press, 2008) on an earlier Australian history of couples passing as husband and wife.
28 Dino Hodge, *Did You Meet Any Malagas? A Homosexual History of Australia's Tropical Capital* (Nightcliff, NT: Little Gem Publications, 1993), 57.
29 Interview with Megg Kelham, 27 February 2013.
30 Interview with Chris Sitka, 3 July 2013.
31 Kukumo Rocks, in *Footsteps and Witnesses: Lesbian and Gay Lifestories from Scotland*, ed. Bob Cant (Edinburgh: Polygon, 1993), 121.
32 Interview with Margaret Jones, 18 September 2007.
33 Interview with Al Garthwaite, 5 July 2019.
34 Jayne Egerton, 'Out But Not Down: Lesbians' Experience of Housing', *Feminist Review* 36 (Autumn 1990): 76.
35 https://www.mmu.ac.uk/equality-and-diversity/doc/gender-equality-timeline.pdf, accessed 21 June 2018; Interview with Margaret Jones, 18 September 2007.

36 Barbara Creed, 'Public Myth Versus Personal Identity', *Papers and Proceedings: First National Homosexual Conference: Melbourne, 16–17 August 1975*, 33.
37 Alison Ravetz, 'Housing the People', in *Labour's Promised Land? Culture and Society in Labour Britain 1945–51*, ed. Jim Fyrth (London: Lawrence and Wishart, 1995); Alison Ravetz, *The Place of the Home: English Domestic Environments, 1914–2000* (London: E. and F.N.Spon, 1995); Jon Lawrence, *Me, Me, Me?: Individualism and the Search for Community in Post-War England* (Oxford: Oxford University Press, 2019).
38 'More Housing for Single Women', *The Times*, 20 October 1955, 7.
39 See, for example, Laura Hutton, *The Single Woman and Her Emotional Problems* (London: Bailliere, Tindall and Cox, 1935); M. B. Smith, *The Single Woman of Today: Her Problems and Adjustment* (London: Watts & Co., 1951); 'The Loneliness of the Unmarried Woman', *Medical News*, 30 August 1963.
40 Egerton, 'Out But Not Down', 76.
41 Sarah F. Green, *Urban Amazons: Lesbian Feminism and Beyond in the Gender, Sexuality and Identity Battles of London* (Basingstoke: Macmillan Press Ltd, 1997), 28.
42 Murphy and Probert, 'Anything for the House', 288. See also Sophie McNamara and John Connell, 'Homeward Bound? Searching for home in Inner Sydney's share houses', *Australian Geographer* 38, no. 1 (2007): 71–91. Jon Lawrence, *Me, Me, Me* similarly depicts the new post-war housing estates in Britain as communities which were dominated by nuclear families.
43 NSA, HCC (C456/97) Dorothy Cooper.
44 Kennetta Hammond Perry, *London Is the Place for Me: Black Britons, Citizenship, and the Politics of Race* (Oxford: Oxford University Press, 2015), 83–5.
45 Beverley Bryan, Stella Dadzie and Suzanne Scafe, *Heart of the Race: Black Women's Lives in Britain* (London: Verso, 2018 [1985]), 161.
46 Pet Brien, 'The DO IT Therapy', *Arena Three* 7, no. 6 (July 1970): 6.
47 Interview with Margaret, 28 October 2014.
48 Carey-Ann Morrison, 'Heterosexuality and Home: Intimacies of Space and Spaces of Touch', *Emotion, Space and Society* 5 (2012): 11.
49 Isabel Miller, *Patience and Sarah* (London: The Women's Press, 1979).
50 NSA, HCC (C456/40) Gilli Salvat.
51 'Mary and June', in *Footsteps and Witnesses*, ed. Cant, 84.
52 Anon, *Lesbian Territory* 9 (1993): 12.
53 Letter from Asphy Xia, 'Young Dykes Have Their say', *Labrys Newspaper* (September 1991), 13. On home as a restrictive space for lesbians, see Sarah A Elwood, 'Lesbian Living Spaces', *Journal of Lesbian Studies* 4, no. 1 (2000): 11–27.
54 See Rebecca Jennings, 'Womin Loving Womin: Lesbian Feminist Theories of Intimacy', in *Intimacy, Violence and Activism: Gay and Lesbian Perspectives on Australasian History and Society*, ed. Graham Willett and Yorick Smaal (Melbourne: Monash University Publishing, 2013).
55 Egerton, 'Out But Not Down', 81–4; Green, *Urban Amazons*, 71–6; Matt Cook, '"Gay Times": Identity, Locality, Memory and the Brixton Squats in 1970s London', *Twentieth Century British History* 24, no. 1 (March 2013): 84–109; Rachael Scicluna, 'Thinking through Domestic Pluralities', *Home Cultures* 12, no. 2 (2015): 169–91; Christine Wall, 'Sisterhood and Squatting in the 1970s: Feminism, Housing and Urban Change in Hackney', *History Workshop Journal* 83, no. 1 (April 2017): 79–97.
56 See, for example, FWTR, Interview with Frankie Green.

57 Interviews with Chris Sitka, 3 July 2013; Chris Pearce, 6 November 2007; Diane Minnis, 30 January 2012; Alex Kaufman, 23 August 2014; Sandra Mackay, 2 July 2007; Valerie Odewahn, 20 May 2008.
58 'Conflicts ... on Becoming a Lesbian Feminist', *Rouge* 8 (June/July 1980).
59 Interview with Chris Pearce, 6 November 2007.
60 Cook, 'Gay Times'.
61 Wall, 'Sisterhood and Squatting in the 1970s', 82–3. Rachael Scicluna also discusses the ways in which British lesbian feminists troubled notions of the kitchen as a space of women's inequality and discrimination by holding political discussions around the kitchen table and sharing the production of food. Scicluna, 'Thinking through Domestic Pluralities', 180–6.
62 Interview with Alex Kaufman, 23 August 2014.
63 Interview with Chris Sitka, 3 July 2013.
64 NSA, HCC (C456/97) Dorothy Cooper.
65 Interview with Sandra Mackay, 2 July 2007.
66 Lynda Johnston and Gill Valentine, 'Wherever I Lay My Girlfriend, That's My Home: The Performance and Surveillance of Lesbian Identities in Domestic Environments', in *Mapping Desire: Geographies of Sexualities*, ed. David Bell and Gill Valentine (London: Routledge, 1995), 109.
67 Interview with Helen Pausacker by Graham Willett, 27 December 1996, Australian Queer Archives.
68 Rebecca Jennings, '"A Meeting of Different Tribes"? Travelling Women and Mobility between European and Australasian Women's Lands', *Women's History Review* 31, no. 1 (2022): 88–106.
69 Melbourne Radicalesbians, 'The Radicalesbian Manifesto' (1973), https://cv.vic.gov.au/stories/a-diverse-state/out-of-the-closets-into-the-streets/gay-womens-group-and-radicalesbians/the-radicalesbian-manifesto/, accessed 22 June 2018.
70 Interview with Sand Hall, 30 January 2017.
71 Interview with Chris Sitka, 3 July 2013.
72 Interview with Sand Hall, 30 January 2017.
73 Sand Hall, ed., *Amazon Acres, You Beauty: Stories of Women's Lands, Australia* (Wollongong: Shall Publishing, 2016). See Rebecca Jennings, 'Creating Feminist Culture: Australian Rural Lesbian-Separatist Communities in the 1970s and 1980s', *Journal of Women's History* 30, no. 2 (Summer 2018): 88–111.
74 Jenny, 'Rules and Relationships', papers from the Radicalesbian Conference, Sorrento, Victoria, 1973, http://www.reasoninrevolt.net.au/objects/pdf/d2103.pdf, accessed 22 June 2018.
75 Interview with Jean Taylor, 22 September 2012.
76 Interview with Sylvia Kinder, 11 June 2012.
77 Interview with Megg Kelham, 27 February 2013.
78 Interview with Sally, 6 October 2012.
79 Interview with Jai Forde, Haringey Vanguard.
80 Andrew Gorman-Murray, 'Reconciling Self: Gay Men and Lesbians Using Domestic Materiality for Identity Management', *Social and Cultural Geography* 9, no. 3 (2008): 288.
81 bell hooks, *Yearning: Race, Gender, and Cultural Politics* (Boston: South End Press, 1991); Divya Tolia-Kelly, 'Materializing Post-colonial Geographies: Examining the Textural Landscapes of Migration in the South Asian Home', *Geoforum* 25 (2004): 675–88; Andrew Gorman-Murray, 'Contesting Domestic Ideals: Queering the Australian Home', *Australian Geographer* 38, no. 2 (2007): 195–213; Andrew

Gorman-Murray, 'Queer Politics at Home: Gay Men's Management of the Public/Private Boundary', *New Zealand Geographer* 68, no. 2 (2012): 111–20.
82 Johnston and Valentine, 'Wherever I Lay'.
83 Interview with Megg Kelham, 27 February 2013.
84 Jan Rawlins-Tully, Review of Kerry Lobel, ed., 'Naming the Violence: Speaking Out about Lesbian Battering' (Washington: The Seal Press, 1986), *Labrys Newspaper*, December 1990, 12.
85 'Domestic Violence in Lesbian Relationships: A COAL First Discussion Paper', Prepared by Looking Out for Each Other, The Lesbian Domestic Violence Project Collective (Thirroul, NSW: Coalition of Lesbian Activists, 1997).
86 Gaye McCulloch, 'Violence – Our Responsibility', *Labrys Newspaper*, October 1991, 19.
87 Vera Ray, 'Violence in Dyadic Lesbian Relationships', *Journal of Australian Lesbian Feminist Studies* (June 1991).
88 Interview with Jennifer Partington, 30 April 2012.
89 Leonore Davidoff, "The Rationalization of Housework", in *Dependence and Exploitation*, ed. D. L. Barker and S. Allen (London: Longman Press, 1976); Joanna Bourke, 'Housewifery in Britain, 1850–1914', *Past and Present* 143 (May 1994), 167–97.
90 Carla Barrett, 'Lesbians at Home: Gender and Housework in Lesbian Coupled Households', in *Lesbian Geographies: Gender, Place and Power*, ed. Kath Browne and Eduarda Ferreira (London: Routledge, 2016), 56.
91 Susan Kentlyn, '"Who's the Man and Who's the Woman?" Same-sex Couples in Queensland "Doing" Gender and Domestic Labour', *Queensland Review* 14, no. 2 (2007), 120. See also Sarah Oerton, '"Queer Housewives?": Some Problems in Theorising the Division of Domestic Labour in Lesbian and Gay Households', *Women's Studies International Forum* 20, no. 3 (1997): 421–30.
92 NSA, HCC (C456/68) Rene Sawyer.
93 Willson, *Between Me and Myself*, 65.
94 Ibid., 66.
95 'Pat James', in *Women Like Us*, ed. Suzanne Neild and Rosalind Pearson (London: The Women's Press, 1992), 60.
96 For example, Paull, 'A Letter', 174.
97 NSA, HCC (C456/01) Sharley McLean.
98 Anne Hughes, 'Psychological "Masculinity"', *Arena Three* 3, no. 6 (July 1966): 17–18.
99 *Arena Three* 7, no. 2 (February 1970): 7.
100 NSA, HCC (C456/15), Diana Chapman.
101 See, for example, Ellen Malos, ed., *The Politics of Housework* (London: Allison & Busby, 1980) for a collection of articles from this debate.
102 Maud Anne Bracke, 'Between the Transnational and the Local: Mapping the Trajectories and Contexts of the Wages for Housework Campaign in 1970s Italian Feminism', *Women's History Review* 22, no. 4 (August 2013): 625–42; Jenefer Coates, 'Shared Housework', *Spare Rib* 25 (July 1974): 28–9; Wendy Whitfield, 'His and Her Housework', *Spare Rib* 45 (April 1976): 6–7.
103 Kerryn Higgs and Barbara Bloch, 'Beyond the Cliches: A Reappraisal of Feminism', *Scarlet Woman* 3 (February 1976): 18.
104 'Wimin Living with Wimin', *Rouge* 8 (June/July 1980): 26.
105 NSA, HCC (C456/97) Dorothy Cooper.
106 Interview with 'Clare', 7 May 2012.
107 Interview with Sally, 6 October 2012.

108 Interview with Lou Wilson, 29 May 2012.
109 Conversation with Andrée Bellamy.
110 *Arena Three* 6, no. 3 (March 1969): 7.
111 *Arena Three* 6, no. 4 (April 1969): 7.
112 Interview with Jan Aitkin, 5 June 2012.
113 'A Radicalesbian Lifestyle', *Refractory Girl* (Summer 1974): 13.
114 Interview with Lava Kohaupt, 19 April 2017.
115 Janet Wahlquist, 'Living Collectively', *Scarlet Women* 3 (February 1976): 9, 13.
116 For example, Letter from J. M. I. and J. B. F. (Berkshire), *Arena Three* 5, no. 9 (September 1968): 11.

Chapter 3

1   Julie McCrossin, '"Always a Bridesmaid, Never a Bride" – Recognising Same-Sex Relationships', *Sydney Papers* 11, no. 3 (1999): 145.
2   Barbara Baird, '"Gay Marriage", Lesbian Wedding', *Gay and Lesbian Issues and Psychology Review* 3, no. 3 (2007): 161–70; Barbara Baird, 'The Politics of Homosexuality in Howard's Australia', in *Acts of Love and Lust: Sexuality in Australia from 1945–2010*, ed. Lisa Featherstone, Rebecca Jennings and Robert Reynolds (Newcastle: Cambridge Scholars Publishing, 2014).
3   Lisa Duggan, 'The New Homonormativity: The Sexual Politics of Neoliberalism', in *Materializing Democracy: Toward a Revitalized Cultural Politics*, ed. Russ Castronovo and Dana D. Nelson (Duke University Press, 2002), 182, 190, 179.
4   Judith Butler, 'Is Kinship Always Already Heterosexual?', *Differences* 13, no. 1 (2002): 20; Wendy Brown, *States of Injury: Power and Freedom in Late Modernity* (Princeton: Princeton University Press, 1995), 126.
5   Alison Oram, *Her Husband Was a Woman! Women's Gender-Crossing in Modern British Popular Culture* (London: Routledge, 2013); Ruth Ford, 'They "Were Wed, and Merrily Rang the Bells": Gender-Crossing and Same-sex Marriage in Australia, 1900–1940', in *Australian Gay and Lesbian Perspectives 5*, ed. Graham Willet and David Phillips (Sydney: Australian Centre for Lesbian and Gay Research, 2000).
6   El Chenier, 'Freak Wedding: Lesbian Marriage as a Pleasure Practice in Post-WWII Toronto', unpublished paper given at the ESSHC, 1 March 2008, 2 and 5. El Chenier, 'Love-politics: Lesbian Wedding Practices in Canada and the United States from the 1920s to the 1970s', *Journal of the History of Sexuality* 27, no. 2 (2018): 294–321.
7   Jeffrey Weeks, *Sex, Politics and Society: The Regulation of Sexuality since 1800*, 4th edn. (London: Routledge, 2017), 260.
8   'Myrtle Solomon' in *Inventing Ourselves: Lesbian Life Stories*, ed. Hall Carpenter Archives Lesbian Oral History Group (London: Routledge, 1989), 16.
9   *Arena Three* 6, no. 2 (February 1969): 6.
10 Robyn Kennedy, 'Civil Liberties and the Lesbian', Papers and Proceedings: First National Homosexual Conference, Melbourne, 16–17 August 1975, 12.
11 Sandra Willson, *Between Me and Myself: A Memoir of Murder, Desire and the Struggle to be Free*, ed. Rebecca Jennings (Melbourne: Text Publishing, 2022), 63.
12 I. F., 'Compact', *Arena Three* 4, no. 5 (May 1967): 8.
13 Interview with Eileen Hickey by Esther Singer, 2 August 2011, AQA.
14 *Sappho* 5, no. 5 (1977): 12.

15 Pam Nilan, 'I Was Never a Dress Person', in *Out in the Valley: Hunter Gay and Lesbian Histories*, ed. Jim Wafer, Erica Southgate and Lyndall Coan (Newcastle: Newcastle Region Library, 2000), 225.
16 Eustace Chesser, *Odd Man Out: Homosexuality in Men and Women* (London: Victor Gollancz, 1959), 102–3.
17 'Another Kind of Loving', *Manchester Daily Express*, 16 January 1978; Michael Brennan, 'It's a Miserable Life When You're Gay Says Dr Tim', *News of the World*, 16 July 1978.
18 K. H., 'What Makes It Last?', *Arena Three* 1, no. 4 (March 1964): 3.
19 *Sappho* 5, no. 10 (1977): 10–11.
20 Letters to Forum Adviser (undated), Folder 73, Gay Counselling Service of NSW Papers, ML MSS 5836.
21 Conversation with Andrée Bellamy.
22 Paddy Byrnes, '"La Vie en Rose" 1956', in *Words from the Same Heart*, ed. Margaret Bradstock and Louise Wakeling (Sydney: Hale & Iremonger, 1987), 26.
23 'Helen Lilly', in *Inventing Ourselves*, ed. Hall Carpenter, 116.
24 'Eight Days Hard', *Mejane* 1 (March 1971): 6–7.
25 *Sheffield Morning Telegraph*, 9 December 1966.
26 '"Bridegroom" Was Woman', *Aberdeen Press and Journal*, 19 October 1971, 4.
27 Oram, *Her Husband Was a Woman*.
28 *Arena Three* 4, no. 12 (December 1967): 9.
29 *Arena Three* 5, no. 12 (December 1968): 6.
30 *Arena Three* 2, no. 11 (November 1965): 16.
31 *Arena Three* 2, no. 12 (December 1965): 21.
32 *Arena Three* 2, no. 12 (December 1965): 2–3.
33 Miss D. F., 'Towards a Christian View of Lesbians', *Arena Three* 3, no. 1 (January 1966), 20–1.
34 Margot Whitehead, 'Towards a Homosexual View of Christianity', *Arena Three* 3, no. 2 (February 1966): 11.
35 *Arena Three* 5, no. 3 (March 68): 15.
36 *Arena Three* 5, no. 12 (December 68): 7.
37 'Happily Ever after?', *Spare Rib*, March 1976.
38 Interview with Gerlin, *Shrew* 3, no. 8 (September 71): 12.
39 'The Radicalesbian Manifesto', *Melbourne Gay Liberation* Newsletter 4 (September 1973), 8.
40 Rebecca Jennings, 'Womin Loving Womin: Lesbian Feminist Theories of Intimacy', in *Intimacy, Violence and Activism: Gay and Lesbian Perspectives on Australasian History and Society*, ed. Graham Willett and Yorick Smaal (Melbourne: Monash University Publishing, 2013).
41 Vivienne C. Cass, submission no. 462, folder 285, box 27, Elizabeth Evatt, Records of the Royal Commission on Human Relationships, National Archives of Australia. See also Lesbian Action Group newsletter, 19 December 1978, Chris Sitka papers, State Library of NSW, MLMSS 8866.
42 Dennis Altman, *Homosexual: Oppression and Liberation* (London: New York University Press, 1993 [1971]), 75.
43 Cass, 'Report on Homosexuality', 9–10.
44 Baden Hickman, 'A Plea for Homosexual Marriages', *Guardian*, 5 October 1971, 7.
45 Elsa Beckett, 'Holy Matrimony', *Sappho* 1, no. 1 (undated): 5–6.
46 *Sappho* 1, no. 4, 6.

47 *Sappho* 2, no. 5 (August 1973): 9.
48 *Sappho* 1, no. 7, 7.
49 Mark D. Jordan, *Blessing Same-Sex Unions: The Perils of Queer Romance and the Confusions of Christian Marriage* (Chicago: University of Chicago Press, 2005).
50 See Jeffrey Weeks, *Coming Out: Homosexual Politics in Britain, from the Nineteenth Century to the Present* (London: Quartet Books, 1977), 164.
51 Graham Willett, *Living Out Loud: A History of Gay and Lesbian Activism in Australia* (Sydney: Allen & Unwin, 2000), 98–100. See also Malcolm Cowan, '"Knowing" Sodom? Australian Churches and Homosexuality', in *Gay and Lesbian Perspectives III*, ed. Garry Wotherspoon (Sydney: Australian Centre for Lesbian and Gay Research, 1996).
52 Max Denton, 'Sexual Identity and Christian Same-Sex Weddings in Britain, c.1970–2000' (MPhil diss., Cambridge University, 2017), 29.
53 'Christian Group Debates Homosexual Marriages', *The Guardian*, 22 September 1978.
54 Colin Cross, 'Church Vows for Gays', *The Observer*, 8 October 1978. This culminated in the publication of a pamphlet, *Exploring Lifestyles: An Introduction to Services of Blessing for Gay Couples* (London: Gay Christian Movement, 1980). Earlier in the decade, an Australian clergyman, Rev Colin James Leane, mapped out a possible structure for a gay wedding service in *William and John*: 'Christian Viewpoint: Marriage and the Homosexual', *William and John* 1, no. 2 (February 1972), 37–8.
55 'The Forbidden Love', *Sunday Observer*, 19 July 1970, 22.
56 'Homosexuality: A Christian View', *Forum* 4, no.11 (1976), 52.
57 Letter to Forum Adviser, undated (c.1980s), Gays Counselling Service of NSW Papers, Mitchell Library, MSS5836, Folder 73, State Library of NSW.
58 Jo McVay-Abbott, 'With this ring …', *Focal*, December 1973, 8–10.
59 Jane Clements, 'Tying the Knot', *Lesbians on the Loose* 10 (October 1990): 10–11.
60 *The Age*, 9 May 1973. The ceremony caused some controversy in the church and in 1977, a Study Group on Homosexuality, established by the Union of Congregational Churches in response to Rev Schoenmaker's actions, reported to the Royal Commission on Human Relationships that they did not consider such ceremonies to be appropriate but that individual pastors should use their judgment in counselling homosexuals, for whom a committed homosexual relationship may be regarded as preferable to a promiscuous lifestyle.
61 *Saturday Evening Mercury* (Hobart), 16 June 1973. See also, Rev Robert John, 'Free to Love … Same-Sex Marriage', CentreCOMM, May 1996, http://www.ica.org.au/962gay1.html, accessed 20 May 2022.
62 'Vicar Who "Weds" Gay Couples', *Sunday People*, 2 March 1975, 13.
63 'A Church "Wedding" for Gays', *Sunday Mirror*, 21 May 1978.
64 Max Denton, '"Marriage without a Man": Understanding the Emergence of Same-Sex Marriage in Australia' (Honours diss., University of Melbourne, 2014), 32.
65 Lyndall Coan, 'Gay Times, Good Times, Females United and Women with No Frills', in *Out in the Valley*, ed. Wafer et al., 248–9.
66 'This Baby Has 2 Mums …', *The People*, 1 December 1996.
67 'Lesbian Marriage', *Labrys Newspaper*, August 1991, 21.
68 Jill Jones, 'The Politics of Love and the Art of the Possible: Recognising Our Relationships', in *Queer City: Gay and Lesbian Politics in Sydney*, ed. Craig Johnston and Paul van Reyk (Sydney: Pluto Press, 2001), 128.
69 See Barbara Baird, '"Kerryn and Jackie": Thinking Historically about Lesbian Marriages', *Australian Historical Studies* 36, no. 126 (2005): 253–71.
70 Kirsty Machon, 'Justify My Love', *LOTL* 77 7, no. 5 (May 1996): 8.

71 Liz Stuart, 'Wedding Alarm Bells', *Diva*, 1 August 1995, 47.
72 Frances Rand, 'Lobbying for Lesbian Love Rights', *LOTL* 46 4, no. 9 (October 1993): 1.
73 'Two Sides of the Same Coin', *PanDA* 2, no. 1 (November 1993): 4.
74 Emma Healey, 'The Curse of Coupledom', *Diva*, June 1994, 17.
75 Rachel Giese, 'Let's Stay Together', *Diva*, October 1997, 35.
76 Beverley Kemp, 'Coupledom versus Solo', *Diva*, January 1999, 23.
77 Ibid., 24.
78 Larry Galbraith, 'The ABC and De Facto Equality', *Campaign* 105 (September 1984): 5–6; Letter from Helen Pausacker to Ken Meyer, 19 September 1984, Papers of Helen Pausacker, Australian Queer Archives.
79 Peter de Waal, *Lesbians and Gays Changed Australian Immigration: History and Herstory* (Darlinghurst: Gay and Lesbian Immigration Task Force NSW, 2002).
80 Madeline Shaw, 'Our Relationships and the Law', *Lesbians on the Loose* 28 (April 1992): 9.
81 Jones, 'The Politics of Love'; Lesbian and Gay Legal Rights Service, 'The Bride Wore Pink: Legal Recognition of Our Relationships: A Discussion Paper' (Darlinghurst: Gay and Lesbian Rights Lobby, 2003); Rand, 'Lobbying for Lesbian', 1.
82 Jenni Millbank, 'Recognition of Lesbian and Gay Families in Australian Law – Part One: Couples', *Federal Law Review* 34 (2006): 1–44.
83 Jeffrey Weeks, Brian Heaphy and Catherine Donovan, *Same Sex Intimacies: Families of Choice and Other Life Experiments* (London: Routledge, 2001).
84 Jeffrey Weeks, *The World We Have Won: The Remaking of Erotic and Intimate Life* (London: Routledge, 2007), 183.
85 Paul Baker, *Outrageous! The Story of Section 28 and Britain's Battle for LGBT Education* (London: Reaktion Books, 2022).
86 Jones, 'The Politics of Love', 114.
87 'Lesbian Marriage', *Labrys Newspaper*, August 1991, 20.
88 Ibid.
89 Jane Clements, 'Tying the Knot', *Lesbians on the Loose* 10 (October 1990): 10–11; Robert Kellaway, 'This Baby Has Two Mums', *The People*, 1 December 1996.
90 Clements, 'Tying the Knot'.
91 'Lesbian Marriages – Lesbian Weddings?!', *Labrys Newspaper*, August 1991, 21.
92 Elin O'Connell, 'Tying the Knot on the Reef', *LOTL* 80 7, no. 8 (August 1996): 29–32.
93 Carol Richardson, 'We're One Big Happy Family', *Bella*, 17 August 1991.
94 Interview with Lou Wilson, 29 May 2012.

Chapter 4

1 Hilary Benno, 'Scouting for … The Public Image', *Arena Three* 1, no. 1 (January 1964): 4.
2 *Arena Three* 2, no. 1 (January 1965): 11.
3 *Arena Three* 8, no. 3 (October 1970): 3.
4 Interview by Ruth Ford with Elizabeth, 6 May 1992, Australian Queer Archives (AQA). See also interview by Sandra Mackay and Rebecca Jennings with Jan McInnies and Margaret Cummins, Pride History Group (PHG).
5 *Lesbianon* 6 (1975).

6   Lauren Jae Gutterman, *Her Neighbor's Wife: A History of Lesbian Desire within Marriage* (Philadelphia: University of Pennsylvania Press, 2019), 24.
7   Jane Lewis, 'Marriage', in *Women in Twentieth-Century Britain: Social, Cultural and Political Change*, ed. Ina Zweiniger-Bargielowska (London: Routledge, 2014), 72.
8   Ibid., 70–1.
9   Gordon A. Carmichael, 'Bust After Boom: First Marriage Trends in Australia', *Demography* 24, no. 2 (May 1987): 246; Frank Bongiorno, *The Sex Lives of Australians: A History* (Collingwood, VIC: Black Inc, 2015), 235.
10 Carmichael, 'Bust after Boom', 253.
11 Hera Cook, *The Long Sexual Revolution: English Women, Sex and Contraception, 1800–1975* (Oxford: Oxford University Press, 2004), 323–4.
12 Bongiorno, *The Sex Lives*, 200. See, for example, Teri Chettiar, '"More Than a Contract": The Emergence of a State-Supported Marriage Welfare Service and the Politics of Emotional Life in Post-1945 Britain', *Journal of British Studies* 55 (July 2016): 566–91.
13 Janet Finch and Penny Summerfield, 'Social Reconstruction and the Emergence of Companionate Marriage, 1945–59', in *Marriage, Domestic Life and Social Change: Writings for Jacqueline Burgoyne, 1944–88*, ed. David Clark (London: Routledge, 2019), 6.
14 Royal Commission on Marriage and Divorce, Report 1951–1955, 7.
15 For example, Geoffrey Gorer, *Exploring English Character* (London: Cresset, 1955); Geoffrey Gorer, *Sex and Marriage in England Today: A Study of the Views and Experiences of the Under-45s* (London: Nelson, 1971); Eliot Slater and Moya Woodside, *Patterns of Marriage: A Study of Marriage Relationships in the Urban Working Classes* (London: Cassell, 1951); A. P. Elkin, ed., *Marriage and the Family in Australia* (Sydney: Angus and Robertson, 1957).
16 Claire Langhamer, *The English in Love: The Intimate Story of an Emotional Revolution* (Oxford: Oxford University Press, 2013), 179–81.
17 David Morgan, 'Ideologies of Marriage and Family Life', in *Marriage, Domestic Life*, ed. Clark, 97–116.
18 Finch and Summerfield, 'Social Reconstruction', 6.
19 Elkin, ed., *Marriage and the Family*, 210, 208.
20 Bongiorno, *The Sex Lives*, 200–1. See also Stephen Brooke, 'Gender and Working Class Identity in Britain during the 1950s', *Journal of Social History* 34, no. 4 (Summer 2001): 773–95.
21 Claire Langhamer, 'Love, Selfhood and Authenticity in Post-War Britain', *Cultural and Social History* 9, no. 2 (2012): 278.
22 Bongiorno, *The Sex Lives*, 235–6.
23 *Sappho* 3, no. 2 (May 1974): 12.
24 Kirsten Blanch, 'The Shy Homosexual Woman', *Cleo*, July 1974, 72.
25 Megan Forrest, 'Falling Apart and Coming Together', in *Words from the Same Heart*, ed. Margaret Bradstock and Louise Wakeling (Sydney: Hale & Iremonger, 1987), 53.
26 Ibid., 53–5.
27 Margaret Simpson, 'The Simpson Case', *Campaign* 67 (July 1981): 12.
28 *Sappho* 1, no. 9 (1972): 10.
29 Interview with 'Sue', 23 April 1993.
30 'Firsthand – a publication of MRG', enclosed in *Arena Three* 4, no. 3 (March 1967).
31 Interview by Sandra Mackay with Rae Morris, 4 December 2008, PHG.
32 Megan, in *Words*, ed. Bradstock and Wakeling, 55.

33 Reverend Herbert Gray, 'Preparation for Marriage', in *Sex in Social Life*, ed. Sybil Neville-Rolfe (London: George Allen & Unwin, 1949), 300.
34 Langhamer, 'Love, Selfhood and Authenticity'.
35 *Sappho* 3, no. 9 (1975): 11.
36 *Arena Three* 6, no. 2 (February 1969): 5.
37 *Cleo* (July 1974): 74.
38 *Campaign* 67 (July 1981): 12.
39 *Arena Three* 2, no. 6 (June 1965): 11–12.
40 Langhamer, 'Love, Selfhood and Authenticity', 281.
41 *Arena Three* 2, no. 3 (March 1965): 14.
42 *Lesbianon* 4 (1975): 15.
43 *Arena Three* 8, nos. 7–12 (1971): 7.
44 For example, *Sappho* 1, no. 12 (March 1973): 7, 20.
45 *Lesbianon* 4 (1975): 15.
46 *Sappho* 3, no. 3 (June 1974): 27.
47 *Arena Three* 3, no. 6 (July 1966): 15.
48 Ibid.
49 Esme Langley to Barbara Gittings, 6 November 1964, 1–2, box 57, folder 12, Barbara Gittings and Kay Lahusen Papers, New York Public Library.
50 *Arena Three* 3, no. 11 (December 1966): 14.
51 NSA, HCC (C456/15), Diana Chapman.
52 *Arena Three* 2, no. 3 (March 1965): 14.
53 *Arena Three* 1, no. 11 (December 1964): 12.
54 *Arena Three* 4, no. 10 (October 1967): 11.
55 *Arena Three* 6, no. 2 (February 1969): 6.
56 Phoenix, 'Review of Charlotte Woolff, Bisexuality', *Sappho* 6, no. 3. See also *Sappho* 3, no. 1 (April 1974): 9–10; *Sappho* 6, no. 5 (1978): 9–11.
57 *Sappho* 6, no. 5 (1978): 9; *Sappho* 6, no. 5 (1978): 10.
58 *Arena Three* 2, no. 9 (September 1965): 10.
59 *Sappho* 3, no. 5 (1974): 10.
60 Lauren Jae Gutterman, '"The House on the Borderland": Lesbian Desire, Marriage and the Household, 1950–1979', *Journal of Social History* 46, no. 1 (2012): 2–3, 3. See also Gutterman, *Her Neighbor's Wife*.
61 NSA, HCC (C456/73), Margaret Cranch.
62 *Arena Three* 6, no. 4 (April 1969): 6.
63 *Cleo* (July 1974): 74.
64 *Campaign* 67 (July 1981): 12.
65 *Arena Three* 4, no. 7 (July 1967): 12.
66 *Arena Three* 2, no. 9 (September 1965): 10.
67 *Arena Three* 3, no. 9 (October 1966): 18–19.
68 *Sappho* 2, no. 12 (March 1974): 12.
69 'An Affair', *Evening Argus*, Brighton, 9 September 1969.
70 *Sappho* 2, no. 7 (October 1973): 25.
71 Marilyn Archer, 'Gay Wives and Mothers', *Spare Rib* 31 (January 1975): 26.
72 *Sappho* 1, no. 11 (February 1973): 4, 18.
73 'Classified Advertisements', *Arena Three* 1, no. 11 (December 1964): 9.
74 Elizabeth Wilson, 'Memoirs of an Anti-heroine', in *Radical Records: Thirty Years of Lesbian and Gay History*, ed. Bob Cant and Susan Hemmings (London: Routledge, 1988), 42.

75 Interview by Sandra Mackay with Rae Morris, 4 December 2008, PHG.
76 *Sappho* 7, no. 2 (undated, c.1979): 8.
77 *Arena Three* 2, no. 7 (July 1965): 10.
78 Letter from R. J. to Society Five, received 20 April 1975, AQA, Box 13/5.
79 Victoria Brittain, 'Easing the Isolation of Lesbianism', *The Times*, 2 November 1970, 8.
80 'Not a Label', *Forum* 4, no. 12 (December 1976): 61.
81 Interview with Jan Aitkin, 5 June 2012.
82 Megan, in *Words*, ed. Bradstock and Wakeling, 55-7.
83 Ibid., 57-8.
84 Rights of Women Lesbian Custody Group, *Lesbian Mothers' Legal Handbook* (London: The Women's Press Handbook Series, 1986), 19.
85 Interview with Lynne Roberts, 24 February 2012, Pride in our Past collection (PioP), Plymouth.
86 Interview with 'Joan' by Lucy Chesser, 23 April 1993, AQA.
87 *Sappho* 6, no. 5 (1978): 10.
88 *Sappho* 7, no. 2 (undated, c.1979): 8.
89 Letter to Cleo Adviser, *Cleo* 41 (March 1976): 76.
90 *Arena Three* 8, nos. 7-12 (1971): 7.
91 Gardner v Gardner [1947] 1 AER 630.
92 Helen McCarthy, *Double Lives: A History of Working Motherhood* (London: Bloomsbury Publishing, 2020).
93 *Campaign* 67 (July 1981): 12.
94 Interview with Lynne Roberts, 24 February 2012, PioP.
95 Rights of Women, *Lesbian Mothers on Trial: A Report on Lesbian Mothers and Child Custody* (London: Rights of Women, 1984), 25.
96 Megan, in *Words*, ed. Bradstock and Wakeling, 58.
97 *Sappho* 1, no. 9, 10-11.
98 *Sappho* 1, no. 11 (February 1973): 4, 18.
99 Gillian E. Hanscombe and Jackie Forster, *Rocking the Cradle: Lesbian Mothers* (London: Sheba Feminist Publishers, 1982), 67. On violence by husbands and ex-husbands toward lesbian mothers see ROWLCG, *Lesbian Mothers' Legal Handbook*, 19-20; Interview with Lynne Harne, 18 July 2019.
100 Ruth Ford, '"Filthy, Obscene and Mad": Engendering "Homophobia" in Australia, 1940s-1960s', in *Homophobia: An Australian History*, ed. Shirleene Robinson (Sydney: The Federation Press, 2008), 97-101. The mother lost both custody and access in this case.
101 See Shurlee Swain, *Born in Hope: The Early Years of the Family Court of Australia* (Sydney: UNSW Press, 2012); Rebecca Jennings, 'Lesbian Mothers and Child Custody: Australian Debates in the 1970s', *Gender & History* 24, no. 2 (2012): 502-17.
102 Robyn Plaister, 'Lesbian Mothers', *Campaign* 42 (April 1979): 13.
103 See Ellen Goodman, 'Homosexuality of a Parent: A New Issue in Custody Disputes', *Monash University Law Review* 5 (June 1979): 305-15; O. C. Giles, 'Two Recent Australian Custody Cases', *International and Comparative Law Quarterly* 25 (April 1976): 440-4.
104 Rights of Women, *Lesbian Mothers on Trial*, 3-4; Janet Fink, 'Natural Mothers, Putative Fathers and Innocent Children: The Definition and Regulation of Parental Relationships Outside Marriage in England 1945-1959', *Journal of Family History* 25 (2000): 178-95.
105 See, for example, Re F (1969) 2 All ER 766.

106 B v B (Court of Appeal) (1975) Family Law 6 (1976), 42; Re K (1977) 1 All ER 647.
107 'Lesbian and Her Lover can Keep Girl of Five', *Daily Telegraph*, 22 July 1982.
108 A number of feminist commentators regarded this silence as a continuation of the historic attempt to limit public discussion around lesbianism. See Rights of Women, *Lesbian Mothers on Trial*, 9; Jill Radford, 'The Lesbian Custody Project', *Health Care for Women International* 13, no. 2 (1992): 236.
109 Eleanor Stephens, 'Out of the Closet into the Courts', *Spare Rib* 50 (1976): 7.
110 S. Cohen, S. Green, L. Merryfinch, G. Jones, J. Slade and M. Walker, *The Law and Sexuality* (Manchester: Grass Roots Books, 1978); Julia Brophy, 'Motherhood, Lesbianism and Child Custody', unpublished manuscript, University of Essex (1979), cited in Diane Richardson, 'Lesbian Mothers', in *The Theory and Practice of Homosexuality,* ed. John Hart and Diane Richardson (London: Routledge and Kegan Paul, 1981), 152.
111 Rights of Women, *Lesbian Mothers on Trial*, 26.
112 Campbell v. Campbell (1974) *SASR* 9, 28.
113 Tony James, 'The Real Life Story of Barb and Helen', *Campaign* 29: 10.
114 Martha Kirkpatrick, Catherine Smith and Ron Roy, 'Lesbian Mothers and Their Children: A Comparative Survey', *American Journal of Orthopsychiatry* 51, no. 3 (1981): 545–51; Richard Green, 'Sexual Identity of 37 Children Raised by Homosexual or Transsexual Parents', *The American Journal of Psychiatry* 135, no. 6 (June 1978): 692–7.
115 Susan Golombok, Ann Spencer and Michael Rutter, 'Children in Lesbian and Single-parent Households: Psychosexual and Psychiatric Appraisal', *Journal of Child Psychology and Psychiatry* 24, no. 4 (1983): 551–72.
116 Moira Steel, *Lesbian Mothers, Custody Disputes and Court Welfare Reports* (Norwich: University of East Anglia, 1990).
117 NSA, HCC (C456/106) Gillian Butler.
118 For example, Robyn Plaister, 'Lesbian Mothers and Custody Cases', in *Living Together: Family Patterns and Lifestyles: A Book of Readings and Reports*, ed. Dorothy Davis, Geoff Caldwell, Margaret Bennett and David Borer (Canberra: Centre for Continuing Education, ANU, 1980), 149–54; Vivienne Cass, 'Lesbian Mothers and the Role of Professionals', in *Women in Jeopardy: Papers of the Women's Electoral Lobby Conference, Murdoch University, Perth, 20th and 21st November 1981*, ed. Barbara Buick (Perth: Women's Electoral Lobby, 1981), 51–4.
119 'Action for Lesbian Parents', *Sappho* 4, no. 12 (1976).
120 Sue Allen and Lynne Harne, 'Lesbian Mothers: The Fight for Child Custody', in *Radical Records*, ed. Cant and Hemmings.
121 Margaret McMann, 'Interview with a Lesbian Mother', *Gay Solidarity Newsletter* 1, no. 1 (1979).
122 *Sappho* 3, no. 9 (1975): 11.

Chapter 5

1 'Editorial Note', *Sappho* 6, no. 3 (1978): 3.
2 Carol Finlay, 'Women as Parents', *Campaign* 82 (October 1982): 16–17.
3 Barbara Baird, 'An Australian History of Lesbian Mothers: Two Points of Emergence', *Women's History Review* 21, no. 5 (2012): 855.

4   Damien W. Riggs, *Priscilla, (White) Queen of the Desert: Queer Rights/Race Privilege* (New York: Peter Lang, 2006), 82.
5   Wendy Webster, *Imagining Home: Gender, 'Race' and National Identity, 1945–64* (London: UCL Press, 1998), 127.
6   Hannah Charnock discussed similar themes in her, 'Teenage Girls, Hopes for the Future and Contraceptive Practice, 1950–1980', conference paper given at MBS, University of Birmingham, 4 July 2019.
7   Rebecca Jennings, *Tomboys and Bachelor Girls: A Lesbian History of Post-war Britain 1945–71* (Manchester: Manchester University Press, 2007).
8   Interview with Sharyn Walters, 20 April 2013.
9   Amy Tooth Murphy, '"I Conformed; I Got Married. It Seemed like a Good Idea at the Time": Domesticity in Postwar Lesbian Oral History', in *British Queer History: New Approaches and Perspectives*, ed. Brian Lewis (Manchester: Manchester University Press, 2013), 169, 170.
10 Ibid., 176–9.
11 *Arena Three* 7, no. 6 (July 1970): 8.
12 For example, William Vogt, *Road to Survival* (New York: William Sloane Associates, 1948); Paul R. Ehrlich [and Anne Ehrlich], *The Population Bomb* (New York: Ballantine Books, 1968); https://www.smithsonianmag.com/innovation/book-incited-worldwide-fear-overpopulation-180967499/
13 *Arena Three* 7, no. 10 (October 1970), 5. See also Alison J. Laurie, 'Unusual Solutions', *Sappho* 3, no. 12 (1975): 19.
14 'The "Facts" as Presented by Mother Magee', *Arena Three* 2, no. 4 (April 1965): 8–9.
15 L. G., 'Butch Beef', *Sappho*, reproduced in *Sapphic Woman* 7 (1975).
16 Prue Borthwick and Barbara Bloch, *Mothers and Others: An Exploration of Lesbian Parenting in Australia* (Sydney: Jam Jar Publishing, 1993) similarly point to the dominance of childless lesbian identity models.
17 NSA, HCC (C456/68) Rene Sawyer.
18 Marion Paull, 'A Letter from Australia', in *The Persistent Desire: A Femme-Butch Reader*, ed. Joan Nestle (Boston: Alyson Publications Inc, 1992), 177. See also Interview with Sharyn Walters, 20 April 2013.
19 Interview with Margaret, 28 October 2014.
20 Kathleen Kiernan, Hilary Land and Jane Lewis, *Lone Motherhood in Twentieth-Century Britain* (Oxford: Oxford University Press, 1998); Helen McCarthy, *Double Lives: A History of Working Motherhood* (London: Bloomsbury Publishing, 2020), 255–7; April Gallwey, 'Love Beyond the Frame: Stories of Maternal Love Outside Marriage in the 1950s and 1960s', in *Love and Romance in Britain, 1918–1970*, ed. Alana Harris and Timothy Willem Jones (London: Palgrave Macmillan, 2015).
21 Barbara Farrelly, 'Spirited Away', *LOTL* 75 7, no. 3 (March 1996): 30–1. Twenty-six years later Mary was reunited with her daughter, who also identified as a lesbian.
22 'Betty', in *Words from the Same Heart*, ed. Margaret Bradstock and Louise Wakeling (Sydney: Hale & Iremonger, 1987), 98.
23 NSA, HCC (C456/43) Liz Naylor.
24 Martin Richards, 'Artificial Insemination and Eugenics: Celibate Motherhood, Eutelegenesis and Germinal Choice', *Studies in History and Philosophy of Biological and Biomedical Sciences* 39 (2008): 211–21; Simone B. Novaes, 'Social Integration of Technical Innovation: Sperm Banking and AID in France and in the United States', *Social Science Information* 24 (1985): 570.

25 Carol Finlay, 'Women as Parents', *Campaign* 82 (October 1982): 16–17; Barbara Wishart, 'Motherhood within Patriarchy—A Radical Feminist Perspective', in *All Her Labours*, ed. Women and Labour Conference (Sydney: Hale and Iremonger Pty Ltd, 1984), 90.
26 'My AID Son – By a Lesbian', *Observer*, 8 January 1978, 1–2.
27 Interview with Katharine Mather, 26 March 2019.
28 'Unto Us a Child Is Born', *Sappho* 1, no. 9 (December 1972): 12.
29 Ibid., 15.
30 Ibid.
31 'My AID Son – By a Lesbian', *Observer*, 8 January 1978, 1–2.
32 See, for example, Gillian E. Hanscombe and Jackie Forster, *Rocking the Cradle: Lesbian Mothers – A Challenge in Family Living* (London, 1982), 31.
33 *Evening News* (London), 5 January 1978, 1.
34 Babs Todd, 'Easter '74 A.I.D. A.D.', *Sappho* 3, no. 2 (May 1974): 14.
35 NSA, HCC (C456/87) Jackie Forster; From a Whisper to a Roar (FWTR) oral history collection, interview with Mairi. http://www.whisper2roar.org.uk/oral-history-archive/.
36 Carol Finlay, 'Women as Parents', *Campaign* 82 (October 1982): 16–17.
37 Wishart, 'Motherhood within Patriarchy', 90.
38 Deborah Dempsey, 'Beyond Choice: Family and Kinship in the Australian Lesbian and Gay "Baby Boom"' (PhD diss., La Trobe University, Melbourne, 2006), 55.
39 'AI Denied to Lesbians at All but One Hospital', *Campaign* 70 (October 1981): 7.
40 Cited in Shani Keane and Lasandra Kurukulasuriya, 'Conceivable Options', *Refractory Girl* 52 (Summer/Winter 1997): 37.
41 'No Help in NT on Lesbian Fertility', *PanDa* 8 (June/July 1993): 2.
42 There were also calls for legislation in some states e.g. in 1985 the Country Women's Association called on the NSW government to legislate against donor sperm being made available to lesbians. 'CWA Decrees on Sperm', *The Star Observer*, 17 May 1985, 6. On the legal framework governing access to donor insemination, see Adiva Sifris, 'Dismantling Discriminatory Barriers: Access to Assisted Reproductive Services for Single Women and Lesbian Couples', *Monash University Law Review* 30, no. 2 (2004): 229–68. On access to IVF see Anita Stuhmcke, 'Lesbian Access to In Vitro Fertilisation', *Australasian Gay and Lesbian Law Journal* 7 (1997): 15–40.
43 Dempsey, 'Beyond Choice', 54–5.
44 Anne Scahill, 'Outlaw', *LOTL* 39 4, no. 3 (March 1993): 11.
45 Kat Costigan, 'DI Test Case Win Good News for Lesbians', *LOTL* 83 7, no. 11 (November 1996): 7.
46 'Lesbian Mothers: Getting Pregnant', *Labrys Newspaper* (November 1991): 8. See also Keane and Kurukulasuriya, 'Conceivable Options', 37.
47 Interview with Maxine Drake, 22 January 2013.
48 Ruth McNair, Deborah Dempsey, Sarah Wise and Amaryll Perlesz, 'Lesbian Parenting: Issues, Strengths and Challenges', *Family Matters* 63 (Spr/Sum 2002): 43. However, the figures were growing, with 33 per cent of the forty-three prospective parents they surveyed stating that they intended to use clinic-based insemination to conceive.
49 *Evening News* (London), 5 January 1978, 1.
50 'Ban These Babies', *Evening News* (London), 6 January 1978.
51 Rebecca Jennings, 'Lesbian Motherhood and the Artificial Insemination by Donor Scandal of 1978', *Twentieth Century British History* 28, no. 4 (2017): 570–94.

52   Philip Jordan, 'Lesbians Stage Protest over Babies Story', *The Guardian*, 7 January 1978; 'Editor Made to Explain Anti-lesbian "Trickery"', *Morning Star*, 7 January 1978.
53   'Lesbians Reply to the Evening News', *Evening News* (London), 10 January 1978.
54   Beverley Bryan, Stella Dadzie and Suzanne Scafe, *Heart of the Race: Black Women's Lives in Britain* (London: Verso, 2018), 100–7.
55   See Laura Tisdall, 'Education, Parenting and Concepts of Childhood in England, c. 1945 to c. 1979', *Contemporary British History* 31, no. 1 (2017): 24–46; Christina Hardyment, *Dream Babies: Three Centuries of Good Advice on Child Care* (London: Harper and Row, 1983); Michal Shapira, *The War Inside* (Cambridge: Cambridge University Press, 2013).
56   Frederick Whitehead, 'Ill-conceived Ambitions', *Birmingham Post*, 11 January 1978, 4.
57   Norman St John-Stevas, 'Vexed Question of Insemination for Lesbians', *Catholic Herald*, 20 January 1978; 'Speak Up for the Child', *The Journal* (Newcastle-upon-Tyne), 9 January 1978.
58   Joanna Patyna, 'The Most Remarkable Family in Britain', *London Evening News*, 6 January 1978; 'No Father but Three "Mums" for Test Tube Baby Michael', *Liverpool Echo*, 7 January 1978.
59   'The City Lesbian Family Who Want a Baby', *Liverpool Echo*, 12 January 1978, 3.
60   Lucy Orgill, 'Their Right to Bear Children?', *Derby Evening Telegraph*, 17 January 1978. Pat Arrowsmith made a similar argument in a radio debate on Charing Cross Hospital Radio, reprinted in Robert Edison, 'In Praise of Lesbian Mothers', *London Evening News*, 25 January 1978.
61   *Sappho* 6, no. 3 (1978): 11.
62   Ibid., 9.
63   Baird, 'An Australian History'; Mel Irenyi, 'Lesbian Mothers: (Re)creating Family through Discourse and Identity' (Ph.D. diss, Deakin University, Victoria, 2005).
64   'BMA for Lesbian AID', *Family Planning Today*, December 1978.
65   Interview with Al Garthwaite, 5 July 2019.
66   Interview with Clare, 7 May 2012.
67   'Lesbians Splaid', *Sydney Women's Liberation Newsletter*, September 1978 [unpaginated].
68   *Sappho* 3, no. 4 (July 1974): 11.
69   'The City Lesbian Family Who Want a Baby', *Liverpool Echo*, 12 January 1978, 3.
70   Interview with Al Garthwaite, 5 July 2019.
71   'Longing for a Baby', *Love Affair*, 20 February 1982; *Daily Mirror*, 26 January 1982.
72   *The Sunday Times*, 11 April 1982, 31.
73   Jill Radford, 'The Lesbian Custody Project', *Health Care for Women International* 13, no. 2 (1992): 229–37; Jill Radford, 'Rights of Women – Twenty Years of Feminist Activism', in *Feminist Activism in the 1990s*, ed. Gabriele Griffin (London: Taylor and Francis, 1995): 51–64.
74   Kim Sengupta, 'Docs Slated over Test-tube Babies for Lesbians', *Daily Star*, 2 July 1994, 4.
75   'Reproductive Rights under Attack Again', *Rouge*, Summer 1990, 5.
76   Tracey Reynolds, *Caribbean Mothers: Identity and Experience in the UK* (London: Tufnell Press, 2005).
77   Amina Mama, 'Black Women, the Economic Crisis and the British State', *Feminist Review* 17 (Autumn 1984): 30.

78 Chris Everingham, 'Motherhood', in *Australian Feminism: A Companion*, ed. Barbara Caine (Melbourne: Oxford University Press), 230.
79 Simone de Beauvoir, *The Second Sex*, ed. and trans. H. M. Parshley (Harmondsworth: Penguin, 1972); Shulamith Firestone, *The Dialectic of Sex: The Case for Feminist Revolution* (London: The Women's Press, 1970). On the relationship between Australian feminism and maternity, see Catherine Kevin, 'Maternity and Freedom: Australian Feminist Encounters with the Reproductive Body', *Australian Feminist Studies* 20, no. 46 (2005): 3–15; Kerreen M. Reiger, *Our Bodies, Our Babies: The Forgotten Women's Movement* (Melbourne: Melbourne University Press, 2001).
80 Pam Stein, 'Women's Oppression', *Sydney Gay Liberation Newsletter* 1, no. 6 (December 1972): 7–8.
81 Linda Freeland, 'Lesbian Nation Revisited', *Liberaction* 26 (June 1974): 5.
82 Everingham, 'Motherhood'; Kevin, 'Maternity and Freedom'.
83 Terry Lovell, ed., *British Feminist Thought: A Reader* (Oxford: Basil Blackwell, 1990); Sarah Crook, 'Writing about Motherhood and Childcare in the British Women's Liberation Movement, 1970–85', in *Women's Periodicals and Print Culture in Britain, 1940s–2000s*, ed. Laurel Forster and Joanne Hollows (Edinburgh: Edinburgh University Press, 2020).
84 'Up the Mainstream with a Mop, Hi Ho!', *Gossip* 2, 34–5.
85 Ibid., 35.
86 Sheila Shulman, 'Lesbian Feminists and the Great Baby Con', *Spinster* 4 [undated, c.1981/2], 22.
87 Ibid., 22–3.
88 Wishart, 'Motherhood within Patriarchy', 85.
89 Ibid., 86.
90 Janet Ree in *Once a Feminist: Stories of a Generation*, ed. Michelene Wandor (London: Virago, 1990), 97.
91 Ibid., 101.
92 'As Feminists, as Lesbians, as Mothers', *Scarlet Woman* 4 (July 1976): 20.
93 Ibid.
94 Wishart, 'Motherhood within Patriarchy', 86.
95 *Gossip: A Journal of Lesbian Feminist Ethics* 2 (1986): 8–9.
96 *Sappho* 3, no. 4 (July 1974): 11.
97 Letter from Jessica Wood, *Spinster* 6 (Winter 1983/4): 3–4.
98 Janet Dixon, 'Separatism: A Look Back at Anger', in *Radical Records: Thirty Years of Lesbian and Gay History*, ed. Bob Cant and Susan Hemmings (London: Routledge, 1988), 81.
99 Greta Rensenbrink, 'Parthenogenesis and Lesbian Separatism: Regenerating Women's Community through Virgin Birth in the United States in the 1970s and 1980s', *Journal of the History of Sexuality* 19, no. 2 (May 2010): 288–316.
100 Ibid., 307.
101 Dixon, 'Separatism', 80–1.
102 Angela, 'Lesbian Mothers Conference: A Black Lesbian View', first published in *In Print: Newsletter of Peckham Black Women's Group* 2, reproduced with permission by Lesbian Custody Project, in 'Lesbian Custody Project' papers, The Women's Library, LSE, 7HEF/02/05 Box 2.
103 The Feminist Self Insemination Group, *Self Insemination* (London, c.1979?), 8–9.
104 Ibid., 9.
105 Interview with Chloe Bardsley, 1 May 2012.

106 Anne Robinson, 'The City Lesbian Family Who Want a Baby', *Liverpool Echo*, 12 January 1978, 3.
107 Ibid.
108 'Betty', in *Words*, ed. Bradstock and Wakeling, 98; Peter Read, 'The Return of the Stolen Generation', *Journal of Australian Studies* 22, no. 59 (1998): 8–19; Anne Manne, 'What Mary Bennett Knew: The Whispering in Her Heart', in *Australian Mothering: Historical and Sociological Perspectives*, ed. Carla Pascoe Leahy and Petra Bueskens (Cham: Palgrave Macmillan, 2019), 127–52.
109 Mary Braid, 'Lesbian Couple Win Parenting "Rights"', *The Independent*, 30 June 1994. See also George Hill, 'Fury over Lesbians', *Daily Star*, 1 July 1994.
110 Louise Wakeling and Margaret Bradstock, eds., *Beyond Blood: Writings on the Lesbian and Gay Family* (Sydney: BlackWattle Press, 1995), 35.
111 Ibid.
112 Borthwick and Bloch, *Mothers and Others*, 21–2.
113 ACON Women's Team, *Lesbian Sex* (AIDS Council of NSW, Women's Team, 1994), 27–8.
114 The Feminist Self Insemination Group, *Self Insemination*, 3.
115 Jalna Hanmer and Elizabeth Powell-Jones, 'Who's Holding the Test-tube?', *Trouble and Strife* 3 (Summer 1984): 44–9; Marge Berer, 'Breeding Conspiracies: Feminism and the New Reproductive Technologies', *Trouble and Strife* 9 (Summer 1986): 29–35; 'Letters', *Trouble and Strife* 10 (Spring 1987): 2–5; Alison Caddick, 'Feminism under Glass – The Reproductive Technologies Debate', *Scarlet Woman* 19 (1985): 11–17; Rebecca Albury, 'The New Reproductive Technologies: Liberation or Loss for Women', *Womanspeak* 10, no. 2 (August–September 1986): 6–7; 'FINRRAGE Responds to Surrogacy Report', *Womanspeak* 12, no. 5 (December 1989–January 1990): 4–7. See also Jana Sawicki, *Disciplining Foucault: Feminism, Power, and the Body* (London: Routledge, 1991), 67–94.
116 Interview with Clare, 7 May 2012.
117 Lisa Saffron, *Challenging Conceptions: Planning a Family by Self-Insemination* (London: Cassell, 1994).
118 Interview with Miriam Zukas by Jeska Rees, 27 February 2006, FAN.
119 For example, Cheri Pies, *Considering Parenthood: A Workbook for Lesbians* (San Francisco: Spinsters Ink, 1985) and Lisa Saffron, *Getting Pregnant Our Own Way: A Guide to Alternative Insemination* (London: Women's Health Information Centre, 1987). There was also a surge in discussion of the issue in the lesbian press in 1990/1991. See 'Becoming Pregnant', *Lesbians on the Loose* 16 (April 1991): 10–11.
120 'Artificial Insemination for Lesbians', *Campaign* 61 (January 1981): 5.
121 McNair, Dempsey, Wise and Perlesz, 'Lesbian Parenting', 43. Of those planning to conceive, 44 per cent intended to use self-insemination, 33 per cent clinic-based insemination, 13 per cent IVF or GIFT and 2 per cent heterosexual intercourse, reflecting a significant shift in practices of conception in the late 1990s and early 2000s.
122 The Feminist Self Insemination Group, *Self Insemination*, 11.
123 Borthwick and Bloch, *Mothers and Others*, 19. Margaret Bradstock also refers to this technique as the most widely practised when her partner, Louise Wakeling was attempting to conceive in the early 1980s: Wakeling and Bradstock, *Beyond Blood*.
124 The Feminist Self Insemination Group, *Self Insemination*, 13.
125 Manja Vishedyke, 'Cummer Waltzing', *Hecate* X, no. ii (1984): 75.
126 Ibid., 76.
127 Ibid., 73.

128 Ibid., 77.
129 Sally Williams, 'The Loving Spoonful That Cuts Out the Middleman', *The Observer*, 25 April 1993, 52.
130 Interview with Clare, 7 May 2012.
131 Borthwick and Bloch, *Mothers and Others*, 37.
132 'Immaculate Conception', *Time Out*, 25 February 1982, 7.
133 'When Did You Last See Your Donor?', *The Independent*, 1 April 1993, 27.
134 '"Bizarre Peril" of Children by Proxy', *Daily Mail*, 19 August 1983, 9. See Lucy Delap, 'Uneasy Solidarity: The British Men's Movement and Feminism', in *Women's Liberation Movement: Impacts and Outcomes*, ed. Kristina Schulz (New York: Berghahn, 2017) and 'Feminism, Masculinities and Emotional Politics in the Late Twentieth Century', *Cultural and Social History* 15, no. 4 (2018) on anti-sexist men.
135 'When Did You Last See Your Donor?'.
136 'Christmas Virgin Birth for Lesbian DIY Mum', *Express and Star Wolverhampton*, 25 November 1994. The agreement mentioned in this article would not have been legally binding as, from 1993, the Child Support Agency could require mothers to provide the name of a donor father and require those men to pay maintenance for the child.
137 See Damien W. Riggs, 'Lesbian Mothers, Gay Sperm Donors, and Community: Ensuring the Well-being of Children and Families', *Health Sociology Review* 17, no. 3 (October 2008): 226–34; Paul van Reyk, 'Donor Dads: The Sperm Givers' View', in *Beyond Blood*, ed. Wakeling and Bradstock, 82.
138 The Feminist Self Insemination Group, *Self Insemination*, 12.
139 Jean Taylor, *Lesbians Ignite! In Victoria in the 1990s* (Brunswick East: Dykebooks Inc, 2016), 37.
140 Heather Welford, 'Gay Pride and Joy', *The Guardian*, 4 January 1994.
141 Paul van Reyk, 'Baby Love: Gay Donor Father Narratives of Intimacy', in *Out in the Antipodes: Australian and New Zealand Perspectives on Gay and Lesbian Issues in Psychology*, ed. Damien W. Riggs and Gordon A. Walker (Bentley, WA: Brightfire Press, 2004).
142 Saffron, *Challenging Conceptions*, 147.
143 Kelvin Fontaine, 'Gay Mothers Fight for Right to Parenthood', *The Weekly Journal*, 30 June 1994.
144 Barbara Farrelly, 'Julie McCrossin Unplugged', *LOTL* 107 9, no. 11 (November 1998): 23.
145 Riggs, 'Lesbian Mothers', 228. See also M. Kaye and J. Tolmie, 'Discoursing Dads: The Rhetorical Devices of Fathers' Rights Groups', *Melbourne University Law Review* 22 (1998): 162–94.
146 Borthwick and Bloch, *Mothers and Others*, 36.
147 Ibid., 31.
148 The Feminist Self Insemination Group, *Self Insemination*, 6.
149 Saffron, *Challenging Conceptions*, 30.
150 Interview with Linda, 30 May 2019.
151 'Happy Families', *Sappho* 2, no. 9 (December 1973): 11–12.
152 Reproduced in 'Letters', *Camp Ink* 2, no. 11: 3.
153 Tisdall, 'Education, Parenting'; Hardyment, *Dream Babies*; Shapira, *The War Inside*.
154 *Sappho* 1, no. 11 (February 1973): 12–13, 15.
155 Ibid., 5.
156 'Unto Us a Child Is Born', *Sappho* 1, no. 9 (December 1972): 12.
157 Ibid., 13–14.

158 Ibid., 13.
159 'Double Standards on Fostering: Four Quit', *Sydney Star Observer* 118 (17 November 1989): 5.
160 Ibid., 12.
161 *Sappho* 2, no. 2 (May 1973): 6.
162 *Sappho* 2, no. 12 (March 1974): 10.
163 'Can a Lesbian Be a Good Parent?', *Daily Telegraph*, 23 April 1993.
164 'Gays, Lesbians Can't Foster or Adopt: Govt', *Sydney Star Observer* 118 (17 November 1989): 5.
165 Helen Campbell, 'Legal Issues for Lesbian Mothers', *Lesbians on the Loose* 16 (April 1991): 12.
166 Deborah Taylor, 'Fostering and Adoption Denied', *Lesbians on the Loose* 3 (March 1990): 4.
167 'Urged to Hate Their Fellow Human', *Hackney Gazette*, 29 January 1985; 'Leader Defends "Gay" Policy', *East London Advertiser*, 1 February 1985; 'Gays Are Not Child Molesters', *Hackney Gazette*, 5 February 1985; 'Ridiculous to Place Children with Gays', *Hackney Gazette*, 12 February 1985. Rotherham Council faced a similar backlash to their attempt to recruit gay foster parents in 1996: Harry Cooke, 'Outrage at Bid to Recruit Gay Foster Parents', *Daily Express*, 21 September 1996; Neil Tweedle, 'Gays Are Sought as Foster Parents', *Daily Telegraph*, 21 September 1996.
168 'Gay Adoption Policy "Illegal"', *The Leader* (Ealing and Chiswick), 20 June 1986; 'Go-ahead for Gay Adoption', *Greenford-Northolt Gazette*, 13 June 1986; 'Have a Go!', *The Sun*, 24 January 1985. Bexley, however, reiterated its ban on gay adoption: 'Homosexuals Need not Apply', *Kentish Times*, 28 June 1985; 'Gay Anger at Council Foster Ban', *Bexley Comet*, 28 June 1985. 'Fury on "Lesbians as Parents"', *Birmingham Evening Mail*, 25 November 1986; 'Family Rights of Children', *Birmingham Evening Mail*, 26 November 1986.
169 For example, 'Lesbian Care Boy Rolled Own Joint', *Daily Express*, 3 April 1992.
170 'Town Hall Strike Threat over Homosexual Foster Parents', *Wandsworth Borough News*, 27 September 1991.
171 Justin Strong, 'Silent Secret of Child Care', *The News* (Portsmouth), 19 December 1992.
172 'Sadness of Lesbians in Foster Wrangle', *The Echo* (Southampton), 7 January 1993. See also Steve Boggan, 'Lesbians Faced Fostering Bias', *The Independent*, 7 January 1993; Ann Clayton, 'Lesbians Win Fight to Become "Parents"', *The Echo* (Southampton), 20 April 1993. See also 'Gays Can Adopt Children', *Croydon Advertiser*, 18 October 1991.
173 'Longing for a Baby', *Love Affair*, 20 February 1982.
174 'Lesbian Couple Adopts Baby', *Lesbian Territory* 6 (August 1993): 10.
175 Robert Shrimsley, 'Row on Adoption by Homosexuals', *Daily Telegraph*, 30 December 1993. In 2000, Tony Blair's government took a similarly pragmatic approach to lesbian and gay adoption in the context of insufficient demand to adopt children: Eben Black, 'Blair to Let Gay Couples Adopt', *Sunday Times*, 23 April 2000.

Chapter 6

1 Frank Bongiorno, *The Sex Lives of Australians: A History* (Collingwood, VIC: Black Inc, 2015), 288.
2 Barbara Baird, 'An Australian History of Lesbian Mothers: Two Points of Emergence', *Women's History Review* 21, no. 5 (2012): 858.

3   Jacqui Gabb, 'Lesbian Motherhood: Strategies of Familial-linguistic Management in Lesbian Parent Families', *Sociology* 39, no. 4 (2005), 590.
4   Baird, 'An Australian History', 861.
5   Dr Clair Isbister, 'The Rights of Children', paper delivered at the 'Population, Development and the Role of Women': International Council of Women Regional Conference and the National Council of Women Triennial Conference, Sydney, 24 October–1 November 1973, 3, Mitchell Library, Q301.32 23.
6   Angela Davis, *Modern Motherhood: Women and Family in England, 1945–2000* (Manchester: Manchester University Press, 2012), 177; Carla Pascoe, 'Mum's the Word: Advice to Australian Mothers since 1945', *Journal of Family Studies* 21, no. 3 (2015): 218–34; Sue Sheridan, *Who was that Woman? The Australian Women's Weekly in the Postwar Years* (Sydney: UNSW Press, 2001).
7   John Bowlby, *Child Care and the Growth of Love* (London: Penguin, 1953). For a detailed discussion of Bowlby's work, see Denise Riley, *War in the Nursery: Theories of the Child and Mother* (London: Virago, 1983). On the influential concept of child-centred parenting see Laura Tisdall, 'Education, Parenting and Concepts of Childhood in England, c. 1945 to c. 1979', *Contemporary British History* 31, no. 1 (2017): 24–46; Christina Hardyment, *Dream Babies: Three Centuries of Good Advice on Child Care* (London: Harper and Row, 1983); Michal Shapira, *The War Inside* (Cambridge: Cambridge University Press, 2013).
8   Dolly Smith Wilson, 'A New Look at the Affluent Worker: The Good Working Mother in Post-War Britain', *Twentieth Century British History* 17, no. 2 (2006): 210–11.
9   S. Dex, *Women's Attitudes towards Work* (New York: St Martin's Press, 1988), 34, cited in Smith Wilson, 'A New Look', 210. See also Davis, *Modern Motherhood*.
10 Isbister, 'The Rights of Children', 3–4.
11 Laura King, *Family Men: Fatherhood and Masculinity in Britain, 1914–1960* (Oxford: Oxford University Press, 2015).
12 John Tosh, 'Domesticity and Manliness in the Victorian Middle Class', in *Manful Assertions,* ed. Michael Roper and John Tosh (Oxford: Routledge, 1991).
13 See, for example, Shapira, *The War Inside*; Mathew Thomson, *Lost Freedom: The Landscape of the Child and the British Post-war Settlement* (Oxford: Oxford University Press, 2013).
14 Wendy Webster, *Imagining Home: Gender, 'Race' and National Identity, 1945–64* (London: UCL Press, 1998).
15 Pascoe, 'Mum's the Word'.
16 Davis, *Modern Motherhood*, 56–8.
17 Diane Richardson, 'Lesbian Mothers', in *The Theory and Practice of Homosexuality*, ed. John Hart and Diane Richardson (London: Routledge, 1981), 153.
18 Tanya Evans, 'The Other Woman and Her Child: Extra-marital Affairs and Illegitimacy in Twentieth-Century Britain', *Women's History Review* 20, no. 1 (2011): 48.
19 April Gallwey, 'Love beyond the Frame: Stories of Maternal Love Outside Marriage in the 1950s and 1960s', in Alana Harris and Timothy Willem Jones, *Love and Romance in Britain, 1918–1970* (London: Palgrave Macmillan, 2015); Christin Quirk, 'Never-married Women versus the Records: Archives, Testimony and the History of Adoption Practices at the Royal Women's Hospital', *Melbourne Historical Journal* 40, no. 1 (2012): 169–84. This issue is also raised in several lesbian oral history interviews. See Interview with Margaret Jones, 31 August 2007.

20 OECD, Job and Family: measures to help women fulfil a dual role (Geneva, 1965), cited in Smith Wilson, 'A New Look', 208. However, Helen McCarthy notes the increasing articulation of a narrative of 'guilt' by working mothers in the 1970s: Helen McCarthy, *Double Lives: A History of Working Motherhood in Modern Britain* (London: Bloomsbury Publishing, 2020), 329.
21 Karen Rowlingson, 'Lone-Parent Families', in *The Blackwell Encyclopedia of Sociology*, ed. George Ritzer (Malden, MA: Blackwell, 2007). On single mothers in Australia, see also Christin Quirk, 'Historicizing the Marginalization of Single Mothers', in *Motherhood and Single-Lone Parenting: A 21st Century Perspective*, ed. Maki Motapanyane (Bradford, ON: Demeter Press, 2016) and Shurlee Swain and Renate Howe, *Single Mothers and Their Children: Disposal, Punishment and Survival in Australia* (Cambridge: Cambridge University Press, 1995).
22 *Sappho* 2, no. 9 (December 1973): 8.
23 *Sappho* 6, no. 9 (1978): 10.
24 'Happy Families', *Sappho* 2, no. 9 (December 1973), 11–12.
25 Sue Allen and Lynne Harne, 'Lesbian Mothers: The Fight for Child Custody', in *Radical Records: Thirty Years of Lesbian and Gay History*, ed. Bob Cant and Susan Hemmings (London: Routledge, 1988), 182.
26 Conversation with Andrée.
27 *Arena Three* 6, no. 3 (March 1969), 6.
28 Paul Bathurst, 'Is the Gay Family a Real Alternative?', *The Sunday Times*, 3 July 1994.
29 *Sappho* 3, no. 2 (May 1974), 13.
30 Robyn Plaister, 'Lesbian Mothers', *Campaign* 42 (April 1979): 13.
31 Ben Griffin, *The Politics of Gender in Victorian Britain: Masculinity, Political Culture and the Struggle for Women's Rights* (Cambridge: Cambridge University Press, 2012), 137–63.
32 G v D, unreported, Court of Appeal 16 February 1983. Cited in Rights of Women (hereafter ROW), *Lesbian Mothers on Trial: A Report on Lesbian Mothers and Child Custody* (London: Rights of Women, 1984), 14.
33 Eleanor Stephens, 'Out of the Closet into the Courts', *Spare Rib* 50 (1976): 7.
34 'A Case of Heads He Wins – Tails She Loses?', *Family Law Journal* 6 (1976): 230. Cited in ROW, *Lesbian Mothers on Trial*, 10–11, using mother's notes taken in court. Robyn Plaister argued that, in Australia, the need for an appropriate male role model was regarded as particularly important for boys: Robyn Plaister, 'Lesbian Mothers and Custody Cases', in *Living Together: Family Patterns and Lifestyles. A Book of Readings and Reports*, ed. Dorothy Davis, Geoff Caldwell, Margaret Bennett and David Boorer (Canberra: Centre for Continuing Education, ANU, 1980), 152.
35 Stephens, 'Out of the Closet', 6.
36 See advice in ROW, *Lesbian Mothers on Trial*, 51–3.
37 For a report of an Australian case in which an unmarried mother sought to challenge the conventional nuclear family environment, see 'Child Custody', *Rouge* 9 (October 1980): 14.
38 See advice in ROW, *Lesbian Mothers on Trial*, 58.
39 Campbell v. Campbell (1974) *SASR* 9, 29.
40 In the marriage of Spry, B. A. and Spry, R. W. (1977) FLC 90–271 at 76442; In the marriage of Brook, G. E. and Brook, H. L. (1977) FLC 90–325 at 76710; In the marriage of Schmidt, R. G. and Schmidt, M. D. (1979) FLC 90–685 at 78652; In the marriage of Cartwright, B. H. and Cartwright, M. (1977) FLC 90–302 at 76601.

41 Kate Harrison, 'Lesbian Custody – a Personal Account', *Refractory Girl* (October 1980), 4.
42 See, for example, Stephens, 'Out of the Closet', 7.
43 Cartwright 1977 FLC 90-302.
44 3 Fam LR 11, 334. See also Powell v Powell (1976).
45 ROW, *Lesbian Mothers on Trial*, 9–10. See also the case of S v S 1 FLR 143 (Court of Appeal 21 June 1978).
46 ROW, *Lesbian Mothers on Trial*, 74.
47 Harrison, 'Lesbian Custody', 5.
48 See, for example, 'Lesbian Mother Wins Custody', *Spare Rib* 54 (January 1977): 17.
49 Interview with Lynne Harne, 18 July 2019; Interview with Marit, 6 October 2012; NSA, HCC (C456/92) Angela Chilton.
50 ROW, *Lesbian Mothers on Trial: A Report on Lesbian Mothers and Child Custody* (London: Rights of Women, 1984).
51 Rights of Women Lesbian Custody Group (ROWLCG), *Lesbian Mothers' Legal Handbook* (London: The Women's Press Handbook Series, 1986), 24–5.
52 *Campaign* 28, 56.
53 Lesley Wilson, 'Lesbian Mothers Conference', *Sappho*, 10.
54 Carmen, Gail, Shaila and Pratibha, 'Becoming Visible: Black Lesbian Discussions', *Feminist Review* 17 (Autumn 1984): 72.
55 NSA, HCC (C456/46/01–02), Ellen Noor.
56 NSA, HCC (C456/92) Angela Chilton.
57 Interview with Marit, 6 October 2012.
58 *Campaign* 28, 56.
59 Vivienne Cass, 'Lesbian Mothers and the Role of Professionals', in *Women in Jeopardy: Papers of the Women's Electoral Lobby Conference, Murdoch University, Perth, 20th and 21st November 1981*, ed. Barbara Buick (Perth: Women's Electoral Lobby, 1981), 51–2.
60 'Unto Us a Child Is Born', *Sappho* 1, no. 9 (December 1972): 14.
61 Stephens, *Out of the Closet*, 7.
62 ROWLCG, *Lesbian Mothers' Legal Handbook*, 24.
63 'Media Shorts', *Sydney Women's Liberation Newsletter* (March 1978): 7; 'In the Best Interests of the Children', *Sydney Women's Liberation Newsletter* (November 1979): 8; 'Jane's Column', *Campaign* 33, 48; 'In the Best Interests of the Children', *Spare Rib* 74 (September 1978): 39.
64 Alison Lyssa, 'Pinball', in *Australian Gay and Lesbian Plays*, ed. Bruce Parr (Sydney: Currency Press, 1996), 202.
65 Margaret Bradstock, 'A Different Kind of Ballgame', *Gay Information* 8 (Summer 1981/82): 38.
66 http://www.unfinishedhistories.com/history/companies/gay-sweatshop/care-and-control/.
67 Rachel Smith's speech at the House of Commons, 6 March 1978, Hall Carpenter Archives, Women's Library@LSE, HCA/Ephemera/315.
68 Wages Due Lesbians, London, 'Lesbian Autonomy and the Gay Movement', Hall Carpenter Archives, Women's Library@LSE, HCA/Ephemera/315.
69 Interview with Linda, 30 May 2019.
70 ROWLCG, *Lesbian Mothers Legal Handbook*, 53.
71 On feminist creches, see also 'Sharing Childcare', *Spare Rib* (January 1980): 31–4.
72 Interview with Lynne Harne, 18 July 2019.
73 Interview with Chloe Bardsley, 1 May 2012.

74 'Changing with My Daughter', *Spare Rib* 60 (July 1977): 42–6.
75 Interview with Jean Taylor, 22 September 2012.
76 Linda, 'The Politics of Parenting – Lesbian Mothers Out on a Limb?', *Spare Rib*, August 1987.
77 'As Feminists, as Lesbians, as Mothers', *Scarlet Woman* 4 (July 1976): 21. See also 'Living with a Male Child', *Rouge* 8 (June/July 1980): 27.
78 S. Golombok, A. Spencer and M. Rutter, 'Children in Lesbian and Single Parent Households: Psychosexual and Psychiatric Appraisal', *Journal of Child Psychology & Psychiatry* 24, no. 4 (1983): 551–72.
79 Nigel Bunyan, 'Lesbian Pair Win Rights as Parents', *The Daily Telegraph*, 30 June 1994.
80 Interview with Clare [pseudonym], 7 May 2012.
81 Gipsy Hosking and Margie Ripper, 'In the Best Interests of the (Silenced) Child', *Australian Feminist Studies* 27, no. 72 (2012): 171–88.
82 Linda, 'The Politics of Parenting'.
83 Susannah Hayward, 'Boys and Girls Come Out and Say … We're Really Glad Our Mums Are Gay', *LOTL* Issue 107 9, no. 11 (November 1998): 26–7. Sue Allen and Lynne Harne also note that a workshop for the daughters of lesbian mothers was included in the 1981 Edinburgh conference on feminist childcare practice: Allen and Harne, 'Lesbian Mothers', 190.
84 Clare, 'Why I Would Like to Destroy the Nuclear Family', *Vashti's Voice* 10 (Autumn 1975): 8.
85 CAMP NSW, 'Homosexuals and Human Relationships', Submission to the Royal Commission on Human Relationships, September 1975, State Library of NSW.
86 Interview with Lynne Harne, 18 July 2019.
87 'My Four Mums', *The Guardian*, 4 July 2009.
88 Response to recommendation on adoption by NSW Law Reform Commission, undated, Chris Sitka papers, State Library NSW.
89 'Lesbian Custody and the New Myth of the Father', *Trouble and Strife* 3 (Summer 1984): 12–15.
90 Interview with Megg Kelham, 27 February 2013.
91 Interview with Linda, 30 May 2019.
92 Letter from Jean Freer, 'Lesbian Co-parenting', *Trouble and Strife* 6 (Summer 1985): 4–5.
93 Interview with Megg Kelham, 27 February 2013.
94 Interview with Lynne Harne, 18 July 2019.
95 Interview with Al Garthwaite, 5 July 2019.
96 'My Four Mums', *The Guardian*, 4 July 2009.
97 Interview with Al Garthwaite, 5 July 2019.
98 Ruth Wallsgrove, 'Thicker than Water?', *Trouble and Strife* 7 (Winter 1985): 27.
99 Ibid.
100 Ibid., 28.
101 Ibid.
102 'Mothering Is Mothering, Not Power', *Trouble and Strife* 8 (Spring 1986): 3.
103 Ibid., 4
104 Ibid., 3.
105 Ibid., 4.
106 Joanna Patyna, 'The Most Remarkable Family in Britain', *Evening News* (London), 6 January 1978, 10.
107 Manja Vishedyke, 'Cummer Waltzing', *Hecate: A Women's Interdisciplinary Journal* x, no. ii (1984): 72.

108 Ibid., 74.
109 Ibid., 76.
110 Interview with Chloe Bardsley, 1 May 2012.
111 Marion Paull, 'A Letter from Australia', in *The Persistent Desire: A Femme-Butch Reader,* ed. Joan Nestle (Boston: Alyson Publications Inc, 1992), 177–8.
112 Interview by Ruth Ford with Elizabeth on 6 May 1992, AQuA.
113 Interview with Chloe Bardsley, 1 May 2012.
114 Paul Bathurst, 'Is the Gay Family a Real Alternative?', *The Sunday Times*, 3 July 1994.
115 Hunter Davies, 'My "Mothers" Loved Me', *Daily Mail*, 22 April 1993.
116 Interview with Clare, 7 May 2012.
117 'Unequal Society Upholds "Roles"', *Newham Recorder*, 4 December 1986.
118 From a Whisper to a Roar (FWTR) oral history collection, interview with Elizabeth Wilson. http://www.whisper2roar.org.uk/oral-history-archive/.
119 Helen Campbell, 'Legal Issues for Lesbian Mothers', *LOTL* 16 (April 1991), 12. This situation continued through the decade: Gay and Lesbian Rights Lobby, 'And then … the brides changed nappies' (April 2003), 9.
120 Barbara Guthrie and Andrea Malone, 'The Case of the $150,000 Turkey Baster', *LOTL* 75 7, no. 3 (March 1996): 17.
121 Report on the 'Lesbian and Gay Parenting' Conference, London Lesbian and Gay Centre, 11 October 1986, Women's Library@LSE.
122 Lynne Harne and Rights of Women, *Valued Families: The Lesbian Mothers' Legal Handbook* (London: The Women's Press, 1997), 15.
123 *Lesbians on the Loose* 17 (May 1991), 10.
124 Interview with Katharine, 26 March 2019.
125 Pearlie McNeill, 'Oh Susannah!', *Gossip: A Journal of Lesbian Feminist Ethics* 2 (1986), 72.
126 Marie McShea, 'Great Expectations', *Gossip* 3, 47.
127 McNeill, 'Oh, Susannah!', 70.
128 Interview with Megg Kelham, 27 February 2013. On the experience of jealousy of the child, see also 'Parent at Your Peril', *Wicked Women* 26 (July 1995), 25.
129 Interview with Clare, 7 May 2012.
130 Anne Robinson, 'The City Lesbian Family Who Want a Baby', *Liverpool Echo*, 12 January 1978.
131 Interview with Jenny Robertson, 25 August 2012.
132 Lucy Orgill, 'Mainly for Women', *Derby Evening Telegraph*, 18 January 1978.
133 'Christmas virgin birth for lesbian DIY mum', *Express and Star* (Wolverhampton), 25 November 1994.
134 Paull, 'Letter from Australia', 178.
135 Interview with Katharine, 26 March 2019.
136 Interview with Maxine Drake, 22 January 2013.
137 'How Can a Baby's Father be Her Mother and Be Her Father Again? We Tell You How …', *The People*, 23 July 1995, 6; 'Four Gay Parents "Are Bizarre and Abnormal"', *The Sun*, 7 May 1996.
138 Richard Littlejohn, 'Must We Pay Lesbians to Conceive by Pickle Jar?', *Daily Mail*, 15 May 1997; See also 'We're Both Mum to Our Daughter', *News of the World*, 27 October 1996; Kamal Ahmed, 'A Harsh Judgment on Home Affairs', *Scotland on Sunday*, 12 May 1996, 18.

139 Paul Baker, *Outrageous! The Story of Section 28 and Britain's Battle for LGBT Education* (London: Reaktion Books, 2022).
140 This has been widely noted in education research such as Jen Skattebol and Tania Ferfolja, 'Voices from an Enclave: Lesbian Mothers' Experiences of Child Care', *Australian Journal of Early Childhood* 32, no. 1 (March 2007): 10–18; Lucy Mercier and Rena Harold, 'At the Interface: Lesbian-Parent Families and Their Children's Schools', *Children and Schools* 25, no. 1 (2003): 35–47; Damien W. Riggs and Indigo Willing, '"They're All Just Little Bits, Aren't They: South Australian Lesbian Mothers' Experiences of Marginalisation in Primary Schools', *Journal of Australian Studies* 37, no. 3 (2013): 364–77. See also Jacqui Gabb, 'Locating Lesbian Parent Families: Everyday Negotiations of Lesbian Motherhood in Britain', *Gender, Place and Culture: A Journal of Feminist Geography* 12, no. 4 (2005): 419–32.
141 ROW, *Lesbian Mothers on Trial*, 32.
142 Report on the 'Lesbian and Gay Parenting' Conference, London Lesbian and Gay Centre, 11 October 1986, Women's Library@LSE.
143 Interview with Lynne Harne, 18 July 2019.
144 Will Harris, 'Lesbian Parents: Challenging School Bigotry', *Sydney Star Observer* 190 (21 August 1992): 19.
145 Yvette Taylor, *Lesbian and Gay Parenting: Securing Social and Educational Capital* (Basingstoke: Palgrave Macmillan, 2009); Catherine Ann Nixon, 'Working-Class Lesbian Parents' Emotional Engagement with Their Children's Education: Intersections of Class and Sexuality', *Sexualities* 4, no. 1 (2011): 79–99.
146 Anne Simpson, 'The Family Lesbians', *Glasgow Herald*, 16 January 1978.
147 Daniel Winunwe Rivers, *Radical Relations: Lesbian Mothers, Gay Fathers, and Their Children in the United States since World War II* (Chapel Hill: University of North Carolina Press Books, 2013), 5.

Chapter 7

1 Interview with Robyn Plaister, 20 December 2007.
2 Matt Cook, *Queer Domesticities: Homosexuality and Home Life in twentieth-century London* (London: Palgrave Macmillan, 2014), 92.
3 Alison Oram, 'Love "Off the Rails" or "Over the Teacups"? Lesbian Desire and Female Sexualities in the 1950s British Popular Press', in *Queer 1950s: Rethinking Sexuality in the Postwar Years*, ed. Heike Bauer and Matt Cook (London: Palgrave Macmillan, 2012), 53–4.
4 Kath Weston, *Families We Choose: Lesbians, Gays, Kinship* (New York: Columbia University Press, 1991), 22.
5 Heather Murray, *Not in the Family: Gays and the Meaning of Kinship in Postwar North America* (Philadelphia: University of Pennsylvania Press, 2012), 2.
6 Cook, *Queer Domesticities*.
7 Paul Baker, *Outrageous! The Story of Section 28 and Britain's Battle for LGBT Education* (London: Reaktion Books, 2022).
8 Terry Sanderson, *Mediawatch* (London: Continuum, 1995), 68; 'A Lesbian Mother's Terror Rule', *Daily Express*, 8 May 1987.
9 Margaret Thatcher, Speech to Conservative Party conference, Blackpool, 9 October 1987, https://www.margaretthatcher.org/document/106941
10 'Princess in Lesbian Demo', *Irish Independent*, 13 July 1990.

11 Jennifer Connell, 'The International Year of the Family: Over and Out', *LOTL* 61, vol. 6, no. 1 (January 1995).
12 Weston, *Families We Choose*, 27.
13 Jeffrey Weeks, Brian Heaphy and Catherine Donovan, *Same Sex Intimacies: Families of Choice and Other Life Experiments* (London: Routledge, 2001).
14 Interview with Sally, 6 October 2012.
15 Interview with Rachel, 19 May 2012.
16 Interview with Virginia Binning and Ruth Ritchie by Sandra Mackay and Rebecca Jennings, 7 April 2007, Pride History Group.
17 Sandie, Brighton Ourstory Project, *Daring Hearts: Lesbian and Gay Lives of 50s and 60s Brighton* (Brighton: QueenSpark Books, 1992), 26. See also Barbara Bell, *Just Take Your Frock Off: A Lesbian Life* (Brighton: Ourstory Books, 1999), 42, 54.
18 Interview with Margaret Jones, 18 September 2007.
19 Interview with Laurie Van Camp by Sandra Mackay, 18 February 2008, Pride History Group.
20 Interview with Francesca Curtis by Liz Ross and Gary Jaynes, 7 October 2008, AQuA.
21 NSA, HCC (C456/33) Cynnie Reid.
22 Interview with Margaret Jones, 18 September 2007.
23 Interview with Melisa McLean, Haringey Vanguard.
24 Interview with Phyllis Papps by Liz Ross and Gary Jaynes, 7 October 2008, AQuA.
25 Interview with Angie Stone, Haringey Vanguard.
26 Murray, *Not in the Family*.
27 The Gay and Lesbian Rights Lobby, 'Lesbians and Gay Men Have Families Too! A response to: 'The Heart of the Matter: Families at the Centre of Public Policy. A discussion paper prepared by the National Council for the International Year of the Family', June 1994, 3.
28 KH, 'Looking after Mum', *Arena Three* 2, no. 3 (March 1965): 3–4.
29 Interview with Barbara Williams, 23 September 2012.
30 Interview with Jean Taylor, 22 September 2012.
31 Valerie Mason-John and Ann Khambatta, eds., *Lesbians Talk: Making Black Waves* (London: Scarlet Press, 1993), 24.
32 Carmen, Gail, Shaila and Pratibha, 'Becoming Visible: Black Lesbian Discussions', *Feminist Review* 17 (July 1984): 54.
33 Natalie Thomlinson, *Race, Ethnicity and the Women's Movement in England, 1968-1993* (London: Palgrave Macmillan, 2016), 57.
34 Tracey Reynolds, *Caribbean Mothers: Identity and Experience in the UK* (London: Tufnell Press, 2005).
35 Carmen, Gail, Shaila and Pratibha, 'Becoming Visible', 54.
36 Mason-John and Khambatta, eds., *Lesbians Talk*, 22.
37 Interview with Tokunbo Alijore, Haringey Vanguard.
38 Jeanette Winterson, *Why Be Happy When You Could Be Normal?* (London: Vintage, 2012), 80–1.
39 Interview with Frances Mohan, Haringey Vanguard.
40 Interview with Clare, 7 May 2012.
41 Judith Butler, 'Is Kinship Always Already Heterosexual?', *Differences: A Journal of Feminist Cultural Studies* 13, no. 1 (2002): 14–15.
42 Geoff Dench, Kate Gavron and Michael Young, *The New East End: Kinship, Race and Conflict* (London: Profile Books, 2006), 236–9; Michael Young and Peter Wilmott, *Family and Kinship in East London* (London: Routledge and Kegan Paul, 1957).

43 Angela Davis, *Modern Motherhood: Women and Family in England 1945–2000* (Manchester: Manchester University Press, 2012), 20.
44 Carla Pascoe Leahy, *Becoming a Mother: An Australian History* (Manchester: Manchester University Press, 2023), 154.
45 Emily Struick, '"Why Didn't You Decide You Were a Lesbian before You Became Pregnant?"', *Lesbians on the Loose* 16 (April 1991): 11.
46 Letter from Delphine, Maroochydore, to Jane's Column, *Campaign* 28, 56.
47 'Happy Families', *Sappho* 2, no. 9 (December 1973): 12.
48 Interview with Chloe Bardsley, 1 May 2012.
49 'Happy Families', 13–14.
50 Interview with Clare, 7 May 2012.
51 'Older Wiser Lesbians', *Gay Information* 17–18, 74.
52 *Sappho* 2, no. 9 (December 1973): 6.
53 Interview with Elizabeth by Ruth Ford, 6 May 1992, AQuA.
54 Ibid. See also interview with Jan McInnies and Margaret Cummins by Sandra Mackay and Rebecca Jennings, Pride History Group.
55 Jacqui, 'Gay Wives and Mums Group', *Sappho* 3, no. 2 (May 1974): 8–10.
56 Camp Women's Association Newsheet 13 and 15 (1973), Gays Counselling Service of NSW Papers, Box 3, Folder 25, ML MSS 5836, State Library of NSW.
57 Interview with Robyn Plaister, 20 December 2007. Robyn Plaister spoke at conferences and wrote articles on lesbian motherhood and child custody cases for a number of Australian feminist and lesbian and gay publications in the late 1970s and early 1980s, including: 'Lesbian Mothers and Custody Cases under Family Law', paper presented at Australian women and the law conference, University of Sydney, 25–26 August 1978; 'Lesbian Mothers', *Campaign* 42 (April 1979): 13–14.
58 Jean Taylor, *Stroppy Dykes: Radical Lesbian Feminist Activism in Victoria during the 1980s* (Melbourne: Dyke Books Inc, 2012), 85.
59 Marilyn Archer, 'Gay Wives and Mothers', *Spare Rib* 31 (January 1975): 26.
60 Interview with Lynne Harne, 18 July 2019.
61 Archer, 'Gay Wives and Mothers', 26.
62 Alison Oram and Matt Cook, *Queer beyond London* (Manchester: Manchester University Press, 2022).
63 'We Are Not a Bunch of Perverts Who Are Going to Produce Awful Children', *Wembley Observer*, 28 July 1978; Taylor, *Stroppy Dykes*, 390–3; Barbara Baird, 'An Australian History of Lesbian Mothers: Two Points of Emergence', *Women's History Review* 21, no. 5 (2012): 849–65. Conferences were also considered to be important for the children of lesbian mothers to socialize. See *Gossip* 2, 10; Linda, 'The Politics of Parenting – Lesbian Mothers Out on a Limb?', *Spare Rib*, August 1987. There were also several workshops exploring lesbian mothers' experience, including one of CAMP NSW's workshops on female homosexuality planned for International Women's Year: Flyer, Ge056207 10 June 75. State Library of NSW; 'The Alternative – a group for gay women', *Melbourne Gay Liberation Newsletter* 12 (August 1974); a planned workshop on lesbian mothers at the Sydney Women's Liberation Conference, 1979: *Sydney Women's Liberation Newsletter*, February/March 1979, 4.
64 For example, 'Help with Women's Centre Child Care Arrangements Needed', *Melbourne Gay Liberation* Newsletter 16 (June–July 1975): 11; 'Arty Adelaide', *Rouge* 6 (1980): 15; *Gossip* 2 (1986).

65 For example, Barbara Wishart, 'Motherhood within Patriarchy – A Radical Feminist Perspective', in *All Her labours* (Sydney: Hale and Iremonger Pty Ltd, 1984), Published from the Third Women and Labour Conference, Adelaide, June 1982, 85.
66 *Sydney Women's Liberation* Newsletter, July 1977, 13.
67 Sue Allen and Lynne Harne, 'Lesbian Mothers – the Fight for Child Custody', in *Radical Records: Thirty Years of Lesbian and Gay History*, ed. Bob Cant and Susan Hemmings (London: Routledge, 1988), 189.
68 'Statement from the Lesbianfeminists', July 1975, Chris Sitka papers, Victorian Women's Liberation and Lesbian Feminist Archive, University of Melbourne; See also Minutes on the Lesbian Collective meeting of 30 July 1974 on lesbian mothers, Folder 3, Di Hudson Collection, Box 1 (DH1), Feminist Archive North, Leeds.
69 Interview with Lynne Harne, 18 July 2019.
70 Interview with 'Joan' by Lucy Chesser, 23 April 1993, AQuA.
71 Interview with Linda, 30 May 2019. See also 'Visiting Separatist Houses with a Male Child', *Rouge* 8 (June/July 1980): 27.
72 Victoria Golding, '"We Weren't Asking Permission to Be Lesbians Here": Sexuality, Space and Community in the Upper Calder Valley 1981–1999' (PhD diss, University of Sussex, Falmer, 2021), 176.
73 'Gay Wives and Mothers Collective – a Personal View by a Lesbian Mum', *Sappho* 4, no. 4 (1975): 5; 'Sapphoscene', *Sappho* 2, no. 3 (June 1973): 4.
74 Interview with Sylvia Kinder, 11 June 2012.
75 Interview with Katharine, 26 March 2019.
76 Interview with Linda, 30 May 2019.
77 Interview with Sally, 6 October 2012.
78 'In Search of a Kid-friendly Community', *LOTL* 105, Vol. 9, no. 9 (September 1998): 10.
79 'Our Kids Have Two Mums', Family section, Saturday *Guardian*, 16 February 2013, 2.
80 Conversation with Andrée Bellamy.
81 Vicky, in Brighton Ourstory Project, *Daring Hearts*, 38.
82 Sandie, in Brighton Ourstory Project, *Daring Hearts*, 75.
83 Laura Jackson, Hall Carpenter Archives, eds., *Inventing Ourselves: Lesbian Life Stories* (London: Routledge, 1989), 129. On violence in lesbian relationships, see Rebecca Jennings, '"It Was Quite a Scary Time": Lesbians and Violence in Post-war Australia', in *Gender Violence in Australia: Historical Perspectives*, ed. Alana Piper and Ana Stevenson (Melbourne: Monash University Publishing, 2019).
84 Sandie, in Brighton Ourstory Project, *Daring Hearts*, 29.
85 Interview with Ley Anderson, Haringey Vanguard.
86 Judith Davis, 'The Construction of Family and Social Networks by Old Lesbians', *Journal of Australian Lesbian Feminist Studies* 4 (June 1994): 86.
87 Monika Kehoe, *Lesbians over 60 Speak for Themselves* (New York: Haworth Press, 1989), 56.
88 Gill, in Brighton Ourstory Project, *Daring Hearts*, 48. Myrtle Solomon similarly cared for her friend, Sybil Morrison during her final years: NSA, HCC (C456/10) Myrtle Solomon.
89 'Eleanor' in Suzanne Neild and Rosalind Pearson, *Women Like Us* (London: Women's Press, 1992), 35.
90 Interview with Mairi, From a Whisper to a Roar, http://www.whisper2roar.org.uk/oral-history-archive/
91 Interview with Jean Taylor, 22 September 2012.
92 Golding, '"We Weren't Asking Permission"'.

93 Sara Ahmed, *The Cultural Politics of Emotion* (Edinburgh: Edinburgh University Press, 2004), 156.
94 NSA, HCC (C456/15), Diana Chapman.
95 Interview with Margaret Jones, 18 September 2007. See also NSA, HCC (C456/14) Mabel Hills.
96 Interview with Barbara Williams, 23 September 2012.
97 Interview with Barbara Williams, 23 September 2012.
98 NSA, HCC (C456/01) Sharley McLean.
99 Interview with Maxine Drake, 22 January 2013.
100 For example, Barbara Farrelly, 'Last Rights', *LOTL* 84, vol. 7, no. 12 (December 1996): 22–5.
101 Alice Petherbridge, 'Letting Go Rites/Rights', *Labrys Newspaper* 12 (November 1991): 18.
102 Pavithra Prasad, 'In a Minor Key: Queer Kinship in Times of Grief', *QED: A Journal in GLBTQ Worldmaking* 7, no. 1 (Spring 2020): 114.
103 Interview with Clare, 7 May 2012.
104 Interview with Jean Taylor, 22 September 2012. See also Interview with Helen, 29 May 2012.

Select Bibliography

Ardill, Susan and Sue O'Sullivan. 'Upsetting an Applecart: Difference, Desire and Lesbian Sadomasochism'. *Feminist Review* 23 (Summer 1986): 98–126.
Baird, Barbara. '"Gay Marriage", Lesbian Wedding'. *Gay and Lesbian Issues and Psychology Review* 3, no. 3 (2007): 161–70.
Baird, Barbara. 'The Politics of Homosexuality in Howard's Australia'. In *Acts of Love and Lust: Sexuality in Australia from 1945-2010*, edited by Lisa Featherstone, Rebecca Jennings and Robert Reynolds, 130–50. Newcastle: Cambridge Scholars Publishing, 2014.
Baird, Barbara. '"Kerryn and Jackie": Thinking Historically about Lesbian Marriages'. *Australian Historical Studies* 36, no. 126 (2005): 253–71.
Baird, Barbara. 'An Australian History of Lesbian Mothers: Two Points of Emergence'. *Women's History Review* 21, no. 5 (2012): 849–65.
Baker, Paul. *Outrageous! The Story of Section 28 and Britain's Battle for LGBT Education*. London: Reaktion Books, 2022.
Barrett, Carla. 'Lesbians at Home: Gender and Housework in Lesbian Coupled Households'. In *Lesbian Geographies: Gender, Place and Power*, edited by Kath Browne and Eduarda Ferreira, 55–70. London: Routledge, 2016.
Bennett, Judith M. '"Lesbian-like" and the Social History of Lesbianisms'. *Journal of the History of Sexuality* 9, no. 1/2 (January–April 2000): 1–24.
Bland, Lucy and Laura Doan, eds. *Sexology in Culture: Labelling Bodies and Desires*. Cambridge: Polity, 1998.
Blunt, Alison and Robyn Dowling. *Home*. London: Routledge, 2006.
Bongiorno, Frank. *The Sex Lives of Australians: A History*. Collingwood, VIC: Black Inc, 2015.
Bourke, Joanna. 'Housewifery in Britain, 1850–1914'. *Past and Present* 143 (May 1994): 167–97.
Bourke, Joanna. 'Fear and Anxiety: Writing about Emotion in Modern History'. *History Workshop Journal* 55, no. 1 (2003): 111–33.
Boyd, Nan Alamilla and Horacio N. Roque Ramirez, eds. *Bodies of Evidence: The Practice of Queer Oral History*. Oxford: Oxford University Press, 2012.
Bracke, Maud Anne Bracke. 'Between the Transnational and the Local: Mapping the Trajectories and Contexts of the Wages for Housework Campaign in 1970s Italian Feminism'. *Women's History Review* 22, no. 4 (August 2013): 625–42.
Brooke, Stephen. 'Gender and Working Class Identity in Britain during the 1950s'. *Journal of Social History* 34, no. 4 (Summer 2001): 773–95.
Brown, Wendy. *States of Injury: Power and Freedom in Late Modernity*. Princeton: Princeton University Press, 1995.
Butler, Judith. 'Is Kinship Always Already Heterosexual?'. *Differences: A Journal of Feminist Cultural Studies* 13, no. 1 (2002): 14–44.
Chenier, El. 'Love-politics: Lesbian Wedding Practices in Canada and the United States from the 1920s to the 1970s'. *Journal of the History of Sexuality* 27, no. 2 (2018): 294–321.

Chesser, Lucy. *Parting with My Sex: Cross-Dressing, Inversion and Sexuality in Australian Cultural Life*. Sydney: Sydney University Press, 2008.

Chettiar, Teri. '"More Than a Contract": The Emergence of a State-Supported Marriage Welfare Service and the Politics of Emotional Life in Post-1945 Britain'. *Journal of British Studies* 55 (July 2016): 566–91.

Churchill, David S. 'Transnationalism and Homophile Political Culture in the Postwar Decades'. *GLQ* 15, no. 1 (2008): 31–66.

Clarke, Victoria. 'Feminist Perspectives on Lesbian Parenting: A Review of the Literature 1972–2002'. *Psychology of Women Section Review* 7, no. 2 (2005): 11–23.

Collins, Marcus. *Modern Love: An Intimate History of Men and Women in Twentieth-Century Britain*. London: Atlantic Books, 2003.

Cook, Blanche Wiesen. '"Women Alone Stir My Imagination": Lesbianism and the Cultural Tradition'. *Signs: Journal of Women in Culture and Society* 4, no. 4 (1979): 718–39.

Cook, Hera. *The Long Sexual Revolution: English Women, Sex, and Contraception 1800–1975*. Oxford: Oxford University Press, 2004.

Cook, Matt. 'Warm Homes in a Cold Climate: Rex Batten and the Queer Domestic'. In *Queer 1950s: Rethinking Sexuality in the Postwar Years*, edited by Heike Bauer and Matt Cook, 115–32. London: Springer, 2012.

Cook, Matt. *Queer Domesticities: Homosexuality and Home Life in Twentieth-century London*. London: Springer, 2014.

Cowan, Malcolm. '"Knowing" Sodom? Australian Churches and Homosexuality'. In *Gay and Lesbian Perspectives III*, edited by Garry Wotherspoon, 207–39. Sydney: Australian Centre for Lesbian and Gay Research, 1996.

Davis, Angela. *Modern Motherhood: Women and Family in England, 1945–2000*. Manchester: Manchester University Press, 2012.

Davison, Graeme, Tony Dingle and Seamus O'Hanlon, eds. *The Cream Brick Frontier: Histories of Australian Suburbia*. Melbourne: Monash Publications in History No. 19, 1995.

Denton, Max. 'Sexual Identity and Christian Same-sex Weddings in Britain, c.1970–2000'. MPhil diss., Cambridge University, 2017.

Doan, Laura. *Disturbing Practices: History, Sexuality, and Women's Experience of Modern War*. Chicago: University of Chicago Press, 2013.

Duggan, Lisa. 'The New Homonormativity: The Sexual Politics of Neoliberalism'. In *Materializing Democracy: Toward a Revitalized Cultural Politics*, edited by Russ Castronovo and Dana D. Nelson, 175–94. Durham, North Carolina: Duke University Press, 2002.

Dunne, Gillian A. *Lesbian Lifestyles: Women's Work and the Politics of Sexuality*. London: Macmillan Press Ltd, 1997.

Elwood, Sarah A. 'Lesbian Living Spaces'. *Journal of Lesbian Studies* 4, no. 1 (2000): 11–27.

Evans, Tanya. 'The Other Woman and Her Child: Extra-marital Affairs and Illegitimacy in Twentieth-century Britain'. *Women's History Review* 20, no. 1 (2011): 47–65.

Faderman, Lillian. *Surpassing the Love of Men: Romantic Friendship and Love between Women from the Renaissance to the Present*. London: The Women's Press, 1985.

Featherstone, Lisa. *Let's Talk about Sex: Histories of Sexuality in Australia from Federation to the Pill*. Newcastle: Cambridge Scholars Publishing, 2011.

Finch, Janet and Penny Summerfield. 'Social Reconstruction and the Emergence of Companionate Marriage, 1945–59'. In *Marriage, Domestic Life and Social Change: Writings for Jacqueline Burgoyne, 1944–88*, edited by David Clark, 23–44. London: Routledge, 2019.

Ford, Ruth. '"The Man-Woman Murderer": Sex Fraud, Sexual Inversion and the Unmentionable "Article" in 1920s Australia'. *Gender & History* 12, no. 1 (2000): 158–96.
Ford, Ruth. 'They "Were Wed, and Merrily Rang the Bells": Gender-crossing and Same-sex Marriage in Australia, 1900–1940'. In *Australian Gay and Lesbian Perspectives 5*, edited by Graham Willet and David Phillips, 41–66. Australian Centre for Lesbian and Gay Research, 2000.
Ford, Ruth. '"Filthy, Obscene and Mad": Engendering "Homophobia" in Australia, 1940s-1960s'. In *Homophobia: An Australian History*, edited by Shirleene Robinson, 97–101. Sydney: The Federation Press, 2008.
Gabb, Jacqui. 'Querying the Discourses of Love: An Analysis of Contemporary Patterns of Love and the Stratification of Intimacy within Lesbian Families'. *The European Journal of Women's Studies* 8, no. 3 (2001): 313–28.
Gabb, Jacqui. 'Lesbian m/otherhood: Strategies of Familial-linguistic Management in Lesbian Parent Families'. *Sociology* 39, no. 4 (2005): 585–603.
Gabb, Jacqui. 'Locating Lesbian Parent Families: Everyday Negotiations of Lesbian Motherhood in Britain'. *Gender, Place and Culture: A Journal of Feminist Geography* 12, no. 4 (2005): 419–32.
Gammerl, Benno. *Anders fühlen: Gay and Lesbian Life in the Federal Republic: A History of Emotions*. München: Carl Hanser, 2021.
Gardiner, Jill. *From the Closet to the Screen: Women at the Gateways Club, 1945–85*. London: Rivers Oram Press, 2003.
Giddens, Anthony. *The Transformation of Intimacy: Sexuality, Love and Eroticism in Modern Societies*. Cambridge: Polity Press, 1992.
Giles, Judy. 'A Home of One's Own: Women and Domesticity in England 1918–1950'. *Women's Studies International Forum* 16, no. 3 (1993): 239–53.
Gluck, Sherna Berger and Daphne Patai. *Women's Words: The Feminist Practice of Oral History*. London: Routledge, 2016.
Gorman-Murray, Andrew. 'Contesting Domestic Ideals: Queering the Australian Home'. *Australian Geographer* 38, no. 2 (2007): 195–213.
Gorman-Murray, Andrew. 'Reconciling Self: Gay Men and Lesbians Using Domestic Materiality for Identity Management'. *Social and Cultural Geography* 9, no. 3 (2008): 283–301.
Gorman-Murray, Andrew. 'Queer Politics at Home: Gay Men's Management of the Public/private Boundary'. *New Zealand Geographer* 68, no. 2 (2012): 111–20.
Green, Sarah F. *Urban Amazons: Lesbian Feminism and Beyond in the Gender, Sexuality and Identity Battles of London*. Basingstoke: Macmillan, 1997.
Griffin, Ben. *The Politics of Gender in Victorian Britain: Masculinity, Political Culture and the Struggle for Women's Rights*. Cambridge: Cambridge University Press, 2012.
Gutterman, Lauren Jae. '"The House on the Borderland": Lesbian Desire, Marriage and the Household, 1950–1979'. *Journal of Social History* 46, no. 1 (2012): 1–22.
Gutterman, Lauren Jae. *Her Neighbor's Wife: A History of Lesbian Desire within Marriage*. University of Pennsylvania Press, 2019.
Halberstam, Jack. *Female Masculinity*. Durham: Duke University Press, 1998.
Hall, Lesley. 'Birds, Bees and General Embarrassment: Sex Education in Britain from Social Purity to Section 28'. In *Public or Private Education?: Lessons from History*, edited by Richard Aldrich, 98–115. London: Woburn Press, 2004.
Halperin, David M. *How to Be Gay*. London: Harvard University Press, 2012.
Hardyment, Christina. *Dream Babies: Three Centuries of Good Advice on Child Care*. London: Harper and Row, 1983.

Harris, Alana and Timothy Willem Jones, eds. *Love and Romance in Britain, 1918–1970*. London: Palgrave Macmillan, 2015.

Healey, Emma. *Lesbian Sex Wars*. London: Virago, 1996.

Hodge, Dino. *Did you Meet Any Malagas? A Homosexual History of Australia's Tropical Capital*. Nightcliff, NT: Little Gem Publications, 1993.

hooks, bell. *Yearning: Race, Gender, and Cultural Politics*. Boston: South End Press, 1991.

Hord, Levi C. R. 'Specificity without Identity: Articulating Post-gender Sexuality through the "Non-binary Lesbian"'. *Sexualities* 25, nos. 5–6 (2022): 615–37.

Hosking, Gipsy and Margie Ripper. 'In the Best Interests of the (Silenced) Child'. *Australian Feminist Studies* 27, no. 72 (2012): 171–88.

Houlbrook, Matt. *Queer London: Perils and Pleasures in the Sexual Metropolis, 1918–1957*. Chicago: University of Chicago Press, 2006.

Jackson, Julian. *Living in Arcadia: Homosexuality, Politics and Morality in France from the Liberation to AIDS*. Chicago: University of Chicago Press, 2009.

Jamieson, Lynn. 'Intimacy Transformed? A Critical Look at the 'Pure Relationship'. *Sociology* 33, no. 3 (August 1999): 477–94.

Jennings, Rebecca. 'The Gateways and the Emergence of a Post-Second World War Lesbian Subculture'. *Social History* 31, no. 2 (2006): 206–25.

Jennings, Rebecca. '"It Was a Hot Climate and It Was a Hot Time": Lesbian Migration and Transnational Networks in the Mid-twentieth Century'. *Australian Feminist Studies* 25, no. 63 (2010): 31–45.

Jennings, Rebecca. 'A Room Full of Women: Lesbian Bars and Social Spaces in Postwar Sydney'. *Women's History Review* 21, no. 5 (November 2012): 813–30.

Jennings, Rebecca. 'Lesbian Mothers and Child Custody: Australian Debates in the 1970s'. *Gender & History* 24, no. 2 (2012): 502–17.

Jennings, Rebecca. 'Womin Loving Womin: Lesbian Feminist Theories of Intimacy'. In *Intimacy, Violence and Activism: Gay and Lesbian Perspectives on Australasian History and Society*, edited by Graham Willett and Yorick Smaal, 133–46. Melbourne: Monash University Publishing, 2013.

Jennings, Rebecca. *Unnamed Desires: A Sydney Lesbian History*. Melbourne: Monash University Publishing, 2015.

Jennings, Rebecca. '"A Meeting of Different Tribes"? Travelling Women and Mobility between European and Australasian Women's Lands'. *Women's History Review* 31, no. 1 (2022): 88–106.

Jennings, Rebecca and Liz Millward. '"A Fully Formed Blast from Abroad"? Australasian Lesbian Circuits of Mobility and the Transnational Exchange of Ideas in the 1960s and 1970s'. *Journal of the History of Sexuality* 25, no. 3 (2016): 463–88.

Johnston, Craig and Paul van Reyk, eds. *Queer City: Gay and Lesbian Politics in Sydney*. Sydney: Pluto Press, 2001.

Johnston, Lynda and Gill Valentine. 'Wherever I Lay My Girlfriend, That's My Home: The Performance and Surveillance of Lesbian Identities in Domestic Environments'. In *Mapping Desire: Geographies of Sexualities*, edited by David Bell and Gill Valentine, 99–113. London: Routledge, 1995.

Jordan, Mark D. *Blessing Same-Sex Unions: The Perils of Queer Romance and the Confusions of Christian Marriage*. Chicago: University of Chicago Press, 2005.

Kentlyn, Susan. '"Who's the Man and Who's the Woman?" Same-sex Couples in Queensland "Doing" Gender and Domestic Labour'. *Queensland Review* 14, no. 2 (2007): 111–24.

King, Laura. *Family Men: Fatherhood and Masculinity in Britain, 1914–1960*. Oxford: Oxford University Press, 2015.
Langhamer, Claire. 'The Meanings of Home in Postwar Britain'. *Journal of Contemporary History* 40, no. 2 (April 2005): 341–62.
Langhamer, Claire. 'Love, Selfhood and Authenticity in Post-War Britain'. *Cultural and Social History* 9, no.2 (2012): 277–97.
Langhamer, Claire. *The English in Love: The Intimate Story of an Emotional Revolution*. Oxford: Oxford University Press, 2013.
Lawrence, Jon. *Me, Me, Me?: Individualism and the Search for Community in Post-War England*. Oxford: Oxford University Press, 2019.
Lewis, Jane. *Women in Britain since 1945*. Oxford: Blackwell, 1992.
Lewis, Jane. 'Marriage'. In *Women in Twentieth-Century Britain: Social, Cultural and Political Change*, edited by Ina Zweiniger-Bargielowska, 69–85. London: Routledge, 2014.
Love, Heather. *Feeling Backward: Loss and the Politics of Queer History*. London: Harvard University Press, 2007.
Marcus, Sharon. *Between Women: Friendship, Desire, and Marriage in Victorian England*. Princeton, NJ: Princeton University Press, 2009.
Matthews, Jill Julius, ed. *Sex in Public: Australian Sexual Cultures*. Sydney: Allen & Unwin, 1997.
McCarthy, Helen. *Double Lives: A History of Working Motherhood*. London: Bloomsbury Publishing, 2020.
Minto, David. 'Mr Grey Goes to Washington: The Homophile Internationalism of Britain's Homosexual Law Reform Society'. In *British Queer History: New Approaches and Perspectives*, edited by Brian Lewis, 219–43. Manchester: Manchester University Press, 2013.
Meeker, Martin. *Contacts Desired: Gay and Lesbian Communications and Community, 1940-1970s*. Chicago: University of Chicago Press, 2006.
Millbank, Jenni. 'Recognition of Lesbian and Gay Families in Australian Law – Part One: Couples'. *Federal Law Review* 34 (2006): 1–44.
Moore, Nicole. *The Censor's Library: Uncovering the Lost History of Australia's Banned Books*. St Lucia: University of Queensland Press, 2012.
Morris, George. 'Intimacy in Modern British History'. *The Historical Journal* 64, no. 3 (2021): 796–811.
Morrison, Carey-Ann. 'Heterosexuality and Home: Intimacies of Space and Spaces of Touch'. *Emotion, Space and Society* 5 (2012): 10–18.
Murphy, Amy Tooth. '"I Conformed; I Got Married. It Seemed Like a Good Idea at the Time": Domesticity in Postwar Lesbian Oral History'. In *British Queer History: New Approaches and Perspectives*, edited by Brian Lewis, 165–87. Manchester: Manchester University Press, 2013.
Murphy, Amy Tooth. 'Listening in, Listening Out: Intersubjectivity and the Impact of Insider and Outsider Status in Oral History Interviews'. *Oral History* 48, no. 1 (2020): 35–44.
Murphy, John and Belinda Probert. '"Anything for the House": Recollections of Post-war Suburban Dreaming'. *Australian Historical Studies* 36, no. 124 (2004): 275–93.
Murray, Heather A. *Not in This Family: Gays and the Meaning of Kinship in Postwar North America*. Philadelphia: University of Pennsylvania Press, 2010.
Murray, Heather. '"This Is 1975, Not 1875": Despair and Longings in Women's Letters to Cambridge Lesbian Liberation and Daughters of Bilitis Counselor Julie Lee in the 1970s'. *Journal of the History of Sexuality* 23, no. 1 (2014): 96–122.
Nestle, Joan. 'The Fem Question'. In *Pleasure and Danger: Exploring Female Sexuality*, edited by Carole S. Vance, 232–41. London: Routledge and Kegan Paul, 1984.

Newman, Sally. 'The Archival Traces of Desire: Vernon Lee's Failed Sexuality and the Interpretation of Letters in Lesbian History'. *Journal of the History of Sexuality* 14, nos. 1/2 (January–April 2005): 51–75.
Newman, Sally. 'Sites of Desire: Reading the Lesbian Archive'. *Australian Feminist Studies* 25, no. 64 (2010): 147–62.
Oerton, Sarah. '"Queer Housewives?": Some Problems in Theorising the Division of Domestic Labour in Lesbian and Gay Households'. *Women's Studies International Forum* 20, no. 3 (1997): 421–30.
Oosterhuis, Harry. *Stepchildren of Nature: Krafft-Ebing, Psychiatry and the Making of Sexual Identity*. Chicago: Chicago University Press, 2000.
Oram, Alison. 'Love "Off the Rails" or "Over the Teacups"? Lesbian Desire and Female Sexualities in the 1950s British Popular Press'. In *Queer 1950s: Rethinking Sexuality in the Postwar Years*, edited by Heike Bauer and Matt Cook, 41–60. London: Palgrave Macmillan, 2012.
Oram, Alison. *Her Husband Was a Woman! Women's Gender-crossing in Modern British Popular Culture*. London: Routledge, 2013.
Oram, Alison and Matt Cook. *Queer Beyond London*. Manchester: Manchester University Press, 2022.
Pascoe, Carla. 'Mum's the Word: Advice to Australian Mothers since 1945'. *Journal of Family Studies* 21, no. 3 (2015): 218–34.
Pascoe Leahy, Carla. *Becoming a Mother: An Australian History*. Manchester: Manchester University Press, 2023.
Perry, Kennetta Hammond. *London Is the Place for Me: Black Britons, Citizenship, and the Politics of Race*. Oxford: Oxford University Press, 2015.
Porter, Roy and Lesley Hall. *The Facts of Life: The Creation of Sexual Knowledge in Britain 1659–1950*. London: Yale University Press, 1995.
Porter, Roy and Mikulas Teich, eds. *Sexual Knowledge, Sexual Science: The History of Attitudes towards Sexuality*. Cambridge: Cambridge University Press, 1994.
Quirk, Christin. 'Never-married Women versus the Records: Archives, Testimony and the History of Adoption Practices at the Royal Women's Hospital'. *Melbourne Historical Journal* 40, no. 1 (2012): 169–84.
Quirk, Christin. 'Historicizing the Marginalization of Single Mothers'. In *Motherhood and Single-Lone Parenting: A 21st Century Perspective*, edited by Maki Motapanyane, 207–24. Bradford, ON: Demeter Press, 2016.
Ravetz, Alison. 'Housing the People'. In *Labour's Promised Land? Culture and Society in Labour Britain 1945–51*, edited by Jim Fyrth, 146–62. London: Lawrence and Wishart, 1995.
Ravetz, Alison. *The Place of the Home: English Domestic Environments, 1914–2000*. London: E. and F.N.Spon, 1995.
Rees, Jeska. 'A Look Back at Anger: The Women's Liberation Movement in 1978'. *Women's History Review* 19, no. 3 (2010): 337–56.
Rees, Jeska. '"Are You a Lesbian?" Challenges in Recording and Analysing the Women's Liberation Movement in England'. *History Workshop Journal* 69, no. 1 (2010): 177–87.
Reynolds, Tracey. *Caribbean Mothers: Identity and Experience in the UK*. London: Tufnell Press, 2005.
Riggs, Damien W. and Indigo Willing. '"They're All Just Little Bits, Aren't They: South Australian Lesbian Mothers' Experiences of Marginalisation in Primary Schools'. *Journal of Australian Studies* 37, no. 3 (2013): 364–77.
Riley, Denise. *War in the Nursery: Theories of the Child and Mother*. London: Virago, 1983.

Rivers, Daniel Winunwe. *Radical Relations: Lesbian Mothers, Gay Fathers, and Their Children in the United States since World War II*. Chapel Hill: University of North Carolina Press Books, 2013.

Robb, George. 'Marriage and Reproduction'. In *Palgrave Advances in the Modern History of Sexuality*, edited by H. G. Cocks and Matt Houlbrook, 87–108. London: Palgrave Macmillan, 2006.

Rowlingson, Karen. 'Lone-Parent Families'. In *The Blackwell Encyclopedia of Sociology*, edited by George Ritzer, 2663–7. Malden, MA: Blackwell, 2007.

Scicluna, Rachael. 'Thinking through Domestic Pluralities'. *Home Cultures* 12, no. 2 (2015): 169–91.

Segal, Lynne. *Straight Sex: The Politics of Pleasure*. London: Virago, 1994.

Shapira, Michal. *The War Inside*. Cambridge: Cambridge University Press, 2013.

Sheridan, Sue. *Who Was That Woman? The Australian Women's Weekly in the Postwar Years*. Sydney: UNSW Press, 2001.

Shugar, Dana. *Separatism and Women's Community*. Lincoln, NE: University of Nebraska Press, 1995.

Skattebol, Jen and Tania Ferfolja. 'Voices from an Enclave: Lesbian Mothers' Experiences of Child Care'. *Australian Journal of Early Childhood* 32, no. 1 (March 2007): 10–18.

Smaal, Yorick. 'Sex in the Sixties'. In *The 1960s in Australia: People, Power and Politics*, edited by Shirleene Robinson and Julie Ustinoff, 69–96. Newcastle: Cambridge Scholars Publishing, 2012.

Smith-Rosenburg, Carroll. 'The Female World of Love and Friendship'. In *Disorderly Conduct: Visions of Gender in Victorian America*, edited by Carroll Smith-Rosenburg, 53–76. New York: Knopf, 1985.

Summerskill, Clare, Amy Tooth Murphy and Emma Vickers, eds. *New Directions in Queer Oral History: Archives of Disruption*. London: Routledge, 2022.

Swain, Shurlee. *Born in Hope: The Early Years of the Family Court of Australia*. Sydney: UNSW Press, 2012.

Swain, Shurlee and Renate Howe. *Single Mothers and Their Children: Disposal, Punishment and Survival in Australia*. Cambridge: Cambridge University Press, 1995.

Taylor, Jean. *Stroppy Dykes: Radical Lesbian Feminist Activism in Victoria during the 1980s*. Melbourne: Dyke Books Inc, 2012.

Taylor, Yvette. *Lesbian and Gay Parenting: Securing Social and Educational Capital*. Basingstoke: Palgrave Macmillan, 2009.

Taylor, Yvette. 'The Ties That Bind: Intimacy, Class and Sexuality'. In *Mapping Intimacies: Relations, Exchanges, Affects*, edited by Tam Sanger and Yvette Taylor, 15–34. London: Palgrave Macmillan, 2013.

Teo, Hsu-Ming, ed. *The Popular Culture of Romantic Love in Australia*. Melbourne: Australian Scholarly Publishing, 2017.

Thane, Pat. 'Family Life and "Normality" in Postwar Culture'. In *Life after Death: Approaches to a Cultural and Social History of Europe during the 1940s and 1950s*, edited by Richard Bessell and Dirk Schumann, 193–210. Cambridge: Cambridge University Press, 2003.

Thomlinson, Natalie. *Race, Ethnicity and the Women's Movement in England, 1968–1993*. London: Palgrave Macmillan, 2016.

Thomson, Mathew. *Lost Freedom: The Landscape of the Child and the British Post-war Settlement*. Oxford: Oxford University Press, 2013.

Tisdall, Laura. 'Education, Parenting and Concepts of Childhood in England, c. 1945 to c. 1979'. *Contemporary British History* 31, no. 1 (2017): 24–46.

Tolia-Kelly, Divya. 'Materializing Post-colonial Geographies: Examining the Textural Landscapes of Migration in the South Asian Home'. *Geoforum* 25 (2004): 675–88.
Tosh, John. 'Domesticity and Manliness in the Victorian Middle Class'. In *Manful Assertions*, edited by Michael Roper and John Tosh, 44–73. Oxford: Routledge, 1991.
Traub, Valerie. 'History in the Present Tense: Feminist Theories, Spatialized Epistemologies, and Early Modern Embodiment'. *Representations* 33 (1991): 1–41.
Vicinus, Martha. '"They Wonder to Which Sex I Belong": The Historical Roots of the Modern Lesbian Identity'. *Feminist Studies* 18, no. 3 (Fall 1992): 467–97.
Vicinus, Martha. *Intimate Friends: Women Who Loved Women, 1778–1928*. London: University of Chicago Press, 2004.
Wall, Christine. 'Sisterhood and Squatting in the 1970s: Feminism, Housing and Urban Change in Hackney'. *History Workshop Journal* 83, no. 1 (April 2017): 79–97.
Webster, Wendy. *Imagining Home: Gender, Race and National Identity 1945–64*. London: UCL Press, 1998.
Weeks, Jeffrey. *Coming Out: Homosexual Politics in Britain, from the Nineteenth Century to the Present*. London: Quartet Books, 1977.
Weeks, Jeffrey. *The World We Have Won: The Remaking of Erotic and Intimate Life*. London: Routledge, 2007.
Weeks, Jeffrey. *Sex, Politics and Society: The Regulation of Sexuality since 1800*. 4th edn. London: Routledge, 2017.
Weeks, Jeffrey, Brian Heaphy and Catherine Donovan. *Same Sex Intimacies: Families of Choice and Other Life Experiments*. London: Routledge, 2001.
Weston, Kath. *Families We Choose: Lesbians, Gays, Kinship*. New York: Columbia University Press, 1991.
Willett, Graham. *Living out Loud: A History of Gay and Lesbian Activism in Australia*. Sydney: Allen & Unwin, 2000.
Wilson, Dolly Smith. 'A New Look at the Affluent Worker: The Good Working Mother in Post-war Britain'. *Twentieth Century British History* 17, no.2 (2006): 206–29.
Wilson, Elizabeth. *Only Halfway to Paradise: Women in Post-war Britain 1945–1968*. London: Tavistock, 1980.

Index

abortion 141–2, 148
abuse/abusive relationships 36, 42, 52, 64–66, 118, 122, 228
Action for Lesbian Parents group 125
adoption 5, 19, 127–9, 131, 133, 142, 149, 157–63, 168, 229, 257 n.175
Adoption of Children Act 1958 158
adoptive parents 149, 157, 161–2, 209
age 3, 19, 24, 102, 109, 123, 145, 158, 178, 181, 218–21
AIDS Council of NSW 150
Albany Trust 86–7
alternative insemination 150, 153
Altman, Dennis, *Homosexual: Oppression and Liberation* 87
Amazon Acres 62, 73
Anti-Discrimination Act 1977 136
Ardill, Susan 39
Arena Three magazine 27–8, 43, 47–8, 54, 69, 72, 79–80, 83, 85, 101–2, 104, 107, 109–16, 120, 129–30, 214
Arrowsmith, Pat 253 n.60
artificial insemination (AI) 2, 127–8, 132–41, 146, 152, 191, 193
Artificial Insemination – An Alternative Conception booklet 152
artificial insemination by donor (AID) 127–8, 132–41, 147–9, 151, 170, 189, 193, 196, 198, 213
Australasian Lesbian Movement 90, 205
Australian Broadcasting Corporation 94
autonomy 8–9, 13, 62–3, 69, 72–3, 75, 101, 151, 182, 184, 204, 229

backward feelings 11
Baird, Barbara 77, 127, 139, 165–6
Batten, Rex 202
Beckett, Elsa, 'Holy Matrimony' 88
Bella magazine 96
Bennett, Judith 6
bereavement 94, 208, 210, 221

biological mother/relationship 170, 184–8, 190–94, 196–7, 199–200, 229
Birmingham Post newspaper 137
bisexual 26, 111–12, 144, 177
black feminism 141–2, 157, 208–9
Bongiorno, Frank 103–4, 165
Bowlby, John 167, 184
Boyd, Nan Alamilla 18–19
The Bride Wore Pink magazine 94
Bridge the Gap Forum 215
British Gay Christian Movement 89
British Gay Sweatshop Theatre Company, 'Care and Control' 189
British Medical Association 139
British Pregnancy Advisory Service 140
Brittain, Victoria 117
Brixton Women's Centre 40
butch/femme lesbians 7, 12, 29–32, 39–40, 50–1, 60–1, 67–8, 78, 130, 191, 218, 228
Butler, Judith 7, 210

Campaign Against Moral Persecution (CAMP) 86, 90, 184, 214–5, 265 n.63
Campaign for Access to DI 141
Campaign for Homosexual Equality (CHE) 86, 158
  Women's Campaign Committee 215
Campaign newspaper 105, 108, 113, 121, 124, 127, 135, 152, 176, 178, 212
Camp Women's Association 214
Caprio, Frank, *The Lesbian* 158
Cass, Vivienne 86–7, 125, 178
casual heterosexual relationships 128, 146–50, 152, 158, 255 n.121
celibacy 17, 38–9, 177
censorship laws 18
Chadwick, Virginia 161
Chain Reaction club 40

Chesser, Eustace 28, 81
  Odd Man Out: Homosexuality in Men and Women 26
childcare 59, 132, 141–2, 161, 165–66, 171, 184–8, 216 n.83, 214–16, 221
child-centred parenting 137, 158
child custody 13, 121–6, 129, 141, 151, 215, 229
  losing custody (fear and concealment) 174–180, 215
  and nuclear family 172–4, 179
child development 13, 126, 126, 166–9, 172, 182–3, 185
childlessness, lesbian 129–31, 186
Children Act 1989 156, 193
Child Support Act 1993 156
chosen family 203–4, 224
church-sanctioned marriage 87, 91
Clark, Wendy 30
class, social 4–5, 9–10, 13, 18, 36, 47, 65, 128, 139, 147–8, 157–9, 163, 166, 176, 181, 189, 199
Claudia's Group 105, 214
Cleo magazine 42, 105, 108, 120
clinic-based AID 132–3, 136, 139–41, 156, 252 n.48, 255 n.121. *See also* artificial insemination by donor (AID)
The Clit Club 40
Coalition of Activist Lesbians 135
collective parenting 13, 184–6, 188–90
Collins, Marcus 8
Comfort, Alex, *The Joy of Sex* 8
commitment ceremony 95–7
co-mothers/non-biological mother 13, 134, 180, 187, 189–94, 200. *See also* non-biological children/parenting
companionate marriage 79, 89, 103, 109, 119
consciousness-raising group 34, 74, 86
Cook, Matt 45, 59, 202
co-parents/co-parenting 155, 169, 185–7, 192, 194–7
Cosmopolitan magazine 42
counter-cultures 34–5, 46, 57–8, 75, 184, 189
Country Women's Association 252 n.42
Covenant of Love ceremony 91
Creed, Barbara 29, 53
cultural models of lesbian sex 25–8

Daily Mail newspaper 111, 198
Daily Telegraph newspaper 161–2
Daughter Visions periodical 146
Davis, Angela 166, 211
de Beauvoir, Simone, *The Second Sex* 35, 142
Dempsey, Deborah 135–6
Denton, Max 89, 91
deprivation 52, 167, 169, 180
Derby Evening Telegraph newspaper 138, 196
disabled lesbians 25, 36
discrimination 2, 51, 53–4, 65, 86–7, 141, 161, 179–80, 182
Diva magazine 93
diversity 3, 6, 14, 19, 74, 98, 128, 165
divorce 78, 80, 86, 107–8, 113, 120–2, 141, 166, 172, 201, 214, 227
Dixon, Janet 145–7
Doan, Laura 5–6
domesticity 14, 45–7, 53, 57, 64, 129, 201, 228. *See also* homes/housing
  domestic environment 12, 46–7, 60, 62
  domestic labour 66–71, 180
  domestic roles, allocation of 66–74
  domestic violence 65–6
  and power 64–66
Duggan, Lisa 77
Dunne, Gillian 9, 165

egalitarian/egalitarianism 165
employment 3, 72, 103, 120, 124, 132, 169, 228–9
erotica 39–40
erotic/eroticism 22–5, 27–8, 30, 33, 38–41, 235 n.52
Evening Argus newspaper 115
Evening News newspaper 137–8

family
  biological 185, 204, 208–10, 224
  family structures 13, 132, 151, 163, 170–1, 179, 183–7, 189, 196, 199
  lesbian's relationships with 204–8
  practical/emotional support from 210–13, 221–25
  support during illness and old age 218–21

Family Law Act 1975 122–3
Family Planning Association 152
female husband 7, 83
female sexuality 42
   disabled lesbians 25
   personal narratives on 18–27
   in post-war period 19–22, 29–33
feminine/femininity 28, 30, 32, 37, 45, 50, 67, 69, 130, 144, 168, 172–3, 201
feminism/feminists 6, 30, 42, 235 n.58, 45–47, 53, 56–63, 58, 65, 70–1, 93–4, 129–30, 135, 137, 139, 141, 147, 172–3, 182, 202, 209, 216, 220, 229, 241 n.61
   approaches to lesbian motherhood 141–46
   approaches to lesbian sex 33–8
   approaches to parenting 180–3
   approaches to same-sex marriage 85–8
   black feminists 141, 157, 209
   and family structures 183–7
   feminist politics 38, 58–9, 63, 70–1, 151, 187, 205
   lesbian separatist 36–7, 146–7
   revolutionary feminists 38–9, 187
Feminist International Network of Resistance to Reproductive and Genetic Engineering (FINNRAGE) 151
Feminist Review journal 141, 176, 208
Feminist Self Insemination Group 147, 151–2, 152, 217
fertility/fertility treatment 103, 132, 136, 141, 156
Fertility Society of Australia 135
financial resources 58, 64, 68–74, 132, 158, 217
Finch, Janet 103
Firestone, Shulamith, *The Dialectic of Sex* 142
Forster, Jackie 127, 134, 214, 220
   Rocking the Cradle 122
Forum magazine 42, 90, 118
foster/fostering 3–5, 9, 13, 33, 57–8, 128–9, 131, 133, 149, 157–63, 193, 228
From a Whisper to a Roar (FWTR) collection 4, 237 n.102

Gabb, Jacqui 9–10, 165–6
Gammerl, Benno 11
gay
   adoption 161–3, 163 n.175
   fostering 129, 161–2, 257 n.167
   gay activist approach to marriage 85–8
   gay male sexual culture 41, 236 n.85
   gay marriage 77–7, 83, 91–92
   gay shame 11
   parenting 158–9, 183, 218
Gay and Lesbian Immigration Task Force 94
Gay and Lesbian Rights Lobby (GLRL) 94, 161, 207
Gay Information 179
gender 5, 7, 10, 12–13, 49, 125, 148, 165–6, 171–2, 179–182, 229–30
   conventional 165, 172, 183
   equality/inequality 8–9, 65, 227
   hierarchies 65–7, 185
   and sexuality 7, 12, 14, 125, 182, 230
genital sexuality 6, 17–19, 21–2, 33, 38
Giddens, Anthony 9–10
Glasgow Herald newspaper 199
Golding, Victoria 217, 221
good parent/parenting 128, 178
Gossip 142, 145
Greater London Council, Women's Committee 125
Griffin, Ben 172
Guardianship of Infants Act 1925 123
Guardianship of Minors Act 1973 123
Gutterman, Lauren Jae 102, 113

Halberstam, Jack 18–19
Hall Carpenter Collection (HCC) 4, 42
Haringey Vanguard (HV) 4
Hecate journal 189
hetero-domesticity 129
heteronormative 10, 54, 165, 194
heteropatriarchal models 30, 35, 60, 85, 143
heterosexism 179
heterosexual/heterosexuality 1, 8–10, 28, 30, 33, 36–8, 50, 56, 58, 73, 81, 83, 85–6, 90, 94, 97, 105, 107, 127–8, 130, 133, 136, 138–9, 154, 156, 158, 168–9, 173, 175, 183, 193–4, 196, 200, 207, 212–13, 218, 22, 222
   casual heterosex 128, 146–50, 152, 158, 255 n.121

marriages 13, 50, 73, 78, 80, 83, 85–7, 96, 101, 104, 128–9, 131, 149, 163, 170, 199, 212, 218
nuclear family 13, 127, 166, 168, 188–9, 194
histories of emotion 8–11
HIV/AIDS transmission 42, 95, 149–50
home-schooling 181
homes/housing 12–13, 45–6, 65, 75, 228. *See also* domesticity
  advertisements 54
  allocation of domestic roles 66–74
  difficulties for women in finding 52–57
  and domestic power 64–6
  family home 46, 55–6, 113, 119, 202, 228
  housing shortages 53, 103
  imaginative/imagined 46–8
  landlords and neighbours 48, 50–5
  material environment 46–52, 56, 58–9, 62, 74
  public housing 53–4
  rented housing 53
  shared homes/houseshares 13, 48, 51, 54, 57–64, 70, 73–5, 119, 184–5, 187
  terraced 59
homo-domesticity 129
homonormativity 77, 165, 199
homophile 90, 111, 158
homophobia/homophobic 42, 57, 64–5, 199, 209
homosexual/homosexuality 6, 9–12, 18, 20–1, 25–9, 36, 41, 45, 48, 72, 79, 81–2, 84, 86–7, 86–7, 95, 107, 111, 125, 133, 135–6, 159–60, 162, 171, 173–4, 175, 178, 184, 198, 201–3, 245 n.60, 265 n.63
Homosexual Law Reform Society 111
hooks, bell 65
Hord, Levi CR 7
Howard, John 77, 127
How to Become a Lesbian in 35 Minutes short film 203
Human Fertilisation and Embryology Authority 141
Human Fertility and Embryology Act 1990 140
hypersexual 26–7, 174

immigrant/immigration 45, 94, 128, 180
incest 145
The Independent newspaper 154
Indigenous women 128, 131, 142, 149, 157, 184
Infertility (Medical Procedures) Act 1984 136
intergenerational relationships 10, 102, 202, 213
International Year of the Family (IYF) 203, 207
inter-racial relationships 51
'*In the Best Interests of the Children*' documentary 179
Isbister, Clair 166–7

jealousy 10, 12, 34–5, 60, 80–1, 89, 195, 262 n.128
Jenny Lives with Eric and Martin 203
Jenny, 'Rules and Relationships' 62
Johnston, Jill, *Lesbian Nation* 142

Kemp, Beverley 94
Kennedy, Robyn 79
Khambatta, Ann 208
  Lesbians Talk: Making Black Waves 41–2
kinship 10, 14, 202–3, 210, 221, 224–5, 228, 230

Labrys Newspaper 41, 57, 65, 92, 95–6, 136, 224
Langhamer, Claire 103–4, 107–8
Langley, Esme 69, 101–2, 110–11, 114
Leeds Revolutionary Feminist Group
  Love Your Enemy? pamphlet 39
  'Political Lesbianism' 38
legal cases
  B v B 123
  Campbell v Campbell 124, 173
  Cartwright v Cartwright 174
  Gardner v Gardner 120
  G v D 172
legislation 2, 77, 94–5, 123, 132, 137, 139, 252 n.42, 203, 228
Legitimacy Act 1959 123
Leichhardt Women's Health Centre 153
Lesbian and Gay Families Project 152

Lesbian and Gay Foster and Adoptive Parents group 161
Lesbian and Gay Parenting Conference 193, 198
'Lesbian and Gay Relationships and the Law' forum 94
lesbian bars 50, 214, 218
Lesbian Cancer Support Group 221
lesbian family models 9–10, 13, 127, 130, 155, 165, 182, 198, 230
lesbian feminism. *See* feminism/feminists
lesbian intimacy, defining 5–7
Lesbian Litters group 155
lesbian mothers' conferences 147, 176
lesbian mothers' groups 125, 214–15, 217
lesbian mothers/motherhood 1–2, 5, 13, 25, 105–6, 118–22, 127–30, 163, 165–6, 169, 180–3, 185, 189–92, 194–5, 200, 203, 212, 227, 229, 261 n.83, 250 n.63
    in 1950s and 1960s 129–32, 171
    adoption 5, 19, 128–9, 131, 133, 149, 157–63, 257 n.175
    and AID 2, 127–8, 132–41
    casual heterosexual relationships 128, 146–50
    and child custody (*see* child custody)
    community's perception on 198–9
    feminist approaches to 141–6
    foster/fostering 3–5, 9, 13, 33, 128–9, 131, 133, 157–63
    in post-war period 169–70, 213–18
    redefining 188–90
    challenges of 194–6
    self-insemination 128, 132, 150–4
    and sperm donors 132, 152–7, 252 n.42
    unmarried 170–1
Lesbianon magazine 102, 109
lesbian parents/parenting 1–3, 11, 13, 64, 127–8, 131–2, 135–6, 150, 152, 163, 165–6, 175, 191, 193–4, 200, 217, 229–30. *See also* parenthood
    and child development in post-war period 166–9
    feminist approaches to 180–3
Lesbians Against Sado Masochism group 39
lesbian sex/sexuality 12, 17, 36, 42–3, 122–3
    cultural models of 25–8
    disabled lesbians 25, 36
    feminist approaches to 33–8
    personal narratives on 18–27
    post-war sexual practice 29–33
    sex performances 40–1
Lesbians on the Loose magazine 94, 96, 136
lesbian specificity 7, 10–11
LGBTQ+ people, hate crime against 14
Liberation journal 142
Liverpool Echo newspaper 138, 140, 148, 196
London Evening News newspaper 189
London Feminist Self Insemination Group 151–3, 155, 157
London Lesbian and Gay Centre 39
London Lesbian Line 121
London Women's Liberation Newsletter 39, 151
lone mothers. *See* single (mothers) parent/parenting
LOTL journal 93, 156, 193, 203, 217
Love Affair magazine 140, 162
Love, Heather 11

Magee, Bryan, *One in Twenty: A Study of Homosexuality in Men and Women* 27
Manchester Daily Express newspaper 81
marital home 13, 46, 51, 112–14, 118, 120
marriage 9–10, 12–13, 18, 33, 79–80, 85–6, 97, 103
    church-sanctioned 87, 91
    companionate 79, 89, 103, 109, 119
    disappointment in 106–8
    equality 77, 86, 98
    formal 87
    heterosexual 13, 50, 73, 78, 80, 83, 85–7, 96, 101, 104, 128–9, 131, 149, 163, 170, 199, 212, 218
    hiding same-sex desires 106–8
    love and 104, 108
married lesbians 7, 13, 101–2, 107–112
    and child custody 13, 121–6, 172–180
    decision on breaking the marriage 119–22
    financial consequences of 120–1
    and marital home 112–14
    and motherhood in post-war period 169–70
    search for lesbian community 110–12

Married Women's Correspondence Magazine 110
masculine/masculinity 19, 26, 30, 69, 155, 167–8, 172
Mason-John, Valerie 208
  Lesbians Talk: Making Black Waves 41–2
masturbation 21, 26–8, 33, 39
material environment 46–52, 56, 58–9, 62, 74
McCrossin, Julie 77, 156
Melbourne Radicalesbians 33, 86
Metropolitan Community Church (MCC) 91–2
migrants 5, 54, 128, 168, 184
Miller, Isabel, *Patience and Sarah* 56
Millett, Kate, *Flying* 236 n.79
Minorities Research Group (MRG) 47, 101, 106, 116, 205
  husband's signature for subscription 111
Minorities Research Trust 117
Mirror newspaper 140
monogamy/monogamous 12, 33, 56–7, 60–1, 75, 79, 81, 83–4, 86–7, 93–4, 229. *See also* non-monogamous/-monogamy; serial monogamy
mortgage 53, 103, 160, 227
Murphy, Amy Tooth 3, 129
Murray, Heather 6, 10, 202, 207

National Health and Medical Research Council 136
Nestle, Joan 30
Newham Recorder newspaper 193
new homonormativity 77
News of the World newspaper 81, 101
New Statesman magazine 130
non-biological children/parenting 186, 188, 190–3, 196
non-monogamous/-monogamy 13, 33–5, 57–62, 86, 229. *See also* monogamy/monogamous
non-mothering 188
non-sexual friendships 18
nuclear family 13, 33, 46, 57, 59, 75, 85–6, 122, 125–7, 142, 166, 168–71, 182–5, 199–200, 202–3, 209, 228, 259 n.37
  and child custody 172–4, 179
  heterosexual 13, 127, 166, 168, 172–3, 194

Older Wiser Lesbians group 214
Operation Spanner 42
oppressions/oppressive 25, 30, 33, 38–9, 57, 59, 70, 78, 85, 93, 141, 182–4, 209, 228
oral history, lesbian 2–5, 7, 18, 20, 42, 102, 122, 129. *See also* personal narratives
orgasm 26–9. *See also* vaginal orgasm
O'Sullivan, Kimberley 39–41
O'Sullivan, Sue 39–40
over-sexed lesbian 26, 28

PanDA magazine 93
parenthood 1–2, 4, 127, 131, 142, 146, 155–6, 158, 163, 193, 207. *See also* lesbian parents/parenting
parthenogenesis 146–7
Pascoe Leahy, Carla 211
patriarchy/patriarchal society 34–5, 41, 57, 145, 151, 165, 179, 181–2, 184–5, 229, 236 n.79
penetrative sex 21, 36
The People newspaper 92
personal narratives. *See also* oral history, lesbian
  on AID 134–6, 138–40
  on casual heterosex 150
  on child adoption 162
  on child custody 124–6, 172–7
  on child development 167, 170
  on childlessness 129–32
  on Christian's approach to homosexuality 89–90, 92–3
  on co-parenting 197
  on disappointment in marriage 107–9, 112–14
  on discrimination 86
  on domestic circumstance 48–52, 54–64
  on domestic roles 67–71
  on emotional support from family 212–13, 220–2
  on female sexuality 18–27, 30–3
  feminist perspectives on lesbian sex 33–8
  on finances 72–4
  on homosexual marriage (wedding ceremonies) 82–4, 87–8, 96–7

lesbian feminist 143–5, 184–5, 216
  on multiple relationships 34–5
  on open marriage 115–19
  on physical abuse 65–6
  on pregnancy 148
  on self-insemination 151–3, 155
  on shared lesbian house 219
Plaister, Robyn 122, 125, 172, 215, 259 n.34, 265 n.57
platonic friendship 10, 24, 46
political lesbianism 37–8
polygamy 93. *See also* monogamy/monogamous
porn/pornography 28, 41
possessiveness, sexual 34–5, 81, 236 n.79
post-war period 5–6, 10–13, 18, 27, 45, 48, 53, 58, 67, 78, 101–4, 113, 128–9, 137, 163, 190–1, 203, 205, 211, 225, 228–9
  domestic roles during 67
  female sexuality in 19–22
  financial resources 72
  homosexuality in the Church 89
  lesbian mothers and community in 213–18
  lesbian sexual practice 29–33
  motherhood and married lesbian in 169–70
  parenting and child development 166–9
  same-sex marriage 78–9, 82–3
power relations 59, 66–7, 142
pregnancy (conceiving) 21–2, 25, 127–8, 130–2, 134–6, 138–40, 148–50, 152–3, 212
pre-marital sex 103
Princess Diana 203
privacy 8, 50, 56, 64, 85
promiscuous/promiscuity 25–6, 28, 89, 138–9, 149, 245 n.60
Property (Relationships) Legislation Amendment Act 1999 95
prostitute/prostitution 6, 40–1, 45, 138, 162
psychoanalytic/psychoanalysis 34, 168, 202
psychosexual development 123, 125, 173, 182
pure relationship 9–10

queer 11–12, 18–19, 41, 45, 77–8, 128, 201, 221–2, 224–5
  queer kinship 224, 230
Quim magazine 39–40

race/racial/racism 4, 10, 36, 54–5, 65, 128, 130–1, 142, 149, 157–8, 166, 176–7, 208–10, 225
Radicalesbian Manifesto (1973) 61
Radicalesbians 33, 216
  'Woman-Identified Woman' 37
radical feminists 25, 33, 36–7, 40, 58–9, 73, 142–3, 151, 187
rape, lesbian 40, 42
Reddy, William 8
Refractory Girl journal 73, 173
relationship breakdown 52, 81, 118, 121, 123, 170, 175, 192, 206, 208, 215, 221, 225
religion/religious faith 21, 55, 89–92, 98, 158–60, 208–10
religious ceremonies 89–91, 228
Renault, Mary 129–30
Rensenbrink, Greta 146
reproductive technologies 5, 132–3, 135–6, 140–1, 146, 151, 163, 228
Reproductive Technology Act 1988 136
resistance 11, 45, 78, 132, 151, 200
Riggs, Damien 128, 156
Rights of Women Lesbian Custody Project 124–5, 174–5, 178
  Lesbian Mothers' Legal Handbook 118–19, 125, 180
  Lesbian Mothers on Trial 175
  survey (1984) 198
Robin Hood club 130
Robinson, Anne 148
romantic friendships 18
romantic love 9, 81, 89, 104, 107–8, 119
Rouge magazine 47, 58, 70, 141
Roxon, Sue 36
Royal Commission on Human Relationships 86–7, 184, 245 n.60
Royal Commission on Marriage and Divorce 103
rural women-only communities 58, 61

sadomasochism (SM) 39–42, 81
Saffron, Lisa

Challenging Conceptions: Planning a Family by Self Insemination 152, 155
Getting Pregnant Our Own Way 152
same-sex desire 3–6, 11–13, 18–20, 22, 25–7, 34, 42, 45–52, 56, 64, 78, 101, 104–8, 129, 149, 204, 225, 227
   hiding 108–10
   and marital home 112–14, 118, 120
   and open marriage 115–19
   search for lesbian community 110–12
same-sex marriage 4, 14, 72, 77–81, 105, 228
   Church/Christianity's approach on 84, 87–92
   feminist/gay activist's approaches to 85–8
   official recognition of relationships in 1960s 83–5
   wedding ceremonies 82–3, 95–7
same-sex relationships 1, 9–10, 12–13, 18–19, 23, 30, 46, 51, 53, 55, 77–80, 85–7, 122, 204, 228–9
   activism on relationship recognition 92–5
   domestic roles in 66–74
Sapphic relationships. *See* same-sex relationships
Sappho Gay Wives and Mothers Group 214
Sappho magazine 43, 45 n.52, 80–1, 88, 104–5, 107, 109–11, 114–16, 119, 121, 126–7, 130, 133–4, 138–9, 158–60, 169, 171, 212, 214
Sappho organization 133–4, 137, 139, 145, 159–60
Scarlet Woman magazine 70, 74, 144, 182
Schoenmaker, Mario 91, 245 n.60
Section 28 of the Local Government Act 1988 20, 95, 198, 203
Sedgwick, Eve Kosofsky 11
selfhood 5–8, 12, 104, 108, 120, 148, 202
self-insemination 128, 132, 150–4, 163, 192, 196, 255 n.121
   sperm donors 154–7
Self Insemination booklet 152
separatism/separatist 36–7, 58, 73, 145–7, 216
serial monogamy 93. *See also* monogamy/monogamous

Serious Pleasure magazine 39–40
sex. *See* lesbian sex/sexuality
Sex Discrimination Act, Commonwealth's 136
sex education 20–1
sexism 142, 179, 181, 183
sexology 18, 36, 43
sex performances 40–1
sex positive culture 38–43
Sex Subculture parties 41
sex toys 27–8, 37, 40
sexual experiences 4–5, 11, 20, 33, 41–3, 149, 207, 235 n.52. *See also* personal narratives
sexual identity 3–4, 18–19, 24, 101, 165, 171, 207
sexuality 3–8, 11, 17–18, 30, 37–8, 78, 105, 112, 123–4, 129, 132, 138, 141, 161, 171, 175, 178, 201–2, 205–8, 210, 212, 217, 230
   and gender 7, 12, 14
   personal narratives on female 18–25
   uncontrolled 26–7
Sexually Outrageous Women group 40
shame 10–11, 22, 121
shared parenting 120, 186
Sheffield Morning Telegraph 83
Shrew magazine 86
Shulman, Sheila 143, 145
single (mothers) parent/parenting 54, 108, 125, 131–2, 135, 142, 159, 168–9, 186, 194, 197, 199, 217–18, 259 n.21
social attitudes 4, 13, 124, 168–70, 182–3, 192, 195–6, 198, 200, 204, 218, 225, 228–9
social hostility 13, 56, 128, 227–9
social learning theory 168
social structures 9, 12, 65, 151, 182, 195, 228
social workers 135, 159–62, 167–8, 176–7, 183, 192
Society Five group 117, 119
Spare Rib magazine 85, 115, 123, 179, 182–3
sperm/sperm donors 132, 152–7, 252 n.42
Spinster journal 143
spinsters 48
squats 13, 40, 58–60, 70, 73, 184, 187
Stein, Pam, 'Women's Oppression' 142

Stolen Generations 128, 131, 149, 157
Stonewall Housing Association 52, 64, 95
Stopes, Marie, *Married Love* 8
Stop the Amendment Campaign 141
Storr, Anthony 29
    Sexual Deviation 28
subjectivity, lesbian 5–7
Summerfield, Penny 103
swapping of partners 59–60
Sydney Morning Herald newspaper 203
Sydney Star Observer magazine 199
Sydney Women's Liberation Newsletter 215

Taylor, Yvette 9–10, 199
Teo, Hsu-Ming 8
Thatcher, Margaret 95, 203
Time Out magazine 133, 154
The Times newspaper 117
Towards a Quaker View of Sex 89–90
The Transformation of Intimacy (Giddens) 9
transnational approach 5, 69, 132, 134
Trouble and Strife journal 185–6, 188

unmarried mother 131, 138, 149, 168–71, 259 n.37

vaginal orgasm 29, 36, 235 n.58. *See also* orgasm
Vashti's Voice journal 183
Vicinus, Martha 18
violence 65–6, 119, 145, 218

WACKIT (Women and Children in Transition) 215

Wages for Housework campaign 69, 180
Warnock Report 1984 140
Webster, Wendy 45, 128
wedding ceremonies 81–3, 91–2, 95–7, 228
Weekly Journal newspaper 156
West, D. J. 28
Weston, Kath 201, 203
Wicked Women magazine 40
    Be Wicked parties 40–1
    Ms Wicked competition (1990) 41
Wilmott, Peter, *Family and Kinship in East London* 211
Wilson, Dolly Smith 167, 169
Wilson, Elizabeth 116, 193
Winnicott, Donald 167–8
Wishart, Barbara 135, 143–4
Wittig, Monique 7
    Les Guerilleres 35
Women in Science group 152
Women's Health Centres 152
women's lands 61, 73, 181
Women's Liberation Movement 33, 38, 45, 63, 85, 130, 137, 144, 173, 183, 208, 215, 217
working-class 18, 45, 52, 149, 168, 199, 205
working mothers 158, 167–9, 259 n.20

Young, Michael, *Family and Kinship in East London* 211
youth 81, 86, 141, 149

www.ingramcontent.com/pod-product-compliance
Lightning Source LLC
Chambersburg PA
CBHW071809300426
44116CB00009B/1247